KV-353-853

The Canterbury and York Society
GENERAL EDITOR: PROFESSOR R. L. STOREY

ISSN 0262–995X

DIOCESE OF YORK

Canterbury and York Society Vol. LXXXV

The Register of
William Melton

ARCHBISHOP OF YORK

1317–1340

VOLUME IV

EDITED BY

REGINALD BROCKLESBY, B.A., F.R.Hist.S.

Senior Archivist (retired)
Nottinghamshire Archives Office

The Canterbury and York Society

The Boydell Press

1997

First published 1997

A Canterbury and York Society publication
published by The Boydell Press
an imprint of Boydell & Brewer Ltd
PO Box 9, Woodbridge, Suffolk IP12 3DF, UK
and of Boydell & Brewer Inc.
PO Box 41026, Rochester, NY 14604–4126, USA

ISBN 0 907239 56 0

A catalogue record for this book is available
from the British Library

Details of previous volumes available from Boydell & Brewer Ltd

This publication is printed on acid-free paper

Printed in Great Britain by
St Edmundsbury Press Ltd, Bury St Edmunds, Suffolk

CONTENTS

PREFACE

The first volume of a projected edition of Archbishop Melton's register was published in 1977. In her preface, Professor Rosalind Hill explained that a team of editors would be required for so large an undertaking. Mr. Brocklesby soon joined this team as editor of the section for the archdeaconry of Nottingham, with the intention of first submitting his edition for a higher degree of Nottingham University. His progress in this direction was halted by the death of his wife. Recently, however, Dr. Alison McHardy, the previous general editor, discovered that Mr. Brocklesby had completed a thorough edition of the whole text for the archdeaconry, and she persuaded him to present his large typescript to the society for publication in a somewhat reduced form modelled on the first three published volumes of the planned edition.

Of these, the second, being the section for another unprivileged archdeaconry (Cleveland), bears the closest resemblance to the Nottingham section. Comparison reveals how much use was made of formularies by Melton's scribes, for injunctions following visitations as well as for mandates and commissions; full texts in *Melton* II are not repeated in this volume. Here dates of entries are generally given only once, in modern forms of place, day and year, at the ends of their texts or summaries. In cross-references, other entries are cited by their numbers in bold type.

Grateful thanks are due to Professor David Smith for the long loan of a photocopy and for generously remedying its shortcomings by inspection of the manuscript in St. Anthony's Hall. Responsibility for remaining defects must rest with the present general editor.

ABBREVIATIONS

BRUC	A.B. Emden, *A Biographical Register of the University of Cambridge to 1500*, Cambridge 1963.
BRUO	A.B. Emden, *A Biographical Register of the University of Oxford to A.D. 1500*, 3 vols., Oxford 1957–9.
CCR	*Calendar of Close Rolls*, 47 vols., H.M.S.O. 1900–63.
CPL	*Calendar of Entries in the Papal Registers relating to Great Britain and Ireland: Papal Letters*, 14 vols., H.M.S.O. 1893–1960
CPR	*Calendar of Patent Rolls*, 73 vols., H.M.S.O. 1891–.
EPNS Notts.	J.E.B. Gover, A. Mawer and F.M. Stenton, *The Place-names of Nottinghamshire*, English Place-Name Society 17, 1940.
Fasti	John Le Neve, *Fasti Ecclesiae Anglicanae 1300–1541*, 12 vols., 1962–7.
HBC	*Handbook of British Chronology*, third edition, ed. E.B. Fryde, D.E. Greenway, S. Porter and I. Roy, Royal Historical Society 1986.
Reg. Corbridge	*The Register of Thomas of Corbridge*, ed. W. Brown and A.H. Thompson, 2 vols., Surtees Society 138, 141, 1925–8.
Reg. Greenfield	*The Register of William Greenfield*, ed. W. Brown and A.H. Thompson, 5 vols., Surtees Society 145, 149, 151–3, 1931–40.
Reg. Melton	Borthwick Institute, York, Register 9 (of Archbishop Melton).
Reg. Melton	*The Register of William Melton*, vols. I and III, ed. R.M.T. Hill, 1977, 1988; vol. II, ed. D.B. Robinson, 1978.
VCH	*Victoria County History*.

ARCHDEACONRY OF NOTTINGHAM

[Fo.331; N.F.400] DE ARCHIDIACONATU NOTINGHAMIE PONTIFICATUS DOMINI WILLELMI DE MELTON ANNO PRIMO.[1]

1 [*Commission to determine a cause about possession of West Markham vicarage.*] COMMISSIO SUPER [VICARIA] DE PARVA MARK[HAM].[2] Willelmus permissione divina Ebor' archiepiscopus Anglie primas dilectis filiis . . officiali nostro Ebor' et ejus commissario generali salutem graciam et benedictionem. De vestris circumspectione et industria plenius confidentes, in causa seu negocio que vel quod vertitur seu verti speratur inter dominum Ricardum de Hoton asserentem se vicarium ecclesie de Parva Markham[3] nostre diocesis actorem ex parte una et dominum Ricardum de Roderham possessioni ejusdem vicarie incumbentem[4] reum ex altera super vicaria memorata vobis ad cognoscendum procedendum decernendum diffiniendum pronunciandum et exequendum, necnon ad continuandum processum coram quibuscumque judicibus seu commissariis quorumcumque pluribus aut uno inter easdem partes in causa seu negotio suprascriptis prius habitum processui coram vobis[5] habendo, ac eciam ad omnia et singula facienda et exercenda que in premissis et ea quomodolibet contingentibus necessaria fuerint vel etiam oportuna, conjunctim et divisim vices nostras committimus cum cohercionis canonice potestate. [Beverley, 21 Dec. 1317.]

2 Institution and mandate for induction[6] of Thomas de Sibthorp, acolyte, to Kilvington (*Kilvyngton*) church, now vacant; presented by William de Staunton, kt. Also letters dimissory for his further ordination. Beverley, 22 Dec. 1317.

3 Commission to M. Michael de Harcla and M. Richard de Scardeburgh, clerks (dioc. York), to hear and determine the cause between William de Lee, priest, presented to Blyth (*Blida*) vicarage, plaintiff, and Gregory de Neuton, defendant in possession.[7] Beverley, 28 Dec. 1317.

4 Letters dimissory for holy orders to William de Salford, acolyte, rector of Folkton (*Folketon*) [Y.E.R.], Beverley, 24 Dec. 1317.

[1] In lower margin. Most earlier following folios have, at their feet on both sides, *De archidiaconatu Notinghamie*, often with the pontifical year. Quires are numbered from fo.339 (*Quaternus secundus*) to fo.368 (*Sextus quaternus*). After then (Dec. 1329, **570–86**), these footnotes are limited to *Notingh'* to fo.373 and thereafter are very rare.
[2] Partly illegible.
[3] Presented by the king and instituted, 1313 (*CPR 1307–13*, 526, 558; *Reg. Greenfield*, IV.132 (no.1956). See also **98** and references given there.
[4] In April 1316 he claimed to have been presented and was instituted after Hoton's alleged resignation in September; but Hoton soon resumed the suit (*Reg. Greenfield*, V.274–6, nos.2875, 2878, 2881). See also *CPR 1313–17*, 594, 693.
[5] Interlined.
[6] While the record of institution was generally a letter to the new incumbent, the mandate for his induction immediately following was a memorandum of a letter of the same date, normally (unless otherwise shown in this calendar) to the archdeacon and his official.
[7] Instituted 1315 (*Reg. Greenfield*, IV.198, no.2074); and see **58**, **182**.

5 Commission to the official of York and his commissary-general to hear and determine the cause between John de Stanton, priest, claiming as presentee a mediety of North Muskham (*Northmuskam*) vicarage, and William de Tythebi, priest, in possession.[8] Beverley, 2 Jan. 1318.

6 Commission to the same for the cause in which the prior and convent of Shelford, claiming as patrons, seek to remove William de Tythebi from the above mediety. [Same date.]

7 Licence to study for one year at a *studium generale* to M. John Luterell, D.D., rector of Holme Pierrepont (*Holm juxta Noting'*).[9] Beverley, 12 Jan. 1318.

8 [Fo.331v; N.F.400v] Appointment[10] of M. William de Hundon, rector of Barnburgh (*Barneburgh*) as sequestrator in the archdeaconry of Nottingham and dean of Southwell (*Suwell*) and Laneham (*Lanum*). Beverley, 23 Jan. 1318.

9 Institution and mandate for induction (to the dean of Laneham) of John de Sutton, priest, to Hayton vicarage; presented by M. John Bussh, sacrist of the chapel of St. Mary and the Holy Angels, York. Bishop Burton (*Burton prope Beverl'*), 26 Jan. 1318.

10 Commission to the official of York and his commissary-general to hear and determine the cause between John de Routhecliff, clerk, presented to Hockerton (*Hokerton*) church, plaintiff, and Ralph de Hertford, defendant in possession;[11] continuing the process before M. John de Wodhous, rector of Sutton on Derwent (*Sutton super Derwent'*), official of the court of York, commissary-general of the dean and chapter as custodians of the spiritualities *sede vacante*, and special commissary in this cause.[12] Cawood (*Cawod*), 2 Feb. 1318.

11 Note of letters dimissory for further orders to Hugh de Wilghby, subdeacon, rector of Rempstone (*Rempiston*). Cawood, 8 Feb. 1318.

12 Note of licence to the same to study at a *studium generale* until Michaelmas following.[13] [Same date.]

13 Note of similar licence for one year to Hugh [*recte* Thomas] de Hercy, rector of West Retford (*West Retteford*). Cawood, 13 Feb. 1318.

14 Commission[14] to M. William de Hundon, rector of Barnburgh, sequestrator in the archdeaconry, of the custody of Warsop (*Warsoppe*) church, vacant since 14

[8] Instituted 1312 (*Reg. Greenfield*, IV.120, no.1925). See also ibid. V.277, no.2885.
[9] Then chancellor of Oxford University (*BRUO*, II.1181–2).
[10] Similar in form to no.1 in *Reg. Melton*, II.1.
[11] Presented in 1300 (*Reg. Corbridge*, I.208, no.572).
[12] See *Reg. Greenfield,* V.277, no.2884.
[13] See *BRUO*, III.2051.
[14] In same form as no.5, *Reg. Melton,* II.3.

February by the resignation of the rector[15] under the papal decree against pluralists. Cawood, 14 Feb. 1318.

15 [*Commendation to Clayworth church.*]
COMMENDA ECCLESIE DE CLAWORD. Willelmus etc. dilecto filio magistro Johanni de Notingham sacre pagine professori presbitero salutem [*etc.*]. Ecclesiam parochialem de Claword nostre diocesis, ad quam per reverendum virum magistrum Henricum de Malmesfeld decanum ecclesie Linc' presentatus existis, tibi ad tempus semestre in forma constitutionis edite in concilio Lugdun' novissime celebrato pensantes evidentem utilitatem ipsius ecclesie commendamus. Vale. [Cawood, 18 Feb. 1318.]

16 Mandate to the archdeacon or his official to induct M. John de Notingham or his proctor into corporal possession of the above church [rehearsing **15**. Same date.]

17 Note of commission to M. William de Hundon, sequestrator, of the custody of the sequestration of Tuxford (*Tuxeford*) church 'as in the form for Warsop' [**14**].[16] 18 Feb. 1318.

18 Grant, during pleasure, to John Burdon, clerk, of custody of the sequestration of Warsop church, vacant and in the presentation of John de Somery, kt.; he is to render an account of the fruits and income to the archbishop or his official of York on request. Cawood, 12 Mar. 1318.

19 Note of mandate to M. William de Houndon, sequestrator, to release the above sequestration to John Burdon. Same date.

20 [Fo.332; N.F.401] Licence to study for one year at a *studium generale* to Henry de Sybbethorp, priest, rector of a mediety of Eakring (*Eykeryng'*) church. Cawood, 14 Mar. 1318.

21 Note of letters dimissory to be ordained priest to M. Thomas de Garton, deacon, rector of Misson (*Misyn*).[17] 28 Mar. 1318.

22 [*Mandate to value Farndon church, a prebend in Lincoln cathedral, reporting by 16 April.*]
LITTERA AD INQUIRENDUM DE VERO VALORE ECCLESIE DE FARNDON PREBENDATE IN ECCLESIA LINCOLN'. Willelmus etc. dilecto filio decano nostro de Neuwerk' salutem [*etc.*]. De vero valore ecclesie parochialis de Farndon nostre diocesis in ecclesia Linc' prebendate et in quibus porcionibus consistit certis ex causis volentes effici certiores, tibi committimus et mandamus quatenus aliquo certo die per te assignando ad dictam ecclesiam de Farndon personaliter accedens, per viros fidedignos tam de parochia dicte ecclesie quam aliorum

[15] M. John de Sutton (*BRUO*, III.1820).
[16] William de Bevercotes, instituted to Tuxford in 1300, was dispensed for plurality in 1312 (*Reg. Corbridge*, I.206–7, no.568; *CPL*, II.100).
[17] See *BRUC*, 252.

locorum vicinorum ad numerum sufficientem ipsius ecclesie meliorem habentes noticiam ab antiquo juratos de valore ejusdem ecclesie et in quibus rebus proventus ipsius ecclesie consistunt inquisitionem facias diligentem, designans distincte quantum habent in terris dominicis et redditibus, quantum in decimis garbarum et feni ac aliis decimis minutis et obvencionibus quibuscumque, quantum porciones singule valeant annuatim, necnon et de pensionibus ac aliis oneribus incumbentibus ecclesie memorate, de manso etiam ad dictam ecclesiam pertinente[18] que et quales sint ibi domus situate ac de amplitudine aree ortorum et gardinorum ejusdem et longitudine, ac de aliis ad dictam ecclesiam qualitercumque pertinentibus, per que de statu ejusdem ecclesie et valore possimus plenius informari; premunito primitus per te prebendario seu rectore dicte ecclesie quod die ad inquisicionem hujusmodi faciendam apud Farndon intersit dicte inquisicionis recepcioni si sibi viderit expedire. Nos autem super hiis que feceris et inveneris in premissis citra dominicam in Ramis Palmarum distincte et aperte certiores reddas per tuas clausas litteras harum seriem continentes. Vale. [Cawood, 1 Apr. 1318.]

23 Institution [etc.] of John Burdon, acolyte, to Warsop church, now vacant; presented by John de Somery, kt. Cawood, 4 Apr. 1318.

24 Licence to study until 16 Jan. 1321 at a *studium generale* to Reginald de Sibbethorpe, subdeacon, rector of Hawksworth (*HAUKESWELL*; *Hawkesworth*). Cawood, 4 Apr. 1318.

25 Note of mandate to the dean of Newark (*Neuwerk'*) to value South Scarle (*Scarle*) church, a prebend in Lincoln cathedral, 'as in the form for Farndon' [**22**]; he is to report by 7 May. Cawood, 14 Apr. 1318.

26 [*Ordinance for a vicarage in the prebendal church of Farndon and Balderton. Vicars are to be presented by the prebendary. For their portion they will have all oblations, tithes of curtilages, all other small tithes, dead mortuary payments from both vills and living mortuary payments from Farndon together with its whole tithe of wool and lambs. Prebendaries are to meet all charges, vicars responsible only for the repair of their manse and its outhouses; with provision for its construction.*]
ORDINATIO VICARIE ECCLESIARUM DE FARNDON ET DE BALDRESTON. Universis Christi fidelibus ad quorum noticiam pervenerit hec scriptura Willelmus [*etc.*] salutem in sinceris amplexibus salvatoris. Inter alias sol[l]icitudines quibus officii nostri debito astringimur, illam mentalius amplectimur et prosequi intimur prona mente qua divini cultus augmentum promovere cupimus ad laudem altissimi et decorem ecclesie in ministris. Cum itaque in ecclesia prebendali de Farndon et Baldreston nostre diocesis Linc' ecclesie cui ecclesie animarum cura iminet perpetuus non sit vicarius deputatus nec vicaria perpetua in eadem ecclesia hactenus ordinata juxta canonum instituta, nos ex professionis debito circa curam et regimen subditorum nostrorum ecclesie prebendalis et parochialis predicte sicut et ceterarum ecclesiarum nostre diocesis solliciti semper pro viribus et attenti, ac utilitatem earumdem precordialiter intuentes et pro nostre fragilitatis humane modulo affectantes ut decus sancte matris

[18] MS. *pertinentem*

ecclesie succrescat devocius in subjectis cumuletur etiam et amplificetur per majorem numerum ministrorum qui gratos deo se faciant et ydoneos servitores per divini cultus exercit[i]um in latitudine caritatis prout sanctiones canonice requirunt et exigunt in hac parte, intervenientibus ad hoc consensu et assensu omnium quorum interest et quos dictum negotium tangit, facta inquisicione legitima ad mandatum nostrum super valore dicte ecclesie de Farndon et Balderston prebendalis et pertinentium ad eandem, consideratis considerandis et omnibus equo libramine ponderatis, habita super hiis et premissa deliberacione pleniori, dei nomine invocato, ad instantem peticionem magistri Pandulphi de Sabellis nunc prebendarii ecclesie prebendalis predicte perpetuam vicariam in ecclesia predicta de Farndon et Balderston prebendali auctoritate nostra diocesana ordinamus et disponimus in subscriptis porcionibus particulariter et singulariter, prout sequitur in hunc modum: videlicet quod vicarii qui pro tempore fuerint ad dictam vicariam nobis et successoribus nostris qui pro tempore fuerint ac decano et capitulo Ebor' sede ejusdem vacante per prebendarium prebende predicte cum dicta vicaria vacaverit successivis temporibus presentandi, et per nos ac ipsos ad ipsam vicariam admittendi et instituendi canonice in eadem, habeant et percipiant omnes oblaciones earumdem ecclesiarum ac decimas curtilagiorum in quibuscumque consistentes et omnes alias minutas debitas ad easdem ecclesias pertinentes, omnia eciam mortuaria mortua utriusque ville et insuper omnia mortuaria viva in villa de Farndon una cum tota decima lane et agnorum ejusdem ville, ceteris aliis ad easdem prebendam et ecclesias pertinentibus integraliter reservatis prebendariis memoratis; qui prebendarii omnia onera ordinaria et extraordinaria tocius dicte prebende et ecclesiis predictis et pertinenciis ad easdem incumbencia integraliter subeant et agnoscant, ita quod vicarii ad nulla alia teneantur nisi ad refectionem mansi vicarie sue et domuum spectancium ad eandem; et provideat prebendarius quamcicius [Fo.332^v; N.F.401^v] poterit vicario instituendo ibidem de una placea competenti pro manso dicti vicarii per dictum vicarium edificanda, ad cujus edificacionem solvet prebendarius eidem vicario quatuor marcas, et interim donec de dicta placea sibi realiter sit provisum idem vicarius in domibus prebende hospitetur vel alibi ubi congrue poterit sumptibus prebendarii predicti. Hanc autem ordinacionem nostram in omnibus et singulis suis articulis futuris perpetuo temporibus ratam firmam et illibatam volumus et decernimus permanere. In quorum omnium testimonium sigillum nostrum presentibus est appensum. [Cawood, 15 Apr. 1318.]

27 Note of licence to study (under the constitution *Cum ex eo*) from 19 April to 29 Sept. 1318 and the following year to Hugh Gernoun, acolyte, rector of Elkesley.[19] Also of letters dimissory for his ordination as subdeacon by an English bishop. Bishopthorpe, [19 Apr. 1318].

28 Institution [etc.] of John de Cotegrave, priest, to the vicarage ordained by the archbishop in the prebend of Farndon and Balderton (*Balderston*); presented by M. Francis de Luco, canon of York, and John de Pontesellis, proctors of M. Pandulph de Sabellis, papal notary, canon of Lincoln and prebendary of Farndon and Balderton. Cawood, 30 Apr. 1318.

[19] See *BRUC*, 256.

29 Ordination[20] of vicarage in South Scarle church, a prebend in Lincoln cathedral, at the instance of Thomas de Goldesburgh, its prebendary. Vicars are to be presented [etc.] and for their portion will have all oblations, tithes of wool and lambs, chickens, calves, pigs, milk, cheese, flax, hemp, mills, geese, hens, pigeons, fisheries, bees, honey, fowling, merchandise, and money payments for the tithe of milk, wool and any other small tithes due to the prebendal church and its chapels, mortuary payments live and dead and also the tithes of curtilages of the whole parish and half the tithe hay belonging to the prebendary in the vill of Spalford (*Spaldeford*). The vicar is to have the second best dwelling house in South Scarle for his habitation and another house in Girton (*Gretton*) belonging to the prebend, excepting the half place for the prebendary's byre, but saving to the vicar the house in that place where the parish chaplain usually lived. The vicar will provide two chaplains at his own cost with the option of himself taking the place of one, pay procurations to the archdeacon and synodal dues, maintain lights, books and vestments, but have no other burdens. The prebendary is to have the main dwelling house, demesne lands, manorial court income and the whole tithe of sheaves and hay, except half the tithe hay in Spalford (as mentioned above) and the tithe of curtilages; he is to bear all charges except those allotted above to the vicar. Cawood, 30 Apr. 1318.

30 Institution [etc.] of Robert de Couton, priest (dioc. York), to the vicarage ordained in South Scarle prebendal church; presented by [Thomas] de Goldesburgh, canon of Lincoln and prebendary of South Scarle. Langton (*Langeton*), 12 May 1318.

31 Note of licence to study for one year in a place of his choice in England to Thomas [de Outheby], rector of East Bridgford (*Estbriggeford*). 27 May 1318.

32 [Fo.333; N.F.402] Note of letters dimissory for Hugh Gernoun's ordination as subdeacon [cf. **27**]. Bishop Burton, 10 June 1318.

33 Oath of obedience[21] by Robert, abbot of Rufford [undated].[22]

34 Ordination[23] of vicarage in East Stoke (*Stokes*) church, a prebend in Lincoln cathedral, at the instance of Roger de Northburg', its prebendary. Vicars are to be presented [etc.] and for their portion will have the tithes of flax, hemp, dairy produce and other small tithes and oblations; the whole altarage except live mortuary payments; any profit arising in the vills of East Stoke, Syerston (*Sireston*) and a mediety of Elston (*Ayleston*) and Coddington (*Codington*); the tithe of wool and lambs from the vill of East Stoke and of the mills there; the tithe of a windmill and all the hay of Syerston and the mediety of Elston; the tithes and income due to the prebend from the mills of Newark castle; all the dairy produce (*totius albi*) of the castle and the tithe of the fishery

[20] In same form as **26**.
[21] Identical in form to similar oath in *Reg. Melton*, II.19–20.
[22] This abbot is apparently otherwise unknown (*Rufford Charters*, ed. C.J. Holdsworth, Thoroton Society Record Series, 1972–81), 4 vols., I.lxxxi.
[23] In same form as **26**.

in the [River] Trent below the castle and mills. The vicar is to live in the main dwelling house of the prebend until he is provided with a suitable house in East Stoke at the prebendary's expense; subsequent rebuilding and repair to be at the vicar's cost. He is also to pay procurations to the archdeacon and synodal dues, and to provide three chaplains to celebrate mass–one at East Stoke, another at Syerston and Elston, and the third at Coddington–of whom he may be one. The prebendary is to meet all other charges. Bishopthorpe, 20 June 1318.

35 Institution [etc.] of Richard de Otringham, priest, to Kneeton (*Knyveton*) church, now vacant; presented by the abbot and convent of Newbo. Bishop Wilton (*Wilton)*, 22 June 1318.

36 [*Commission to execute mandate of John XXII (dated Avignon, 15 Mar. 1318) to recover property in York diocese of the Hospital of St. John of Jerusalem in England unlawfully farmed, notwithstanding its leases and their confirmation by the pope.*]
[Fo.333ᵛ; N.F.402ᵛ] COMMISSIO SUPER DECIMIS ET POSSESSIONIBUS PRIORIS ET FRATRUM SANCTI JOHANNIS JEROSOLIM' AUCTORITATE PAPALI. Willelmus permissione divina etc. dilectis filiis priori de Thurgarton et magistro Elie de Couton canonico ecclesie Suwell' salutem [*etc.*]. Litteras apostolicas recepimus in hec verba:

Johannes episcopus servus servorum dei venerabili fratri archiepiscopo Ebor' salutem et apostolicam benedictionem. Ad audienciam nostram pervenit quod tam dilecti filii prior et fratres hospitalis sancti Johannis Jerosolimit' in Anglia quam predecessores eorum decimas terras domos prata pascua nemora molendina aqueductus piscarias maneria grangias redditus possessiones castra stagna lacus jura jurisdictiones et quedam alia bona ipsius hospitalis in civitate et diocesi Ebor' consistencia, datis super hoc litteris confectis exinde puplicis instrumentis factis renunciacionibus juramentis interpositis et penis adjectis, in gravem ejusdem hospitalis lesionem nonnullis clericis et laicis aliquibus eorum ad vitam quibusdam vero ad non modicum tempus et aliis perpetuo ad firmam vel sub censu annuo concesserunt, quorum aliqui dicuntur super hiis confirmacionis litteras in forma communi a sede apostolica impetrasse. Quia vero nostra interest super hoc de oportuno remedio providere, fraternitati tue per apostolica scripta mandamus quatenus ea que de bonis hujus hospitalis ejusdem per concessiones easdem alienata inveneris illicite vel distracta, non obstantibus litteris instrumentis penis et confirmacionibus supradictis, ad jus et proprietatem ejusdem hospitalis legitime revocari procures, contradictores per censuram ecclesiasticam appellatione postposita compescendo. Testes autem qui fuerunt nominati, si se gracia odio vel timore subtraxerint, censura simili appellatione cessante compellas veritatis testimonium perhibere. Datum Avinion' Idus Marcii pontificatus nostri anno secundo.

Nos itaque execucionem dicti mandati variis negociis prepediti intendere seu vacare personaliter non valentes, de vestris fidelitate et industria plenius confidentes, ad cognoscendum procedendum pronunciandum et exequendum juxta naturam vim formam et effectum dicti mandati apostolici contra personas infra archidiaconatum Notingh' constitutas vobis conjunctim et divisim vices nostras committimus cum cohercionis canonice potestate. Valete. [Bishop Burton, 25 June 1318.]

37 Institution [etc.] of Adam de Bajocis, acolyte, to Tuxford church, now vacant [see **17**]; presented by John de Bajocis, Peter Foune and John de Barkesworth, kt. Also letters dimissory for his further ordination. Ottringham (*Otringham*), 30 June 1318.

38 The like of William de Aslakby, priest (dioc. York), to the vicarage ordained in the prebendal church of East Stoke [see **34**]; presented by Roger de Northburgh, prebendary and rector of East Stoke and canon of Lincoln. Bishop Burton, 24 July 1318.

39 Ordination[24] of vicarage in Clifton church, a prebend in Lincoln cathedral. For their portion vicars will have the tithes of milk and dairy products, flax and hemp, curtilages and gardens, oblations and mortuary payments, all the income accruing to the altarage of the church except the tithe of wool and lambs which, together with the tithe of sheaves and hay, demesne lands and tenants' rents due to the church, are reserved to the prebendary, who will be responsible for all charges. The vicar will inhabit the house in South Clifton (*Suthclifton*) belonging to the church and the prebendary will annually provide him with two cartloads of hay and one of fodder. Bishop Burton, 27 July 1318.

40 Institution and mandate for induction of William de Wykenby, priest (dioc. York), to this vicarage; presented by M. Elias de Muskam, prebendary and rector and canon of Lincoln. Bishop Burton, 27 July 1318.

41 [Fo.334; N.F.403] Institution (by proxy, unnamed) and mandate for induction of William de Ilkeston, priest, to the church of St. Nicholas, Nottingham, now vacant; presented by the prior and convent of Lenton. Cawood, 1 Aug. 1318.

42 LITTERA AD MONENDUM DOMINUM CANT' ARCHIEPISCOPUM NE CRUCEM SUAM CORAM SE ERIGI FACIAT VEL DEFERRI IN DIOCESI VEL PROVINCIA EBOR' ETC.[25] Mandate[26] to the archdeacon of Nottingham or his official. The archbishop has heard that the archbishop of Canterbury is about to enter the diocese or province of York with his cross erect, to York's prejudice. It is to be announced in the archdeaconry that no one is to bow at the archbishop of Canterbury's blessing or assist him if he enters the diocese, under pain of excommunication, according to the form of the enclosed bull; informing him that [York] will defend the rights of his church. An interdict is to be imposed on all places through

[24] Similar in form to **26**. The parish was divided in 1874, with the original church in North Clifton.

[25] In the margin beneath this heading is a (contemporary?) drawing of a cross.

[26] Almost identical to the mandate to the deans of Newark and Bingham in 1314 (*Reg. Greenfield*, IV.157–9, no.2018): Melton's text usually has *et (*or *vel) provinciam* after *diocesim*, and *dictum archidiaconatum* instead of *dictos decanatus*. There are four insertions: *moneatis et* before *moneri canonice faciatis*; this is immediately followed by *in forma bulle presentibus intercluso et ei fac' ipsis* (of which the first five words are interlined); also interlined are *in hiis scriptis* after *ecclesiastico supponimus interdicto*; and *archiepiscopo* follows *prefato domino* in the last sentence.

which [Canterbury] passes. Names of subjects disobeying this inhibition are to be reported by letters patent. Cawood, 7 Aug. 1318.

43 MONICIO FACIENDA EIDEM OB CAUSA. Monition[27] of the archdeacon of Nottingham's official forbidding Walter [Reynolds], archbishop of Canterbury, from crossing York diocese or province with his cross erect, under pain of canonical punishment.

44 [*Mandate with more detailed instructions for the execution and delivery of these letters.*]
ALIA LITTERA SUPER EODEM.[28] Willelmus etc. archidiacono Notingh' vel ejus officiali salutem [*etc.*]. Ne per adventum venerabilis patris domini Cantuar' archiepiscopi cum cruce ante se erecta ad nostram diocesim vel provinciam per possessionem pacificam bajulacionis crucis ejusdem juri et libertati nostre Ebor' ecclesie derogetur, nostro incumbit officio multumque nobis insidet animo modis et viis licitis quibus possumus hujusmodi prejudicii[29] obviare. Quocirca vobis in virtute sancte obediencie qua nobis tenemini et sub pena districcionis canonice firmiter injungimus et mandamus quatinus mandatum nostrum vobis super premisso negocio directum cum omni celeritate diligencia et industria per totum archidiaconatum Notingh' execucioni debite demandetis, et monicioneS quarum formam vobis cum presentibus mittimus dicto domino archiepiscopo si ipsum per archidiaconatum predictum transire contingatur sub fidedignorum et notarii testimonio quamcicius de ipsius adventu vobis constare poterit publice faciatis modo pacifico et quieto, ne vobis super premissis quod absit possitis de necligencia reprehendi. Inhibemus autem et per vos inhiberi mandamus ne dicto domino archiepiscopo vel alicui de sua comitiva corporale violencia inferatur.[30] Valete. [Cawood, 7 Aug. 1318.]

45 Memorandum of similar letters to the archdeacon of York or his official, and to the deans of Nottingham, Newark, Retford (*Retteford*) and Bingham (*Byngham*), 'as are fully contained in the register of our immediate predecessor'. Same date.

46 Institution [etc.] of M. John de Notingham, D.D., to Clayworth church, now vacant; presented by M. Henry de Mamesfled, dean of Lincoln. Cawood, 14 Aug. 1318.

47 Note of licence to study for one year to John Burdon, subdeacon, rector of Warsop. 15 Aug. 1318.

[27] Again modelled on Greenfield's monition for the dean of Newark. The last sentence is given in full (repeating *ne per Ebor' . . . evitare*, where the Greenfield text has *ne etc. ut supra.*).
[28] Based on the Greenfield text (*Reg.*, IV.159–60), but with substantial additions.
[29] These two words interlined.
[30] This sentence – one of Melton's additions – has been underlined by another hand. Most other underlinings are of the names of religious houses; in some cases these lines are linked to marginalia in a sixteenth-century hand which name their orders (**278**, **538**, **777**, **803**); and likewise in two entries about synods (**497**, **772**).

48 [Fo.334v; N.F.403v] Institution [etc.] of Thomas son of Ralph de Wyleford, clerk, to Wilford (*Willeford*) church, now vacant; presented by Gervase de Clifton, kt. Also licence (given in full) to study for two years from this day in a *studium generale* and be ordained as far as the subdiaconate. Nottingham, 22 Aug. 1318.

49 LICENCIA PRO CANTARIA HABENDA IN QUADAM CAPELLA INFRA MANERIUM. Licence during pleasure to Roger de Brunnesleye for the celebration of services in the chapel of his manor of Brinsley, provided there is no loss or prejudice to the parish church of Greasley (*Greseleye*), which is distant, with floods impeding access. Arnold by Nottingham, [day and month omitted] 1318.

50 Note of letters dimissory for holy orders to Simon de Briggeford, acolyte. 29 Aug. 1318.

51 Institution [etc.] of M. Ralph de Holbech to Kilvington (*Kilington*) church, now vacant; presented by William de Staunton, kt. Scrooby (*Scroby*), 31 Aug. 1318.

52 Commission to the official of York or his commissary-general to hear and determine the cause between William Brase, a parishioner, and Gregory de Neuton, vicar of Blyth, because the latter excommunicated Alice wife of Thomas le Warde, also a parishioner, without due form (*forma juris omissa*) and against the statutes of the general council, and subsequently celebrated mass, so incurring irregularity. Scrooby, 31 Aug. 1318.

53 Note of licence to study for three years to Thomas de Casterton, priest, rector of a mediety of Cotgrave (*Cotegrave*) church. 10 Sept. 1318.

54 Mandate[31] to the archdeacon or his official to cite the clergy of Nottingham deanery, and two, three or four men from each vill, to attend visitation as follows: on Friday 20 Oct. in Hucknall Torkard (*Hokenale*) church; on Saturday 21 Oct. in Arnold (*Arnhale*) church; and on Monday 23 Oct. in St. Mary's, Nottingham. Cawood, 15 Sept. 1318.

55 Note of letters dimissory for all orders to Thomas son of Ralph de Willeford, clerk, rector of Wilford. 15 Sept. 1318.

56 [*Postponement of the visitation of Worksop priory announced for 17 October.*]
DELACIO VISITACIONIS DOMUS DE WIRSOP. Willelmus etc. priori et conventui de Wirkesop salutem [*etc.*]. Cum propter quemdam tractatum cum domino Cantuar' archiepiscopo super bajulacione crucis sue et nostre habendum, necnon propter parliamentum quod evicino jam instat[32] ut noscis, visitationis officium quod apud vos die Martis proximo post festum sancti Wilfridi nuper mandavimus excercendum complere minime permittamur, aliquam contra nos providenciam faciendi omnino cessetis ista vice. Nam offerente se oportunitate

[31] Identical in form to mandate for Bulmer deanery in *Reg. Melton*, II.6 (no.14).
[32] At York from 20 Oct. (*HBC*, 554); see also **42–4**; **120**.

congrua ad premissa tempestive ad parandum ea que incubuerint vos curabimus premunire. Valete. [Snaith (*Snayth*), 13 Oct. 1318.]

57 [Fo.335; N.F.404] Note of mandate to the archdeacon or his official to cite the clergy and people of Retford deanery to attend visitation as follows: on Tuesday 17 Oct. in Blyth parish church; on Wednesday 18 Oct. in West Retford church; and on Thursday 19 Oct. in West Markham (*Parvamarcham*) church. 13 Oct. 1318.

58 [*Revocation of the commission to hear the cause about Blyth vicarage* (3); *the parties have submitted to arbitration by the archbishop, who is to receive the evidence and documents by 25 October.*]
REVOCATIO PROCESSUS HABITI INTER PRESENTATUM AD VICARIAM DE BLIDA ET INCUMBENTEM POSSESSIONI. Willelmus etc. dilectis filiis magistris Michaeli de Harkele et Ricardo de Scardeburgh vel eorum alteri commissariis nostris inter partes subscriptas specialiter deputatis salutem [*etc.*]. Cum dominus Willelmus de Lee ad vicariam ecclesie parochialis de Blida nostre diocesis per religiosos viros priorem et conventum loci ejusdem presentatus ac dominus Gregorius de Neuton vicarius ejusdem ecclesie possessioni dicte vicarie incumbens ac prefati prior et conventus quantum ad eos attinet coram nobis consenserint et se ordinationi nostre submiserint ut nos, auditis causis vacationis per presentatum predictum contra ipsum incumbentem propositis et pretensis et probationibus earundem de plano absque figura et strepitu judicii et discussis, necnon juribus et defensionibus incumbentis consideratis et equo libramine ponderatis super toto negocio, ut parcium parcatur laboribus et expensis, sentencialiter diffiniamus prout secundum allegata et probata coram nobis et processus jam habiti super hec probationes et instrumenta justicia fieri suadebit; vobis et vestrum alteri injungimus et mandamus quatenus totum processum coram vobis et vestrum altero in dicto negocio, quod ex premissis causis ex certa sciencia ad nostrum examen revocamus, habitum litis coram aliis commissariis quibuscumque cum omnibus instrumentis et munimentis propositionibus actis et attestacionibus omnibusque aliis hinc inde propositis productis et exhibitis prefatum negocium concernentibus nobis citra diem Mercurii proximum ante festum apostolorum Symonis et Jude sub sigillis vestris vel vestrum alterius integraliter et fideliter transmittatis una cum vestris litteris que harum seriem representent. Valete. [Blyth, 17 Oct. 1318.]

59 Note of letters dimissory to John and Robert, sons of Adam the tailor of Blyth, acolytes. Scrooby, 17 Oct. 1318.

60 Mandate to the archdeacon or his official cancelling the intended visitation of Newark deanery 'for certain reasons'. Laneham, 22 Oct. 1318.

61 [*Commission to correct defects etc. discovered in the visitation of Retford deanery.*]
COMMISSIO FACTA PRO CORRECTIONIBUS FACIENDIS IN DECANATU DE RETFORD. Willelmus etc. dilectis filiis magistris Ricardo de Melton ac Willelmo de Hundon nostris clericis ministerialibus salutem [*etc.*]. De vestra industria et fidelitate circumspecta plenius confidentes, ad corrigendum puniendum et reformandum crimina defectus et excessus in visitatione nostra quam nuper

in decanatu de Retford exercuimus ex officio nostro compertos et ad omnia alia exercenda et exequenda que statum salubrem sancte ecclesie ac subjecti nobis populi respicere, videlicet[33] in hac parte vestra discretio nobis fida vobis vices nostras committimus cum cohercionis canonice potestate. In cujus rei testimonium litteras nostras vobis fieri fecimus has patentes. [Laneham, 23 Oct. 1318.]

62 Institution [etc.] of John de Castreton, priest, to a mediety of Cotgrave church;[34] presented by the prior (*sic*) and convent of Swineshead (*Swynesheved*) in an exchange from the chapel of Woodhead (*Wodeheved*; dioc. Lincoln). York, 31 Oct. 1318.

63 Note of licence to study for one year to Gilbert de Sancta Elena, priest, rector of Finningley (*Fyningley*). 3 Nov. 1318.

64 [*Licence for a private confessor to Sir John de Segrave and his wife.*]
LICENCIA PRO DOMINO J. DE SEGRAVE ET UXORE AD CONFITENDUM FRATRI W. DE DRAYTON. Willelmus etc. dilecto nobis in Christo nobili viro domino Johanni de Segrave militi et domine Cristiane uxori sue salutem [*etc.*]. Devocionis vestre precibus favorabiliter annuentes et animarum vestrarum profectui consulere cupientes, ut religioso viro fratri Willelmo de Drayton de ordine predicatorum, de cujus sincera in domino devotione confidimus, peccata vestra confiteri possitis et possit alter vestrum quociens vobis et vestrum alteri videbitur expedire, quodque dictus frater Willelmus de peccatis sibi confessatis vos et vestrum alterum in foro consciencie absolvere valeat et vobis penitencias injungere salutares, casibus a jure nobis specialiter reservatis dumtaxat exceptis, vobis et alteri vestrum sic confitendi et dicto fratri confessiones hujusmodi audiendi ac vobis vestrumque alteri absolutionis beneficium impendendi injungendique penitencias salutares potestatem et licenciam specialem concedimus per presentes ad nostrum beneplacitum duraturas. Valete. [Bishopthorpe, 3 Nov. 1318.]

65 Note of licence to study for one year at a *studium generale* to Robert [son of] Richard Jorce, rector of North Collingham (*Northcolingham*), 'not however in the form of the constitution *Cum ex eo*'. York, 8 Nov. 1318.

66 Note of licence to study for one year to William de Quylly, rector of Eastwood (*Estweyt*). 12 Nov. 1318.

67 [*Commission to enquire into a cause shown in a schedule (not given).*]
COMMISSIO FACTA MAGISTRO THOME DE SANCTO LEONARDO ET DOMINO WILLELMO DE HUNDON AD PROCEDENDUM ET DIFFINIENDUM PROUT CONTINETUR IN LITTERA. Willelmus [*etc.*] dilectis filiis magistro Thome de Sancto Leonardo rectori ecclesie de Egmanton et domino Willelmo de Hundon salutem [*etc.*]. De

[33] Interlined.
[34] Thomas de Casterton (see **53**) had been instituted to this mediety in 1317, despite the incumbency of Henry de Hale since 1310 (*Reg. Greenfield*, IV.111, no.1906; V.276, no. 2882). The exchange was soon reversed (**84**). For Woodhead, see *VCH Rutland,* II.235, an identification kindly supplied by Dr. Nicholas Bennett.

vestris circumspectione et industria plenius confidentes, ad cognoscendum et inquirendum tam ex officio quam ad promocionem partis super articulis in cedula presentibus annexa contentis ac eciam ad procedendum super ipsis prout natura predictorum articulorum exigit et requirit usque ad finalem decisionem eorundem, pronunciacione diffinitiva officiali nostro Ebor' specialiter reservata, vobis vices nostras committimus cum cohercionis canonice potestate. Valete. [Bishopthorpe, 13 Nov. 1318.]

68 [*Licence for a rector to be absent for medical treatment.*]
LICENCIA ABSENTANDI PRO RECTORE MEDIETATIS ECCLESIE DE COTEGRAVE CAUSA INFIRMITATIS. Willelmus etc. dilecto filio domino Willelmo dicto le Palmer de Notingham rectori medietatis ecclesie de Cotegrave[35] nostre diocesis salutem [*etc.*]. Ut occasione morbi quo fidedignorum testimonio diceris languere acerbi, et ex quo tibi nisi ciciori cura medici magis artificialis succurratur mortis tibi jacula cominantur, ab ecclesia tua predicta apud Oxon' vel London' ubi copiam ac facultatem peritiorum invenire valeas medicorum licite possis te transferre pro tua convalescencia et abesse, ne pro non residencia a quibuscumque nostris ministris [inquieris], licenciam tibi de nostra speciali gracia per annum continuum a data presencium concedimus per presentes; ita tamen quod dicta ecclesia tua interim debitis non fraudetur obsequiis nec animarum cura aliquatenus necgligatur, set volumus quod procuratorem idoneum ibidem medio tempore constituas qui ordinariis in singulis respondeat debite loco tui. Vale. [Bishopthorpe, 18 Nov. 1318.]

69 [Fo.335^v; N.F.404^v] Commission to the official of York to hear and determine the *ex officio* cause against Roger son of Nicholas de Misterton, and to continue the proceedings against him before the archbishop at the instance of Cecily Fauke of Misterton, as shown in a schedule. Bishopthorpe, 17 Nov. 1318.

70 Note of letterers dimissory for ordination to all minor orders of William son of Alan de Northleverton. 19 Nov. 1318.

71 Note of letters dimissory for ordination to all minor and holy orders to John de Leverton and William his brother. 22 Nov. 1318.

72 Mandate to the sequestrator in the archdeaconry to sequestrate all goods and revenues in the churches and manors of East (*Magna*) and West (*Parva*) Markham, Harworth (*Hareworth*), Walesby, Lowdham and North Wheatley (*Wheteley*) held by M. Boniface de Saluciis as rector;[36] he is to make a detailed report by letters close. Bishopthorpe, 5 Dec. 1318.

73 Institution [etc.] of Thomas de Bugdene, priest, to Fledborough (*Fletburg'*) church, now vacant; presented by John de Lyseus of Fledborough. Bishopthorpe, 11 Dec. 1318.

[35] This was the mediety in Lenton's gift. William was instituted in 1309 (*Reg. Greenfield*, V.183, no.2661).
[36] See *BRUO*, III.1634.

74 Note of licence to Acard [de Longo Prato[37]], priest, rector of Ordsall (*Ordesale*), to be absent for one year and demise his church to an ecclesiastic of the diocese; its revenues are not to be removed and he is to put in a suitable proctor. Bishopthorpe, 12 Dec. 1318.

75 Note of release of the sequestration of goods of Nicholas de Tykhill, rector of Kelham (*Kelm*), imposed by authority of two royal writs; Richard de Celario, rector of Treeton (*Treton*), his pledge, is to make satisfaction for their value of £7 3s. 15 Dec. 1318.

76 Note of licence to study until Michaelmas [29 Sept. 1319] to M. Thomas de Laford, rector of Cotham (*Cotom*). 20 Dec. 1318.

77 Mandate to the prior of Thurgarton to return Stephen de Langetoft, canon of Marton, banished to Thurgarton as a penance,[38] when his prior sends for him. Cawood, 21 Dec. 1318.

78 RECUPERACIO PRESENTACIONIS MEDIETATIS ECCLESIE DE EKERINGGE VERSUS JOHANNEM DE STIRCHELE. [Common Pleas] writ[39] ***admittatis non obstante reclamacione*** ordering the archbishop to admit a suitable presentee of Marjory, widow of Jordan Foliot', to a mediety of Eakring church because she has recovered the presentation in the king's court against John de Stirchele by default. Tested by W[illiam] de Bereford, Westminster, 28 Nov. 1318.

79 Note of mandate to the sequestrator to release the sequestration of the goods of M. Boniface de Saluciis. 13 Jan. 1319.

80 [*Grant of custody of the hospital of St. Mary Magdalen outside Southwell.*]
COMMISSIO CUSTODIE HOSPITALIS BEATE MARIE MAGDALENE EXTRA SUWELL' Willelmus etc. dilecto filio Henrico Sabbe presbitero salutem [*etc.*]. De tua fidelitate et industria circumspecta confidentes, custodiam hospitalis beate Marie Magdalene extra Suwell cum omnibus juribus et pertinenciis ipsius una cum administracione bonorum hospitalis ejusdem tibi committimus per presentes, proviso quod onera eidem incumbencia juxta ipsius facultates subeas et supportes, ordinacionem primariam hospitalis predicti et voluntatem fundatoris ejusdem quatenus tibi possibile fuerit debite prosequendo. Volumus autem quod cum ipsius hospitalis custodiam qualitercumque dimiseris, ipsum tam in rebus mobilibus quam eciam immobilibus in adeo bono statu vel meliori quod illud reciperis omnimodo dimittas, ut ex tuo labore retribucionem condignam a domino valeas promereri; presentibus pro nostro beneplacito duraturis. Vale. [Cawood, 17 Jan. 1319.]

[37] See note to **143**.
[38] See *Reg. Melton*, II.25–6, nos.51–2.
[39] The writ itself, measuring 24 by 4 cms., is between ff.335–6, and numbered 405 in the new foliation; it cites rot. 443 and is 'signed' *Sobbury*. It is endorsed as received at Cawood, 23 December.

81 Mandate for his induction to the bailiff of Southwell. [Same date?]

82 [Fo.336; N.F.406] Institution and mandate for induction (to the dean of Laneham) of Richard de Shirburn, priest, to East Retford (*Estretford*) vicarage, now vacant; presented by M. John Bussh, sacrist of the chapel of St. Mary and the Holy Angels, York. Bisshopthorpe, 22 Jan. 1319.

83 Institution and mandate for induction of Matthew de Halifax, priest, to Elton church; presented by the prior and convent of Blyth in an exchange from Kirk Sandall (*Parva Sandale*) church (dioc.York). Bishopthorpe, 24 Jan. 1319.

84 Institution (in the person of William de Fratribus, clerk, as proctor) and mandate for induction of Thomas de Casterton, deacon, to a mediety of Cotgrave church; presented by the abbot[40] and convent of Swineshead in an exchange from the chapel of Woodhead (*Wodesheved*; dioc. Lincoln[41]). Bishopthorpe, 8 Feb. 1319.

85 Licence[42] to the king, his lieutenant or lieutenants, to take during Sexagesima the assize of novel disseisin sued by Thomas de Bekering against Adam de Everingham of Laxton, his wife Clarice and others, touching his free tenement in Laxton. Bishopthorpe, 10 Feb. 1319.

86 Note of like licence for assize sued by Thomas Lungevillers against Adam de Everingham and others as above. Same date.

87 Licence to study for one year at a *studium generale* to Thomas de Hercy, rector of West Retford. Bishopthorpe, 13 Feb. 1319.

88 Note of letters dimissory for all orders to William de Radclyve, acolyte. Same date.

89 Commission [*sic*] to Edmund Deyncourt, kt., Richard de Wyleby, kt., and Richard de Whatton, justices of assize in Nottinghamshire, to take during Lent the assize of novel disseisin sued by John le Berett', son of Sir Roger le Berett', and John's wife Alice against Peter de Mountfort, kt., and others, touching his free tenement in Lowdham (*Loudham*), Gunthorpe and Caythorpe (*Cathorp*). Bishopthorpe, 16 Feb. 1319.

90 [*Licence for the vicar of West Markham to visit the Roman Curia.*]
LICENCIA ABSENTANDI PRO VICARIO ECCLESIE DE PARVA MARCHAM. Memorandum quod xiii Kalendas Marcii apud Thorp dominus tolleravit quod dominus Ricardus de Hoton vicarius ecclesie de Parva Markham propter aliqua conscienciam suam tangencia, ut dicebat, posset adire curiam Romanam, ita quod aliquem in sua vicaria dimittat qui curam vicarie sue gerat eo

[40] Corrected from 'prior'; cf. **62**.
[41] *Lincoln' dioc'* interlined. A semi-legible note records that by the chancellor's order (*de precepto cancellarii*) the letter issued *alibi* with corrections.
[42] Identical in form to licence in *Reg. Melton*, II.35, no.70.

absente et procuratorem sufficientem instructum constituat qui ordinariis respondeat singulis debite loco sui, ac eciam quod ad dictam suam vicariam quam cicius poterit expeditis suis negociis redeat. [Bishopthorpe, 17 Feb. 1319.]

91 Licence to study until 29 Sept. 1321 at a *studium generale* to M. John de la Laund, D.C.L., rector of Arnold (*Arnall*).[43] Bishopthorpe, 15 Mar. 1319.

92 [*Commission to claim clerks charged before justices of gaol delivery at Nottingham.*] LITTERA AD PETENDUM CLERICOS APUD NOTINGHAM INCARCERATOS. Willelmus etc. dilecto filio magistro Ade de Pykering rectori ecclesie beate Petri Notingh' decano nostro de Notingh' salutem [*etc.*]. De tua fida industria confidentes, ad petendum et recipiendum clericos quoscumque super quibuscumque criminibus impetitos coram domino nostro rege vel ipsius locum tenentibus ac justiciariis suis quibuscumque assignatis vel assignandis datis vel dandis ad carcerem Notinghamie liberandum tibi cum potestate cohercionis canonice committimus vices nostras, proviso quod clericos quos receperitis sub salva salvari facias custodia quousque quid de illis agendum fuerit judicio ecclesie consulcius ordinetur. In cujus rei testimonium sigillum nostrum presentibus est appensum. Vale. [Bishopthorpe, 12 Mar. 1319.]

93 Note of letter to the king cancelling a request to imprison Roger son of Nicholas de Misterton. Same date.

94 Note of letters dimissory to be ordained priest to Thomas de Casterton, deacon, rector of a mediety of Cotgrave church. Bishopthorpe, 13 Mar. 1319.

95 Note of licence to study for one year to Adam de Bajocis, deacon, rector of Tuxford (*Tokesford*). York, 23 Mar. 1319.

96 Memorandum of oath of obedience[44] to the archbishop, his officials and ministers, by Robert de la Feld of Hemel Hempstead (*Hemelhamstede*), instituted by authority of the cardinals in England[45] to Car Colston (*Kercolston*) church, in an exchange of benefices. Bishopthorpe, 29 Mar. 1319.

97 [Fo.336v; N.F.406v] Note of letters dimissory to be ordained priest to John de Wympton', deacon. Cawood, 1 Apr. 1319.

98 Commission to the official of York to hear and determine the cause between Richard de Hareworth, clerk, presented to West Markham (*West Marcham*) vicarage, plaintiff, and Richard de Hoton, defendant in possession.[46] Cawood, 3 Apr. 1319.

[43] See *BRUO*, III.2168.
[44] Facing fo.336v is an interleaved fragment (N.F.407), measuring 12 by 3 cms., with part of such an oath, without any means of identification remaining.
[45] Gaucelin Deuza and Luke Fieschi (see *CPL*, II.127–32; *Reg. Melton*, III.1–7).
[46] See **1**, **90**, **114**, **130–1**, **397**, **490**, **713**.

99 [*Dispensation to a priest ordained to a fictitious title; by authority of letters (not quoted) of the papal penitentiary.*]
DISPENSACIO JOHANNI DE RADECLIF' PRESBITERO ORDINATO[47] AD FICTUM TITULUM. Willelmus etc. dilecto filio Johanni de Radeclif' super Trentam nostre diocesis presbitero salutem [*etc.*]. Litteras venerabilis patris domini Berengarii miseracione divina episcopi Tusculan' pro te nobis directas recepimus tenorem qui sequitur continentes: Venerabili in Christo patri etc. Nos igitur tecum ab excessu hujusmodi absoluto, injuncta tibi pro modo culpe penitencia salutari teque usque ad festum Pasche proximo futurum exclusive a tuorum ordinum execucione suspenso, tandem[48] suffragantibus tibi meritis et alio canonico non obstante quod sciamus super irregularitate ex premissis contracta et execucione ordinum tuorum auctoritate nobis in hac parte commissa misericorditer dispensamus. Vale. [Cawood, 4 Apr. 1319.]

100 Note of similar dispensation to William de Radeclif, priest. Same date.

101 DECRETUM MONASTERII DE BLIDA. To the prior and convent of Blyth. Injunctions consequent to the archbishop's personal visitation on 16 Oct. 1318 [often in identical words as those for Marton priory dated 26 Jan. 1319[49] on the following subjects, with additions and variations].

(1) Charity and concord (Marton, c.1).

(2) Divine service (Marton, c.2, inserting after *temporum*, 'tam de die quam de nocte').

(3) Silence (Marton, c.3, but ending after *articulis* with 'debite observetur, et illam infringentes seu contravenientes eidem per presidentes in capitulo corrigantur').

(4) Admission of laymen (Marton, c.4).

(5) Strangers in refectory (Marton, c.5).

(6) Alms (Marton, c.10).

(7) Item inhibemus omnibus et singulis monachis in virtute obediencie ne panem vel servisiam ad villam decetero mittant ex quibus elemosina minui poterit absque licencia presidentis.

(8) Moderate expenditure (Marton, c.17, inserting after *officiati* 'et monachi dicti monasterii').

(9) Item compotus decetero omni anno ante festum Natale domini coram tribus vel quatuor discretioribus et maturioribus monachis conventus audiatur distincte et aperte, et eo audito status ejusdem domus tam in mobilibus que habent quam in debitis et creditis ac pensionibus corrodiis et aliis oneribus quibuscumque conventui oneratur.

(10) Item omnes monachi potentes intersint continue divinis obsequiis et sequantur conventum in choro claustro dormitorio et refectorio, ni nisi vel licencia prioris aut alia causa legitima fuerint impediti, et si qui in hiis inobedientes necgligentes vel remissi inventi fuerint absque omni acceptacione personarum per priorem debite corrigantur.

[47] MS. *ordinati*
[48] Interlined.
[49] *Reg. Melton*, II.30–3, no.66.

(11) Revealing secrets (Marton, c.9, with 'monachus' for *canonicus* and ending after *quibuscumque* with 'sub pena districtionis canonice presumat decetero revelare').

(12) Item injungimus priori in virtute obediencie et sub pena excommunicacionis majoris quod a vagacione extrinseca videlicet in cimiterio ac in vicis extra portas monachos suos inhibeat et constringat, ita quod in gardinis et ortis suis inde causa recreacionis spatiari quam opus fuerit permittantur.

(13) Item omnis pecunia undecumque proveniens de bonis monasterii ad manus prioris perveniat et in ejus custodia et dispositione consistat; ita tamen quod per priorem et conventum unus de monachis fidelior et discrecior deputandus, qui rotulum habeat contra priorem, in quo omnes recepciones pecunie inserantur ad testificandum statum prioris in compotis reddendis alias qu[ando]cumque per ordinarium loci super statu domus ipsum poni contigerit ad racionem.

(14) Item officia domus interiora per monachos ejusdem monasterii idoneos et circumspectos regantur decetero prout utilitati domus viderint expedire.

(15) Counsel for prior (Marton, c.15, omitting *conventus sui si comode fieri poterit vel*).

(16) Item injungimus priori et conventui quod numerus monachorum consuetus esse in domo videlicet usque ad xiii, qui nunc deest, citra festum sancti Johannis Baptiste proximo futurum plenarie compleatur.

(17) Chastisement by prior (Marton, c.12).

(18) Grants and alienations (Marton, c.21, omitting *nemorum seu boscorum*).

(19) Item nullus monachus alteri improperet queret aut respondeat de hiis que in hac visitacione dicta sunt per quem seu de quo sub penis inferius annotatis.

(20) Servants (Marton, c.22).

Penalties for disregard of these injunctions (as for Marton, omitting *et inhibilitatis ad quemcumque honorem ac officium quodcumque* and *vel successoribus nostris*).

Similar clause for their being read (omitting clause *quousque . . . fuerit*). Cawood, 2 Apr. 1319.

102 Dispensation for bastardy as the son of unmarried parents to John de Sancto Paulo, clerk (dioc. York), by authority of letters of Arnold, cardinal-bishop of St. Prisca and nuncio, dated London, 1 May 1313; these quote a faculty of Clement V [Fo.337; N.F.408] dated Avignon, 3 Feb. 1313.[50] By order of William [Greenfield], the previous archbishop, the dean of Doncaster enquired about John's associations and merits; his report has been inspected by the [present] archbishop. It is clear to him, however, that his predecessor did not complete the business. Another enquiry has been made to satisfy his conscience and has given evidence of John's honourable life and character. If he does obtain a benefice, he must be promoted to all orders and reside in it. Bishopthorpe, 25 Mar. 1319.

[50] As *CPL*, II.117; not traced in *Reg. Greenfield*.

103 [*Appointment of coadjutor to the aged and incapable rector of Hickling.*] DEPUTACIO CURATORIS RECTORIS ECCLESIE DE HEKELING'. Willelmus etc. dilecto filio domino Simoni de Bilburgh capellano salutem [*etc.*]. Convertentes intuitum ad statum desolabilem domini Hugonis de Halum rectoris ecclesie de Hekeling' nostre diocesis, qui nedum senii set eciam corporis debilitate frangitur adeo quod ad exercendum curam et officium suum in ipsa ecclesia non sufficienter hiis diebus sicut nec quod dolenter referimus sibi ipsi, te de cujus fida industria multum confidimus prefato rectori coadjutorem deputamus et damus cum cohercionis canonice potestate ad dictum officium secundum sanctiones canonicas exequendum ac ad faciendum omnia et singula que ad coadjutoris debeant officium pertinere, proviso quod de statu bonorum prefati rectoris et ecclesie ac qualiter curaveris in eisdem nobis seu officiali nostro Ebor' reddas annis singulis racionem, de qua te tenore presencium oneramus. Vale. [Bishopthorpe, 18 May 1319.]

Et juravit dictus dominus Symon tactis sacrosanctis evangeliis se bene et fideliter omnia bona dicti rectoris et ecclesie sue ministrare et eidem de dictis bonis sua necessaria dare et fidelem compotum omni anno reddere; presentibus domino J[ohanne] de Sutton et R[icardo] Snou[weshill].

104 Note of letters dimissory to William son of William de Grimeston of Nottingham, clerk. Bishopthorpe, 21 May 1319.

105 DIMISSORIE PRO J. DE TYKHILL. The like to M. John Dant' of Tickhill. Bishopthorpe, 23 May 1319.

106 Note of written licence to the subprior and convent of Blyth to sell two liveries of bread and beer for malt for their sustenance *usque novum granum*, provided it is to their benefit. Bishopthorpe, 30 May 1319.

107 Note of letters dimissory for all orders to John Flemyng' of Nottingham, clerk. 6 June 1319.

108 [*Mandate to induct a cardinal provided to the church of Ratcliffe on Soar.*[51]] ARCHIDIACONO NOTINGH' VEL EJUS OFFICIALI AD INDUCENDUM BERTRANDUM CARDINALEM IN ECCLESIA DE RADECLYVE' SUPER SORAM CUM SUIS JURIBUS. Willelmus etc. dilecto filio archidiacono Notinghamie vel ejus officiali salutem [*etc.*]. Cum sanctissimus in Christo pater et dominus noster reverentissimus dominus Johannes divina providencia papa xxii venerabili patri et domino domino Bertrando dei gracia titulo sancti Marcelli presbitero cardinali ecclesiam de Redeclyve' super Sore nostre diocesis cum suis juribus et pertinenciis, quam sive dominus Ludovicus nunc Dunolm' episcopus sive dominus Johannes nunc Wynton' episcopus eam tempore sue electionis tenuerit, motu proprio contulerit per suas certi tenoris litteras et providerit de eadem, certis sibi super hoc per alias suas sibi certi tenoris litteras executoribus deputatis, sicut tam per litteras gracie et executorias quam processus inde nobis presentatas plene liquet; nosque eundem dominum cardinalem in persona domini Johannis de Turberia

[51] See *CPL*, II.194, 234, 471.

procuratoris sui juxta vim formam et tenorem litterarum hujusmodi et processus quatenus ad hoc debeant seu poterant nos artare ac eciam quatenus ad nos attinet receperimus ad ipsam ecclesiam in rectorem; vobis mandamus firmiter injungentes quatenus ipsum venerabilem patrem et dominum dominum Bertrandum vel procuratorem suum ejus nomine in possessionem jurium et pertinencium ejusdem ecclesie sine difficultate qualibet inducatis vel faciatis induci et defendatis inductum. Valete. [Bishopthorpe, 7 June 1319.]

109 Institution [etc.] of Nicholas de Syxtenby, priest, to Marnham vicarage, now vacant; presented by Richard Pavely, prior of the hospital of St. John of Jerusalem in England. Bishopthorpe, 5 July 1319.

110 The like of Adam de Preston, acolyte, to Hickling (*Hikeling'*) church, now vacant; presented by Robert de Holand, kt. Bishopthorpe, 7 July 1319.

111 Commission to M. Alan de Neusom, rector of Bingham, and John de Halughton, rector of Gedling (*Gedeling'*), to hear and determine the matrimonial cause between Maud once wife of Richard de Tudham of Shelford, plaintiff, and John de Stutevill, defendant. Bishopthorpe, 7 July 1319.

112 [*Imposition of penance as required by the papal penitentiary.*]
INJUNCTIO PENITENCIE POST ABSOLUCIONEM. Willelmus etc. dilecto filio Johanni de Boney nostre diocesis clerico salutem [*etc.*]. Litteras fratris Johannis de la More domini pape penitenciarii pro te nobis directas recepimus tenorem qui sequitur continentes: Venerabili in Christo patri etc. Execucio. Juxta quarum litterarum tenorem et formam nos attendentes per inquisicionem legitimam inde factam te passo injuriam satisfecisse competenti, considerata culpa per te ex premissis contracta, tibi per dictum penitenciarium ut premittitur absoluto injunximus penitenciam salutarem prout secundum deum anime tue salute vidimus expedire. In cujus rei testimonium etc.[n.d. See **138**.]

113 (i) Collation to John Burdon, priest, of Twyford church (dioc. Lincoln), quoting a commission of John [Dalderby], bishop of Lincoln (dated Banbury (*Bannebur'*), 2 July 1319), for an exchange of benefices between Burdon, rector of Warsop, and M. John de Sutton, rector of Twyford, in the bishop of Lincoln's patronage. [Fo.337^{v}; N.F.408^{v}] (ii) Certificate to the bishop of Lincoln. (iii) Institution of Sutton to Warsop, in the person of Richard de Snoweshull, clerk, his proctor; presented by John Somery, kt (iv) Mandate for his induction. Bishopthorpe, 18 July 1319.

114 Note of mandate to the official of York's commissary-general and M. Thomas de Cave, receiver of York, to release the sequestration of the goods of [Richard de Hoton] vicar of West Markham (*Parva Marcam*) imposed at his condemnation to pay 100s. to Richard de Harword, Henry le Paintour and Thomas de Stabulo of Blyth [see **98**, **130**]; on paying the debt, the vicar is to be absolved from sentence of greater excommunication imposed on him by the official [*sic*] of Nottingham. Cawood, 31 July 1319.

115 Note of letters dimissory to be ordained priest to Henry Couper of Nottingham, deacon. Cawood, 17 Aug. 1319.

116 Licence for absence for one year to Ralph Rosel, rector of Keyworth (*KEWORTH*, *Keword*) to pursue his business at the Roman Curia. Also letters dimissory to him, subdeacon, for further orders. Cawood, 2 Sept. 1319.

117 Mandate to the archdeacon or his official to cite the clergy and people of Nottingham deanery to attend visitation as follows: on Monday 22 Oct. in Mansfield (*Mamesfeld*) church; on Thursday 25 Oct. in Papplewick (*Papelwyk'*) church; on Friday 26 Oct. in Basford (*Baseford*) church; and on Monday 29 Oct. in St. Mary's, Nottingham. Cawood, 10 Sept. 1319.

118 Note of similar mandate for Newark deanery, for attendance on Tuesday 20 Nov. in Shelton church; on Thursday 22 Nov. in Elston (*Eyleston*) church; on Friday 23 Nov. in Newark church; and on Saturday 24 Nov. in Winthorpe (*Wynthorp*) church. Same date.

119 The like for Bingham deanery, for attendance on Monday 5 Nov. in Holme Pierrepont (*Holm*) church; on Thursday 8 Nov. in Barton in Fabis (*Barton*) church; on Monday 12 Nov. in Costock (*Curtelingstok'*) church; on Wednesday 14 Nov. in Langar church; and on Friday 16 Nov. in Bingham church. Same date.

120 [*Mandate for the visitation of Worksop priory on 10 October.*]
[Fo.338; N.F.409] VISITATIO MONASTERII DE WIRSOP. Willelmus etc. dilectis in Christo filiis priori et conventui monasterii de Wirsop nostre diocesis salutem [*etc.*]. Quia intendimus per dei graciam decimo die mensis Octobris jam instantis vos in capitulo vestro ad recreacionem animarum vestrarum personaliter intueri ac visitationis officium apud vos paternis affectibus exercere, vobis tenore presencium injungimus et mandamus quatinus omnes et singuli dicto die [coram] nobis personas vestras ibidem et votivam presenciam pretendatis, nostra salubria monita correcciones et injuncta debita et devota reverencia recepturi ex quibus altissimus fructum producat placidum qui vobis utinam proficiat sicut pie cupimus ad salutem; fratres vestros nunc absentes ut hujusmodi nostre visitacioni intersint una vobiscum facientes cum celeritate debita premuniri. Et quia per nostrum adventum vestrarum salutem querimus animarum, domus et vestre oneracionem ultra modum debitum propter nostram presenciam minime affectamus, vobis firmiter inhibemus ne de extraneis aut extrinsecis personis nihil utilitatis domui vestre afferentibus ad dictum diem invitaciones aliquas quominus nostro tunc ibidem libere vacare possimus officio aliqualiter sine nostra licencia faciatis. Valete. [Cawood, 10 Sept. 1319.]

121 Memoranda of letters giving notification of visitation of the prior and convent of Thurgarton on 16 Oct.; the prior and convent of Newstead (*Novo Loco in Shirwod*) on 24 Oct.; the prior and convent of Shelford on 31 Oct.; the prioress and convent of Wallingwells (*WELLANDEWELLES*, *Wallandewelles*) on 9 Oct., *mutatis mutandis*; and the prior and convent of Felley on 23 Oct. Same date.

122 Warning[52] to the abbot and convent of Roche (*Rupe*) that the archbishop intends to claim procurations and hospitality there in the course of his visitation, on 6 October. Same date.

123 Memoranda of similar letters to the abbots and convents of Welbeck (*Wellebek'*) for 11 Oct., and Rufford (*Rughford*) for 20 Oct. Same date.

124 [*Postponement of the visitation because of Scottish invasions.*[53]]
DILATIO VISITATIONIS DECANATIBUS DE NOT' BINGHAM ET NEUWERK'. Willelmus etc. dilecto filio archidiacono Noth' vel ejus officiali salutem [*etc.*]. Quia turbacione qua status istarum parcium per ferocem hostilitatem Scotorum hiis diebus impetitur, sicut noscis, ac nonnullis aliis arduis negociis regni occurrentibus propter quod instantem regium apud Ebor' prestolamur adventum,[54] visitationi nostre in decanatibus de Notingham Bingham et Neuwerk' vobis alias per nostras litteras demandate diebus et locis in eisdem nostris litteris comprehensis non[55] possumus interesse, ipsam visitationem hac vice decrevimus suspendendam, vos inde premuniendo tenore presencium litterarum. Valete. [Cawood, 3 Oct. 1319.]

125 Note of similar letters revoking visitations of Thurgarton, Shelford, Felley, Newstead and Rufford. Same date.

126 Note of licence to study *in forma constitutionis* for one year from 1 August to Hugh Gernoun, rector of Elkesley. Cawood, 17 Oct. 1319.

127 Note of licence to study for two years from 29 September to Robert de Sutton, rector of Averham. Bishopthorpe, 19 Oct. 1319.

128 [*Approval of an exchange of property in Nottingham between the chaplain of St. Helen's chapel, Bingham, and the Carmelite friars.*]
PRO FRATRIBUS DE MONTE CARMELI NOTING' PRO QUADAM PLACEA EXCAMBIENDA. Willelmus etc. dilecto filio domino Hugoni capellano capelle sancte Elene in Byngham nostre diocesis salutem [*etc.*]. Cum inter diversa caritatis opera non modicum sit religionis augmentum, jure attestante quo canetur quod summa est ratio que pro religione facitis; nos ad hujusmodi pietatis opus oculum intuentes, vobis innotescimus quod si illam modicam placeam quam in Notingham obtinetis cum religiosis viris priore et fratribus de Monte Carmeli pro octodecim denariis annui redditus quem habent exeuntem de quoddam tenemento ex concessione Laurentii pelliparii in Notingham predicta volueritis legitime permutare, ipsi permutacioni quatenus et prout fieri poterit de jure et absque prejudicio juris nostri ecclesieque nostre Ebor' et cujuslibet alterius

[52] In same form as letter to Byland in *Reg. Melton,* II.5, no.12.
[53] A 'motley force' led by the archbishop was routed by Scots at 'the chapter of Myton' in Swaledale on 20(?) Sept. 1319 (M. McKisack, *The Fourteenth Century* (1959), 56).
[54] Edward II, after an attempt to take Berwick on Tweed, was in York from 5 Oct. (ibid., 56–7; *CPR 1317–21*, 392–3; *Rotuli Scotiae* (Record Comm., 1814–19), I.202).
[55] Interlined.

volumus assentire et in ejus eventu ea prout ad nos pertinet canonice roborare. Valete. [Bishopthorpe, 18 Oct. 1319.]

129 Commission to the official of York to proceed in the cause between Emma widow of Henry le Leker of Bawtry (*Bautre*), guardian (*curator*) of their son Robert in his minority, and the executors of Henry's will. Bishopthorpe, 30 Oct. 1319.

130 Mandate to M. William de Hundon, sequestrator in the archdeaconry, to release sufficient of the sequestrated goods of Richard de Hoton, who acts as vicar of West Markham, to pay Richard de Hareworth 32s. 4d. and Henry le Payntour of Blyth and Thomas de Stabulo 100s.; he was adjudged to owe them these sums before the archdeacon of Nottingham's official [see **114**]. The sequestrator is to report by letters before 6 Dec. Cawood, 12 Nov. 1319.

131 [*Commission to act in the cause of Richard de Hoton, vicar of West Markham, quoting letters of John XXII (dated 27 Apr. 1319) ordering the revocation of acts to his prejudice since his departure for the Curia* (see **90**).]
COMMISSIO PRO VICARIO ECCLESIE DE WEST MARKHAM. Willelmus etc. dilectis filiis magistris Michaeli de Harcla et Thome de Cave receptori nostro Ebor' salutem [*etc.*]. Litteras sanctissimi in Christo patris et domini nostri domini Johannis divina providencia pape vicesimi secundi recepimus in hec verba:

Johannes episcopus servus servorum dei venerabili fratri . . archiepiscopo Ebor' salutem et apostolicam benediccionem. Dilecti filii Ricardi de Hoton perpetui vicarii ecclesie de West Markham Ebor' diocesis apud sedem apostolicam constituti precibus annuentes, presencium tibi auctoritate mandamus quatinus quicquid inveneris in ejus prejudicium temere attemptatum, postquam idem Ricardus causa peregrinacionis et pro quibusdam suis negociis promovendis iter arripuit ad sedem veniendi predictam, in statum debitum legitime revocare procures, contradictores per censuram ecclesiasticam appellacione postposita compescendo. Datum Avinion' v Kalendas Maii pontificatus nostri anno tercio.

De vestris igitur circumspeccione et industria plenius confidentes, vocatis hiis qui evocandi fuerint secundum qualitatem predictarum litterarum, ad cognoscendum procedendum decernendum pronunciandum diffiniendum et exequendum vobis vices nostras committimus cum cohercionis canonice potestate donec eas ad nos duxerimus revocandas. Valete. [Cawood, 13 Nov. 1319.]

132 [*Collation of Mattersey vicarage to a provisor.*]
[Fo.338v; N.F.409v] COLLATIO VICARIE ECCLESIE DE MATHERSEYE. Willelmus permissione etc. dilecto filio domino Thome de Foston presbitero salutem [*etc.*]. Mores et merita quibus diceris insignitus nos excitant propensius et inducunt ut te prosequamur favore gracie papalis amplioris. Hinc est quod vicariam ecclesie de Matherseye nostre diocesis vacantem et ad collationem nostram spectantem tibi, de cujus meritis et virtutibus sinceram in domino fiduciam obtinemus, cum omnibus juribus et pertinenciis suis conferimus intuitu caritatis et te vicarium perpetuum cum onere personalis residencie secundum formam constitucionis legati super hoc edite instituimus canonice in eadem. Vale. [Cawood, 19 Nov. 1319.]

133 Note of mandate to the archdeacon [etc.] for his induction. Same date.

134 Note of letters dimissory for all orders to William Scragg of Retford, acolyte. 1 Dec. 1319.

135 [*Monition to the prior of Thurgarton pay a debt to Nunkeeling priory.*] AD MONENDUM PRIOREM DE THURGARTON QUOD SOLVAT PRIORISSE DE KILLING XIX LIBRAS. Willelmus etc. dilecto filio decano nostro Noting' salutem [*etc.*]. Moneas et efficaciter inducas fratrem Johannem priorem monasterii de Thurgarton nostre diocesis quod de novemdecim libris, in quibus . . priorisse et conventui de Killing juxta confessionem suam coram nobis judicialiter emissam legitime condempnatus existit, infra sex dies a tempore recepcionis presencium proximo numerandos satisfaciat competenter, alioquin ipsum ad idem per suspensionis et excommunicacionis sentencias compellas debite vice nostra. Et quid feceris in premissis nos citra festum Natalis domini reddas certiores per tuas litteras patentes harum seriem continentes. Vale. [Cawood, 11 Dec. 1319.]

136 Mandate[56] to the subprior and convent of Thurgarton to elect a prior in succession to John de Rodeston, whose resignation has been accepted by the archbishop. Cawood, 12 Dec. 1319.

137 Mandate[57] to the dean of Nottingham to proclaim at Thurgarton that objectors to the election of John de Hikeling, canon and subprior, as prior, are to appear before the archbishop wherever he might be in the diocese on the first law day after 25 Jan. Cawood, 4 Jan. 1320.

138 [*Certificate of absolution of a clerk excommunicated for violence* (see **112**).] ABSOLUTIO JOHANNIS DE BONEY CLERICI AB EXCOMMUNICATIONE. Noverint universi quod nos Willelmus permissione etc. Johanni de Boney nostre diocesis clerico a sentencia excommunicationis majoris a canone promulgata, quam propter temerariam manuum injectionem in Willelmum Burgeys de eadem incurrit, auctoritate apostolica absoluto pro modo culpe et excessu hujusmodi penitentiam injunximus salutarem quam peregerat, prout nobis constat ex certificatorio decani nostri de Byngham, ipsumque quantum ad nos attinet restituimus ecclesiasticis sacramentis. [Cawood, 7 Jan. 1320.]

139 AD MONENDUM ARCHIEPISCOPUM CANTUAR' NE BAJULET CRUCEM SUAM IN DIOCESI VEL PROVINCIA EBOR'. Memoranda of mandates to the archdeacons of York, the East Riding (*Estriding'*) and Nottingham, or their officials, to prohibit the archbishop of Canterbury from carrying his cross erect in the diocese or province of York, 'in the form as is written above in the same quire' [see **42–5**]; likewise to the deans of Newark, Bingham, Nottingham and Harthill (*Herthill*). Also of a schedule with [a full text of] the monition to be delivered by the archdeacon of Nottingham's official. 19 Jan. 1320.

[56] Almost identical in form to mandate for Newburgh (*Reg. Melton*, II.7, no.19).
[57] Same form as for Newburgh (ibid., II.10, no.24).

140 Licence to study for two years at a *studium generale* to Henry [de Sibthorp], rector of a mediety of Eakring church, which he may farm [etc.]. Bishopthorpe, 26 Jan. 1320.

141 Note of letters dimissory for all orders to John Houlot of Edwalton, acolyte. Bishopthorpe, 24 Jan. 1320.

142 The like to M. Roger de Heselerton, subdeacon, rector of Thorpe (*Thorp juxta Neuwerk*).[58] Bishopthorpe, 2 Feb. 1320.

143 [*Certificate that a former rector of Ordsall has no benefice in the diocese.*[59]]
[Fo.339; N.F.410] LITTERA TESTIMONIALIS QUOD DOMINUS THOMAS DE BURTON NON HABET BENEFICIUM IN DIOCESI ISTA. Universis sancte matris ecclesie ad quos presentes littere pervenerint Willelmus etc. salutem in autore salutis. Noverit universitas vestra quod licet dominus Thomas de Burton nuper ecclesiam de Ordesale nostre diocesis titulo institucionis aliquo tempore obtinuerit,[60] ipsam tamen postmodum resignavit, nec comperimus ex inspectione registri nostri in presenti ipsum aliquod beneficium ecclesiasticum infra nostram diocesim obtinere. In cujus rei testimonium sigillum nostrum presentibus est appensum. [Bishopthorpe, 31 Jan. 1320.]

144 Sentence quashing the election of John de Hykeling' as prior of Thurgarton because its form was uncanonical (*contra concilium generale*).
[Second] sentence providing John as prior by the archbishop's special grace; a majority of the canons had unanimously voted for him. n.d.

145 [*Mandate to the canons of Thurgarton to obey their new prior.*]
CONVENTUI MONASTERII DE THURGARTON UT PREDICTUM FRATREM JOHANNEM RECIPIANT IN PRIOREM ET EIDEM OBEDIANT UT PRIORI. Willelmus etc. dilectis filiis . . conventui monasterii de Thurgarton nostre diocesis salutem [*etc.*]. Presentatam nobis electionem vestram de fratre Johanne de Hikeling' concanonico domus vestre in priorem dicti monasterii vacantis per cessionem fratris Johannis de Ruddestan ultimi prioris ejusdem factam debito examini subjecimus, quam quia eam invenimus propter defectum forme notorium minus canonice celebratam cassavimus at cassam et irritam pronunciavimus justicia exigente. Et quia ad nos hac vice devoluta est potestas providendi eidem monasterio de priore juxta canonicas sanctiones, nos solicite attendentes unanimem consensum vestrum qui in prefatum Johannem vota vestra unanimiter direxistis, necnon persone ejusdem merita paternis affectibus considerantes quem ad regimen dicti monasterii sufficientem et idoneum reputamus, eidem monasterio vestro vacanti de persona ejusdem fratris Johannis de Hikeling' auctoritate nostra pontificali providimus et ipsum in priorem ejusdem monasterii prefecimus et pastorem, administracionem dicti prioratus eidem tam in

[58] See *BRUC*, 301–2.
[59] Thomas de Burton, instituted in 1301, resigned in an exchange of benefices with Acard de Longo Prato, rector of Newchurch, Kent, in 1314 (*Reg. Corbridge*, I.219, no.615; *CPR 1313–17*, 34; *Reg. Greenfield*, IV.148, no.1998).
[60] MS. *obtinuerat*

spiritualibus quam in temporalibus committentes. Quocirca vobis in virtute obediencie firmiter injungendo mandamus quatinus predictum fratrem Johannem in vestrum priorem et pastorem reverenter admittentes, sibi ut priori vestro intendatis in omnibus et humiliter pareatis. Valete. [Bishopthorpe, 1 Feb. 1320.]

146 [margin] Memorandum of mandate to the archdeacon or his official to instal John as prior. Same date.

147 [*Mandate to Newstead priory to receive Philip de Candelesby, an apostate canon absolved by the archbishop and ordered a (specified) penance.*[61]]
PENITENCIA FRATRIS PHILIPPI DE CANDELESBY DOMUS NOVI LOCI IN SHIRWOD. Willelmus etc. dilectis filiis . . priori et conventui de Novo Loco in Shirwode salutem [*etc.*]. Quia ad instanciam Philippi de Candelesby canonici in vestro monasterio professi, vobis alias vocatis peremptorie ac servato processu qui in hoc casu secundum qualitatem negocii requirebatur, ipsum ad domum suam secundum regularem disciplinam restituendum fore pronunciavimus, quem eciam a sentencia excommunicationis majoris quam pro temeraria habitus mutacione et apostasia involutus fuit absolvimus in forma juris; vobis mandamus in virtute obediencie qua nobis tenemini quatenus cum ad vos in spiritu humilitatis accesserit, ipsum admittatis et juxta dictam regularem disciplinam vestri ordinis pertractetis, cui pro commissis suis quatenus et prout ad nos pertinet infrascriptam injunximus penitenciam salutarem. In primis conventum sequatur in choro claustro refectorio et dormitorio continue nisi gravi infirmitate fuerit impeditus, et ubilibet locum ultimum teneat in conventu. Septa monasterii non exiat quovismodo, nec cum mulieribus at viris secularibus colloquium habeat vel tractatum, nec litteras aliquas nisi quas prius viderit et perlegerit prior vel subprior recipiat vel emittat. Omni quarta et sexta feria a presidente in capitulo unam recipiat disciplinam, et eisdem diebus dicat vii psalmos penitenciales cum letania coram altari beate virginis prostratus humiliter et devote. Omni septimana psalterium unum dicat. Omni die Mercurii jejunando uno genere piscium cum leguminibus et omni die Veneris similiter jejunando leguminibus tantummodo sit contentus, quolibet die Veneris ab ovis lacticiniis et omni genere piscium abstinendo. Nullius officii nec aliquarum rerum monasterii sibi administratio committatur. A ministerio altaris omnino se abstineat donec exigente devocione juxta prioris et conventus testimonium cum eo super hoc duxerimus dispendio. Hec omnia et singula dicto fratri Philippo in virtute sancte obediencie et sub pena districcionis canonice injungimus devote et humiliter facienda completenda et eciam observanda. Valete. [Laneham, 22 July 1320.]

148 Licence (at the request of Roland [Jorz], archbishop of Armagh) to Robert de Jorz, who acts as rector of North Collingham by authority of a papal grace, to be absent from his church and farm it for one year while attending Archbishop Roland. Also letters dimissory for all orders. Bishopthorpe, 12 Feb. 1320.

149 Institution [etc.] of Robert de Derneford, priest, to Bunny (*Boneye*) church, now vacant; presented by Sir Robert de Wodehous. Kirkham, 17 Feb. 1320.

[61] For his return from apostasy in 1313, see *Reg. Greenfield*, IV.138, no.1977.

150 The like of John de Sutteby, clerk, to a mediety of Treswell (*Tereswell*) church, vacant by the resignation of Robert Pygot; presented by William de Musters. Amotherby (*Amunderby*), 21 Feb. 1320.

151 [Fo.339v; N.F.410v] Notes of letters dimissory for holy orders to Roger de Shefeld, acolyte; and for all orders to Robert de Roderham, clerk. Bishop Burton, 25 Feb. 1320.

152 Licence to William de Grendon, rector of Babworth, to be absent for two years in the service of Thomas, earl of Lancaster and Leicester, steward of England; divine service is to be laudably maintained, cure of souls not neglected, and the church demised to a sufficient proctor. Bishop Burton, 16 Mar. 1320.

153 Absolution and restoration to the sacraments of the same rector from sentences of suspension and excommunication imposed on him by the archbishop through the execution of royal writs at the instance of Robert de Crophill. Same date.

154 Note of licence during pleasure to John de Sibthorp to hear divine service in his oratory at Sibthorpe. Bishop Burton, 20 Mar. 1320.

155 [*Request to examine twenty seven witnesses in Stow church (dioc. Lincoln) on articles in a schedule (not given) for a cause about tithes etc. at Thorney (Notts.) brought before the archbishop by Broadholme priory against the vicar of Saxilby (Lincs.); with amendment for the hearing to be at Torksey (Lincs.).*]

ROGATUS MUTUE VICISSITUDINIS OBTENTU AD EXAMINANDUM TESTES EXTRA NOSTRAM DIOCESIM. Willelmus etc. dilecto nobis in Christo . . archidiacono Stauwye vel ejus officiali salutem cum benedictione et gracia salvatoris. Cum in quadam causa decimarum oblacionum et mortuariorum de quibusdam personis animalibus et rebus infra territorium de Brodholm ut dicitur infra parochiam de Thornhagh infra nostram diocesim provenientium auctoritate ordinaria coram nobis pendente inter priorissam et conventum de Brodholm ejusdem nostre diocesis dictam ecclesiam de Thornhagh in proprios suos usus ut dicitur optinentes actores ex parte una et dominum Thomam perpetuum vicarium ecclesie de Saxelby reum ex altera, idem Thomas quosdam testes videlicet xxvii producere intendit de personis in cedula presentibus interclusa[62] nominatis quos sibi necessarios asseruit pro fundacione sue intencionis in quadam exceptione ex parte ejusdem Thome coram nobis proposita in causa predicta, quos etiam asseruit degentes esse infra Linc' diocesim super quibus fidem fecerat coram nobis; quocirca ne probationis copia angustetur vel pereat seu a facultate probandi absque culpa sua aliqualiter excludatur, vos requirimus et rogamus mutue vicissitudinis obtentu quatenus xxvii de predictis testibus quos idem Thomas coram vobis duxerit producendos proxima die juridicali post festum Ascensionis domini proximo futurum in ecclesia de Stowe,[63] ad quos

[62] *presentibus interclusa* underlined (to cancel), with substitution in margin: 'in aliis nostris litteris vobis rogatoriis interclusa'.

[63] *Stowe* preceded by cross and linked to *Thork'* in margin.

diem et locum denunciavimus predicte parti adverse quod memorate receptioni intersit, ac per vos vel per alium super articulis et juxta interrogatoria presentibus[64] interclusis examinari facere velitis, ac nomina et attestationes hujusmodi examinatorum in scriptis redactas nobis vel commissario nostro speciali clausas et etiam sigillo vestro pendente signatas quamcito comode poteritis destinare, ac super omnibus que in hac parte feceritis et faciendum duxeritis nos reddere certiores per vestras patentes litteras harum seriem continentes. Valete. [Leeds (*Ledes*), 15 Apr. 1320.]

156 Note of letter to M. Thomas de Cave not to trouble the rectors of Kirton (*Kirketon in le Clay*)[65] and Babworth (*Babbeworth*) [William de Grendon] for being non-resident; at the request of the earl of Lancaster. Edwinstowe (*Edenestowe*), 30 May 1320.

157 [*Licence for services in private oratories in times of infirmity.*]
LICENCIA PRO NICHOLAO DE WYDMERPOLE AUDIENDI DIVINA. Willelmus etc. dilecto filio Nicholao de Wydmerpol' nostre diocesis salutem [*etc.*]. Ea que sincere devocionis augmentum respiciunt pronis cupimus affectibus promovere. Cum itaque diebus singulis ad dei laudem et anime tue salutem cupias audire divina, ac te frequenter gravi infirmitate impediri contingat quominus domum tuam exire valeas et ad ecclesiam tuam parochialem accedere ad divinum officium audiendum; tibi ut in honestis oratoriis infra septa maneriorum tuorum constructis, quotiens te vel uxorem tuam impediri contigerit quominus absque gravi dispendio tu vel uxor tua ad ecclesiam parochialem possitis accedere, per capellanum idoneum pro te uxore ac familiaribus tuis divina facias cum devocione et honestate debita celebrari licenciam concedimus specialem, ita tamen quod parochialibus ecclesiis in quarum parochiis hujusmodi oratoria situantur in suis minime detrahatur proventibus nec eisdem per hanc nostram licenciam prejudicium aliquod generatur, presentibus tua et exoris tue infirmitate durante in suo robore duraturis. Vale. [Southwell, 1 June 1320.]

158 Institution [etc.] of M. Hugh de Wylughby,[66] priest, to Willoughby on the Wolds (*Wylughby*) church, now vacant; presented by the prior and convent of Worksop (*Wirkesop*). Ossington (*Osington*), 5 June 1320.

159 Note of licence during pleasure to John de Bevercotes, kt., to hear divine service in his oratory at Bevercotes. Laxton, 6 June 1320.

[64] *presentibus* likewise underlined, with margin having: 'in aliis litteris nostris rogatoriis predictis de quibus illud verbum de Scawe per errorem scriptoris scriptum in eisdem detrahimus ab eisdem et hoc verbum Thork' [. .?] ponimus loco ejusdem [. . .?] aliis in eis contentis [dici?]mus in suo robore valituris interclusa etc.'
[65] The previous institution to be traced is of Henry de Walmesford in 1311 (*Reg. Greenfield*, IV.63, no.1813); but cf. letters of protection naming the rector of Kirton as Henry de Athelastre on 28 Mar. 1322, a week after the earl's death, and his soon becoming 'the king's clerk' and an auditor for Lancaster's confiscated estates (*CCR 1318–23*, 454, 531; *CPR 1321–4*, 91); and see **519**. For Grendon, see **305** and note.
[66] Previously rector of Rempstone (cf. **11**, **164**): not noticed in *BRUO*, III.2051.

160 Note of letter to M. Thomas de Cave, receiver of York, not to trouble Adam de Bajocis, rector of Tuxford, for past non-residence in his church, its receipts during the last vacancy, or for any excommunication hitherto sued against him by royal writs. Mansfield (*Mamesfeld*), 10 June 1320.

161 [*Recognition by Rufford abbey that it is obliged to provide archbishops with hospitality on their first coming. A payment of 100s. accepted by Archbishop Melton in lieu will not be considered a precedent.*]
OBLIGATIO . . ABBATIS ET CONVENTUS DE RUGHFORD AD PROCURANDUM QUEMLIBET ARCHIEPISCOPUM EBOR' IN PRIMO SUO ADVENTU. Noverint universi quod nos abbas et conventus monasterii de Rughford tenemur et efficaciter obligati sumus nostrumque monasterium de Rughford est obligatum venerabili patri domino Ebor' archiepiscopo Anglie primati cuicumque qui pro tempore fuerit ad recipiendum ipsum in dicto nostro monasterio et hospitandum ipsum cum tota sua familia decenter nostris sumptibus et expensis omnimodis nomine sui primi adventus per unum diem et unam noctem, videlicet in diem proximo sequentem quo ipsum contigerit recedere ab eodem, cuilibet archiepiscopo Ebor' nomine sui primi adventus debitis et eciam consuetis. Fatemur eciam scienter sponte et pure quod singuli dicti archiepiscopi Anglie primates dictam procuracionem ut premittitur nomine dicti sui primi adventus quo ipsum ad nostrum monasterium declinare contigerit habere consueverant quoque in plena pacifica canonica et sufficienti possessione ipsam in nostro monasterio nostris sumptibus ut premittitur habendi percipiendi et recipiendi fuerant a tempore et per tempus cujus contrarii memoria non existat. Et est sciendum quod nos abbas et conventus predicti concessimus et solvimus venerabili in Christo patri domino Willelmo de Melton dei gracia Ebor' archiepiscopo Anglie primati centum solidos sterlingorum, quos impotencie nostre compaciens de gracia sua speciali hac vice recepit[67] pro expensis quas essemus facturi nomine procuracionis memorate in primo suo adventu, quem denunciaverat nobis se velle facere ut predicitur in nostro monasterio antedicto.[68] Volumus insuper et concedimus scienter et pure quod jus et possessio archiepiscopi predicti et ecclesie sue Ebor' ac successorum suorum qui pro temporibus fuerint quoad hujusmodi procuraciones successivis temporibus singulorum archiepiscoporum nomine primi adventus sui ut predicitur in dicto nostro monasterio percipiendas firma maneant et perpetuis temporibus illibata, non obstante dicte pecunie recepcione et omissione hac vice adventus predicti, quibus juri et possessioni per predictam omissionem et pecunie solucionem non intendimus prejudicare nec eisdem quomodolibet derogare, quod constanter et fideliter promittimus per presentes quas dicto domino archiepiscopo fecimus in premissorum testimonium sigilli nostri communis impressione et munimine roboratas. Datum in monasterio nostro de Rughford xvii die mensis Junii anno gracie MCCCXX.

162 [Fo.340; N.F.411] Institution (in the person of Walter Baudewyne of *Westlee*, clerk, as proctor) and mandate for induction of John called Vanne, clerk, to Epperstone (*Eppreston*) church, now vacant; presented by Thomas de Veer, kt. East Leake (*Leyk'*), 22 June 1320.

[67] MS. *recipere*
[68] See **123**.

163 Licence to Richard [Cokfeld[69]], rector of a mediety of Langar church, to be absent for two years and sell its fruits. Langar, 27 June 1320.

164 Memorandum of oath of canonical obedience by M. Gilbert de Pontefract, rector of Rempstone by papal authority [see **123**]. 25 June 1320.

165 Commission to M. Alan de Neusum, rector of Bingham, M. Thomas de Sancto Leonardo, rector of Egmanton, Hugh [de Crowland], rector of Widmerpool (*Wydmerpol*), and Adam [de Welham], rector of Wollaton, (or two or three of them) to hear and determine the cause between M. Henry de Rotington[70] and Robert de Loghmaban, plaintiffs, and Roger [de Doncaster], vicar of Ruddington (*Rotyngton*), defendant. Cotham (*Cotum*), 9 July 1320.

166 Commission to M. Alan de Neusum, rector of Bingham, M. Thomas de Sancto Leonardo, rector of Egmanton, and M. William de Hundon, rector of Barnburgh, (or two of them) to correct crimes etc. discovered in the visitation of Bingham deanery, as contained in an attached roll, reporting by letters when opportune. Cotham, 9 July 1320.

167 Licence to study for three years at a *studium generale* to Thomas de Outheby, rector of East Bridgford (*Estbrigeford*). Flintham (*Flyntham*), 7 July 1320.

168 Institution [etc.] of M. William de Loudham, priest, to Cotham church; presented by the prior and convent of Thurgarton in an exchange of benefices [as below]. Newark, 12 July 1320.

169 The like of M. Thomas de Lafford, priest, to Gonalston (*Gonaldeston*) church; presented by John de Hyriz, kt., in an exchange of benefices [as above]. Same date.

170 Licence during pleasure for Robert Pirpount, kt., his wife, household and guests to hear divine service celebrated by a suitable chaplain in chapels or oratories within his manors, provided that the parish churches suffer no loss of income or prejudice. Thurgarton, 16 July 1320.

171 The like for Henry le Mouster of Syerston [alone] in respect of a chapel or oratory within his manor of Syerston (*Sireston*). Southwell, 17 July 1320.

172 [*Commission to audit accounts of the executors of Oliver Sutton, sometime bishop of Lincoln (d. 1299).*[71]]
[Fo.340v; N.F.411v] COMMISSIO AD AUDIENDUM COMPOTUM EXECUTORUM DOMINI OLIVERI QUONDAM LINC' EPISCOPI DE BONIS EJUSDEM IN DIOCESI ET PROVINCIA EBOR'. Willelmus etc. discretis viris magistro Egidio de Redemere ac domino Johanni de Scalleby canonicis ecclesie Linc' salutem cum benedictione et gracia salvatoris. De vestris fidelitate ac circumspeccione providis confidentes,

69 Instituted 1309 (*Reg. Greenfield*, V.182, no.2660).
70 Later named as Henry Scot (**190**, **198**). Loghmaban is also a Scottish name.
71 See *Reg. Melton*, III.38, no.74.

ad audiendum et recipiendum compotum ac ratiocinium magistri Gocelini de Kirnyngton thesaurarii ecclesie Linc' executoris testamenti bone memorie domini Oliveri quondam Linc' episcopi ac coexecutorum suorum super administracione bonorum ejusdem defuncti infra nostram jurisdictionem et diocesim inventorum per ipsos, necnon ad allocandum ea eisdem executoribus que rationabiliter fuerint allocanda debitamque eis acquietanciam faciendam ac omnia alia et singula que ad audicionem ejusdem compoti pertinent de consuetudine et de jure, necnon in omnibus et singulis causis negociis articulis et querelis sive ex nostro officio sive ad parcium instancias quarumcumque qualitercumque et quandocumque motis aut movendis dictum testamentum et administracionem bonorum de quibus supra fit mencio qualitercumque contingentibus ad cognoscendum procedendum decernendum pronunciandum diffiniendum et exequendum, et in eventu finalis discussionis administracionis et terminacionis premissorum ipsos executores ab onere administracionis et ulterius reddicionis ratiocinii hujusmodi finaliter exuendos liberandos et absolvendos quatenus ad nos attinet et in nobis est, vobis conjunctim et utriusque vestrum divisim cum potestate cohercionis canonice committimus vices nostras. [Fledborough (*Fledburgh*), 21 July 1320.]

173 Memorandum of oath of obedience and fealty by M. Henry de Mammesfeld, dean of Lincoln, to the archbishop and his successors, their officials and ministers, for churches he has in York diocese, *viz*. Mansfield (*Mammesfeld*) and North and South Leverton (*Northleverton, Suthleverton*). Fledborough, 21 July 1320.

174 [*Request to grant a corrody to a friend of the archbishop.*]
PRO CORRODIO CONCEDENDO A PRIORE ET CONVENTU DE THURGARTON. Willelmus etc. dilectis in Christo filiis et amicis nostris carissimis . . priori et conventui de Thurgarton nostre diocesis salutem [*etc.*]. Grata pietatis opera dilectissimi amici nostri Johannis filii Rogeri dicti Clerici de Wyvelingham nobis exhibita nos excitant et inducunt ut eundem prosequamur speciali favore. Hinc est quod ipsius promotionem et perpetuam sustentationem congruam et honorificam quantum possumus affectantes et de vestris devotione et amicicia confidentes, vos affectuose requirimus precordialiter et rogamus quatinus predicto Johanni unam liberationem qualem pro uno vestro concanonico consueverit liberari cum suis appendiciis, unde victum et vestitum sufficienter et honorifice habere poterit de monasterio vestro percipiendos quamdiu idem Johannes vixerit, velitis concedere et litteras vestras certas super hiis facere nostri contemplatione precibus et amore ac intuitu caritatis, adeo si placet inde facientes ut nos merito astringatis in hiis que poterimus in vestris agendis et ad honorem vestrum et comodum poterunt cedere votis vestris. Nolumus autem per has nostras litteras vobis vel vestris successoribus aliquod prejudicium futuris temporibus generari. Et quid super hiis facere vestre benivolencie placuerit, quesumus per vos rescribi per presencium portitorem. Valete. [Laneham, 22 July 1320.]

175 Licence to study for one year from 30 July at a *studium generale* to Hugh Gernoun, rector of Elkesley, with dispensation from proceeding to the diaconate or priesthood. Clarborough (*Clareburgh*), 25 July 1320.

176 Commission to M. Thomas de Thirnum, vicar of Featherstone (*Fetherstan'*), and John, vicar of Rothwell (*Rothewell*), to examine Adam de Wodusour, William Wytbelt', William son of Robert, Thomas son of Pell, John Monk', John son of William, Robert Wyllecok', William le Hunter, William [*sic*], Hugh de Notton, Robert of the same, Roger le Wodeward, Robert son of Henry de Walton, Adam Wytbelt', Robert de Havercroft, Adam son of Mold and William Prestsone on articles attached; they are witnesses called by the proctor of the community of the vill of Chevet in a cause pending before the archbishop between the community as plaintiff and the prior and convent of Monk Bretton (*Munkebretton)* and the vicar of Royston (*Roston*), defendants.[72] Statements are to be written, shown to no one, and sent to the archbishop, closed, by the third law day after 29 Sept., as required by the plaintiff. Cawood, 5 Aug. 1320.

177 [*Judgment that the inhabitants of Thrumpton should contribute to the repair of Ratcliffe on Soar church and its belfry; with subscription by the archbishop's registrar.*] SENTENCIA CONTRA INCOLAS ET INHABITATORES DE THURMETON PAROCHIANOS ECCLESIE DE RADECLYVE SUPER SORAM. In dei nomine amen. Auditis et intellectis meritis cause que coram nobis Willelmo [*etc.*] in archidiaconatu Notinghamie nostre visitacionis officium excercentibus vertebatur inter Thomam de Radeclyf Thomam de Kirkeby Willelmum filium Rogeri Willelmum Marescallum Rogerum de Richemund Robertum de Langeley et Thomam Scharp incolas et inhabitatores ville de Radeclyf' super Sore nostre diocesis actores ex parte una et Robertum Poutrel Willelmum ad fratres de Sutton et Robertum filium Galfridi incolas et inhabitatores ville de Thurmeton dicte nostre diocesis reos ex altera per modum notorii summarie et de plano absque strepitu et figura judicii, dicta parte actrice petente quod cum omnes incole et inhabitatores de Thurmeton parochiani ecclesie de Radeclyf' predicte capellaque de Thurmeton notorie et totaliter dependens ab eadem ecclesia matrice fuissent per tempus cujus contrarii memoria non existabat, quodque dicta parochialis ecclesia et ipsius campanile refectione et emendatione notorie indigebant ad quorum refectionem et emendationem predicti incole et inhabitatores de Thurmeton contribuere consuevissent una cum suis comparochianis memoratis, quod tamen postea facere recusarunt injuste in animarum suarum pericula, eosdem comparochianos de Thurmeton ad predictas refectionem emendationem et contributionem per nos finaliter condempnari et compelli ac fieri in omnibus quod justum esset, premissa proponente et petente conjunctim et divisim; factaque contestatione per dictos incolas de Thurmeton ad prefatas petitionem et intentionem verbis negativis, ac prestitis hinc et inde juramentis de calumpnia et de veritate secundum premissorum qualitatem, factis etiam quibusdam positionibus et interrogationibus dicte parti ree et secutis responsionibus ad easdem, productis etiam quibusdam testibus per partem actricem quibus per nos receptis juratis et examinatis ac eorum dictis publicatis, prefixoque dicte parti ree termino ad proponendum omnia in facto consistencia in quo quadam exceptione proposita per dictam partem ream ac demum renunciata[73] per eandem partem ream pure et sponte exceptioni eidem et contentis in ea, et etiam de dicendo seu proponendo in dictos testes et eorum

[72] All the places named in this entry are in West Yorkshire.

[73] MS. *renunciato*

dicta ac etiam subsequenter in eadem causa hinc et inde concluso, quia invenimus dictam partem actricem intentionem suam memoratam sufficienter probasse; prefatos incolas et inhabitatores de Thurmeton ut parochianos predicte ecclesie matricis de Radeclyve in personam Roberti Poutrel procuratoris sui ad refectionem emendationem et contributionem de quibus supra fit mencio [Fo.341; N.F.412] sentencialiter et diffinitive condempnamus. Premissa vero per Ricardum de Snoweshull notarium publicum subscriptum scribi et publicari ac signo ejus consueto signari mandavimus et nostri sigilli impressione fecimus communiri. Actis et datis apud Bingham ultimo die mensis Junii anno gracie MCCCXX et pontificatus nostri tercio.

Et ego Ricardus de Snoweshull clericus Wygornien' diocesis apostolica et imperiali auctoritate notarius publicus et dicti domini archiepiscopi scriba omnibus et singulis premissis una cum magistro Johanne de Nassington rectore ecclesie de Kirketon dominis Johanne de Sutton et Ricardo de Melton testibus ad hec vocatis specialiter et rogatis anno indiccione tercia mense die et loco predictis factis habitis atque gestis presens interfui, eaque sic fieri vidi et audivi scripsi et publicavi et in hac publicam formam redegi signoque meo consueto signavi rogatus in fidem et testimonium premissorum. [Bingham, 30 June 1320.]

178 [*Mandate to inquire into the reputation of a clerk charged with homicide and about the crime; with a reply sending reports.*]

INQUISICIO CAPTA SUPER VITA ET CONVERSACIONE ANDREE LE BOTILLER CLERICI [DIFFAMATI] ET INCARCERATI. Willelmus [*etc.*] dilecto filio . . officiali nostro Ebor' salutem [*etc.*]. Ex parte Andree le Boteler clerici in foro seculari super crimine homicidii Thome de Holme nostre diocesis diffamati nostreque carcerali custodie juxta consuetudinem Anglicane ecclesie mancipati nobis est humiliter supplicatum quod, cum ipse super defamatione predicta paratus sit coram nobis canonice se purgare, eum ad purgationem hujusmodi faciendam admittere dignaremur. Volentes igitur de vita conversatione et moribus ejusdem ac qualis nominis et opinionis in suis partibus fuerit et an super dicto crimine culpabilis extiterit vel aliis certiorari primitus et ex causa, devotioni vestre firmiter injungentes mandamus quatinus super singulis dictis articulis et de dicto crimine presertim, vocatis tam clericis quam laicis fidedignis juratis et diligentius examinatis in locis ubi magis conversatus fuerit, inquiratis seu inquiri faciatis diligentius veritatem. Et quid super hiis inveneritis et fieri feceritis nobis ad singulos articulos super quibus vestram oneramus conscienciam respondendo distincte et aperte rescribatis per vestras litteras clausas que harum seriem representent vestro et illorum per quos hujusmodi inquisicio facta fuerit sigillis signatas, ut quod conveniens fuerit ulterius exequamur. Valete. [Doncaster, 15 May 1320.]

Hujus igitur auctoritate mandati vestri reverendi diligentes fieri fecimus inquisitiones in locis ubi idem Andreas magis ut didicimus fuerat conversatus, videlicet per officiales archidiaconatuum Noting' et Estriding' necnon per decanum Holdernes' archidiaconatus Estriding' antedicti, quas vobis mittimus presentibus litteris nostris interclusas sigillis dictorum officialium et decani necnon illorum per quos inquisitiones hujusmodi facte fuerant consignatas. Et sic mandatum vestrum reverendum in omnibus plenarie ut decuit sumus executi. Ad regimen ecclesie sue sancte vos conservet altissimus in prosperis successibus et longevis. [Beverley, 3 July 1320.]

179 [*Certificate that this clerk has been strictly confined in the archbishop's prison.*]
LITTERA PATENS PRO EODEM TESTIMONIALIS. Universis Christi fidelibus presentes litteras inspecturis Willelmus etc. salutem in omnium salvatore. Ad universitatis vestre noticiam deducimus per presentes quod Andreas le Botiler clericus nostre diocesis super quibusdam criminibus in foro seculari coram justiciariis domini nostri regis irretitus circiter festum Purificationis beate Virginis proximo preteritum carcerali custodie tanquam membrum ecclesie extitit liberatus, in quo quidem carcere semper hactenus sub arta custodia detentus extitit continue et existit. In cujus rei testimonium litteras nostras sub sigillo nostro fieri fecimus has patentes. [Bewick (*Bewyk'*), 4 Sept. 1320.]

180 [*Licence to elect a prior of Shelford.*]
SUPPRIORI ET CONVENTUI DE SHELFORD AD ELIGENDUM SIBI PRIOREM. Willelmus etc. dilectis in Christo suppriori et conventui de Shelford nostre diocesis salutem [*etc.*]. Humili requisicioni et peticioni vestre devote per vos litteratorie et ex parte vestra nobis factis ut aliquem de confratribus vestris in priorem vestrum et vestri prioratus per mortem fratris Roberti de Mamesfeld ultimi prioris vestri vacantis eligendi facultatem vobis concedere dignaremur an[n]uendum duximus et licenciam concedimus per presentes, proviso quod talem vobis et vestro prioratui in priorem eligatis qui scit sciens potens et volens ad laborandum pro vobis et domo vestra, circumspectus eciam in spiritualibus et temporalibus deoque et hominibus gratiosus, super quo vestras coram deo consciencias oneramus. Valete. [Poppleton (*Popleton*), 17 Sept. 1320.]

181 Licence to study for one year at a *studium generale* to M. Gilbert de Pontefr', acolyte, rector of Rempstone.[74] Also note of letters dimissory for holy orders. Ripon, 21 Sept. 1320.

182 [*Diffinitive sentence. William de Lee claimed that Blyth vicarage was legally vacant at the time of his presentation because the incumbent had not been instituted etc. Process began before the official of York in the vacancy of the see (1315–17) and continued before the archbishop's commissaries until the parties agreed to accept his award.*[75] *The case is dismissed as unproven.*]
SENTENCIA DIFFINITIVA SUPER VICARIA DE BLIDA PRO DOMINO GREGORIO DE NEUTON POSSESSIONI EJUSDEM INCUMBENTE ET CONTRA WILLELMUM DE LEE AD EAM PRESENTATUM. In dei nomine amen. Dudum super vicaria de Blida nostre Ebor' diocesis inter dominum Willelmum de Lee presbiterum se per religiosos viros . . priorem et conventum de Blida ad predictam vicariam presentatum pretendentem actorem ex parte una, et dominum Gregorium de Neuton dicte vicarie possessioni incumbentem reum ex altera, coram discreto viro magistro Johanne de Nassington juniore officiali Ebor' vacante sede venerabilium virorum . . decani et . . capituli ejusdem tunc custodum spiritualitatis archiepiscopatus Ebor' commissario in hac parte speciali suborta materia questionis, predictis partibus coram eo legitime comparentibus, tradito libello per partem actricem parti ree sub hac forma:

In dei nomine amen. Coram vobis magistro Johanne de Nassington juniore officiali curie Ebor' venerabilium virorum dominorum . . decani et capituli

[74] See *BRUO*, III.1497.
[75] See *Reg. Greenfield*, V.276, no.2281; and **3**, **58** above.

ecclesie beati Petri Ebor' vacante sede ejusdem inter partes infrascriptas commissario speciali dicit et in jure proponit procurator domini Willelmi de Lee de Blida presbiteri quod cum ipse per religiosos viros . . priorem et . . conventum de Blida veros patronos vicarie ecclesie de Blida et in possessione presentandi ad eandem vicariam existentes canonice sit et fuisset presentatus, ipsaque vicaria tempore dicte presentationis notorie vacavit et adhuc vacat ex eo videlicet quod dictus Gregorius de Neuton ad ipsam vicariam dudum vacantem per mortem domini Roberti de Burton per religiosos predictos presentatus absque inquisitione contra formam constitutionis legati super hoc edite et sine institutione et absque inductione canonicis dictam vicariam propria temeritate fuit et est ingressus eamque sic tenet de facto occupatam, et admissioni dicti Willelmi presentati pro quo inquisicio ad presentationem factam de eadem sufficienter operatur cui presentato et ejus admissioni quamvis nichil canonicum obsistat dictus Gregorius indebite se opponit, que sunt publica notoria et manifesta in partibus de Blida et locis evicinis; quare petit probatis de jure probandis dictum Gregorium nullum jus in dicta vicaria habuisse nec habere ipsamque vicariam vacantem fuisse et esse per vos domine judex pronunciari et declarari ipsum Gregorium ab eadem amoveri, dictumque Willelmum ad eam admittendum fore decerni et per eum ad quantum pertinet cum effectu admitti et in ea institui et fieri in omnibus quod est justum. Premissa dicit proponit et petit ac probare intendit conjunctim et divisim, juris beneficio semper salvo.

Factaque contestatione ad libellum ejusdem verbis negativis: 'dico narrata prout narrantur vera non esse et petita fieri non debere', posicionibus traditis responsionibusque secutis ad easdem, factoque contrario per partem ream suo termino proposito, productisque hinc inde testibus admissis et examinatis et eorum dictis publicatis, datoque die ad dicendum in testes et dicta, propositis per partem ream quibusdam [Fo.341v; N.F.412v] exceptionibus in testes et dicta, exhibitisque per partem actricem quibusdam copiis instrumentorum originalium residentium penes decanum et capitulum predictos, invocatoque registro eorumdem ad probationem contentorum in copiis predictis, nonnullis instrumentis per partem ream exhibitis, dato die ad dicendum contra exhibita, proposita per partem actricem quadam exceptione contra exhibita partis adverse, necnon quibusdam aliis exceptionibus ac replicationibus per utramque partem tam coram . . officiali curie Ebor' sede tunc plena quam coram magistris Michaele de Harcla et Ricardo de Scardeburgh specialibus commissariis in dicto negocio deputatis factis [et?] positionibus et responsionibus ad easdem, productisque testibus necnon et exhibitis instrumentis dictisque testium et instrumentis publicatis, partibusque decreta copia dato die ad dicendum tam contra testes quam instrumenta et in facto mixtim; demum partes predicte ac prior et . . conventus de Blida predicti expresse consenserunt ac se ordinationi nostre submiserunt alte et basse ut simpliciter et de plano absque strepitu et figura judicii, auditis causis [tempore?] visitationis dicte vicarie per dictum presentatum contra ipsum incumbentem propositis et pretensis et probationibus earumdem discussis, necnon juribus et defensionibus incumbentis consideratis et equo libramine ponderatis, super toto negocio ut partium parceretur laboribus et expensis diffiniremus et faceremus quod justicia suaderet.

Quorum submissione per nos admissa, viso et rimato processu dicti negocii, auditis et discussis dicte cause seu negocii meritis et plenius ponderatis hincinde propositis et probatis, communicatoque juris peritorum consilio invocataque spiritus sancti gracia, nos Willelmus permissione divina Ebor' archiepiscopus Anglie primas, quia invenimus partem actricem suam intentionem sufficienter non probasse, partem ream ab impetitione ejusdem sentencialiter et diffinitive absolvimus in hiis scriptis, et dictum actorem in expensis etiam condempnamus quarum taxationem nobis specialiter reservamus. Lecta lata et in scriptis pronunciata fuit ista sentencia vicesimo sexto die mensis Januarii anno gracie millesimo trecentesimo decimonono indictione tercia apud Thorp prope Ebor', quam per Ricardum de Snoweshill notarium publicum scribi et publicari mandavimus et signo ejusdem solito consignari ac sigilli nostri impressione fecimus communiri.

Et ego Ricardus de Snoweshill [etc., similar to **176**]; witnessed by John de Sutton, John de Guthemundham, Thomas de Barneby and Richard de Otringham. [Bishopthorpe, 26 Jan. 1320.]

183 Commission to the official of York to hear and determine the cause begun before the archbishop between M. John de Not', rector of Clayworth, plaintiff, and John son of Ralph, William de Beltoft' and Hugh de Suththorp, parishioners of Clayworth, defendants. Bishop Monkton (*Munketon prope Rypon'*), 25 Sept. 1320.

184 Note of licence to M. Adam de Agmodesham, rector of Barton in Fabis (*Barton super Soram*), to be absent for two years.[76] Thirsk (*Thresk*), 28 Sept. 1320.

185 Note of licence to study for two years to Henry,[77] chaplain, rector of Barnby in the Willows (*Barnby juxta Neuwerk'*). Rudby (*Ruddeby*), 2 Oct. 1320.

186 The like for one year to M. Hugh de Wylughby, priest, rector of Willoughby on the Wolds. Whitby (*Whiteby*), 15 Oct. 1320.

187 Licence to study for one year at a *studium generale* to Thomas [de Hercy], rector of West Retford (*Retford in le Clay*). Brompton (*Brumpton*), 21 Oct. 1320.

188 Mandate to the dean of Bingham to cite objectors to the election of William de Breton, canon and subprior, as prior of Shelford, to appear before the archbishop on the first law day after St. Martin's [11 Nov.]. Kirby Misperton (*Kirkeby Misperton*), 23 Oct. 1320.

189 Licence to M. Geoffrey Golias, rector of Sturton le Steeple (*Stretton*), to be absent for one year; he may sell two portions of the tithes of his church, *viz.* of Fenton and Littleborough (*Littelburgh*). Bishopthorpe, 14 May 1322.

190 [*Commissaries are inhibited from proceeding following the defendant's appeal to the archbishop on their refusal to cite him to a safer place and provide him with counsel; the appealed party is to be cited to York* (see **165**, **198**).]

[Fo.342; N.F.413] SUGGESTIO DOMINI ROGERI DE DONCASTR' VICARII ECCLESIE DE RUTINGTON. Willelmus etc. dilectis filiis magistris Alano de Neusum de

[76] See *BRUO*, I.32.

[77] *Recte* Hervey (de Sutton), instituted 1310 (*Reg. Greenfield*, IV.64, no.1817).

Byngham et Thome de Sancto Leonardo de Egmanton ecclesiarum rectoribus una cum discretis viris dominis Hugone de Wydmerpole et Ada de Wollarton ecclesiarum rectoribus in causa mota inter Henricum Scot' et Robertum de Loghmaban actores ex parte una et dominum Rogerum de Donc' perpetuum vicarium ecclesie parochialis de Rutington nostre diocesis reum ex altera nostris commissariis alias deputatis salutem [*etc.*]. Sua nobis Rogerus vicarius predictus gravi conquestione monstravit quod cum vos in dicta causa procedentes, locum videlicet Estbriggeford dicto vicario et suis propter insidias copiose multitudinis inimicorum et adversariorum suorum indies sibi insidiantium minime tutum ubi corporum sui et suorum cruciatus verisimiliter timuit et metum habuit qui cadere debuit in virum constantem quibus resistere non potuit nec audebat quod de novo ad sui noticiam pervenit sibi assignaveritis[78] ut dicit, idemque vicarius coram nobis congrue excipiendo proposuisset et etiam allegasset dictum locum sibi et suis minus tutum[79] ut premittitur fuisse et esse ad quorum probationem in forma juris quatenus requirebatur obtulit se paraturum, petens sibi et suis locum tutum et insignem necnon et consilium advocatorum vel saltem advocati pro defensione sua cum hujusmodi consilium non habuerat quoquomodo licet hujusmodi consilio indiguerat in hoc casu per nos deputari et ut convenit assignari; vos tamen sibi tutum locum et insignem ac consilium hujusmodi deputare et assignare ac ipsum super hiis audire et justiciam facere non curastis set potius recusastis, propter que predictus vicarius sentiens se ex hiis et eorum quolibet per vos indebite pregravari, nos ut asserit legitime appellavit. Quocirca vobis inhibemus et per vos ceteris omnibus quibus jus exigit et permittit inhiberi volumus et mandamus ne pendente hujusmodi appellationis causa coram nobis[80] quicquid in dicte partis appellantis prejudicium quomodolibet attemptetis quominus appellationem suam libere prosequi valeat ut intendit. Citetis insuper seu citari faciatis peremptorie dictam partem appellatam quod compareat coram nobis vel commissariis nostris uno vel pluribus in ecclesia nostra beati Petri Ebor' primo die juridico post festum sancti Andree apostoli in predicta appellationis causa processurus et facturus ulterius secundum qualitatem premissorum quod justicia suadebit. Et certificetis nos de die recepcionis presencium et quid feceritis et faciendum duxeritis in premissis ad dictos diem et locum vel commissarium seu commissarios nostros per vestras patentes litteras harum seriem continentes. Valete. [Gilling (*Gylling'*), 28 Oct. 1320.]

191 Commission to M. Denis Avenel, official of York, and M. Thomas de Cave, canon of Ripon, to hear and determine an *ex officio* cause against Robert Jorz who acts as rector of North Collingham [see **194**, **231**]. Bishop Monkton, 2 Nov. 1320.

192 Commission to M. Alan de Neusum, rector of Bingham, M. Thomas de Sancto Leonardo, rector of Egmanton, and M. William de Hundon, rector of Barnburgh, to correct crimes etc. discovered in the visitation of Nottingham

[78] MS. *assignavit*
[79] MS. *totum*
[80] Interlined.

archdeaconry, as contained in attached rolls, reporting by letters when opportune. Bishop Monkton, 4 Nov. 1320.

193 To the prior and convent of Newstead. Injunctions consequent to the archbishop's personal visitation on 12 June 1320 [like **101** in its similarity to the introduction and c.1 of the decree for Marton. The following clauses, however, do not appear elsewhere]:

(2) Item injungimus vobis . . priori et conventui in virtute obediencie et sub pena excommunicacionis majoris quod ea, que in decreto predecessoris nostri quod penes vos residet continentur,[81] in singulis articulis diligencius observentur et capitulo vestro cum hoc presenti decreto nostro legantur singulis Kalendis juxta ipsorum continentias et tenores.

(3) Item quia invenimus domum vestram variis pensionibus liberacionibus corrodiis et aliis quampluribus debitis graviter oneratam, injungimus priori et omnibus canonicis de conventu quod vivatis et expendatis juxta facultates domus adeo mediocriter et secundum modum taliter ordinandum et prefiniendum per priorem et ceteros domus officiarios, quod annis singulis aliqua certa porcio fructuum reddituum et proventuum reservetur et deputetur ad es alienum solvendum, ut ipsa domus annuatim sic particulariter ab ere alieno valeat respirare.

(4) Item injungimus ut compotus domus reddatur annis singulis per omnes et singulos officiarios priori et duobus vel tribus de sanioribus et senioribus dicte domus, ac exhibeatur idem compotus sub compendio videlicet pes ipsius conventui ut status domus omnibus de ipso conventu et singulis innotescat, et si compotus non sit redditus a quadriennio jam elapso injungimus quod reddatur citra festum sancti Hillarii proximo futurum.

(5) Item ordinamus et injungimus quod sint duo bursarii in domo, quorum unus sit celerarius, qui de visu et competenti testimonio socii sui ac tallie seu indenture inter eos conficiende totam pecuniam recipiat ac priori et ceteris officiariis urgentibus necessitatibus officiorum suorum ministret seu solvat quantitates indigenciarum suarum, et reddant singuli de omnibus et singulis suis receptis compotum ut superius annotatur et secundum dispensationem prioris

(6) Item injungimus quod decetero sit unus infirmarius qui habeat ex liberacione cel[l]arii competenter ad procurandum infirmos prout domus permiserint facultates.

(7) Item injungimus ut decetero in omnibus et per omnia regula observetur, et quod vos prior et subprior studeatis vigilanter quod eam faciatis assidue observari sub pena amocionis ab officiis memoratis et quod delinquentes contra eam graviter puniatis.

(8) Item injungimus priori et conventui quod omnes canonici et fratres conversi domus extra ipsam commorantes temporibus visitacionum vocentur ut hujusmodi visitacionibus personaliter intersint una cum ceteris de conventu, et ipsas subeant et agnoscant.

(9) Item injungimus vobis priori et conventui quod canonici qui de domo apostatando recesserunt, si ad eam redierunt, nullo modo admittantur sine

[81] Injunctions by Greenfield have not been traced (*Reg. Greenfield*, V.xxvi). This may refer to injunctions by Corbridge in 1304 (*Reg. Corbridge*, I.280–2, esp. its monition, p.282).

nostro precepto [Fo.342v; N.F.413v] vel licencia speciali, in quo casu parati erimus justiciam exhibere.

(10) Item injungimus omnibus et singulis canonicis de conventu quod quilibet eorum reddant compotum camerario domus de illa marca quam recipiunt pro indumentis, et si quid ex ea residuum fuerit id reddant et restituant camerario supradicto.

(11) [Forbids admission of canons and *conversi*, grants of pensions etc., sales of woods and long leases of manors, without archiepiscopal licence.[82]]

Correctiones autem personales per nos in capitulo vestro factas secundum formam injunctionum nostrarum et institucionem regularem injunctas pro variis modis excessuum observari volumus et compleri, ac omnia statuta nostra injuncta etiam et precepta salubria supradicta in virtute sancte obediencie sub excommunicatione etiam et aliis penis canonicis transgressoribus premissorum per nos prout regulari discipline convenit infligendis plene ac per omnia precepimus inviolabiliter custodiri, et in capitulo vestro coram vobis omnibus articulatim et distincte semel singulis mensibus ut singulorum vestrum informantur mentibus recitari, ita quod ex hac visitatione nostra in proximo in dicto monasterio per dei graciam exercenda de vobis fructum attendamus placidum pro quo promptam devocionis vestre obedienciam pronis debeamus affectibus in deo commendare. Valete. [Bishop Monkton, 5 Nov. 1320.]

194 COMMISSIO EX OFFICIO CONTRA PERSONAM ECCLESIE DE NORTH COLINGHAM [repeating **191** but adding a third commissary, *viz.*] John de Hemmyngburgh, rector of St. Wilfrid's, York; two of them may act. Bishop Monkton, 10 Nov. 1320.

195 Institution [etc.] of William de Lincoln, canon of St. Katherine's outside Lincoln (order of Sempringham), D.D., priest, to Newark vicarage, now vacant; presented by the prior and convent of St. Katherine's. Bishop Monkton, 18 Nov. 1320.

196 (i) Sentence quashing the election of William Breton, canon of Shelford, as prior of Shelford in succession to Henry[83] de Mamesfeld, because of a technical irregularity. (ii) Provision of William as prior. (iii) Mandate to the canons. (iv) Mandate to the archdeacon.[84] Bishopthorpe, 26 Nov. 1320.

197 [N.F.414[85]] [King's Bench] writ *admittatis*. William Bardolf recovered the advowson of Shelford priory for himself and his heirs in a plea against Adam de Everingham in the court of Henry III before Hugh le Bygot, justiciar of England, taking pleas in various counties between 24 June and 6 October 1258. His heir Thomas Bardolf claimed that Adam de Everingham, heir of Adam, deforced him of the advowson. Adam was summoned [to King's Bench] on 26 November but gave no reason why Thomas should not have the

[82] Almost identical to c.24 of decree for Whitby two weeks later (*Reg. Melton*, II.66).

[83] Cf. Robert in **180**.

[84] Same forms as in **144–6**.

[85] Interleaved facing fo.342v, a writ measuring 24 by 8.5 cms.; it quotes rot. 153 and is 'signed' *Monsel.* See Public Record Office, Coram Rege Roll, Michaelmas 14 Edward II, m.153; *VCH Nottingham*, II.117.

advowson. The archbishop is ordered to admit a prior presented by Thomas. Tested by H[enry] le Scrope, Westminster, 6 [Dec]ember 1321.

[dorse] Memorandum that on 9 Aug. 1322, at Lowdham near Thurgarton, Henry de Neuton, esq., delivered this writ in the presence of Richard de Wylughby, kt., M. Adam de Heselbech, *me et pluribus aliis. R. de M.* [Richard de Melton?]

198 [Fo.343; N.F.415] Commission to the official of York to hear and determine an appeal cause between Roger de Donec', vicar of Ruddington, appellant, and Henry Scot' and Robert de Loghmaban, the party appealed [see **190**]. Bishopthorpe, 28 Nov. 1320.

199 Licence to study for one year at a *studium generale* to M. John de Luterell, D.D., rector of Holme Pierrepont. Bishopthorpe, 6 Dec. 1320.

200 [*Summons of objectors to the purgation of a clerk accused of homicide, following enquiries about his reputation* (see **178**)*; also of the victim's widow.*]
PROCLAMACIO SI QUIS VELIT OPPONERE PURGACIONI ANDREE LE BOTILLER CLERICI INCARCERATI FACIENDE cujus inquisicio scribitur supra in secundo folio precedenti. Willelmus etc. dilecto filio . . archidiacono Notingh' vel ejus officiali salutem [*etc.*]. Ex parte Andree le Botiler clerici in foro seculari super crimine homicidii Thome de Holm nostre diocesis diffamati nostreque carcerali custodie juxta consuetudinem Anglicane ecclesie mancipati, de cujus vita conversacione et moribus ac qualis nominis et opinionis in suis partibus extitit et an super dicto crimine culpabilis fuerat vel aliis inquiri fecimus diligenter que sufficienter operatur pro ipso, nobis est sepius supplicatum humiliter et devote quod cum a dicto crimine sit immunis ut asseritur et de ipso crimine cupiat se canonice purgarare, dignaremur dictam purgacionem suam recipere et juxta qualitatem negocii sibi justiciam exhibere.Quocirca nos volentes cuilibet exhibere justiciam ut tenemur, vobis mandamus quatenus tam in singulis ecclesiis quam in mercatis et foris ac locis aliis publicis per singulos decanatus dicti archidiaconatus constitutis proclamare faciatis et eciam publicari denunciando solempniter quod si[86] quis quicquam justum proponere voluerit quominus ad admissionem purgationis predicte procedere debeamus, proximo die juridico post festum sancti Nicholai proximo futurum in ecclesia nostra beati Petri Ebor' coram nobis vel commissariis nostris vel commissario uno vel pluribus comparens quatenus canonicum fuerit cum complemento justicie audietur. Citetis insuper peremptorie ex habundanti relictam predicti Thome de Holm quod compareat coram nobis vel dictis commissariis nostris uno vel pluribus die et loco predictis causam racionabilem si quam habeat et proponere voluerit quare ad dictam purgationem recipiendam procedere minime debeamus propositura et ut convenit ostensura et factura ulterius secundum qualitatem negocii quod justicia suaderet. Et nos super hujusmodi execucione mandati et citacionis dicte mulieris sic facte ac quid feceritis et inveneritis in premissis citra dictum diem certificetis distincte et aperte per vestras patentes et clausas litteras harum seriem continentes impressioneque sigilli officii vestri pendente signatas. Valete. [Bishop Monkton, 10 Nov. 1320.]

[86] Interlined.

Memorandum quod eisdem die et loco emanavit consimilis littera officiali archidiaconatus Estriding' excepta illa clausula: citetis insuper ex habundanti relictam etc.

201 Commission to M. Denis Avenel, official of York, and M. William de Stanes, the archbishop's clerk, rehearsing the above summons of objectors for 8 December; they are empowered to receive Andrew's purgation on that day and proceed as need requires, certifying the archbishop [see **286–91**]. Bishopthorpe, 6 Dec. 1320.

202 Institution [etc.] of Robert de Warsop, priest, to Eaton (*Eton*) vicarage, now vacant; presented by Walter de Sesyriaco, proctor of M. Gerard de Sesyriaco, canon of Southwell and prebendary of Eaton. Bishopthorpe, 9 Dec. 1320.

203 The like of Reginald de Sibthorp, subdeacon, to Strelley church; presented by Robert de Stralley, kt., in an exchange of benefices [as below]. Cawood, 3 Jan. 1321.

204 The like of M. Roger de Aslacton, priest, to Hawksworth (*Hokesworth*) church; presented by the prior and convent of Thurgarton in an exchange [as above]. Same date.

205 [*Transfer of a canon of Thurgarton to St. Oswald's, Gloucester* (see **229**).]
MISSIO FRATRIS HUGONIS DE NOTINGH' CANONICI DOMUS DE THURGARTON AD DOMUM SANCTI OSWALDI DE GLOUC'. Willelmus etc. dilectis filiis . . priori et . . conventui de Thurgarton nostre diocesis salutem [*etc.*]. Cum nuper fratrem Robertum de Kydermunstr' canonicum domus sancti Oswaldi Gloucestrie ad vos certis ex causis miserimus pro nostro vobiscum beneplacito moraturum, ne vobis sit mora hujusmodi onerosa vestris beneplacitis condescendere cupientes, volumus et mandamus quatinus infra triduum a tempore recepcionis presentium fratrem Hugonem de Notingham concanonicum domus vestre ad dictam domum sancti Oswaldi Gloucestr' transmittatis inibi ad tempus per nos moderandum loco dicti fratris Roberti expensis mutuis moraturum. Scribimus quippe priori et conventui sancti Oswaldi Gloucestr' supradictis quod dictum fratrem Hugonem inter se admittant et fraterne in domino pertractent caritate. Valete. [Bishopthorpe, 17 May 1322.]

206 [*Request to Worksop priory to send indentures about a corrody.*]
[Fo.343v; N.F.415v] PRIORI ET CONVENTUI DE WIRKSOP PRO WILLELMO DE BRONGELFLET'. Willelmus etc. dilectis filiis priori et conventui de Wirkesop salutem [*etc.*]. Regraciamur vobis corditer de eo quod Willelmo de Brongelflet' pauperi consanguineo nostro victum et vestitum in domo vestra caritatis intuitu et nostri interventu rogaminis graciosius concessistis. Et quia ex relatu ejusdem Willelmi accepimus quod litteras dicte concessionis indentatas fecistis et earundem partem alteram signari sigillo ejusdem Willelmi utramque tamen partem penes vos retinuistis hucusque, licet dicte partis signate tenorem non intellexerit sufficienter ut dicit; eapropter devotionem vestram et benevolenciam

de qua magnam gerimus fiduciam affectuose rogamus quatinus predictas litteras utrasque per aliquem de quo confiditis, vel litteras alias quales competentius pro ipsius securitate facere volueritis, predicta parte signata sibi restituta, nobis destinare curetis ut[87] ex earum inspectione scire possimus quantas graciarum actiones vobis merito debeamus referre et nos ad vestra beneplacita promptiores. Et quid super hiis faciendum duxeritis quamcitius nobis rescribi per presentium portitorem. Valete. [Cawood, 5 Jan. 1321.]

207 [*Request to Newburgh priory to present a clerk of the archbishop to Epworth church (Lincs.); a previous request had been withdrawn in favour of Sir John de Moubrey's nominee, whose commendation has now expired.*]
PRIORI ET CONVENTUI DE NOVO BURGO PRO ECCLESIA DE EPPEWORTH. Willelmus etc. dilectis filiis . . priori et conventui de Novo Burgo nostre diocesis salutem [*etc.*]. Nuper vacante ecclesia de Eppeworth vos rogavimus affectuose pro dilecto clerico nostro domino N[icholao] de Notingh' ut ipsum ad dictam ecclesiam dignaremini presentare, effusis nostris precibus pro ipso ydoneo pro quo tam de jure licuit quam meritis suis exposcentibus decuit preces effundere tali casu, vosque nobis supplicastis ut semota cujuslibet offense nostre materia gratanter tacitis impedimentis ex parte vestra permitteremus quod dominum Willelmum Moigne nobilis viri et venerabilis domini Johannis de Moubrey clericum presentaretis ea vice vacationis ejusdem, nosque ob dilectionem sinceram quam erga dictum nobilem gerimus in dicta parte annuimus votis vestris. Promisistis insuper bona fide vestra quod alia proxima vice vacationis ejusdem ecclesie neminem presentaretis absque nostro petito beneplacito et obtento consensu, ipsam submittentes nostre dispositioni pro aliquo de nostris secunda vice vacationis predicte que vos priorem credimus non latere. Cumque intellexerimus quod bina vice vacationis subsequenter prefatum dominum Willelmum ad ipsam ecclesiam presentastis, quodque nunc finita commenda ejusdem domini W. vacet ecclesia sepedicta; hinc est quod vos corditer requirimus et rogamus quatinus de premissis recolentes et ea congrue considerantes, prefatum clericum nostrum ad dictam ecclesiam in presenti vacantem presentare dignemini interventu nostri rogaminis et intuitu caritatis, recogitantes interea quod non decet super contrariis reprehendi quodque gratitudo in aliis gratos interpellans invenit promptiores. Et quid super hiis vobis placuerit quamcitius nobis rescribi per presentium portitorem vel saltem quantum poteritis indilate. Valete. [Bishopthorpe, 9 Jan. 1321.]

208 [*Mandate to enforce penances imposed on the previous prior of Thurgarton and three canons as a result of the archbishop's visitation.*]
PENITENCIA QUORUNDAM CANONICORUM MONASTERII DE THURGARTON. Willelmus etc. dilecto filio priori de Thurgarton salutem [*etc.*]. Super quibusdam compertis in visitatione nostra, quam ad animarum vestrarum salutem vestreque religionis et ordinis honestatem apud vos dudum exercuimus, decretum nostrum correctiones et injuncta nostra salubria continens et statuta ad vos misimus non est diu nonnullos articulos personarum diversarum excessus et crimina continentes, que famam vestram ac vestri ordinis honestatem deformiter macularunt ac contra vos et vestrum monasterium populare obloquium probo-

[87] MS. *et ut*

sius suscitarunt, deliberandi gracia hactenus differentes. Que quidem crimina et excessus etsi in eisdem personis utpote religiosis multum reprehensibilia et detestabilia nostre considerationi reddantur, in persona tamen fratris Johannis de Rudstan immediati pre[de]cessoris vestri hujusmodi illicebra secundum carnem eo dampnabiliora atque magis execrabilia sunt censenda, quo ipse per erroris sui devia ac sue insolencie impudenciam easdem personas duxit in foveam quibus exemplo bone vite pudicicie ducatum debuit prestitisse. Ne igitur malorum nutrix negligentia nos redarguat quam sub famoso clamore similata connivencia non excusat, nos volentes quantum cum deo possumus dictarum personarum insolencias disciplina ecclesiastica cohercere ac penitencia salutari lang[u]oribus animarum suarum mederi, volumus et injungimus sub pena canonice ultionis, quam contravenientes singuli quicumque fuerint poterunt versimiliter formidare, quod persone subscripte hanc penitenciam subeant et sustineant subsequentem.

Idem videlicet frater Johannes de Rudstan in choro refectorio dormitorio capitulo et in claustro sequatur conventum. Septa monasterii non exeat. Et quia jam instat tempus misericordie et salutis quo per penitenciam lege fit remissio singulis sua commissa deflentibus et contritis, idem frater Johannes durante Quadragesima singulis septimanis quatuor dicat psalteria, quatuorque disciplinas presente conventu in capitulo de manu recipiat presidentis, et singulis quartis feriis ab esu piscium se abstinens in sextis feriis in pane et aqua jejunet. Extra Quadragesimam vero duo dicat psalteria septimanis singulis, et duas in forma predicta recipiat disciplinas, et singulis quartis et sextis feriis ab esu piscium se abstinens se pane et legumine tantummodo contentetur.

Fratres vero Johannes de Crophill et Nicholaus de Suwell alibi de incontinencia convicti septa monasterii non exeant. Continue sequantur conventum. Nullis recreationibus intersint. Singulis septimanis durante Quadragesima dicat quilibet tria psalteria, tresque disciplinas presente conventu in capitulo de manu recipiat presidentis, et singulis quartis feriis ab esu piscium se abstinens singulis sextis feriis in pane et aque jejunet. Ac extra Quadragesimam quilibet unam recipiat disciplinam, et unum dicat psalterium singulis septimanis, ac singulis sextis feriis ab esu piscium se abstinens pane et legumine contentetur.

Et quia frater Hugo de Notingham concubitum cum quadam muliere solus cum sola confessus super crimine incontinencie juris interpretacione convictus presumitur atque reus, in choro refectorio dormitorio capitulo et claustro sequatur conventum, singulisque sextis feriis infra Quadragesimam in pane et aqua et extra Quadragesimam in pane et legumine jejunet, singulisque septimanis unum psalterium dicat et unam recipiat disciplinam presente conventu in capitulo de manu presidentis, et illam penitenciam per annum continuum subeat et sustineat humiliter et devote.

Sicque omnes et singule persone prenotate, quibus omnimodas administrationem ac confabulationem cum mulieribus interdicimus nisi evidens necessitas vel utilitas id exposcat, et tunc de licencia presidentis seu custodis ordinis ac in eorum presencia seu alicujus boni viri approbate honestatis et vite ad hoc deputandi ab ipso, quem sibi assistere volumus et audire quicquid dictitur aut fiat.

Hiis penitenciis et aliis orationum ac piorum operum suffragiis se studeant excerere deinceps annis singulis quousque signis contritionis apparentibus in eisdem et aliis sue devotionis meritis exigentibus uberiorem de nobis graciam in premissis meruerint obtinere, quod nos ex sua conversatione ac devotionis promptitudine in premissis gratum gustantes odorem deliniendi dictam penitenciam laudabilibus suis exigentibus meritis excitemur. Per has enim disciplinas per nos eis injunctas pro suis demeritis atque culpis eas excusari nolumus, quominus disciplinas institutas ab ordine nichilominus recipere debeant ut tenentur. Et ne dicti fratres dictas injunctiones nostras tradant neglectui [Fo.344; N.F.416*] vel declinent, omnia et singula supradicta vobis priori sub pena canonica ac depositionis a statu committimus cum potestate cohertionis canonice exequenda, volentes quod nos de nominibus rebellium et nonparentium si qui fuerint in premissis certificetis distincte, et nos eorum conatus demeritos sic curabimus cohercere quod pene eorum cedent ceteris ad terrorem. Valete. [Ripon, 20 Feb. 1321.]

209 [*Commission to admit (unnamed) canons of Thurgarton to purgation on articles shown in schedule (not given); with warning against perjury, conspiracy, etc.*]
COMMISSIO AD RECIPIENDUM PURGATIONEM QUORUNDAM CANONICORUM DE THURGARTON. Willelmus etc. dilectis filiis priori de Thurgarton ac magistro Simoni de Curto Majori canonico nostre ecclesie Suwell' salutem [*etc.*]. De vestra circumspectione provida ac conscientiarum vestrarum puritate confisi, ad recipiendum purgationem quorundam canonicorum prioratus ejusdem super articulis in cedula hiis inclusa contentis prout quemlibet eorum contingunt, et ad certificandum nos plene et distincte de hiis omnibus que feceritis et inveneritis in hac parte, vobis cum potestate cohertionis canonice committimus vices nostras; sub obtestatione divini nominis firmiter inhibentes, ac per vos omnibus et singulis de gremio ac collegio dicti prioratus firmiter inhiberi volumus et mandamus sub pena excommunicationis majoris quam eos qui secus fecerint canonica premissa monitione incurrere volumus ipso facto, nequis prece vel precio favore vel odio suam in hac parte conscienciam quam exnunc coram deo oneramus in purgationibus hujusmodi violet vel degeret, sicut coram deo in summo et extremo judicio inde voluerit respondere. Nos enim ex habundanti omnes colligationes pactiones et federa quacumque firmitate vallata auctoritate nobis tributa a jure erumpimus atque solvimus in hiis scriptis, volentes per vos in pleno ipsius loci capitulo exprimi et edicto publice proponi quod quibuslibet de perjuris hujusmodi quorum absolutionem nobis specialiter reservamus januam claudere intendimus nostro tempore atque gradum cujuslibet insignii et honoris. Valete. [Ripon, 20 Feb. 1321.]

210 [N.F.416[88]] Commission to the prior of Thurgarton and M. Alan de Neusum, rector of Bingham, to audit the accounts of the executors of Agnes de la Cressenere and her son Robert, reserving final acquittance to the archbishop. n.d.

211 [*Order to pay procurations for the dedication of the churches of Hickling and Willoughby on the Wolds; with note of payments.*]
[Fo.344 *continued*] MONICIO FACTA PAROCHIANIS ECCLESIARUM DE HIKELING' ET WILUGHBY AD SATISFACIENDUM DOMINO PRO DEDICACIONE EARUNDEM. Will-

[88] Inserted facing fo.343ᵛ. It is neatly written but with many corrections, and is 22.5 by 9.5 cms. The text is similar to no.227 in *Reg. Melton*, II.87–8.

elmus etc. decano nostro de Byngham salutem [*etc.*]. Tenore presencium tibi committimus et mandamus quatinus ad ecclesias de Hikeling' et de Wilughby nostre diocesis personaliter accedens, parochianos ecclesiarum earundem moneas efficaciter et inducas quod illi, videlicet parochiani ecclesie de Hikeling' de quinque marcis ac parochiani ecclesie de Wylughby de aliis quinque marcis nobis ratione procuracionis pro nostro officio in dedicacione earundem ecclesiarum impenso debitis et nobis subtractis a non modico tempore impudenter, infra xv dies a tempore monicionis hujusmodi continue numerandos satisfaciant tibi nostro nomine competenter. Alioquin dictorum quindecim dierum spacio effluxo, dictas ecclesias quas exnunc prout extunc ecclesiastico interdicto supponimus in hiis scriptis sic interdictas denuncies et facias publice nunciari, dictisque parochianis divine laudis organa subtrahi sub pena juris, quousque de procurationibus nostris solitis nobis vel tibi nostro nomine fuerit plenarie satisfactum. Et nos super execucione hujusmodi mandati ac omni eo quod feceris in premissis distincte et oportune certifices per tuas litteras que harum seriem representent. [Harlsey (*Herlesey*), 28 Jan. 1321.]

[margin] Memorandum quod parochiani de Hikeling solverunt v marcas magistro Thome de Cave receptori Ebor' et super hoc habent litteras suas acquietancie. Item parochiani de Wylughby solverunt alias v marcas domino W. de Hundon sequestratori in archidiaconatu Not' prout per certificatorium decani de Byngham nobis constet.

212 [*Order to Broadholme priory to surrender fleeces and lambs received during a tithe cause with the vicar of Saxilby* (see **155**).]

MONITIO FACTA PRIORISSE ET CONVENTUI DE BRODHOLM AD RESTITUENDUM PERCEPTA MEDIO TEMPORE LITE PENDENTE INTER IPSAS ET VICARIUM DE SAXELBY EIDEM VICARIO. Willelmus permissione etc. decano nostro de Neuwerk' salutem [*etc.*]. Cum in causa decimarum mota coram nobis inter priorissam et conventum monasterii de Brodholm nostre diocesis et dominum Thomam de Cave perpetuum vicarium ecclesie de Saxelby fuisset petita ex parte dicti vicarii restitutio quarundem decimarum lane et agnorum quibus se pretendebat dicta lite pendente spoliatum, et contra dictam peticionem ex parte predictarum religiosarum exceptum seu replicatum, ac testes hincinde super hiis producti habitaque discussione aliquali; tandem dicte partes consenserunt quod decime predicte lane et agnorum per dictas religiosas ultimo tempore decimandi occupate sub nostro sequestro remaneant, et quod custos dicti nostri sequestri hujusmodi decimas in futurum provenientes percipiat dicta lite pendente parti que in dicta causa obtinuerit in eventu restituendas. Et quia rimatis probationibus predictis invenimus dictos priorissam et conventum percepisse et occupasse decem vellera et tres agnos ultimo tempore decimandi preterito ipsa lite pendente, tibi mandamus quatenus moneas et efficaciter inducas dictos priorissam et conventum quod predictos tres agnos et decem vellera sic per eos occupatos si extent alioquin valorem eorundem tibi infra octo dies a tempore monicionis eis facte reddant liberent et restituant, alioquin ipsas ad id per suspensionis et excommunicationis sentencias canonice compellas vice nostra; et quod te, quem custodem nostri sequestri in hac parte deputamus dicta lite pendente, decimas hujusmodi libere percipere colligere et custodire permittant in futurum, certificans nos super hiis quid feceris et inveneris in premissis cum per nos aut ex parte nostra fueris congrue requisitus. Vale. [Bishopthorpe, 4 Mar. 1321.]

213 Note of letters dimissory to be ordained priest to John Vanne, deacon, rector of Epperstone. Bishopthorpe, 16 Mar. 1321.

214 Memorandum of admission of William de Ryseley to Misson (*Misne*) church, by collation of John XXII,[89] and of his oath of obedience. Bishopthorpe, 25 Mar. 1321.

215 Licence for absence to M. Richard de Aston, rector of Sutton Bonington (*Bonynton*), at the request, and while in the service, of Stephen [Gravesend], bishop of London.[90] Bishopthorpe, 5 Apr. 1321.

216 Institution [etc.] of John de Bekingham, acolyte, to Winthorpe (*Wynthorp*) church, now vacant; presented by the prior and convent of Elsham (*Ellesham*; dioc. London). Sherburn (*Shirburn*) in Elmet, 10 Apr. 1321.

217 Licence to study for one year at a *studium generale* to M. Hugh de Wylughby, rector of Willoughby on the Wolds. Cawood, 29 June 1321.

218 Note of licence to study (*in forma constitutionis*) for two years to Hugh Gernon, subdeacon, rector of Elkesley. Bishopthorpe, 4 Sept. 1321.

219 [*Dispensation to a priest ordained to a fictitious title, quoting letters of the papal penitentiary dated 19 Mar. 1321.*]
[Fo.344v; N.F.416*v] DISPENSATIO JOHANNIS DE ROSINGTON PRESBITERI ORDINATI AD FICTUM TITULUM. Willelmus etc. dilecto filio domino Johanni de Rosington nostre diocesis presbitero salutem [*etc.*]. Litteras venerabilis patris domini Berengarii miseratione divina episcopi Tusculani nobis pro te directas recepimus, tenorem qui sequitur continentes:

Venerabili in Christo patri dei gracia archiepiscopo Ebor' vel ejus vicario in spiritualibus Berengarius miseratione divina episcopus Tusculanus salutem et sinceram in domino caritatem. Sua nobis Johannes de Rosington presbiter vestre diocesis lator presentium petitione monstravit quod cum ipse olim vellet ad sacros ordines promoveri et sufficientem titulum non haberet, cuidam militi qui ipsum ad suum titulum presentavit promisit corporali prestito juramento quod pretextu presentationis hujusmodi non impeteret super provisione sua nec molestaret eundem, et sic ad presentationem hujusmodi fuit per fictum titulum alias tamen rite ad omnes sacros ordines promotus. Et ex hoc tanquam simplex et juris ignarus excessisse non credens in sic susceptis ordinibus ministravit et alias divinis officiis se ingessit. Cognita tandem culpa per alterius sibi prudenciam revelata, sedem apostolicam adiens provideri sibi super hiis per eam humiliter supplicavit. Nos igitur auctoritate domini pape cujus penitenciarie curam gerimus, circumspectioni vestre committimus quatinus si est ita et in tales non fuit excommunicationis sentencia promulgata, injuncta inde sibi absolutione previa ab excessu hujusmodi penitencia salutari, eoque ad tempus prout expedire videritis a sic susceptorum ordinum[91] executione sus-

[89] See provision in *CPL*, II.203.
[90] See *BRUC*, 20–1.
[91] Interlined.

penso, demum suffragantibus sibi meritis alioque canonico non obstante super irregularitate inde contracta et sic susceptorum executione ordinum cum ipso misericorditer dispensetis. Datum Avinion' xiiii Kalendas Aprilis pontificatus domini Johannis pape xxii anno quinto.

Nos igitur tecum ab excessu hujusmodi absoluto, injuncta tibi pro modo culpe penitencia salutari teque usque ad tempus prout vidimus expedire a tuorum ordinum execucione suspenso, tandem suffragantibus tibi meritis et alio canonico non obstante quod sciamus super irregularitate ex premissis contracta et execucione ordinum tuorum auctoritate nobis in hac parte commissa misericorditer dispensamus. Vale. [Cawood, 27 May 1321.]

[margin] Et quia[92] dictus presbiter ordinatus fuit per episcopos Linc' et Elien', juravit coram domino tactis sacrosanctis evangeliis quod in tales non fuit sentencia excommunicationis lata in suis diocesibus; inquisita primitus veritate de mandato domini super contentis in littera per decanum de Retford in quo decanatu traxit originem.

220 Licence (at the request of the archbishop's friend, Robert de Wodehous, canon of Southwell) to Robert de Derneford, rector of Bunny, to be absent for one year while in the service of the king or Wodehous. Cawood, 10 June 1321.

221 Memorandum that, by papal authority, the archbishop dispensed Alan son of John de Barneby to be promoted to all orders and hold a benefice, provided he resides, despite his illegitimate birth. Cawood, 11 June 1321.

222 [*Cancellation of the penance imposed on a canon of Thurgarton and mitigation for three others* (see **208**).]
MITIGACIO PENITENCIARUM FRATRIBUS DE THURGARTON INJUNCTARUM. Willelmus etc. dilecto filio . . priori de Thurgarton salutem [*etc.*]. Cum juxta juris doctrinam sive plectendo sive ignoscendo hoc solum bene agatur ut vita hominis corrigatur, nos ad cordis contricionem ac devotam obedientiam quibus dilecti filii fratres Johannes de Ruddestan Nicholaus de Suwell Johannes de Crophill et Hugo de Not' vestri concanonici commissa sua preterita deflevisse penitentiam canonicam eis nuper indictam pro suis reatibus pacienter subeundo ac humiliter sustinendo delatum ad nos per vos . . priorem testimonium perhibet, nostrum intuitum convertentes, penitentiam canonicorum eorundem equanimiter sic duximus moderandum, fratrem videlicet Nicholaum de Suwell ut per hanc nostram graciam in eo fervor devocionis et correctionis deinceps pululet uberius atque crescat ab injuncta penitentia absolventes, et penitentias fratribus Johanni de Ruddestan Johanni de Crophill et Hugoni de Not' injunctas laxantes preterquam disciplinas quas in Quadragesima et in singulis vigiliis apostolorum et singulis septimanis quatuor temporum eos subire volumus devote atque facere, quousque aliud a nobis inde receperitis[93] in mandatis. Benedictionem et diu in domino[94] valeatis. [Bishopthorpe, 3 July 1321.]

[92] Interlined.
[93] MS. *receperint*
[94] Interlined from *in*

223 [*Citation of the master of Bawtry hospital to answer for his absence, neglect and waste.*]
CITACIO CONTRA CUSTODEM HOSPITALIS DE BAUTR'. Willelmus etc. dilecto filio . . decano nostro de Retford salutem [*etc.*]. Insinuatione clamosa nostris est auribus inculcatum quod quidam dominus Petrus de Sandale pro custode hospitalis nostri de Bautr' se gerens, ipso hospitali deserto cantariaque septimanis singulis in dicto hospitali pro animabus fundatorum ejusdem et aliorum fidelium salubriter instituta una cum ceteris operibus caritatis solitis exhiberi in ipsa omnino tradita neglectui et relicta, in locis aliis inhoneste et in scandalum sui ordinis evagatur, ea que ad dictum hospitale pertinent ut prodigus dilapidat et consumit in tantum quod edificia et domus dicti hospitalis pro defectu custodie ruinam funditus comminantur, jura etiam et libertates decidunt inconsulte ac exinanicio terrarum et rerum aliarum ad dictum hospitale pertinentium irreparabiliter apparet in janúis nisi occuratur cicius et salubrius ex adverso. Quocirca tibi firmiter injungendo mandamus quatinus dictum Petrum si personaliter poterit inveniri, alioquin edicto tam in dicto hospitali quam in capella de Bautr' astante populi multitudine in eadem publice proposito ne ignoranciam in hac parte pretendere valeat in eventum, cites peremptorie quod compareat coram nobis proximo die juridico post instans festum sancti Michaelis ubicumque tunc fuerimus in nostra diocesi[95] titulum siquem habeat canonicum super retentione ac custodia dicti hospitalis pro termino peremptorio exhibiturus ac super premissis legitime responsurus [et] facturus ulterius quod canonicis convenerit institutis. Terminum vero hujusmodi peremptorium cum divini cultus diminucio ac perniciosum exemplum aliorum atque pluriorum scandalum dictique hospitalis manifestum prejudicium atque dampnum in hac parte vertatur sic duximus moderandum. Et super hujus execucione mandati citra [dictum] diem nos tempestive certifices et distincte per tuas patentes litteras harum seriem continentes. Vale. [Bishop Wilton (*Wylton*), 10 July 1321.]

224 [*Citation of Richard Gluwe to answer for occupying Marnham vicarage.*]
CITACIO CONTRA INTRUSOREM VICARIE ECCLESIE DE MARNHAM. Willelmus etc. dilecto filio . . decano nostro de Neuwerk' salutem [*etc.*]. Querelam domini Nicholai de Sixtenby perpetui vicarii ecclesie de Marnham nostre diocesis gravem recepimus continentem quod licet ipse in perpetua vicaria ejusdem ecclesie per nos canonice institutus fuisset[96] ac in ipsius corporalem possessionem cum suis juribus et pertinenciis de mandato nostro per ipsius loci archidiaconum seu ejus officialem inductus ipsamque sic aliquamdiu possedisset canonice ac in ipsius possessione notorie fuisset, quidam tamen Ricardus dictus Gluwe in eandem vicariam absque cause cognicione immo propria temeritate se intrusit ipsamque absque titulo canonico sic detinet illicite occupatam, fructus proventus et obvenciones ejusdem occupavit et occupat, predictumque vicarium prefata sua possessione spoliavit spoliarive mandavit et fecit ac spoliationem nomine suo factam et ratam habuit ex postfacto, non absque nostre auctoritatis ordinarie contemptu ac predicti vicarii prejudicio manifesto, super quibus idem vicarius peciit sibi per nos de oportuno remedio

[95] Interlined from *ubicumque*
[96] See **109**.

provideri et sibi in premissis debitam justiciam exhiberi. Quocirca nos non valentes in dicta peticione deesse qui sumus justicie debitores, tibi mandamus quatinus cites peremptorie prefatum Ricardum, et etiam hujus citacionis ex habundanti in predicta ecclesia et duabus ecclesiis evicinis edicto peremptorio dum populi multitudo affuerit publice proposito, quod compareat coram nobis proximo die juridico post festum sancte Fidis virginis ubicumque unc fuerimus in nostra diocesi per se vel procuratorem predicto vicario ac nobis super premissis et ea tangentibus ad correctionem et salutem anime sue personaliter [Fo.345; N.F.417] responsurus, ac titulum incumbencie seu causam si quem aut quam habeat in predicta vicaria et quicquid canonicum pretendere voluerit sibi competere in eadem exhibiturus seu ut convenit ostensurus, facturusque ulterius secundum qualitatem premissorum quod justicia suadebit. Terminum vero et personalem comparitionem de quibus premittitur cum premissorum qualitas hec exposcat sic duximus moderandum. Et ad probationem hujus mandati nostri totaliter adimpleti remittas nobis ad dictum diem presentes impressione sigilli officii tui pendente signatas. Vale. [Skerne, 15 Sept. 1321.]

225 Note[97] of licence to study in a suitable place for one year to Thomas de Castirton, rector of a mediety of Cotgrave. Bishop Monkton, 5 Oct. 1321.

226 Note of licence to study for two years to Andrew Luterel, rector of West Bridgford (*Brigeford*). York, 24 Sept.1321.

227 COPIA ORDINATIONIS SUPER VICARIAM ECCLESIE DE BLIDA.[98] Copy [undated and without explanation] of composition between the priory and vicar of Blyth in 1287.

228 Institution [etc.] of John de Creton, priest, to Orston vicarage, now vacant; presented by the dean and chapter of Lincoln. Bishop Monkton, 12 Oct. 1321.

229 Note[99] of mandate to the prior and convent of Thurgarton to admit Robert de Kydermynstr', former prior of St. Oswald's, Gloucester, as a canon of the house, with the Gloucester house defraying the expenses, as it has promised in writing. Cawood, 14 Apr. 1322.

230 [Fo.345v; N.F.417v] Institution (in the person of Edmund de Grymmesby, clerk, as proctor) and mandate for induction of Roger de Sutton, priest, to North Collingham church; presented by Edward II by reason of the vacancy of

[97] This entry is an insertion at the foot of fo.344v.

[98] Printed from the text in British Library, Harleian MS 3759, in *The Cartulary of Blyth Priory*, ed. R.T. Timson, Thoroton Society Record Series, vols.27–8 (1973), II.354–6. There are slight variations in field and place-name forms (e.g. *Hyldertrewong*) and wording. The Melton text supplies the words lost by rubbing in the cartulary (p.355): 'in decima agnorum et argenti dati pro decima agnorum, in decima lane ac argenti dati pro decima lane in villa de Blida, . . .'.

[99] Like the first mandate in this exchange (**205**), this entry is out of sequence. Both are at the feet of folios, suggesting late insertion.

Peterborough abbey,[1] in an exchange of benefices [as below]. Bishopthorpe, 24 Oct. 1321.

231 (i) Institution of Robert Jorce, subdeacon, to Stow church (dioc. Lincoln), by authority of a commission of Henry [Burghersh], bishop of Lincoln (quoted; dated Banbury, 30 Oct. 1321) for an exchange of benefices between Robert, rector of North Collingham [see **191**], and Roger de Sutton, rector of Stow. (ii) Certificate to the bishop of Lincoln that Robert was instituted to Stow, being presented by Nicholas de Segrave, kt. Bishopthorpe, 6 Nov. 1321.

232 Institution [etc.] of Peter de Bekering', clerk, to Tuxford church, now vacant; presented by Thomas de Bekering', kt. Bishopthorpe, 15 Nov. 1321.

233 Memorandum that, by papal authority, the archbishop dispensed Alexander son of John Kayser of Newark, clerk, to be promoted to all orders and hold a benefice with cure of souls, provided he resides, despite his illegitimate birth. Bishopthorpe, 11 Dec. 1321.

234 Institution [etc.] of William de Ilkeston, priest, to Selston (*SELYSTON, Seliston*) church, now vacant; presented by Nicholas de Cantilupo, kt., lord of Greasley (*Greseley*). Also note [in margin] that he had a letter to the dean of Nottingham to enquire into defects of houses, etc. Bishopthorpe, 15 Dec. 1321.

235 The like of Geoffrey de Wilford, chaplain, to the church of St. Nicholas, Nottingham, now vacant; presented by the prior and convent of Lenton. Cawood, 10 Jan. 1322.

236 [*Order for Richard Gluwe to restore Marnham vicarage to Nicholas de Sixtenby, after judgment* (see **224**).]
[Fo.346; N.F.418] SENTENCIA CONDEMPNATORIA SUPER RESTITUTIONE VICARIE ECCLESIE DE MARNHAM. Willelmus etc. dilecto filio . . officiali archidiaconi Not' salutem [*etc.*]. Cum nos in causa restitutionis que nuper inter dominum Nicholaum de Sixtenby perpetuum vicarium ecclesie de Marnham nostre diocesis actorem ex parte una et Ricardum dictum Gluwe reum ex altera coram nobis super inferius contentis aliquamdiu vertabatur legitime procedentes, dictum Ricardum Gluwe ad restitutionem vicarie ejusdem ecclesie de Marnham et rerum inibi contentarum, videlicet viginti quarteriorum ordei xii quarteriorum siliginis unius quarterii et dimidii avenarum, dicto domino Nicholao vicario predicto de consensu ejusdem Ricardi plenarie faciendam, quiquidem Ricardus dictum vicarium de rebus pretaxatis se spoliasse coram nobis judicialiter fatebatur suamque hujusmodi confessionem secuti per sentenciam precepti rite condempnavimus justicia suadente, dicte vicarie et rerum predictarum possessionem dicto vicario restituendam fore ac reformandam canonice decernentes, eamque restituimus eidem et reformavimus per nostram sentenciam antedictam, condempnacionem expensarum ea occasione in lite factarum nobis expressius reservantes; vobis mandamus quatenus dictum

[1] *CPR 1321–4*, 24.

Ricardum vice nostra monea[ti]s et efficaciter induca[ti]s quatenus prefatam vicariam statim ac ceteras res supranominatas memorato domino Nicholao vicario predicto infra x dies a dato presencium continue numerandos realiter ac plenarie restituat secundum formam nostre sentencie antedicte, alioquin dictum Ricardum ad id faciendum per sentencias excommunicacionum extunc per vos in eundem Ricardum fulminandarum de diebus in dies canonice compellatis. Et de omni eo quod feceritis in premissis ac qualiter hanc nostram sentenciam fueritis executi nos citra festum Purificationis beate Marie Virginis distincte et aperte certificetis per litteras vestras patentes harum seriem continentes. Valete. [Bishopthorpe, 21 Dec. 1321.]

237 [*Deprivation of the master of Bawtry hospital; he had ignored his original citation* (see **223**) *and two others, the last being an inquest into dilapidations.*]
PRIVACIO PETRI DE SANDALE DE HOSPITALI DE BAUTR'. In dei nomine amen. Cum nos Willelmus [*etc.*] in visitacione nostra quam nuper in archidiaconatu Not' exercuimus comperimus clamosa insinuacione seu fama vehementissima referente quod quidam Petrus de Sandale qui se gerit pro custode hospitalis nostri de Bautre, ipsum hospitale et ejus custodiam quasi totaliter deserens, bona inibi tunc existencia miserabiliter consumpsit et dilapidavit, cantariam que inibi consuevit et adhuc deberet inveniri et alia opera pietatis ibidem consueta exhiberi subtraxit, domos et edificia ad dictum hospitale pertinentia tendere permisit funditus in ruinam, in anime sue periculum et cultus divini diminucionem aliorumque perniciosum exemplum; quorum occasione dictum Petrum propositurum titulum si quem haberet in hospitalis custodia memorati ad certos diem et locum pro termino preciso et peremptorio ex causa legitima in hujusmodi citatorio nostro expressa coram nobis legitime fecimus evocari, quibus ipso Petro nullatenus comparente sed contumaciter absente, ipsum pronunciavimus contumacem et in penam hujusmodi sue contumacie sibi viam quicquem ulterius proponendi in hac parte exclusimus per decretum; cumque eundem Petrum ad proponendum si quod canonicum haberet quare a dicti hospitalis custodia minime deberet amoveri iterum peremptorie ad certos diem et locum coram nobis legitime fecerimus evocari, sicuti prius tunc se contumaciter absentavit, ipsoque contumace pronunciato, licet ad ejus amocionem de custodia predicta potuimus processisse ad ejus convincendam maliciam, de statu dicti hospitalis et de dilapidacione bonorum ejusdem inibi facta per eundem ipso in hac parte legitime evocato inquirere fecimus in forma juris, ipsumque ex habundanti ad audiendum super premissis pronunciacionem finalem ad certos diem et locum coram nobis legitime fecimus evocari, quibus dicto Petro nullatenus comparente sed contumaciter absente, ad pronunciacionem finalem procedimus in hunc modum:

In dei nomine amen. Nos Willelmus [*etc.*] in negotio seu causa ex officio nostro contra Petrum de Sandale qui se gerit pro custode hospitalis nostri de Bautr' legitime procedentes, habita deliberacione sufficienti nobiscum et cum juris peritis, quia invenimus eundem Petrum in dicti hospitalis custodia nullum jus habuisse vel habere in presenti, eundem in eodem hospitali nullum jus habuisse vel habere per hanc nostram sentenciam pronunciamus et etiam declaramus. Et quia eundem Petrum crimen dilapidacionis in bonis dicti hospitalis et circa ea invenimus notorie commisisse, ipsum omni jure si quod habuit vel habeat in presenti in hospitalis custodia memorati sentencialiter et diffinitive privamus exuimus et amovemus [et] privatum exutum et amotum pronunciamus et declaramus in hiis scriptis.

Lecta lata et in scriptis pronunciata fuit ista sentencia apud Cawod Ebor' diocesis[2] xix die mensis Januarii anno gracie MCCCXXI indictione quinta, presentibus domino Ricardo de Melton et Willelmo de Wakefeld clericis testibus etc. R'. R. Snou' etc. [Cawood, 19 Jan. 1322.]

238 [*Licence for a canon of Newstead under penance* (see **147**) *to do outdoor work for the house and go to the archbishop to be ordained.*]
MITIGACIO PENITENCIE FRATRIS PHILIPPI DE CANDELBY CANONICI DE NOVO LOCO IN SHIRWOD. Willelmus etc. dilectis filiis priori et conventui monasterii de Novo Loco in Shirwode nostre diocesis salutem [*etc.*]. Licet alias fratri Philippo de Candelby concanonico vestro pro suis demeritis inter cetera injunxerimus quod septa monasterii vestri non exiret, attendentes tamen quod idem frater Philippus super premissis quodammodo penituit ut dicebat et quod per eundem negocia vestra extrinseca attenta sui corporis ad laborandum potencia aliquociens poterunt promoveri, ad exeundum dicti monasterii vestri septa si et quando pro utilitate domus vestre vobis videbitur expedire super quo consciencias vestras oneramus, et ut valeat ad ordines sibi convenientes suscipiendos ad nos accedere dumtamem sibi aliquod canonicum non obsistat, eidem liberam in domino concedimus facultatem, aliis penitenciis nostris eidem per nos injunctis in suo robore duraturis. Valete. [York, 1 Mar. 1322.]

239 Licence to study (*in forma constitutionis*) for two years at a *studium generale* to Peter de Bekering', acolyte, rector of Tuxford, with dispensation from proceeding to orders beyond the subdiaconate; [beside the usual requirement to provide a vicar, etc.] he is to see that five quarters of hard grain, *viz.* two of corn, two of barley and one of beans, are annually distributed among his poor parishioners. Cawood, 9 Apr. 1322.

240 Appointment, during pleasure, of Walter de Fery of Beckingham (*Bekingham*), the archbishop's serjeant in North Soke (*North Soken*), as attorney to claim and withdraw the archbishop's tenants from cases in any county or wapentake courts in Nottinghamshire, arrange for them to be heard according to justice or custom, and receive the archbishop's rents from North Soke tenants.

[margin] Note that Walter swore before the archbishop that he would serve him faithfully and do justice and not harm to rich and poor. Cawood, 13 Apr. 1322.

241 [Fo.346^{v}; N.F.418^{v}] AUGMENTACIO VICARIE ECCLESIE DE STOKES. Decree. The vicar of East Stoke claimed that the portion assigned in the ordination of the vicarage [cited; see **34**] was insufficient to support him, his chaplains and his other charges. On being called, the rector or prebendary made no canonical objection to any augmentation. An inquisition confirmed the inadequacy of the vicarage. The archbishop, after taking expert counsel, therefore decrees that vicars are to have all tithes, oblations and revenues due to the altar which were not mentioned in the original ordination, namely live mortuaries and tithes of

[2] Interlined.

wool and lambs in the parish of the church and its chapels (*viz*. Syerston, Elston, Coddington and Newark castle), *i.e.* the whole altarage of the parish. The rest of the original ordination is to stand. Cawood, 24 Mar. 1322.

Subscription by Richard de Snoweshull, clerk (dioc. Worcester), notary and the archbishop's scribe; witnessed by M. Adam de Hesellebech', Richard de Otringham and Richard de Melton, the archbishop's familiar clerks.

242 Institution [etc.] of Lancelot de Coreberto, acolyte, to the church of St. Peter, Nottingham, now vacant; presented by the prior and convent of Lenton. Bishopthorpe, 11 May 1322.

243 Dispensation to John Traveys, clerk (dioc. York), to hold a benefice with cure of souls, despite his illegitimate birth, provided that he takes orders at statutory times and resides; quoting letters of John XXII (dated Avignon, 1 May 1318). Bishopthorpe, 9 May 1322.

244 Notes of licence to study (*in forma constitutionis*) to Lancelot [de Coreberto], acolyte, rector of St. Peter's, Nottingham, for one year from the date of his institution; and of letters dimissory for all orders. Bishopthorpe, 17 May 1322.

245 [N.F.419[3]] Oath of obedience of John de Notingham, abbot of Welbeck, subscribed by his own hand [see **250**]. Bishopthorpe chapel, 23 May 1322.

246 [Fo.347; N.F.420] Institution [etc.] of Walter de Carleton in Lyndrik', priest, to Walkeringham (*Walkringham*) vicarage, now vacant; presented by the prior and convent of Worksop (*Wirsop*). Bishopthorpe, 18 May 1322.

247 The like of Alexander de Chaggele, priest, to a mediety of Gedling (*Gedelyng'*) church, now vacant; presented by Lady Isabel Bardolf. Also note of licence to be absent for one year in a suitable place. Bishopthorpe, 20 May 1322.

248 Note of licence to study for one year from 5 October to Thomas de Casterton, rector of a mediety of Cotgrave. Same date.

249 Note of licence for absence for one year in a suitable place to M. Stephen de Kynardesley, priest, rector of Sibthorpe. Bishopthorpe, 23 May 1322.

250 [*Report by Premonstratensian abbots that John de Notingham has been elected abbot of Welbeck.*]

PRESENTACIO ELECTI IN ABBATEM DE WELLEBEK' AD BENEDICENDUM PER ABBATEM DE NEUHUS. Reverendo in Christo patri domino W. dei gracia archiepiscopo Ebor' Anglie primati suus humilis et devotus frater Johannes ejusdem paciencia . . abbas de Neuhus ordinis Premonstr' salutem cum omni humilitate reverencia et honore. Venerande paternitati vestre duximus significandum quod cum ecclesia de Wellebeck' nostre ordinis vestre diocesis que est nostra filia

[3] Interleaved facing fo.346^v, measuring 22 by 3.5 cms. A cross follows *subscribo,* the last word of the oath. The memorandum of the date, the last line, appears to end with a signature – *R' R' Snou' notar'*.

spiritualis per spontaneam cessionem domini Willelmi de Kendale quondam abbatis ejusdem ecclesie nuper esset pastore viduata, ad ipsam ecclesiam visitandam assumptis nobiscum venerabilibus confratribus nostris dominis de Bellocapite et de Dala ecclesiarum abbatibus novique abbatis electionem celebrandam personaliter accessimus ut decebat, ubi invocata spiritus sancti gracia observatisque omnibus et singulis secundum ritum nostri ordinis ad electionem canonicam spectantibus canonici omnes et singuli dicte ecclesie de Wellebeck' in capitulo congregati pari voto et unanimi assensu fratrem Johannem de Notingham dicte ecclesie concanonicum virum utique providum in spiritualibus et temporalibus discretum in patrem et pastorem concorditer elegerunt, cujus electione coram nobis in forma juris probata et auctoritate paterna legitime confirmata administracionem tam spiritualium quam temporalium ad eandem ecclesiam de Wellebeck' spectancium commisimus eidem, ipsumque electum a paternitate vestra sui plenitudine officii recepturum vobis presentamus, excellenciam vestram attencius exorantes quatinus munus benedictionis vestre eidem dignemini impartiri et ipsum admittere in graciam et favorem. Ut autem dictis electioni et confirmacioni fidem adhibeatis pleniorem, presentes litteras sigillo nostro et sigillis venerabilium confratrum nostrorum de Bellocapite et de Dala ecclesiarum abbatum nobis in dictis electione et confirmacione assistencium signatas vestre reverencie duximus destinandas. Valeat excellencia vestra semper in domino. Datum in monasterio predicto die Jovis proxima post festum sancti Johannis ante portam latinam anno domini MCCCXXII. [Welbeck, 13 May 1322.]

251 [*Special licence for the prior of Thurgarton's visit to the Roman Curia.*]
LICENCIA PRO PRIORE DE THURGARTON VISITANDI CURIAM ROMANAM. Universis pateat per presentes quod nos Willelmus etc. ad expiandum reatus qui suam premunt conscienciam fratri Johanni de Hikeling' priori monasterii de Thurgarton nostre diocesis sedem apostolicam personaliter[4] visitandi licenciam concedimus specialem, quem in eundo morando et redeundo omnibus Christi fidelibus specialiter commendamus. In cujus rei testimonium sigillum nostrum presentibus est appensum. [Bishopthorpe, 24 May 1322.]

252 Mandate to the official of York not to trouble Robert de Hikeling', vicar of Granby (*Graneby*),[5] for being non-resident while detained at the Curia, with the archbishop's special licence, about matters on his conscience. Same date.

253 Institution [etc.] of John de Cotes, priest, to East Stoke vicarage, now vacant; presented by Roger de Northburgh, canon of Lincoln and prebendary of East Stoke. Bishopthorpe, 24 June 1322.

254 Note of licence for absence for one year in a suitable place to Robert de Derneford, rector of Bunny. Bishopthorpe, 10 June 1322.

[4] Interlined.
[5] Died by 13 Feb. 1331, when Walter de Groby, priest, was instituted to Granby, presented by Thurgarton priory (Reg. Melton, fo.581; N.F.723).

255 Note [interlined] of licence allowing him to be absent for a year from 10 June 1323. Cawood, 10 Apr. 1323.

256 [*Mandate for the repair of the rectories of Orston, Whatton, East Bridgford, Clifton, Colston Bassett, Bunny, (East?) Leake and Barton in Fabis.*]
PRO REPARACIONE RECTORIARUM IN ARCHIDIACONATU NOTING'. Willelmus [*etc.*] dilecto filio officiali archidiacono Notingh' salutem [*etc.*]. Cum persone ecclesiastice que de suis ecclesiis et ecclesiasticis beneficiis multa bona recipiant domos et cetera eorum edificia juxta qualitatem eorundem beneficiorum integra teneantur conservare ac dirupta prout indignerint sufficienter restaurare, ac nos dudum dictum archidiaconatum Notingh' visitantes inter cetera comperimus quod edificia rectoriarum de Orston Whatton Estbriggeford Clifton Colstonbasset Boney Leyk' et Barton sunt minus idonea et secundum qualitatem eorundem beneficiorum penitus insufficiencia et sic ea necgligenter permittunt insufficiencia dirupta pariter et infecta, unde ipsarum ecclesiarum status deformitas et multa incommoda subsecuntur in animarum suarum periculum et perniciosum exemplum aliorum; nos igitur prout nostro incumbit officio pastorali volentes in premissis remedium apponere oportunum, vobis in virtute obediencie firmiter injungendo mandamus quatinus visis presentibus quamcito commode poteritis predictarum ecclesiarum rectores moneatis peremptorie et efficaciter inducatis (videlicet de Orston sub pena xl s., de Whatton quinque marcarum, Estbriggeford quinque marcarum, Clifton x marcarum, Colstonbasset x marcarum, Boney xx marcarum, Leyk x marcarum et Barton C s.) quod citra festum Pentecostes proximo futurum predictas domos et edificia prout indignerint sufficienter reparent et reficiant ut tenentur, alioquin extunc sumptibus dictorum rectorum de fructibus eorundem beneficiorum predictas domos et edificia reparare ac reficere intendimus juxta formam constitucionis legati super hoc edite, penis autem predictis in suo robore nichilominus duraturis. De die vero recepcionis presencium ac monicionum per vos in hac parte factarum ac omni eo quod feceritis in premissis et qualiter prefati rectores monitis vestris paruerint in hac parte nos citra dictum diem Pentecostes reddatis certiores distincte et aperte per vestras [litteras] patentes harum seriem continentes. Valete. [Acaster Malbis (*Acastre Malebys*), 18 June 1322.]

[margin] Memorandum quod postea scriptum fuit dicto officiali quod supersedeat quoad rectorem ecclesie de Boney, videlicet ad festum Nativitatis domini proximo futurum sub dato apud Cawod Kalendis Marcii anno gracie etc. xxii et pontificatus domini sexto. Et ista ad rogatum domini Roberti de Wodehous.[6] [Cawood, 1 Mar. 1323.]

257 [*Appointment of coadjutor to the aged rector of Clifton, a canon of Lincoln.*]
[Fo.347v; N.F.420v] DEPUTACIO COADJUTORIS PRO RECTORE ECCLESIE DE CLIFTON. Willelmus etc. dilecto nobis in Christo Willelmo de Graham rectori ecclesie de Somerby Linc' diocesis salutem cum benediccione et gracia salvatoris. Cum magister Elyas de Muskham ecclesiam parochialem de Clifton nostre diocesis nobisque jure ordinario subjectam canonicatui suo quem habet in ecclesia Lincolnien' assignatam optinens penes nos ut rector ejus debilitate visus et senio adeo sit confractus quod ad sui ipsius regimen ut accepimus non sufficit

[6] See **220** for his interest.

nec suorum; nos ex officii nostri debito tam dicte ecclesie parochiali quam persone prefati magistri Elye quatenus ratione ejusdem ecclesie parochialis nobis subesse dinoscitur providere volentes de tuaque fidelitate fiduciam obtinentes, dumtamen prefatus magister Elyas nobis consenserit in hac parte, te eidem magistro Elye ad ipsius prout nobis subest et suorum in dicta nostra diocesi existentium regimen et ad curam dicte ecclesie sue tam in temporalibus quam in spiritualibus peragendam coadjutorem tenore presencium deputamus, mandantes tibi quatinus de bonis prefati Elye prout jurisdictioni nostre subsunt et ecclesie sue parochialis predicte nunc extantibus et futuris inventario per te fideliter facto, eundem magistrum Elyam secundum facultates suas quarum curam et administrationem in forma pretacta tibi committimus competenter exhibeas et custodias curamque parochie predicte ecclesie si et quatenus ipsum concernit et onera eidem incumbencia peragi facias et agnosci; te in hac parte taliter habiturus ut quamcicius poteris ad nos personaliter accedas de facto tuo in premissis fidelem reddendi in eo eventu rationem juxta juris exigenciam nobis cautionem ydoneam prestaturus quo ex parte nostra fueris congrue requisitus. Vale. [Bishopthorpe, 4 July 1322.]

258 Institution [etc.] of John de Spaldyng, canon of Welbeck (*Wellebek'*), priest, to Whatton vicarage, now vacant; presented by the abbot and convent of Welbeck. Bishopthorpe, 11 July 1322.

259 [*Monition against persons detaining a testator's goods; they are to be cited to appear before the archbishop on 5 July.*]
MONICIO IN GENERE CUM CITACIONE CONTRA OCCUPATORES BONA ALICUJUS DEFUNCTI. Willelmus etc. dilecto filio . . officiali archidiaconi Notingh' salutem [*etc.*]. Ad nostrum nuper pervenit auditum quod quidam iniquitatis filii sue salutis immemores ac proprii honoris persecutores bona domini Johannis de Halghton dudum [rectoris] medietatis ecclesie de Gedeling' defuncti occultant occupant et minus juste detinuerunt et detinent occupata, quominus dicti defuncti ultima voluntas cujus liber debet esse stilus suum debitum sortitur effectum quin verius ex hoc impeditur et graviter perturbatur, cujus occasione perturbacionis dicta bona defuncti illicite ut premittitur occupantes sentenciam majoris excommunicationis in nostra sancta synodo Ebor' auctoritate constitutionis super hoc inibi edite promulgate et in forma juris publicate proinde latam dampnabiliter incurrebant ipso facto.[7] Quocirca vobis mandamus firmiter injungentes quatenus omnes et singulos qui dicta bona prefati defuncti occultarunt celarunt aut quovismodo maliciose detinuerunt seu detinent occupata contra debitum justicie et ultimam voluntatem dicti defuncti memoratam in genere moneatis et efficaciter inducatis et per alios moneri et induci faciatis diebus et locis quibus ex parte executorum dicti defuncti congrue fueritis requisiti, quatenus dicta bona memoratis executoribus infra x dies a tempore monicionis sibi in hac parte legitime facte quatenus ad eos devenerunt plenarie restituant ut est justum, alioquin ipsos dictam sentenciam dampnabiliter incurrisse diebus et locis de quibus premittitur quatenus de jure fuerit faciendum in genere nuncietis seu per alios faciatis nunciari; inquirentes

[7] See *Councils and Synods, II A.D. 1205–1313*, ed. F.M. Powicke and C.R. Cheney, 2 vols. (Oxford, 1964), I.495 (c.39).

nihilominus de nominibus dicta bona detinentium et injuste occupancium, et quos in hac parte culpabiles inveneritis citetis seu citari faciatis personaliter quod compareant coram nobis die Lune proximo post festum apostolorum Petri et Pauli ubicumque tunc fuerimus in nostra diocesi dictis executoribus occasione premissa de justicia responsuri ac penitenciam condignam pro suis demeritis ulteriusque recepturi quod justicia suadebit. Et de omni eo quod in premissis feceritis ac qualiter presens mandatum nostrum fueritis executi nos, cum per dictos executores congrue super hoc fueritis requisiti, curetis reddere certiores per vestras patentes litteras harum seriem continentes. Valete. [Bishopthorpe, 16 June 1322.]

260 ORDINACIO PERPETUARUM CANTARIARUM IN CAPELLA BEATE MARIE DE HETHEBETHBRIGG' ET IN ECCLESIA SANCTE ELENE DE STAPELFORD. Letters patent of the archbishop inspecting:

(1) Letters patent of Edward I.[8] Licence for alienation in mortmain by John le Palmere of Nottingham and Alice his wife of £6 13s. 5d. rent in Nottingham to two chaplains celebrating daily in St. Mary's chapel on Hethbeth bridge [Nottingham] for their souls, and the souls of their ancestors and all Christians assisting the bridge's upkeep. Laneham, 16 Apr. 1303.

(2) Letters patent of Edward II.[9] Similar licence for Alice to grant 5 messuages and 5 bovates of land in Barton [in Fabis] and Stapleford to a chaplain celebrating daily in St. Helen's church, Stapleford, for the souls of Hugh de Stapelford, Alice, their ancestors and all the faithful departed. [Fo.348; N.F.421] Westminster, 16 Nov. 1320.

(3) Charter of Alice le Palmere of Nottingham, confirming her grant of £6 13s. 5d. annual rent in Nottingham to Hugh del Coulane and John de Neustede of Nottingham, chaplains, and their successors, celebrating daily for ever for the souls of John le Palmere, Hugh de Stapulford, Alice, her parents and benefactors, and the benefactors of Hethbeth bridge. The rent is received from the following tenants of Alice, their heirs and assigns, with their services: John de Gra[nt]ham, for a messuage in the daily market, Nottingham, 36s.; Laurence le Pelter, for a messuage in the same place, 2s. 3d., with a cock and 2 hens; Henry de Wolloton, for a messuage in the same place, 4s. 4d.; Marjory de Crophill, for a cellar once William le Spicer's in the same place, 2s.; Richard son of Gervase, for a messuage once Lettice Curzon's in Castle Gate (*vico Castri*), Nottingham, 2s. 6d.; Richard de Grymeston, for a messuage once Emma Doubuldent's towards the Bar (*barram*), 2s. with 2 hens; William de Dembulby, for a messuage in the Saturday market, 10s.; Ellis de Loquinton, for a messuage in the same place, 6s. 8d., a cock and 2 hens; Robert de Warewyk', for a messuage in the same place, 2s. 6d.; Hugh de Wolloton, for a messuage once William son of Stephen's in the same place, 2s. and a hen; Robert le Shereman, for a messuage in the same place, 4s. 8d.; Emma la Barker, for a messuage in Cookstool Row (*Cukestoldam*), 12s.; Roger le Boustringer, for a messuage in the same place, 18s.; Roger de Hempsel, for a messuage in the same place, 2s. 6d.; John de Rasin, for a messuage in Bridlesmith Gate (*vico lorimariorum*), 26s. Granted with warranty. Witnesses: Laurence le Spicer, mayor of Nottingham,

[8] As in *CPR 1301–7*, 133.
[9] As in *CPR 1317–21*, 529.

John le Colier and William Godinogh, bailiffs of the same, Robert de Cropphill, Robert Ingram, John le Palmere, William de Cropphill and others. Nottingham, 20 Feb. 1320.

(4) Charter of Alice confirming her grant to Richard de Stapulford, chaplain, and his successors [as in second licence], with warranty. Witnesses and date [as above].

Approval and confirmation by the archbishop of these three perpetual chantries, ordaining that Alice is to present the said three chaplains and their successors in her lifetime, and afterwards the prior and convent of Newstead are to present other chaplains to the archbishop, his successors, and custodians of the diocese *sede vacante*, for their institution and to receive their obedience. Patronage will lapse to the archbishop, etc., when presentations are not made within a month of vacancies occurring. Cawood, 25 Aug. 1322.

261 Commission to the official of York and M. John de Wodehous, rector of Sutton upon Derwent, to hear and determine an *ex officio* cause against Ralph Dode of Newark concerning the administration of the goods of his wife Joan, who died intestate; they are to report. Bishopthorpe, 19 Nov. 1322.

262 [Fo.348v; N.F.421v] LITTERA STUDENDI PRO RECTORE DE REMPSTONE IN FORMA CONSTITUCIONIS.[10] Licence to study at a *studium generale* for two years to M. Gilbert de Pontefracto, subdeacon, rector of Rempstone, without proceeding to further orders, provided that he deputes a vicar. Bishop Burton, 5 Sept. 1322.

263 Institution [etc.] of Rocelinus, canon of St. Katherine's priory outside Lincoln, priest, to Newark vicarage, now vacant; presented by the prior and convent of St. Katherine's. Beverley, 18 Sept. 1322.

264 The like of John de Kendale, priest, to Selston (*Seleston*) church, now vacant; presented by Nicholas de Cantilupo, lord of Ilkeston. Bishop Burton, 20 Sept. 1322.

265 Licence to study to M. Gilbert de Pontefracto [as in **262**] with provision that if he does not spend the time at a *studium generale* he must proceed to all holy orders at the statutory times.[11] Bishop Burton, 5 Sept. 1322.

266 Note of licence to study for one year to M. William de Loudham, rector of Cotham, provided that he feeds his poor parishioners. Kirby Hill (*Kirkeby super moram*),[12] 4 Oct. 1322.

[10] This licence follows another to Gilbert of the same date which has been cancelled, with a marginal note *Vacat quia statim inferius*. The cancelled licence was in the form *Precibus tuis favorabiliter inclinati*, while the existing entry begins *Attendentes tue indolis humilitatem tuumque propositum laudabile insistendi scolasticis disciplinis* etc. The former required performance of the rector's obligations in the church and his appointment of a proctor.

[11] Without the requirement for a vicar.

[12] Near Boroughbridge (see *Reg. Melton*, I.16, no.46).

267 [*Restoration of canons to Thurgarton and Gloucester* (see **205**, **229**).]
AD REVOCANDUM FRATREM HUGONEM DE NOT' AD DOMUM SUAM DE THURGARTON. Willelmus etc. dilecto filio . . priori de Thurg' salutem [*etc.*]. Ex parte fratris Hugonis de Notingham concanonici domus vestre nobis est graviter querelatum quod idem frater Hugo absque magna causa urgente seu rationabili a domo sua in qua suam emisit professionem ad vestri instanciam est amotus, et cum jam causam habeat legitimam nostram presenciam aut curiam Romanam ut asserit propter aliqua que suam monent[13] conscienciam personaliter visitare, volumus et vobis mandamus quatenus ipsum ad domum suam reduci faciatis tempestive ut beneficium absolucionis a sentencia excommunicationis quam incurrerat auctoritate apostolica a vobis cui absolvendi eundem eadem auctoritate potestas est ut dicitur attributa recipere valeat ut est justum, deinceps inter vos canonice moraturum ac observancie vestre regularis statuta una cum penitencia salubri quam ob sua demerita sibi debite duxeritis injungenda humiliter subiturum. Et quia ob certas causas fratrem Robertum de Kyderminstr' ad domum suam remitti volumus ista vice ibidem deinceps sub ordinis sui regulari observancia moraturum, expedit ut credimus ut una eademque equitatura vestra dictis fratribus Hugoni et Roberto redeundo ac veniendo deserviat alternatim. Valete. [Laneham, 20 Oct. 1322.]

268 Appointment of Sir William de Sutton as coadjutor to Roger de Sutton, rector of North Collingham, who is paralysed and incapable of conducting business, at the latter's request and with his written consent. An inventory is to be made of the spiritual and temporal goods of the rector and his church. The coadjutor is to render an account when required, meanwhile giving sufficient security. Same date.
Note that the coadjutor gave security on this day, with an oath on the Gospels.

269 Note of licence to William Ouly, rector of Eastwood, to study for two years. Bishopthorpe, 31 Oct. 1322.

270 Note of licence to study for two years to John de Sutreby, rector of a mediety of Treswell (*Tireswell*). Bishopthorpe, 2 Nov. 1322.

271 Institution [etc.] of Laurence de Hercy, clerk, to Ordsall church, now vacant; presented by Hugh de Hercy. Pontefract (*Pontemfractum*), 10 Nov. 1322.

272 [Fo.349; N.F.422] Institution and mandate for induction (to the dean of Laneham) of Thomas called Sweton, priest, to Clarborough vicarage, now vacant; presented by M. John Bussh, sacrist of the chapel of St. Mary and the Holy Angels, York. Sherburn in Elmet, 9 Nov. 1322.

273 Note of licence to M. Adam de Amundesham, rector of Barton in Fabis (*Barton juxta Neuwerk*[14]), to be absent for a year from 29 Sept. 1321.[15]

[13] Or *movent?*
[14] An error (see **184**).
[15] This undated entry is squashed between **272** and **274**.

274 Institution [etc.] of Robert de Aston, subdeacon, to Sutton Bonington (*Bonyton*) church, now vacant; presented by John de Segrave, kt. Also note of letters dimissory for his further ordination by any English bishop. Bishopthorpe, 16 Nov. 1322.

275 Note of licence for the same to be absent in a suitable place for a year after his institution. Cawood, 7 Dec. 1322.

276 Institutions (all in the person of Hugh de Wyverton as proctor) and mandates for inductions of John de Novo Loco of Nottingham and Hugh de Coulane, chaplains, to the perpetual chantries newly established in the chapel of St. Mary, Hethbeth bridge, and of Richard de Stapelford, chaplain, to the new chantry in St. Helen's, Stapleford; presented by Alice le Palmere of Nottingham [see **260**]. Bishopthorpe, 23 Nov. 1322.

277 [*Order to commissaries appointed subsequent to the archbishop's visitation to levy fines* (see **192**).]
CORRECTORIBUS IN ARCHIDIACONATU NOT' AD LEVANDUM PENAS PER EOS IMPOSITAS. Willelmus etc. dilectis filiis magistris Alano de Neusom Thome de Sancto Leonardo et Willelmo de Hundon de Byngham de Egmanton et de Barneburgh ecclesiarum rectoribus ac nostris dudum in archidiaconatu Notingh' super certis compertis in eodem correctoribus deputatis salutem [*etc.*]. Cum vos in corrigendo hujusmodi comperta que vobis misimus a diu est diversas plerisque penas imposueritis atque mulctas que post certa tempora per vos statuta jam effluxa sunt commissa, prout nobis per litteras vestras certificatorias necnon rotulos hujusmodi comperta correctiones penas atque mulctas continentes nobis per vos missos constat evidenter, vestram sollicitudinem requirimus quatinus de hujusmodi mulctis diligenter inquiratis et quas sic inveneritis commissas quamcicius poteritis nostro nomine levari faciatis ac levari faciat quilibet vestrum. Contradictores autem et rebelles adhoc per censuras ecclesiasticas canonice compellatis et quilibet vestrum compellat vice nostra. Et quid in premissis duxeritis faciendum nos distincte oportuno tempore reddatis cerciores. Valete. [Cawood, 14 Oct. 1322.]

278 Commission to the prior of Thurgarton to execute letters of John XXII [not quoted] to the archbishop, enquiring whether Ralph [son] of the late Robert de Keworth, a poor clerk (dioc. York), is of good repute, not beneficed or otherwise canonically barred; in which case he is to be provided and inducted to a benefice usually held by secular clerks, with or without cure of souls, in the presentation of the abbot and convent of Welbeck (Premonstratensian) in York city or diocese. Cawood, 15 Dec. 1322.

279 [Fo.349ᵛ; N.F.422ᵛ] Institution (in the person of Thomas de Wylton, clerk, as proctor) and mandate for induction of William de Dalton, clerk, to Bulwell church, now vacant; presented by Edward II.[16] Cawood, 10 Jan. 1323.

[16] *CPR 1321–4*, 221.

280 The like of Edmund le Brun, priest, to Rossington (*Rosyngton*) church,[17] vacant by the resignation of Thomas de Stayngrave; presented by Peter de Malo Lacu, fourth lord of Mulgrave (*Mulgreve*). Same date.

281 The like of M. Henry de Wylton, acolyte, to Gamston (*Gameleston*) church, now vacant; presented by the prior and convent of Mattersey (*Mathersay*). Note that he swore fealty and obedience like other rectors and vicars. York, 26 Jan. 1323.

282 The like of Walter de Tuddyngton, priest, to Averham church, vacant by the resignation of Robert de Sutton; presented by Agnes de Sutton, lady of Averham, widow of Sir James de Sutton. Same date.

283 The like of William de Aselakby, priest, to Sibthorpe church, now vacant; presented by Thomas Larthier, prior of the hospital of St. John of Jerusalem in England. Cawood, 14 Feb. 1323.

284 The like of Henry de Mammesfeld, priest, to Mansfield church, now vacant; presented by M. Henry de Mammesfeld, dean of Lincoln. Cawood, 28 Feb. 1323.

285 The like of Roger son of Richard Belegrant of Staunton, priest, to Colwick church, now vacant; presented by William de Collewyk', kt. Cawood, 2 Mar. 1323.

286 [*Certificate of the purgation of Andrew le Botiler* (see **200–1**); *after witnesses were heard, the dead man's widow withdrew her opposition.*]
CERTIFICATORIUM COMMISSARIORUM SUPER PURGATIONE ANDREE LE BOTILER CLERICI. Venerabili [*etc.*] sui humiles et devoti filii Dionisius Avenell officialis curie Ebor' et Willelmus de Stanes clericus in negotio purgacionis Andree le Botiler nuper com[m]issarii vestri specialiter deputati obedienciam reverenciam et honorem. Mandatum vestrum nuper recepimus in hec verba:

Willelmus [*etc.* with full quotation of their commission, almost identical to **201** but omitting a date for appearance in York Minster, and dated Bishop Burton, 29 July 1321.]

Nos vero Dionisius et Willelmus comissarii predicti processum vestrum processui nostro continuantes et cognoscentes judicialiter super briga oppositionibus seu objectionibus per Petronillam relictam dicti Thome contra dictum Andream nuper super morte ipsius Thome consensu et assensu ad mortem ejusdem in foro seculari diffamatum et ipsius purgationis admissioni se opponentem propositis, predictis oppositionibus et objectionibus per nos sub modo admissis et quibusdam testibus super eisdem productis et etiam sub modo admissis juratis et examinatis, et demum ipsa Petronilla omnibus et singulis objectionibus et oppositionibus memoratis ac omni processui et prosecutione qualitercumque per partem ipsius Petronille factis et qualitercumque habitis et habendis necnon et omnibus impeditis et causis per quas et que ipsius Andree purgatio impediri possit quomodolibet vel differri

[17] Rossington was in Retford deanery although in Yorkshire. See also **813**.

judicialiter sponte et pure et scienter tam personaliter quam per procuratorem renunciante, ac depositionibus testium predictorum coram nobis exhabundanti recensitis, propositis insuper ex parte dicti Andree quibusdam exceptionibus corruptionis et subornationis contra dictos testes et eorum attestaciones ac ipsis per nos admissis, productis etiam ex parte ejusdem quibusdam testibus per nos receptis juratis et examinatis et eorum dictis publicatis, exhibitis etiam certificatoriis inquisitionum super fama vita et conversatione ejusdem Andree habitarum, necnon omnibus et singulis ipsum negotium contingentibus per nos diligenter rimatis discussis et intellectis ac juris ordine qui in hoc casu requirebatur in omnibus observato, dictum Andream admittendum fore ad purgandum se de impositis decrevimus et pronunciavimus sentencialiter et diffinitive in scriptis, qui se de morte dicti Thome consensu et assensu ad mortem ipsius juxta formam pronunciacionis nostre cum xviii manu clericorum bone fame existencium canonice se purgavit; unde ipsum inculpabilem fuisse et esse de morte consensu et assensu predictis quantum ad nos attinuit pronunciavimus et ipsum ad bonam famam suam restituimus per decretum, que omnia et singula paternitati vestre tenore presencium intimamus. In quorum testimonium presentibus sigilla nostra sunt appensa. [York, 14 May 1322.]

287 [Fo.350; N.F.423] Certificate to the archbishop from the dean of Christianity of York that Andrew le Botiler, clerk, defamed before the king's justices at York of assenting to the death of Thomas de Holm, was delivered by them to the archbishop's prison on 29 Jan. 1320 and received by the dean. Under his seal, York, 22 Jan. 1323.

288 Certificate to the archbishop from Denis Avenel and William de Stanes, commissaries [as in **286**], that the date of Andrew le Botiler's purgation in York Minster was 2 Jan. 1322. Under their seals, York, 22 Jan. 1323.

289 Writ of Edward II ordering the archbishop to certify the dates when Andrew le Botiler of Stainton (accused and convicted of felonies before Henry le Scrop and other justices) was delivered to the archbishop and of his purgation. York, 13 May 1322.

290 [*Reply to this writ(?)*]
DOMINO REGI PRO LIBERACIONE BONORUM DICTI ANDREE ET DE DIE PURGATIONIS SUE.[18] Serenissimo principi domino suo domino Edwardo dei gracia regi Anglie illustri domino Hibernie et duci Aquitanie Willemus [*etc.*] salutem in eo qui servire perhenniter est regnare. Quia Andreas le Botiler clericus parochianus noster nuper coram dilectis et fidelibus vestris Henrico le Scrop et sociis suis justiciariis vestris ad placita coram vobis tenenda assignatis super crimine homicidii Thome de Holm nostre diocesis diffamatus et nobis ad requisitionem nostram juxta privilegium clericale per dictos justiciarios vestros die Mercurii proximo ante festum Purificationis beate Marie Virginis anno gracie millesimo CCC decimonono liberatus, post plures proclamationes in omnibus locis huic negotio op[p]ortunis sollempniter et publice promulgatas, demum cum nullus

[18] This description is curious. For a pardon to Andrew, dated 3 June 1323, see *CPR 1321–4*, 290.

esset qui per viam accusationis vel alio modo dictum crimen contra eum prosequi attemptaret, de prefato crimine sibi imposito coram nobis in ecclesia nostra beati Petri Ebor' in crastino Circumcisionis Domini anno gracie millesimo CCC vicesimo primo canonice se purgavit, per quod nos ipsum Andream a prefato crimine inculpabilem sententialiter pronunciavimus et immunem, eundem pristine fame restitutentes exigente justicia utpote dicti criminis penitus innocentem. Conservet vos ecclesie et populo suo deus per tempora longiora. [Cawood, 3 Mar. 1323.]

291 [*Letters patent certifying this purgation dated 22 Jan. 1323; with note of their reissue, amended at the requirement of justices itinerant, dated 23 Nov. 1329.*]
LITTERA PATENS SUPER PREMISSIS PENES DICTUM ANDREAM RESIDENDA. Universis sancte matris ecclesie filiis quorum interest seu poterit interesse Willelmus permissione etc. ut supra salutem in eo qui est omnium salus vera. Universitati vestre notum facimus per presentes quod cum Andreas le Botiler clericus nostre diocesis nuper super crimine homicidii consensu et assensu mortis Thome de Holm nostre diocesis dudum interfecti coram dominis Henrico le Scrop et sociis suis domini nostri regis justiciariis ad placita sua tenenda assignatis diffamatus, nobisque ad requisicionem nostram juxta privilegium clericale nostre carcerali custodie mancipandus per prefatos justiciarios die Mercurii proximo ante festum Purificationis beate Marie Virginis anno gracie MCCCXIX fuisset liberatus; idem Andreas coram magistris Dionisio Avenel curie nostre Ebor' officiali et Willelmo de Stanes nostris commissariis ad hoc specialiter deputatis[19] de prefato crimine sibi imposito in ecclesia nostra beati Petri Ebor' in crastino Circumcisionis Domini anno gracia MCCCXXI canonice se purgavit, prout per certificatorium dictorum commissariorum nostrorum nobis constat evidenter.[20] In cujus rei testimonium litteras nostras eidem Andree fieri fecimus has patentes sigilli nostri impressione munitas. Datum apud Cawode xi Kalendas Februarii[21] anno gracie MCCC vicesimo secundo[22] et pontificatus nostri sexto.[23]

[margin] Memorandum quod dictus Andreas habuit litteram prout in interlinearibus continetur quia justiciarii domini regis itinerantes apud Notingh' noluerunt allocare primam litteram 'coram commissariis' nisi diceret 'coram nobis'.

292 Institution [etc.] of John son of William Cosyn, deacon, to the vicarage of St. Mary's, Nottingham, now vacant; presented by the prior and convent of Lenton. Cawood, 12 Mar. 1323.

293 [*Despatch of a monk of Blyth to the mother house at Rouen for transmission to the Curia to seek absolution for again consecrating the host.*]
TRANSMISSIO FRATRIS THOME DE BROUNETOFTE MONACHI DE BLIDA AD CURIAM ROMANAM ABSOLVENDI EO QUOD CORPUS CHRISTI SEMEL CONSECRATUM ITERATO CONSECRAVIT IN ALTARI. Willelmus etc. dilecto nobis in Christo domino . . abbati sancte Katherine de monte Rothomag' ordinis sancti Benedicti

[19] Underlined (to cancel) from *magistris,* with *nobis* interlined.
[20] Underlined from *prout.*
[21] Underlined from *Cawode,* with *Suwell' ix Kalendas Decembris* interlined.
[22] Underlined, with *nono* interlined.
[23] Underlined, with *xiii* interlined.

Rothomag' diocesis salutem cum benedictione et gracia salvatoris. Intimavit nobis frater Thomas de Brounetofte monachus domus vestre quod ipse nuper corpus Christi prius debite consecratum iterum in altari non ex contemptu sed ex juris ignorantia verbis congrue ad hoc institutis coram clero et populo publice consecravit, idque ut moris est levavit eisdemque clero et populo patencius ostendebat, illud venerabile sacramentum iterando. Quocirca dictum fratrem Thomam vobis transmittimus, vestre consulentes solicitudini quatenus ipsum sedi apostolice cum suis expensis necessariis prout sui exigit status ordinis et persone mittere non tardetis ejusdem status sui reformacionem occasione premissa in forma juris humiliter recepturum. Valete. [Cawood, 22 Mar. 1323.]

294 Letters patent. In response to papal letters, an inquest found that William de Cotyngton, a poor priest, had a good reputation, held no benefice before the pope wrote for him, and no canonical obstacle was known. Cawood, 31 Mar. 1323.

295 Note of licence to Robert de Helpeston, rector of Hawton (*Houton*), to be absent for one year. Cawood, 17 Apr. 1323.

296 Note of letters dimissory for Richard de Alferton, acolyte, canon of Thurgarton, to be ordained subdeacon by the bishop of Lincoln or by the bishop of Coventry and Lichfield. Cawood, 21 Apr. 1323.

297 [*Appointment of M. Thomas de Sancto Leonardo as sequestrator in the archdeaconry and dean (with judicial powers) of Southwell and Laneham; with note of a second, amended commission.*]
[Fo.350v; N.F.423v] CREACIO SEQUESTRATORIS IN ARCHIDIACONATU NOTINGH' AC DECANI DECANATUUM SUWELL' ET LAN'. Willelmus etc. dilecto filio magistro Thome de Sancto Leonardo rectori ecclesie de Egmanton nostre diocesis salutem [*etc.*]. De tuis circumspectione et industria plenius confidentes, te sequestratorem nostrum in archidiaconatum Not' ac decanum Suwell' et de Lanum preficimus ac etiam deputamus, tibique ad cognoscendum procedendum statuendum interloquendum diffiniendum et exequendum in omnibus et singulis causis et negociis tam ex officio quam ad instanciam partium infra dictos decanatus de Suwell et de Lanum qualitercumque contingentibus, et infra eosdem decanatus ad inquirendum de excessibus quorumcumque subditorum nostrorum eosque reformandos corrigendos et puniendos, ac etiam ad exercendum officium sequestratoris predicti in dicto archidiaconatu in omnibus et singulis articulis qui de jure vel consuetudine illud concernunt officium[24] vices nostras committimus cum cohercionis canonice potestate; decanis nostris et aliis ministris ceterisque subjectis nostris universalibus per predictos archidiaconatum et decanatus constitutis firmiter injungentes ut tibi in hiis que ad hujusmodi officia pertinent humiliter pareant et intendant.[25] [Cawood, 2 May 1323.]

[24] Interlined here is *ita quod de testamentis aut eorum probationibus que ultra x libros sterlingorum se extendant nullatenus te intromittatis*
[25] Interlined here is *aliam commissionem nostram alias in hac parte tibi factam tenore presencium expressius revocantes.*

[margin] Memorandum quod ista commissio prout interliniatur mutata et moderata sub dato apud Cawod vi Kalendas Junii anno supradicto [27 May 1323].

298 Acquittance to William de Claworth, formerly bailiff of North Soke (*Northsok'*), for 100s. in part payment of arrears on his last account, received by the hands of William de Feriby, the archbishop's familiar clerk. Cawood, 2 May 1323.

299 Licence for unlimited absence without molestation to M. Elias de Muskham, canon of Lincoln and prebendary of Clifton, who is afflicted by weakness and age; he may stay in a suitable place provided he puts in a competent proctor. Cawood, 5 May 1323.
[margin] Granted at the request of the dean and chapter of Lincoln.

300 Note of licence to study for two years to Nicholas de Tikhill, rector of Kelham. Cawood, 12 May 1323.

301 Note of licence to Robert [de Kirkeby on Asshefeld[26]], rector of Kirkby in Ashfield (*Kirkeby*), to be absent for one year. Cawood, 27 May 1323.

302 Institution [etc.] of Thomas de Sibthorp, priest, to North Collingham church, now vacant; presented by the abbot and convent of Peterborough. Cawood, 18 May 1323.

303 Mandate to the prior and convent of Newstead to relax the penance of their canon, Philip de Candelesby [see **147**, **238**]; he is now to be scourged only once a week and his fast every Friday on bread and water is commuted to bread and weak ale (*tenuem cervisiam*). Cawood, 22 May 1323.

304 Note of commission to M. John de [Woodhouse?] and M. Richard de Grimeston to audit the accounts of the executors of John de Rouclif, clerk, on the administration of the goods of Acard [de Longo Prato], late rector of Ordsall, allowing their expenses and reporting when opportune. Cawood, 27 May 1323.

305 [*Commission to examine receipts of William de Grendon, a former sequestrator who abused his office, and hear and remedy complaints against him.*]
COMMISSIO AD AUDIENDUM QUOSCUMQUE QUERALENTES DE DOMINO WILLELMO DE GRENDON NUPER SEQUESTRATORE IN ARCHIDIACONATU NOTYNGH' ET AD FACIENDUM EISDEM JUSTICIE COMPLEMENTUM. Willelmus etc. dilectis filiis magistris Thome de Sancto Leonardo et Rogero de Ak' in archidiaconatibus Noting' et Estriding' sequestratoribus nostris salutem [*etc.*]. Quia dominus Willelmus de Grendon[27] nuper sequestrator noster in archidiaconatu Notingh'

[26] Instituted 1316 (*Reg. Greenfield*, V.275, no.2878).
[27] Corrected from *Grandon*. His appointment is seemingly not recorded. M. William de Hundon, appointed 23 Jan. 1318 (**8**), is last named as sequestrator early in 1321 (**211**); the

predicto in officio suo male se habuit, vires sue commissionis sibi facte per nos in hac parte multitociens excedendo non absque gravamine multorum ut accepimus, fama vehementi nimium referentes; volentes insolencias hujusmodi dicti domini Willelmi debite compescere ac unicuique pro viribus facere super premissis per omnia quod est justum, ad inquirendum[28] de quibuscumque receptis per dictum dominum Willelmum a quibuscumque personis seu locis officio suo de quo premittitur durante occasione seu colore quocumque hujusmodi officii sui, necnon ad audiendum quoscumque querelas deponere volentes contra eundem et hujusmodi querelas examinandas ac vocatis vocandis plene discuciendas et hujusmodi querelantibus omnibus et singulis plenarie faciendum justicie complementum, vobis vices nostras committimus cum cohercionis canonice potestate, omnibus et singulis decanis et aliis ministris et subditis nostris firmiter injungentes quatenus in premissis vobis pareant et intendant et prout vobis expediens videbitur vestre assistant in hac parte solicitudini si et quando per vos fuerint requisiti; proviso quod de omni eo quod inveneritis et feceritis in premissis nos certificetis distincte et aperte tempore oportuno per vestras patentes litteras harum seriem continentes. Valete. [Cawood, 30 May 1323.]

306 Note of licence to John [de Clifton], rector of Clifton, to be absent for one year; at the request of the earl of Mar. Cawood, 3 June 1323.

307 Note of licence to study for two years from 5 Oct. next to Thomas de Casterton, rector of a mediety of Cotgrave; at the request of Clement de Casterton.[29] Cawood, 7 June 1323.

308 [*Order that Thomas de Brounetoft is not to return to Blyth from Rouen* (cf. **293**).] NE FRATER THOMAS DE BROUNETOFT MONACHUS DE BLIDA DIUCIUS TOLERATUR IN DOMO PROPTER SUAM REBELLIONEM ET INSOLENCIAM. Willelmus etc. dilectis filiis priori et conventui de Blida nostre diocesis salutem [*etc.*]. Cum nostra incumbat solicitudini officii pastoralis tranquillitatem religionis quantum cum deo possumus confovere ut eo devocius divinis valeant intendere obsequiis et tanto quiecius domino famulari; sane ad nostrum deduxit auditum relacio fidedigna quod frater Thomas Brunetoft conmonachus vester ita se tumultuosum exhibet inter fratres ac inter vos pariter discordiam jurgia repetiter et iracundie materiam sepissime subministrat, adeoque vestre fraternitatis unitatem nititur segregare quod absque domus vestre scandalo inter vos amplius non poterit tolerari. Vobis mandamus quatinus si ita est dictum fratrem Thomam, si circa premissa incorrigibilem se ostenderit, inter vos deinceps minime admittatis. Cum sua mora non absque nostri contumelia creatoris si premissa veritate nitantur nullatenus poterit sustineri. Valete. [Cawood, 8 June 1323.]

next recorded appointment was in May 1323 (**297**). Grendon, a non-graduate, rector of Babworth, was serving Thomas of Lancaster in 1320 (**152**, **156**). He may have been appointed 'our' sequestrator after the earl's death (22 Mar. 1322).

[28] MS. *inquiredo*

[29] Followed by *host*[*illarii?*]

[margin] Memorandum quod super hoc scribebatur quasi consimilis littera abbati et conventui sancte Katerine Rotomagens' ut ipsi retineant ipsum Thomam penes se.

309 [Fo.351; N.F.424] Institution [etc.] of Robert de Bilburgh, priest, to South Leverton vicarage, now vacant; presented by M. Henry de Mammesfeld, dean of Lincoln. Cawood, 10 June 1323.

310 [*Dispensation by authority of letters of the papal penitentiary to Robert de Sutton, who had incurred disqualification by becoming rector of Averham while a minor.*[30]] DISPENSACIO AUCTORITATE APOSTOLICA CUM DOMINO ROBERTO DE SUTTON PRESBITERO SUPER INHABILITATE SI QUAM CONTRAXIT EO QUOD ECCLESIAM DE AVERHAM ADMISIT MINOR ANNIS EXISTENS. Willelmus etc. dilecto filio domino Roberto de Sutton nostre diocesis presbitero salutem [*etc.*]. Litteras reverendi patris et domini domini Berengarii dei gracia episcopi Tusculani pro te nobis directas recepimus in hec verba:

Venerabili in Christo patri dei gracia . . archiepiscopo Ebor' vel ejus . . vicario in spiritualibus Berengarius miseracione divina episcopus Tusculan' salutem et sinceram in domino caritatem. Sua nobis Robertus de Sutton presbiter vestre diocesis lator presencium peticione monstravit quod ipse olim minor annis existens parochialem ecclesiam de Haverham vestre diocesis extitit aliter tamen canonice assecutus, ad cujus titulum se fecit infra annum juxta statuta Lugdunen' concilii ad omnes sacros ordines statutis a jure temporibus et rite aliter per omnia promoveri, et in ipsis non tamen in contemptum clavium sepius ministravit et aliter inmiscuit se divinis ipsamque ecclesiam per plures annos tenuit, fructus percipiens ex eadem; tandem culpam suam super hiis recognescens, predictam ecclesiam libere resignavit. Verum cum sit paratus de fructibus perceptis satisfacere ut tenetur, sedem adiens apostolicam supplicavit humiliter sibi per eam super hiis de oportuno remedio misericorditer provideri. Nos igitur hujusmodi supplicacionibus favorabiliter annuentes, auctoritate domini pape cujus penitenciarie curam gerimus ipsum presbiterum ad vos duximus remittendum, vestre circumspectioni auctoritate[m] committentes predictam quatinus si est ita, postquam de predictis fructibus sic perceptis juxta vestre discrecionis arbitrium satisfecerit competenter in evidentem utilitatem ipsius ecclesie fideliter convertendis, injuncta inde sibi pro modo culpe absolucione previa ab excessu hujusmodi penitencia salutari et aliis que ei de jure videritis injungenda, super inhabilitate si quam ex premissis contraxit quodque dictum beneficium si sibi conferatur de novo canonice vel aliud possit licite obtinere dispensetis misericorditer cum eodem, dummodo aliud ei non obviet de canonicis institutis. [Avignon, 16 Mar. 1323.]

Quarum auctoritate litterarum super premissis articulis omnibus et singulis in forma juris diligentius inquisito juxta eorum qualitatem pariter et naturam, quia invenimus suggestionem tuam veritatem per omnia continere nec aliud a suggestione tua tibi obviare de canonicis institutis, de predictis fructibus sic perceptis per te satisfacto primitus competenter in evidentem utilitatem ejusdem ecclesie fideliter convertendis, injuncta inde tibi per nos pro modo culpe absolutione previa ab excessu hujusmodi penitencia salutari et aliis que tibi

[30] Instituted 1316 (*Reg. Greenfield*, IV.274, no.2874). See also **282**, **313**.

de jure vidimus injungenda, super inhabilitate si quam ex premissis contraxisti quodque dictum beneficium si tibi conferatur de novo canonice vel aliud possis licite obtinere tecum misericorditer dispensamus. In cujus rei testimonium sigillum nostrum presentibus est appensum, quas per Ricardum de Snoweshull notarium publicum scribi et publicari mandavimus et signo ejus solito consignari. Acta et data apud Cawode decimo die mensis Junii anno gracie MCCC vicesimo tercio indiccione sexta et pontificatus nostri anno sexto; presentibus magistris Ada[31] de Heselbech et Johanne de Nassington ac dominis Ricardo de Otringham et Ricardo de Melton clericis testibus ad premissa vocatis specialiter et rogatis.

[Subscription by Richard de Snoweshull, clerk and notary, the archbishop's scribe. Cawood, 10 June 1323.]

311 Institution [etc.] of William de Skeryngton, priest, to Lambley (*Lameley*) church, now vacant; presented by Robert de Sallowe as proctor of Sir Ralph de Crumwell. Cawood, 23 June 1323.

312 The like of John de Clatford, priest, to Kneeton church, now vacant; presented by the abbot and convent of Newbo. Cawood, 19 June 1323.

313 The like of Robert de Sutton, priest, to Averham church, now vacant [see **282**, **310**]; presented by Agnes de Sutton, lady of Averham. Bishopthorpe, 28 June 1323.

314 DIMISSORIE PRO JOHANNE DE NOT'. Note of letters dimissory for all orders to John le Cominger of Nottingham. Bishopthorpe, 4 July 1323

315 LICENCIA PRO RECTORE DE KERCOLSTON. Note of letter to the receiver of York not to trouble Robert de Hemelhamsted, rector of Car Colston, for non-residence while he is in the king's service. Same date.

316 Licence to the prior and convent of Felley to sell a corrody to relieve their house. 1 July 1323.

317 Note of letters dimissory to William de Dalton, deacon, rector of Bulwell. Bishopthorpe, 10 July 1323.

318 Note of mandate to M. William de Stanes, R. [omitted] and J. de Sutton to suspend proceedings against the prior and hospitallers of St. John of Jerusalem and their churches until the third law day after Michaelmas [8 Oct.]. Bishopthorpe, 16 July 1323.

319 Mandate to the dean of Retford to deliver all sequestrated goods of Sir John de Merkyngfeld, deceased,[32] to his executors; with them he is to list and value the goods, reporting to the archbishop. Bishopthorpe, 18 July 1323.

[31] MS. *Adam*

[32] Possibly the canon of York known to have died by 31 July 1323 (*Fasti*, VI.86).

320 [Fo.351v; N.F.424v] Collation [etc.] of Matthew de Halifax, priest, as custodian of the hospital of St. John the Baptist, Nottingham, vacant by the resignation of Roger son of Richard de Whatton. Southwell, 17 Sept. 1323.

321 Institution [etc.] of Roger de Whatton, acolyte, to Elton church, now vacant;[33] presented by the prior and convent of Blyth. Cuckney, 23 Sept. 1323.

322 Licence to the prior and convent of Newstead to admit two novices who are 'well behaved, honest and suited to religion'. Cawood, 1 Oct. 1323.

323 Commission to the sequestrator in the archdeaconry and the archdeacon's official to hear and determine the cause between the parishioners of West (*Parva*) Markham, plaintiffs, and Richard de Hoton, defendant, who acts as vicar [see **98**]; reporting to the archbishop by letters patent with their process attached. East (*Magna*) Markham, 21 Sept. 1323.

324 Letters patent. By authority of letters of the papal penitentiary [not quoted], the archbishop has absolved John Torald, deacon (dioc. York), from excommunication incurred by violence to Hugh le Souter, priest, and sacrilege in St. Peter's church, Nottingham; enjoining [unspecified] penance. Braithwell (*Braythewell*), 23 Sept. 1323.

325 [*Sentence ordering that the marriage of Beatrice la Alblaster, plaintiff, and Thomas de Ormesby be solemnised; he has failed to prove an alleged precontract.*]
SENTENCIA LATA IN CAUSA MATRIMONIALI INTER BEATRICEM LA ALBLASTER ET THOMAM DE ORMESBY. In dei nomine amen. In causa matrimoniali que coram nobis Willelmo permissione divina etc. vertitur inter Beatricem la Alblaster actricem ex parte una et Thomam de Ormesby reum ex altera, dictis partibus coram nobis legitime constitutis, pars actrix predicta articulum proposuit vocetenus in hunc modum 'Quia tu Thomas de Ormesby mecum formam ecclesie consuetam fecisti et postea me carnaliter cognovisti, peto te mihi in virum adjudicari', quaquidem peticione mox in scriptis redacta. Pars rea litem contestabatur affirmative intencionem partis actricis expressius faciendo excepto tamen quod eam habere non potuit, pro eo quod antequam cum dicta Beatrice contraxit cum quadam Johanna filia Roberti de Marnham de Grimesby adhuc superstite precontraxit. Jurato hincinde de calumpnia et de veritate dicenda, quesitum fuit a parte rea si habuit testes ad probandum dictum precontractum, ipsaque parte rea asserente palam quod nullus testis presens fuit in hujusmodi precontractu; datoque die parti ree ad probandum dictam exceptionem et utrique parti ad proponendum quicquid juris haberent in causa memorata, nulloque teste producto super probatione dicte exceptionis seu alio genere probationis interveniente. Demum concluso in causa partibus presentibus coram nobis, rimato processu habitaque deliberacione cum juris peritis, quia invenimus partem actricem intencionem suam in hac parte legitime fundasse dictamque partem ream in probatione exceptionis sue de qua premittitur defecisse, dictum Thomam partem ream prefate Beatrici parti actrici dei

[33] An exchange of benefices: see **83**, **320**

nomine invocato in virum sentencialiter et diffinitive adjudicamus, matrimonium inter ipsos fuisse et esse legitime initum sentencialiter declarantes et ipsum matrimonium debere inter eosdem solempnizari in facie ecclesie decernentes. Lecta lata et scriptis pronunciata fuit ista sentencia apud Cawode primo die mensis Octobris annno gracie MCCCXXIII indictione septima; presentibus domino Ricardo de Melton prebendario in ecclesia de Osmund' Henrico de Hes[. . . .][34] et Willelmo de Wakefeld ac Johanne Danyel testibus ad premissa vocatis etc. [Cawood, 1 Oct. 1323.]

326 [*Order that the marriage be solemnised within ten days.*]
MONICIO ET EXECUCIO SUPER DICTO MATRIMONIO. Willelmus etc. dilecto filio decano nostro de Retford salutem [*etc.*]. Quia in causa matrimoniali inter Beatricem la Alblaster actricem ex parte una et Thomam Wa[. . . .][35] de Ormesby reum ex altera coram nobis nuper aliquamdiu agitata pro ipso matrimonio inter eosdem legitime inito et contracto pronunciavimus sentencialiter et diffinitive justicia exigente, tibi mandamus firmiter injungentes quatenus dictum Thomam moneas et efficaciter inducas quod dictum matrimonium quantum ad eum pertinet infra x dies a tempore hujus monicionis sibi facte in forma juris solempniet, alioquin ipsum ad id faciendum per quascumque censuras ecclesiasticas in singulis ecclesiis tui decanatus canonice[?] compellas, ad que omnia et singula tibi vices nostras committimus cum cohercionis canonice potestate. Et de omni eo quod in premissis feceris nos tempore oportuno certifices per tuas patentes litteras harum seriem continentes. Vale. [Cawood, 1 Oct. 1323.]

327 Institution [etc.] of Robert de Allerton, priest, to South Leverton vicarage, now vacant; presented by M. Henry de Mamesfeld, dean of Lincoln. Cawood, 4 Oct. 1323.

328 Note of licence to study (*in forma constitucionis*) to Roger de Whatton, subdeacon, rector of Elton, for one year from his institution. Cawood, 5 Oct. 1323.

329 Note of licence to Michael [Normand], rector of Linby (*Lyndeby*), to be absent for one year from 29 Sept. Southwell, 17 Sept. 1323.

330 Note of licence to study (*infra regnum vel extra*) for one year to M. John de Laland, rector of Arnold. Southwell, 18 Sept. 1323.

331 Note of licence to William de Hundon, rector of Barnburgh, to be absent for three years. North Laithes (*les Northlathes juxta Rughford*), 19 Sept. 1323.

332 The like to William de Aslacby, rector of Sibthorpe, until the next feast of St. John the Baptist. Same date.

333 Note of dispensation for bastardy to William de Averham, with permission to hold a benefice and proceed to all minor orders. Southwell, 18 Sept. 1323.

[34] Illegible.
[35] Illegible.

334 The like for Richard de Flyntham. Kirton (*Kirketon in Hatfeld*), 20 Sept. 1323.

335 [Fo.352; N.F.425] To the sequestrator in the archdeaconry. If it is true that M. Boniface de Saluciis is dead, all churches and chapels in the diocese belonging to the chapel of Tickhill, which he held, and belong to the archbishop during vacancies, are to be sequestrated until further notice to prevent dilapidation; their goods are to be listed and reported. Bishopthorpe, 7 Oct. 1323.

336 Institution [etc.] of William de Wylughby, clerk, to St. Peter's, Nottingham, now vacant; presented by the prior and convent of Lenton. Bishopthorpe, 10 Oct. 1323.

337 Note of licence to study (*in scolis*) for one year to M. William de Loudham, rector of Cotham. Bishopthorpe, 19 Oct. 1323.

338 Note of licence to M. John de Landa, rector of Arnold, to be absent for one year [cf. **330**]. Southwell, 13 Oct. 1323.

339 Collation and mandate for induction (to the dean of Retford) of John de Barneby, priest, to the custody of the hospital of St. Mary Magdalene, Bawtry, now vacant.[36] Scrooby, 28 Oct. 1323.

340 Institution [etc.] of John de Ludham, acolyte, to Ruddington church, now vacant; presented by Alice, widow of Richard de Byngham, kt. North Muskham, 3 Nov. 1323.

341 Note of licence to M. Adam de Amundesham, rector of Barton in Fabis, to be absent for one year from 29 Sept. last. Nottingham, 10 Nov. 1323.

342 Note of licence to study for one year to Alexander de Chaggeley, rector of a mediety of Gedling. Gedling, 15 Nov. 1323.

343 [*Order to collect Peter's Pence from the parishioners of Beckingham.*]
MONICIO PRO DENARIIS BEATI PETRI FACTA PAROCHIANIS DE BEKYNGHAM. Willelmus etc. decano nostro de Lanum salutem [*etc.*]. Moneas et efficaciter inducas vicarium ecclesie de Bekyngham nostre diocesis quod a parochianis dicte ecclesie denarios beati Petri exigat et colligat vice nostra ipsosque tibi liberet oportune. Execuciones etiam sentenciarum et monicionum per nos et nostros ministros factas et etiam faciendas faciat ut est justum, que si facere contempserit ipsum ad hoc per quascumque censuras ecclesiasticas nostro nomine debite compellere non omittas. Vale. [Southwell, 20 Nov. 1323.]

344 LICENCIA PRO RECTORE DE ROTYNGTON. Note of letter to the receiver of York not to trouble John de Ludham, rector of Ruddington, for his non-residence until 29 Sept. next. Southwell, 19 Nov. 1323.

[36] See **237**. John resigned by 8 Sept. 1326, when Adam de Usflett', chaplain, was collated (Reg. Melton, fo.573; N.F.713).

345 Note of licence to Robert de Helperston, rector of Hawton (*Houton juxta Newerk*), to be absent in the service of the bishop of Llandaff for one year from 25 Dec. next. Southwell, 22 Nov. 1323.

346 Note of licence to study for one year at a *studium generale* to Robert de Aston, rector of Sutton Bonington. Edwinstowe, 25 Nov. 1323.

347 [*Order that the numerous chaplains celebrating in St. Mary's, Nottingham, should participate in all services there and not themselves celebrate masses before the preface to the parish mass.*[37]]
MONICIO FACTA CAPELLANIS CELEBRANTIBUS IN ECCLESIA BEATE MARIE NOTINGH' QUOD INTERSINT SINGULIS HORIS IN DICTA ECCLESIA. Willelmus etc. decano nostro Not' salutem [*etc.*]. Cum deceat operarios in vineam domini missos tanta solicitudine tantaque promptitudine diligencius operari quanto fideliter operantibus largiora premia promittuntur dormientibus vero et pigris immania suplicia pretenduntur prospicere sibi debent, ne cum venerit paterfamilias illos inveniat otiosos ipsosque a premii retribucione quod absit eternaliter excludat. Sane ad nostrum deduxit auditum relacio plurimorum fama super hoc nimia creb[r]escente quod nonnulli sacerdotes in ecclesia parochiali beate Marie Not' celebrantes, quibus succrescente devocione fidelium ipsorum munificencia diurna stipendia subministrant[ur] ut pro animabus parentum amicorum et omnium benefactorum suorum ac omnium fidelium defunctorum seu pro vivis vel ex aliis piis causis satagant indies celebrare, seorsum in cameris suis vel in campis vagando seu alibi in locis minus congruis matutinas et alias suas horas canonicas certatim cincopant et transcurrunt, et quod dolencius referimus de quibusdam timere poterit quod ipsas hujusmodi horas prorsus quandoque transiliunt ac ad missas suas celebrandas ante missam parochialem inchoatam prepropere se transferunt minus digne de eorum subsidio ministris supradicte ecclesie in dictis horis canonicis ut deceret aliquotiens impendendo non carentes quinimmo eorum missis non competenti tempore ut premittitur auditis, dicti parochiani ea occasione ut accepimus nonnulli interdum ecclesie limina exeuntes, mandata et injuncta nostra salubria et ministrorum nostrorum quandocumque verbum dei et alia que ad salutem pertinent animarum audire totaliter dedignantur et alia devocionis sue pia opera consueta eo pretextu subtrahere non verentur. Cumque premissa in divini cultus diminucionem ac suppreme magestatis offensum ut verisimiliter credi poterit et multorum periculum animarum non absque prejudicio rectoris et vicarii ecclesie memorate tendere dinoscantur, nos ad honorem dei et sui laudem nominis altissimi tantos excessus et errores cupientes paterna solicitudine pro viribus reformare, tibi committimus et mandamus in virtute obedientie firmiter injungentes quatenus omnes et singulos sacerdotes in dicta ecclesia divina quomodolibet celebrantes moneas et efficaciter inducas quod singulis diebus per annum et presertim diebus dominicis et festivis matutinis et aliis horis canonicis tractim et devote ut convenit psallendo seu etiam dicendo in ipsa ecclesia personaliter intersint, nisi ex causa legitima aliquotiens petita tamen prius vicarii loci seu ejus locum tenentis licencia speciali se duxerint non tam voluntarie quam necessario

[37] For a similar mandate for St. Mary's in 1363, see A.H. Thompson, *The English Clergy and their organization in the later middle ages*, Oxford 1947, 145.

forsitan absentandos, nec missas suas incipiant nisi demum cum ad prefacionem misse parochialis processum fuerit cum effectu. Credimus enim per hoc cultum augmentare divinum ac devocionem fidelium eo propensius excitare quo tot dei ministros simul perpenderint seriosius divina ac seriosius pertractare. Volumus etiam presens mandatum nostrum in singulis ecclesiis parochialibus Not' et ejusdem diaconatus ubi expediens fuerit firmiter observari sub pena suspensionis a divinis si quis eidem mandato nostro presumpserit contraire. Vale. [Bishopthorpe, 12 Dec. 1323.]

348 Note of licence to study (*in forma constitutionis Cum ex eo*) from 4 Sept. [1323] to 25 July [1324] to Hugh Gernoun, subdeacon, rector of Elkesley. Bishopthorpe, 14 Dec. 1323.

349 [Fo.352v; N.F.425v] COMMISSIO AD LEVANDUM PENAS COMMISSAS DE ECCLESIIS INFRASCRIPTIS VIDELICET QUAS HABENT PRIOR ET CONVENTUS DE THUR' IN PROPRIOS USUS. Commission to M. William de Stanes, the archbishop's familiar clerk, to correct and punish excesses and defects described in attached letters and proceed against the rectors of Sutton in Ashfield (*Asshefeld*) and Hoveringham, in Nottingham deanery, and Granby and Owthorpe (*Outhorp*), in Bingham deanery, or the religious claiming to have appropriated these churches, about the penalties and other articles in these letters, reporting when opportune. Cawood, 17 Jan. 1324.

350 Institution [etc.] of M. Robert de Nassington, acolyte, to Epperstone church, now vacant; presented by Thomas de Veer, kt. Also note of licence to study (*in forma constitutionis*) for two years. Cawood, 20 Jan. 1324.

351 [*Commission to examine witnesses about M. Oliver de Kirkeby's ordination.*] COMMISSIO AD RECIPIENDUM ET EXAMINANDUM TESTES SUPER RECEPTIONE ORDINIS ACOLITATUS MAGISTRI OLIVERI DE KIRKEBY. Willelmus etc. decano nostro Not' salutem. De tuis industria et fidelitate plenius confidentes, ad recipiendum in forma juris testes quotquot magister Oliverus de Kirkeby clericus coram te duxerit producendos super recepcione ordinum suorum ordine subdiaconatus quorumcumque inferiorum necnon ad examinandum ipsos testes juxta periciam a deo tibi datam, videlicet ubi dictus magister Oliverus extitit oriundus, et a quo episcopo fuerat ordinatus, et ad quos ordines, in quo loco quo die et quo anno ordines recepit, ac de aliis circumstanciis hujusmodi negotium contingentibus, necnon ad inquirendum in forma juris de vita moribus et conversatione ejusdem magistri Oliveri, tibi vices nostras committimus cum cohercionis canonice potestate; mandantes quatenus de omni eo quod in premissis feceris una cum attestacionibus et nominibus testium quos coram te produci contigerit nos certifices tempore oportuno per tuas litteras patentes harum seriem continentes, quibus dictas attestaciones sub signo tuo clausas consui volumus aut annecti. [Cawood, 25 Jan. 1324.]

352 Letters patent testifying that the archbishop has learnt by lawful proof that M. Oliver de Kirkeby, clerk (dioc. York), having the first tonsure, was ordained acolyte on 21 Sept. 1297 by H[enry] de Neuwerk, once archbishop of York; his life and associations were and are respectable. Bishopthorpe, 3 Feb. 1324.

353 [*Provision for the maintenance of John de Rudestan, former prior of Thurgarton, following the convent's failure in this respect* (see **136**, **208**).]

ORDINACIO PROVISIONIS FACTE FRATRI JOHANNI DE RUDESTAN QUONDAM PRIORI MONASTERII DE THURGARTON. Willelmus etc. dilectis filiis . . priori et conventui monasterii de Thurgarton nostre diocesis salutem [*etc.*]. Cum sita legum equitate subnixa innuant manifeste quod hii sunt aliis preponendi ac merito aliquociens venerandi quos labor prolixior et majora stipendia fecerant anteire, sane de vestra memoria sicuti nec de nostra minime credimus excidisse qualiter frater Johannes de Rudestan quondam prior domus vestre in eo statu adversa diu sustinens pariter et labores, demum ab eodem statu se sponte dimisit et deinceps tamquam obediencie filius jam per aliquot annos inter vos velut simplex canonicus humilitatis indicia plurimum ut accepimus ostentans hactenus extitit laudabiliter conversatus. Et licet sibi occasione premissa per vos uberius fore censu[er]imus providendum, de hujusmodi provisione sibi facienda prout in casu simili fieri consueverat non curastis, propter quod vos ad certos diem et locum coram nobis fecimus evocari in forma juris ostensuros ac etiam propósituros quare dicto fratri Johanni per nos in vestri defectum minime deberet lacius provideri; et cum vos coram nobis nullatenus comparentes reputaverimus contumaces et in penam contumacie vestre, vobis contra dictum fratrem Johannem seu ejus provisionem per nos canonice ordinandam viam quicquid ulterius proponendi precluserimus per decretum in vestri negligentiam et defectum, eidem fratri Johanni modo providimus infrascripto.

In dei nomine amen. Nos Willelmus permissione etc. fratri Johanni de Rudestan dudum priori monasterii de Thurg' nostre diocesis pro sua provisione porciones subsequentes in ejusdem monasterii prioris et conventus defectum ordinamus et sibi de eisdem canonice providemus. In primis habeat idem frater Johannes cameram ab aliis separatam infra septa monasterii de Thurg' antedicti decentem prout statui et honori dicti monasterii magis videbitur convenire pro se et uno concanonico suo sui arbitrio prioris sibi proinde assignando. Habeat etiam et percipiat idem frater Johannes pro victualibus suis in omnibus quantum duo canonici ejusdem monasterii percipiunt in eodem. Habeat nichilominus dictus frater Johannes pro indumentis suis de communi sicut unus de suis concanonicis antedictis. Percipiat etiam de communi pro speciebus xx solidos annuatim. Habeat insuper candelas et focale et alia minuta necessaria de communi prout eisdem dinoscitur indigere. Item habeat unum garcionem qui sibi deserviat et ministret, cui in necessariis de communi provideatur universis sicuti uni de prioris garcionibus antedicti.

Presentem ordinationem ex causis legitimis mutandi augendi seu minuendi prout dicti fratris Johannis merita seu demerita ac dicti monasterii facultates exegerint in futurum potestatem[38] nobis expressius reservamus, vos priorem et conventum in domino exhortantes vobisque in virtute obedientie firmiter injungendo mandantes quatinus sepefato fratri Johanni de supradicta provisione nostra in omnibus et singulis faciatis plenius responderi sibique de eadem congrue ministrari ac debite deserviri prout nostram indignationem et canonicam ulcionem volueritis evitare. Valete. [Bishopthorpe, 11 Feb. 1324.]

[margin] Memorandum quod ista littera fuit duplicata, quarum una remanet penes dictos priorem et conventum et alia penes dictum fratrem Johannem, et iii

[38] Interlined.

Nonas Aprilis anno etc. xxiiij apud Thorp prope Ebor' transmisse fuerant ambe littere predicte dicto fratri Johanni per quemdam garcionem suum quem misit pro eis. [Bishopthorpe, 3 Apr. 1324.]

354 Mandate to the bailiff of Southwell to keep in safe custody clerks received from [the commissaries named in **356**]. Pontefract, 21 Feb. 1324.

355 Note of licence to Robert de Anesly, rector of Bilsthorpe (*Bildesthorp*), to be absent for one year; also that he was excused payment of one mark, the fine for his non-residence in 1322, a letter about this being written to the receiver of York. Southwell, 27 Mar. 1324.

356 COMMISSIO AD PETENDUM ET RECIPIENDUM CLERICOS APUD NOT' INCARCERATOS.[39] Commission to John de Trowell, rector of a mediety of Trowell, and Matthew de Halifax, keeper of the hospital of St. John the Baptist, Nottingham, to claim, receive and securely hold clerks charged before justices of gaol delivery at Nottingham. Kirton, 20 Sept. 1323.

357 Mandate to the sequestrator in the archdeaconry to release the sequestration of goods of M. Boniface de Saluciis: his will has been proved and administration of his goods in the diocese granted to his executor by proxy. Bishopthorpe, 3 Apr. 1324.

358 [*Reply to the archbishop's order to his commissary to explain why he freed John Touke, a clerk convicted of robbery: he was freed by Archbishop Greenfield's commissary and later pardoned.*]

[N.F.426[40]] Venerabili suus humilis et devotus in Christo patri ac domino domino Willelmo dei gracia Ebor' archiepiscopo Anglie primati Johannes de Trouwell obedienciam reverenciam et honorem. Mandatum vestrum reverendum nuper in hec verba recepi:[41]

Willelmus [*etc.*] dilecto filio domino Johanni rectori medietatis ecclesie de Trouwell nostre diocesis salutem [*etc.*]. In nostrum nuper non sine turbacione multiplici devenit auditum quod Johannes filius Walteri Touke de Kelum clericus dudum coram domino Waltero de Goushill et sociis suis domini nostri regis ad gaolam Notinghamie deliberandam tunc justiciariis de quadam roboria Gilberti Gerdlere de Neuwerk' facta convictus tibi virtute commissionis nostre tibi facte de petendo et recipiendo clericos hujusmodi extitit liberatus, qui postea absque purgacione aliqua a tua custodia abire permissus jam in comitatu Notinghamie vagatur pro sue libito voluntatis in grave nostri periculum infuturum, ex quo tuam colligimus simplicitatem ne dicamus maliciam sive dolum. Quocirca tibi mandamus in virtute obediencie firmiter injungentes quatenus de forma indictationis dicti Johannis quando et qualiter tibi vel alteri extitit liberatus, quomodo eciam absque purgacione

[39] The marginal headings for **354** and **356** are preceded by framed capitals B and A respectively, indicating that they are in reverse order.

[40] Interleaved facing fo.352v. While this folio (measuring 23.5 by 10 cms.) might well be the commissary's letter, its hand is very similar to that of the register.

[41] Interlined.

canonica sic vagatur et cur eum sic recedere permisisti, ac de aliis hujusmodi facti circumstanciis que nos informare poterunt in hac parte, nos quamcicius poteritis[42] distincte et aperte per tuas litteras clausas harum seriem continentes reddas per latorem presencium cerciores. Vale. [Bishopthorpe, 20 June 1327.]

Pater reverende, in ultima visitacione vestra super illo articulo fui impetitus, et tunc vobis dixi et adhuc dico quod dictus Johannes Touke in tempore bone memorie predecessoris vestri liberatus fuit domino Henrico de Halum tunc vicario ecclesie beate Marie Notinghamie commissario dicti patris predecessoris vestri[43] et idem dominus Henricus predictum Johannem abire permisit cum securitate et obligatorio sufficienti, ut sibi videbatur. Et postmodum idem Johannes impetravit cartam domini regis de pace[44] ut intellexi, et sic de illo nichil intromisi. Valeat vestra reverenda paternitas feliciter atque diu. Scriptum apud Notingham die Mercurii in octabas Nativitatis beati Johannis Baptiste anno domino supradicto. [1 July 1327.]

359 [Fo.353; N.F.427] To Robert Stuffyn of Skegby, priest (dioc. York), quoting letters of Gaucelin, cardinal-priest of SS. Marcelinus and Peter, papal penitentiary (dated Avignon, 2 Jan. 1324). When an acolyte, Robert wished to be promoted to holy orders. Not having a title with his parents, he went to the prior and convent of Felley, to whom he bound himself and his parents in a sum of money that he would not trouble them to make him a provision and that he would return the title as soon as he was ordained priest. This title was accidentally burnt. On its strength, however, he was promoted to holy orders, otherwise rightly, and ministered in them, not being excommunicate. He came to the papal court for a remedy, and is now sent back to the archbishop to be absolved from perjury and this excess, given a penance and dispensed [as in **219**]. The archbishop, after verifying Robert's statement by an inquest held by the dean of Nottingham, accordingly absolves and dispenses him. Womersley (*Wilmersley*), 31 Mar. 1324.

360 Note of licence to Robert de Derneford, rector of Bunny, to be absent for one year from 10 June next. Bishopthorpe, 8 Apr. 1324.

361 Institution [etc.] of William de Walkyngham, acolyte, to Greasley church, now vacant; presented by Nicholas de Cantulupo. Note [in margin] that he had a letter to enquire into defects. Sancton, 12 May 1324.

362 The like of Hugh de Bardelby, acolyte, to Bulwell church, now vacant; presented by Edward II.[45] Also note of letters dimissory for all orders. North Ferriby (*Northfferiby*), 14 May 1324.

363 Note of licence to study (*in forma constitutionis*) for one year from his institution to William de Walkyngham, subdeacon, rector of Greasley. Bewick, 9 June 1324.

[42] *Sic.*
[43] For a commission to him and Trouwell dated 5 Aug. 1313 see *Reg. Greenfield*, IV.134 (no.1962).
[44] Dated 22 Nov. 1323 (*CPR 1321–4*, 351).
[45] *CPR 1321–4*, 406.

364 Mandate to the dean of Nottingham to enquire about John de Melton Moubray, clerk, accused before the king's justices of burgling William de Beston's house in Nottingham and now in the archbishop's prison, reporting by closed letters [as in **178**]. Bishopthorpe, 2 July 1324.

365 Mandate to the same to proclaim that objectors to John's purgation should appear in Southwell minster on 23 July [as in **200**]. Brayton, 12 July 1324.

366 Commission to M. Elias de Couton, canon of Southwell, and M. Thomas de Sancto Leonardo, sequestrator in the archdeaconry, to hear etc. objections as above, if any, and admit John to purgation, reporting by letters patent.[46] Ousefleet (*Usflet*), 18 July 1324.

367 [*Commission to Roland [Jorz], archbishop of Armagh,*[47] *to confer the first tonsure and confirm children and adults.*]
COMMISSIO ARCHIEPISCOPO ARMACHANO AD CONFERENDUM PRIMAM TONSURAM ET CONFIRMANDUM PARVULOS. Venerabili in Christo patri domino Rolando dei gracia archiepiscopo Armachano Willelmus etc. salutem et fraternam in domino caritatem. De vestra sincera devocione in domino confidentes, cum per archidiaconatum Not' nostre diocesis vos transire contigerit, ad conferendum personis idoneis litteratis videlicet liberis et legitimis et etatis legitime primam tonsuram ordinis clericalis, necnon ad confirmandum parvulos et adultos dicti archidiaconatus ad vestram propter hoc presenciam accedentes, vobis tenore presencium committimus vices nostras pro nostro beneplacito duraturas. Conservet vos etc. [Malton, 24 June 1324.]

368 Note of licence to study (*in forma constitutionis*) for one year to Roger de Whatton, subdeacon, rector of Elton. Cawood, 21 Sept. 1324.

369 [Fo.353^{v}; N.F.427^{v}] Institution [etc.] of Robert de Beverl', canon of Worksop, to Worksop vicarage, now vacant; presented by the prior and convent of Worksop. Cawood, 28 Sept. 1324.

370 Note of licence to study for one year to M. Hugh de Wylughby, rector of Willoughby on the Wolds. 29 Sept. 1324.

371 Note of licence to study in a *studium generale* for three years to M. Gilbert de Pontefracto, rector of Rempstone. Scrooby, 10 Oct. 1324.

[46] The archbishop petitioned the king to restore John's lands etc on 9 Dec. 1330, stating that he had received the purgation at Southwell on 20 July 1324 (Reg. Melton, fo.578; N.F.720; see also *CCR 1330–3*, 81). The dates of **366** and no.250 of *Reg. Melton,* II.103, however, show he was then in Yorkshire.

[47] Said to have resigned the archbishopric by 22 Aug. 1322, when proceedings, apparently for his deprivation, had just been initiated (*CPL*, II.219, which lists charges). He had certainly been replaced before this commission (*HBC*, 335). In another commission to him on 19 Nov. 1326 he was addressed as 'Roland late (*nuper*) archbishop of Armagh', with *dei gracia* interlined to precede *nuper* (Reg. Melton, fo.574^{v}; N.F.714^{v}).

372 Appointment of Gregory Fairfax, rector of Headon, as sequestrator in the archdeaconry and dean of Southwell and Laneham [as in **297** without interlineations].

Note of a letter to M. Thomas de Sancto Leonardo, rector of Egmanton, the previous sequestrator and dean, ordering him to deliver to Gregory without delay, by indenture, the rolls and muniments of these offices and any money in hand from them. Doncaster, 16 Nov. 1324.

373 [*Request to examine fourteen witnesses in St. Mary's, Oxford, in a cause about possession of Elkesley church before the official of York* (see **425**).]
ROGATUS AD EXAMINANDUM TESTES IN CAUSA PENDENTE SUPER ECCLESIA DE ELKESLEY. Willelmus etc. discreto viro . . archidiacono Oxon' vel ejus . . officiali salutem et paratam in juris subsidium ad mutua obsequia voluntatem. Cum in causa seu negotio que vel quod coram . . officiali curie nostre Ebor' et ejus . . commissario generali conjunctim et divisim ex commissione nostra vertitur in curia nostra memorata super ecclesia de Elkesley nostre diocesis inter magistrum Johannem Lambok' clericum ad eandem ecclesiam nobis presentatum actorem ex parte una et dominum Hugonem Gernoun possessioni ejusdem ecclesia incumbentem[48] reum ex altera, ad peticionem partis ejusdem incumbentis pro missione ad vos facienda ad recipiendum in forma juris et examinandum testes infrascriptos infra jurisdictionem vestram et sub districtu vestro ut dicitur degentes et ad probationem intencionis sue necessarios (videlicet Henricum clericum de Kydelington, Johannem de Aulone, Robertum Drewe, Willelmus Ketele, Johannem Felip, Johannem atte Barre, Willelmum Best', Galfridum de Islep, Edmundum de Isle, Willelmum Lingistre, Johannem Dymmok', Nicholaum de Cherton, magistrum Willelmum de Luham et magistrum Lambertum de Trikingham), tempore messium non obstante, de consensu partis dicti presentati diebus et locis infrascriptis per dictos . . commissarios nostros fit decretum; vestram rogamus discrecionem mutue vicissitudinis optentu et in juris subsidium quatinus per vos seu alium dictos testes in ecclesia beate Marie Oxon' proximo die juridico post festum Decollacionis sancti Johannis Baptiste cum continuacione et prorogacione quatuorum dierum proximo subsequencium recipere et examinare velitis in forma juris super articulis et partis adverse interrogatoriis quos vobis mittimus presentibus interclusis, depositiones eorundem testium in scriptis redactis neutri parcium proditas sub sigillo vestro inclusas nobis vel dictis . . commissariis nostris aut eorum alteri aliisve nostris in hac parte commissariis deputatis vel deputandis pluribus aut uni citra diem Mercurii proximo ante festum sancti Luce Evangeliste proximo futurum si placet seriosius cum tenore presencium transmittentes. Denunciarunt quidem commissarii predicti parti presentati predicti quod recepcioni eorundem dictis diebus et locis intersit si sibi viderit expedire. Testes vero supradictos si se gracia odio vel favore subtraxerint, compellere velitis veritati testimonium perhibere. Benedictionem. Valete. [Kippax (*Kypas*), 1 Aug. 1324.]

374 Notes of the like to the same to examine witnesses for the plaintiff [Lambok]; and to the prebendary of Coombe and Harnham (dioc. Salisbury),

[48] Instituted 1317 (*Reg. Greenfield*, V.277, no.2885); and see **378**.

or its custodian, to examine other witnesses for the defendant in Salisbury cathedral on 14 Dec., reporting by 11 Jan. 1325. Bishopthorpe, 20 and 21 Nov. 1324.

375 Institution (in the person of Thomas de Halughton, clerk, as proctor) and mandate for induction of Hugh Leveryk' of Southwell, priest, to Kelham church, now vacant; presented by the abbot and convent of Welbeck. Bishopthorpe, 2 Dec. 1324.

376 Note of licence to John de Loudham, rector of Ruddington, to be absent for one year.[49] Bishopthorpe, 30 Nov. 1324.

377 The like to William de Loudham, rector of Cotham. Grantham (*Graham*), 15 Oct. 1324.

378 Note of letters dimissory to Hugh Gernoun, subdeacon, rector of Elkesley, for his further ordination by an English bishop. The archbishop's manor by Westminster, 3 Nov. 1324.

379 Note of licence to the prior and convent of Shelford, as rector of a mediety of North Muskham church, to demise its fruits, income and offerings for five years. Southwell, 26 Apr. 1327.

380 [*Commission to absolve pupils of Newark grammar school excommunicated for fighting.*]
COMMISSIO SUPER ABSOLUCIONE SCOLARIUM SCOLARUM GRAMMATICALIUM DE NEUWERK'. Willelmus etc. dilecto filio fratri Rocelino perpetuo vicario ecclesie de Neuwerk' nostre diocesis salutem [*etc.*]. De vestris circumspectione et industria confidentes, ad impendum in forma juris beneficium absolucionis omnibus et singulis scolaribus scolarum grammaticalium de Neuwerk' quociens in majoris excommunicationis sentenciam auctoritate canonis 'Si quis suadente diabolo' se adinvicem violenter percuciendo seu manus violentas temere iniciendo inciderint quatenus nostra potestas se extendit in hac parte, ac injungendo eisdem et eorum cuilibet pro modo culparum suarum penitencias salutares, vobis tenore presencium committimus vices nostras pro nostro beneplacito duraturas. Valete. [Southwell, 26 Apr. 1327.]

381 [Fo.354; N.F.428] (i) Certificate of Henry [Burghersh], bishop of Lincoln, that he has executed a commission of the archbishop (quoted; dated at the archbishop's manor by Westminster, 23 Oct. 1324) for an exchange of benefices between Thomas de Sibthorp, rector of North Collingham, and John de Sibthorp, rector of Shenley (*Shenle*; dioc. Lincoln), enclosing the report of an enquiry ordered by the archbishop. John was instituted to North Collingham in the person of Hugh de Bardelby, clerk, his proctor; presented by the abbot and convent of Peterborough. Thomas was instituted to Shenley in the person of Richard de Skerington, clerk; presented by Edward II.[50]

[49] In margin, under heading, is *xl s.*
[50] *CPR 1321–4*, 288; *CPR 1324–7*, 2.

(ii) Letter of the bishop of Lincoln instituting John [as above]. Sleaford (*Lafford*), 9 Dec. 1324.

382 Mandate for John's induction; also notes of his oath of obedience to the archbishop by his proctor, Hugh de Bardelby; and of licence to study (*stare in scolis*) until 29 Sept. 1325. Bishopthorpe, 14 Dec. 1324.

383 Note of licence to M. Adam de Amundesham, rector of Barton in Fabis (*Barton super Trentam*), to be absent until 29 Sept. 1325. Bishopthorpe, 19 Dec. 1324.

384 Sentence quashing the election of William de Thurgarton, canon of Newstead, as prior of Newstead in succession to Richard [de Grange?[51]], who had resigned; with provision of William by devolved right. [n.d. but see **386**.]

385 Mandate to the subprior and convent of Newstead to elect, with the king's licence, a prior in succession to Richard who, broken with age, has resigned to the archbishop. Bishopthorpe, 9 Dec. 1324.[52]

386 (i) Mandate to the same to obey William as their prior. (ii) Mandate to the archdeacon's official to install him. [Fo.354^{v}; N.F.428^{v}] (iii) Letters to Edward II reporting the election and appointment of William, and asking [for the restoration of the temporalities].[53] Cawood, 5 Jan. 1325.

387 Mandate to the dean of Nottingham to cite objectors to William's election to appear before the archbishop wherever he might be in the diocese on 5 January, reporting by that day. Cawood, 22 Dec. 1324.

388 Mandate to the commissary-general of the official of York and Richard de Grymston, receiver of York, to cease process against Alice de Rouclyf', mother and executrix of the will of John de Rouclyf', for £10 in which he was bound to the archbishop for the sale of the fruits of Kelham church in 1320; they are to restore the bond for £10 to her, and also to destroy in her presence a bond for 40 marks concerning the goods of Acard [de Longo Prato], late rector of Ordsall [see **304**]. Any ecclesiastical censures are to be relaxed. Bishopthorpe, 30 Jan. 1325.

389 Note of licence to Adam de Preston, rector of Hickling (*Hicling'*), to be absent for one year. Laneham, 24 Feb. 1325.

390 Mandate to the sequestrator to release the goods of Roger Elger of Misterton who died intestate to his widow Alice and their free-born children; the goods had lapsed to the archbishop as ordinary, and he makes this gift by grace. Same date.

[51] *VCH Nottingham*, II.117; cf. *Reg. Greenfield*, IV.154, no.2011, and V.xxvi.
[52] The marginal headings for **384** and **385** are preceded by capitals B and A respectively, indicating that they are in reverse order.
[53] Ordered 10 Jan. 1325 (*CPR 1324–7*, 85). See ibid. 61 for the licence.

391 Note of licence to study for one year to John de Sibthorpe, rector of North Collingham. Bishopthorpe, 7 Mar. 1325.

392 Collation [etc.] of William de Feriby, priest, to Carlton in Lindrick (*Carleton in Lyndrik'*) church, now vacant. Bishopthorpe, 9 Mar. 1325.

393 Commission to M. Robert de Pykeryng, dean of York, M. Richard de Erghum, M. Walter de Yarwell, canons of York, and M. William de Gotham, D.D. (or two or three of them), to proceed etc. in an appeal cause between Nicholas de Sixtenby, who acts as vicar of Marnham, appellant, and John Godehous, layman, the party appealed, concerning rejection of an exception of alleged excommunication (*super rejectione cujusdam exceptionis majoris excommunicationis facta ut pretendatur*) by M. John de Wodhous, the archbishop's commissary deputed in this case together with the official of York; they are to report. Bishop Wilton, 19 Mar. 1325.

394 Institution [etc.] of Richard de Stapilford, priest, canon of Newstead, to Hucknall Torkard (*Hokenal Torkard*) vicarage, now vacant; presented by the prior and convent of Newstead. Bishop Burton, 21 Mar. 1325.

395 Licence to the subprioress and convent of Wallingwells to elect a prioress in succession to Denise, who has resigned to the archbishop because of age and other lawful reasons. Bishop Burton, 27 Mar. 1325.

396 Institution [etc.] of John de Westretford, priest, to Bilsthorpe church, now vacant; presented by John Bret, kt. Laneham, 16 Apr. 1325.

397 [N.F.429] Copy[54] of two Chancery writs of prohibition *ne teneatis*:

(1) Edward III to the archbishop, his official and their commissaries. Richard de Hoton, clerk, holding the vicarage of West Markham by the king's advowson, is sued in court Christian by Richard de Hareworth, who claims the vicarage by the advowson of Boniface de Saluciis.[55] As the king could thus lose his advowson, the cause is not to be held in a church court until it has been determined in the king's court whether the advowson of the vicarage belongs to the king or Boniface. Westminster, 6 Feb. 1327.

(2) Edward III to the same. William de Melton and M. John de Wodehous are said by Richard de Hoton, chaplain, to have sued him for chatttels and debts before the archbishop in a church court although such pleas (excluding testament and marriage) pertain only to the king; with prohibition [as above, *mutatis mutandis*]. Westminster, 12 Feb. 1327.

398 [Fo.355; N.F.430] Mandate to the archdeacon or his official to cite the clergy and four or six men from each vill of Bingham deanery to attend visitation[56] as follows: on Saturday 4 May in Thoroton (*Thurverton*) chapel; on

[54] Apparently in the same hand as the register. The parchment is 23 by 7.3 cms., interleaved facing fo.345v.

[55] See notes to **1** and **98**.

[56] The marginal headings for **398–403** describe these as second visitations.

Monday 20 May in Owthorpe (*Outthorp*) church; on Tuesday 21 May in Stanton on the Wolds (*Stanton super le Wald*) church; on Wednesday 22 May in Bunny church; and on Thursday 23 May in Wilford church. Laneham, 16 Apr. 1325.

399 Note of similar mandate for Newark deanery, for attendance on Friday 26 Apr. in Laxton church; on Saturday 27 Apr. in Kneesall church; on Monday 29 Apr. in Kelham church; and on Tuesday 30 Apr. in Newark church. Same date.

400 Mandate to the dean of Southwell to cite the clergy and people of his deanery to appear for visitation in Southwell minster on Thursday 9 May, with three or four men from each vill and two or three from each street (*vicus*) of Southwell. Laneham, 17 Apr. 1325.

401 Mandate to the prior and convent of Shelford for their visitation on Friday 17 May; absent brethren are to be recalled. Same date.

402 Note of mandate to the archdeacon or his official for the visitation of Nottingham deanery as follows: on Wednesday 5 June in Hoveringham (*Overyngham*) church; on Friday 7 June in Gedling church; on Monday 10 June in St. Mary's, Nottingham; and on [omitted] in Warsop church.[57] Ossington, 27 Apr. 1325.

403 Notes of mandates to the prior and convent of Thurgarton for visitation on Monday 3 June; the prior and convent of Worksop for Saturday 15 June; and the prior and convent of Newstead for Wednesday 12 June. Norwell, 28 Apr. 1325.

404 [*Appointment by John de Grandisson, archdeacon of Nottingham, of M. John de la Launde as his official and vicar-general.*]
COMMISSIO SEU DEPUTACIO OFFICIALIS ARCHIDIACONI NOTINGH' PER ARCHIDIACONUM FACTA DE MAGISTRO JOHANNE DE LA LAUNDE. Johannes de Grandissino archidiaconus Not' in ecclesia Ebor' discreto viro magistro Johanni de la Launde rectori ecclesie de Arnale juris civilis professori salutem in auctore salutis. De vestris fidelitate circumspectione et industria plenam et indubitatam noticiam obtinentes, vos officialem nostrum ac vicarium generalem in archidiaconatu nostro predicto preficimus et ordinamus ad audiendum et fine debito terminandum omnes et singulas causas lites et querelas quarum cognicio ad nos pertinet ratione archidiaconatus nostri predicti, necnon ad comparendum in convocacionibus quibuscumque et consenciendum licitis ordinacionibus et statutis tam editis quam edendis et prestandum in animam nostram cujuslibet generis licitum sacramentum, synodosque celebrandos et contumacias absencium puniendas acetiam inquirendum et reformandum nostrorum excessus subditorum et procedendum in judicio et extra judicium tam ex officio quam ad parcium instanciam, ac generaliter omnia alia et singula facienda exercenda et expedienda que ad hujusmodi officialatus quomodolibet spectant officium et que nobis incumbunt inibi facienda de consuetudine vel de jure committimus vices nostras cum cohercionis canonice potestate; revocantes ex certa sciencia commissionem aliis quibuscumque in premissis seu circa ea datam et con-

[57] Probably between Newstead on 12 and Worksop on 15 June (**403**).

cessam ante datam nostrarum presencium litterarum. In cujus rei testimonium sigillum nostrum archidiaconatus nostri predicti presentibus litteris sive instrumento publico apposuimus. Et ad majorem et pleniorem premissorum fidem presentes litteras per magistrum Thomam de Exon' clericum publicum auctoritate apostolica notarium infrascriptum scribi fecimus et publicari ac signo suo et subscripcione communiri. Datum in hospicio habitacionis nostre Avinion' mense Februarii die xxvi anno domini ab incarnacione MCCCXXV indictione octavo; presentibus testibus domino Roberto Jolyf presbitero et Willelmo Crescy domicello nostro Ebor' diocesis ad premissa vocatis specialiter et rogatis.

Et ego Thomas dictus de Exon' clericus Exon' diocesis publicus auctoritate apostolica notarius premissis omnibus et singulis anno indictione mense die et loco predictis unacum testibus suprascriptis presens interfui ac de mandato reverendi viri domini Johannis de Grandissono archidiaconi predicti scripsi presentes litteras seu instrumentum publicum in hanc publicam formam redegi meoque signo consignatum in testimonium premissorum. [Avignon, 26 Feb. 1325.]

405 [*Presentation of this commission to the archbishop; with the official's oath of obedience.*]

DIES NOTIFICATIONIS. Memorandum quod primo die mensis Maii anno gracie MCCCXXV indictione octavo apud Stok' Ebor' diocesis magister Johannes de la Launde predictus venerabili in Christo patri et domino domino Willelmo dei gracia Ebor' archiepiscopo Anglie primati insinuavit et notificavit litteras originales copie suprascripte; presentibus magistris Ada de Heselbech et Johanne de Thoresby ac dominis Johanne de Sutton et Johanne de Trowell testibus etc.

FORMA JURAMENTI PRESTITI. Ego Johannes de la Launde officialis et vicarius domini Johannis de Grandissono archidiaconi Not' juro ad sancta dei evangelia corporaliter per me tacta quod fidelis ero vobis venerabili [*etc.*] et successoribus vestris ac officialibus et ministris in canonicis mandatis, nichilque scienter faciam seu attemptabo quod in prejudicium vestrum vel jurisdictionis vestre cujuscumque cedere poterit quovismodo. Sicut deus me adjuvet et sancta dei evangelia. [Stoke,[58] 1 May 1325.]

406 [*Declaration by the archbishop at the official's admission to office.*]

[Fo.355^{v}; N.F.430^{v}] INHIBICIONES ET INJUNCTIONES FACTE OFFICIALI ARCHIDIACONI NOT' IN ADMISSIONE SUA. In dei nomine amen. Nos Willelmus etc. tibi magistro Johanni de la Launde juris civilis professori officiali et vicario generali domini Johannis de Grandissono archidiaconi Notinghamie in virtute sancte obediencie nobis jurate et sub pena districtionis canonice inhibemus injungimus et mandamus ne aliqua monasteria vel loca religiosa virorum aut mulierum dicti archidiaconatus ingrediaris causa visitacionis exercende vel jurisdictionis alterius cujuscumque. Item inhibemus tibi ut supra ne in dicto archidiaconatu vice seu nomine dicti archidiaconi quovismodo te intromittas nec jurisdictionem seu correctionem aliquam exerceas in casibus seu articulis episcopis reservatis. Item injungimus tibi ut supra quod in exercitacione jurisdictionis archidiaconi

[58] Probably East Stoke, or perhaps Stoke Bardolph, as the archbishop planned to be in Newark on the previous day (**399**).

in dicto archidiaconatu sacros canones et sanctorum patrum statuta cures inviolabiliter observare. Item inhibemus tibi ut supra ne correctiones quorumcumque excessuum subditorum nostrorum dicti archidiaconatus seorsum in absencia nostrorum decanorum facias quovismodo. Item injungimus tibi ut supra quod nichil penitus in prejudicium jurisdictionis nostre ordinarie seu metropolitane exerceas seu attemptes.

407 [*Mandate to the clergy and people of the archdeaconry to obey the official.*]
CLERO ET POPULO DICTI ARCHIDIACONATUS QUOD OBEDIANT EIDEM. Willelmus etc. dilectis filiis . . decanis nostris ecclesiarum rectoribus vicariis capellanis et aliis ecclesiarum ministris ceterisque parochianis nostris quibuscumque tam clericis quam laicis per archidiaconatum Not' constitutis salutem [*etc.*]. Cum per litteras patentes domini Johannis de Grandissono archidiaconi Not' sigillo suo pendente signatas nobis constet evidenter quod idem dominus Johannes archidiaconus magistrum Johannem de la Launde rectorem ecclesie de Arnale nostre diocesis juris civilis professorem suum creavit officialem in archidiaconatu predicto ac vicarium generalem, commissionem quibuscumque personis in hac parte prius factam ex certa sciencia penitus revocando, vobis injungimus et mandamus quatenus prefato magistro Johanni de la Launde tamquam officiali et vicario archidiaconatus predicti prout et quatenus tantum humiliter pareatis et etiam intendatis. Valete. [Stoke, 1 May 1325.]

408 DISPENSATIO CUM TRIBUS CLERICIS GENITIS DE SOLUTIS ET SOLUTIS. Note of dispensation for illegitimacy, with permission to receive all minor orders and hold a benefice without cure of souls, to Robert de Byngham, John de Kynalton and Walter de Cotegrave; they also received the first tonsure. Bingham, 16 May 1325.

409 The like [interlined] to Richard and John de Stapelford. Bilborough (*Bilburgh*), 11 June 1325.

410 Note of licence to study for three years from 29 Sept. 1325 in a *studium generale* in or outside England to M. John de Nassington,[59] rector of Screveton (*Kirketon*[60]). Keyworth, 21 May 1325.

411 Dispensation [as in **408**] to John Fraunkeleyn of Keyworth, scholar; and note of another to Henry de Sutton of Rempstone. Clifton, 22 May 1325.

412 The like to William de Cotegrave, Ralph de Crophill, Hugh de Plumtre and Thomas son of Eve. Radcliffe on Trent (*Radeclyf' super Trentam*), 19 May 1325.

413 Notes of licence to study for one year to Thomas de Wilford, rector of Wilford; and that he was excused the fine (*mulctam*) incurred by his absence in the previous year without licence. Colwick (*Collewyk'*), 23 May 1325.

[59] See *BRUO*, II.1337.
[60] The name of a manor in Screveton (see R. Thoroton, *The Antiquities of Nottinghamshire* (1677), ed. J. Throsby, 3 vols., 1790–6, repr. 1972, I.244–52; *Reg. Greenfield*, V.xviii).

414 Commission to the prior of St. Andrew's [York], order of Sempringham, M. Richard de Eryom, canon of York, and M. William de Gotham, D.D., rector of Althorpe (dioc. Lincoln), (or two of them) to hear and determine the appeal cause between Nicholas de Sixtenby, who acts as vicar of Marnham, appellant, and John Godehous, layman, appealed; Nicholas has appealed to the archbishop's audience from a definitive sentence by the commissary-general of the official of York (who were both deputed to act in this cause) depriving him of the vicarage, and from his condemnation by the commissary [cf. **393**]. These sentences are to be confirmed or quashed, with frivolous delays rejected (*frivolis dilationibus penitus amputatis*), and a report made. Southwell, 28 May 1325.

415 Note of licence to study in a *studium generale* for one year from 1 Aug. 1325 to Peter de Bekering, rector of Tuxford. Southwell, 2 June 1325.

416 PRO WILLELMO AMYAS DE NOT' UT ANIMALIA SUA IN HOSPITALI SANCTI JOHANNIS NOT' REPOSITA REPETERE POTERIT QUANDO VOLUERIT. To the archdeacon, his official, the archbishop's sequestrator, deans, other ministers, and all the faithful. The hospital of St. John outside Nottingham, founded for paupers, is so impoverished that it can scarcely support one priest. William de Amyas, burgess of Nottingham, in his zeal to assist the hospital, wishes to put there his sheep and other animals which are his own, corn and other things, to be removed at his will. The archbishop orders those addressed, and in particular the master or keeper of the hospital, or his successors, under pain of excommunication, that William should not be prevented from recovering any of these goods, even if the present master dies or is removed from the house, provided that they are listed by indenture. Greasley, 11 June 1325.

417 [*Remission of fines imposed in visitations of Thurgarton priory in return for its grant of a corrody to John de Essh.*]
REMISSIO PENARUM FACTA PRIORI DE THURGARTON. Noverint universi quod nos Willelmus etc., inspectis rotulis visitationis nostre prime in archidiaconatu Not' facte et bone memorie domini Willelmi de Gren[efeld] predecessoris nostri immediati super compertis contra religiosos viros . . priorem et conventum de Thurgarton nostre diocesis et super correctionibus subsecutis, comperimus quod mulcte et pene pro diversis defectibus in locis et rebus ad ipsos spectantibus repertis et eciam confessatis legitime imposite et commisse ad CXX marcas se extendunt, quam pecunie summam pro quodam corrodio Johanni de Essh servienti nostro Suwell' per eosdem religiosos concesso ac etiam divine pietatis intuitu eisdem remittimus per presentes, quibus sigillum nostrum apponi fecimus in testimonium veritatis. [Burton Joyce, 6 June 1325.]

418 [*Testimonial of Walter de Notyngham's renunciation of Judaism and baptism in St. Mary's, Nottingham, on 10 June 1325.*[61]]
[Fo.356; N.F.431] LITTERA TESTIMONIALIS SUPER BAPTISMO ET CONVERSIONE CUJUSDAM JUDAEI AD FIDEM CHRISTIANAM CONVERSI. Universis sancte matris [*etc.*] Willelmus etc. salutem in amplexibus salvatoris. Ut in publicum prodiat leticiam Christiane professionis augmentacio a cunctis merito fidelibus puris

[61] See *Reg. Melton*, III.139, no.237, giving his former name as Hagyn.

affectibus appetenda, universitati vestre plenius innotescat quod Walterus de Notyngham exhibitor presencium nuper judeus ut asseruit abjecto judaice cecitatis errore ad fidem catholicam spontanee se convertens, expositisque sibi majoribus articulis fidei ipsos singulos credere firmiter se affirmans, die Lune proximo post octabas sancte Trinitatis anno gracie MCCCXXV ad humilis et devote ut apparuit sue requisicionis instanciam in ecclesia beate Marie Not' nostre diocesis extitit in forma ecclesie canonice baptizatus, suscipientibus tunc ipsum de sacro fonte baptismatis nobilibus viris dominis Waltero de Goushill et Ricardo de Whatton militibus unacum Orframina uxore Roberti Ingram de Notyngham, assistente cleri et populi multitudine copiosa de hujusmodi conversione spiritualiter in Christo plurimum recreata; qui quidem Walterus subsequenter per nos dictis die et loco signo sancte crucis ac crismate salutis rite fuerat confirmatus. In cujus [*etc.* Newstead, 12 June 1325.][62]

419 Note of licence to study for three years at a *studium generale* to M. Robert de Shirburn, acolyte, rector of Normanton on Soar; also letters dimissory for all holy orders. Bishopthorpe, 23 Aug. 1326.

420 Institution [etc.] of John de Stanton of Lancaster, priest, to Colwick church, now vacant; presented by William de Collewyk, kt. Bishop Burton, 28 Aug. 1326.

421 Commission to Gregory [Fairfax], rector of Headon, to examine and confirm the forthcoming election of a prioress of Wallingwells, commit its administration and install her, reserving her obedience to the archbishop, and report. Bishop Burton, 29 Aug. 1326.

422 Institution [etc.] of Alan de Rothewell, priest, to St. Michael's, Sutton Bonington, now vacant; presented by Lady Christine, widow of John de Segrave, kt. Bishop Burton, 30 Aug. 1326.

423 Note of mandate to Gregory [Fairfax], sequestrator in the archdeaconry, to sequestrate the fruits of the above church from 24 July, when Robert de Aston, the last rector, resigned, until Alan's induction. Same date.

424 Commission to John de Trowell, rector of a mediety of Trowell, and Matthew de Halifax, keeper of the hospital of St. John the Baptist, Nottingham, to claim and receive into safe custody clerks charged before the king's justices at Nottingham. Bishopthorpe, 17 Sept. 1326.

425 To the abbot of Meaux (*Melsa*). Commission by the archbishop as sole judge delegate in a cause between John de Lambok' of Nottingham, rector of

[62] There are *acta* after this date in a register *extra diocesim* and there are also registers of vicars-general (D.M. Smith, *Guide to Bishops' Registers of England and Wales*, Royal Historical Society 1981, 237; *Reg. Melton*, I.viii). Melton was Edward II's treasurer from 3 July 1325 to 14 Nov. 1326 (*HBC*, 105).

Elkesley (*Ilkesley*), appellant, and Hugh Gernoun, clerk, appealed.[63] The abbot is to proceed in accordance with the papal letters [not quoted], which are transmitted with the bearer of this commission. Bishopthorpe, 18 Sept. 1326.

[margin] Note that [Richard de] Snoweshull has a copy of the bull.

426 Copy of bull of John XXII to Thomas son of the late Richard de Byngham, kt., clerk (dioc. York), and an unmarried woman, dispensing him to hold a benefice provided that he receives orders at statutory times. Avignon, 28 Sept. 1326.[64]

427 Note of licence to study for a year at a *studium generale* to M. John Lambok' of Nottingham, deacon, rector of Elkesley. Cawood, 6 Mar. 1327.

428 [*First ordinance for the chantry founded at Sibthorpe by Thomas de Sibbethorp.*] [Fo.356v; N.F.431v] VACAT.[65] ORDINACIO SUPER CANTARIA IN ECCLESIA DE SYBTHORP. Universis [- caritatis].[66] Sane dilectus filius dominus Thomas de Sibbethorp clericus dum lucem habet volens in lucem securius ambulare, et dum per hujus vite brevis curricula in carnis sue miseriis agitatur anime sue saluti divina favente clemencia consulcius providere, quamdam capellam in honore beate Marie matris dei[67] Virginis gloriose in cimiterio ecclesie de Sibbethorp nostre diocesis eidem ecclesie ex parte boriali annexam ob devocionem quam penes eam gessit erigi fecit suis sumptibus et parari, qui terras et tenementa que inferius memorantur pro quadam cantaria in eadem capella pro salubri statu suo dum vixerit et cum subtractus fuerit ab hac luce pro anima sua et animabus infrascriptorum modo qui subsequitur perpetuis temporibus celebranda plenius adquisivit, que domino Johanni Notebroun capellano et successoribus suis capellanis ad perpetuo celebrandum in dicta capella juxta formam ordinacionis nostre infrascriptam contulit et donavit, prout de eisdem terris et tenementis tam in carta domini nostri regis quam in carta[68] dicti domini Thome et aliorum, quarum tenores ad majorem evidenciam una cum quoddam fine seu concordia inferius continentur plenius poterit apparere. Tenores ipsarum cartarum finis seu concordie tales sunt:

(1) Final concord made in the king's court at Westminster, 29 Apr. 1324, before W[illiam] de Bereford, John de Mitford, William de Herle, John le Busser and Walter de Friskeney, justices, between Thomas de Sibbethorp, clerk, plaintiff, and John son of John Campion of Hawksworth, defendant, concerning a messuage, a toft, 42½ acres of land and three of meadow in Hawksworth in a plea of covenant. John conceded the same to Thomas for 40 marks of silver.

[63] See **373**. The official of York was ordered to institute John to Elkesley on 6 Mar. 1326, and on 11 June commissaries to proceed in the cause to Hugh's deprivation. On 25 June another commission was appointed to hear John's appeal (Reg. Melton, ff.567v, 571; N.F.705v, 711).

[64] As in *CPL*, II.254.

[65] Because of the new foundation in 1335: see **798**.

[66] As in the second ordinance, printed in Thompson, *The English Clergy*, 254.

[67] MS. *die*

[68] For *cartis*?

(2) Charter of Robert son of Nicholas de Orston of Hawksworth and Letitia his wife granting Thomas de Sybthorp, clerk, his heirs and assigns, a messuage and ten acres in Hawksworth which Robert has by his father's gift. Witnesses: Simon de Sibthorp, Robert le Graunt of Hawksworth, William le Clerk of the same, Robert de Scritelinton of Sibthorpe, Geoffrey atte Lane, William son of Hugh atte Grene. n.d.

(3) Quitclaim of John son of Nicholas de Orston of Hawksworth to Thomas [etc.] of his right in the messuage and ten acres which Thomas has by the gift of Robert, John's brother, which his father gave John by his charter. Witnesses [as above, adding William son of Geoffrey de Sibthorpe and Thomas his brother; with variations, Robert de *Scridington*, William atte Grene *of Sibthorpe*]. Sibthorp, 18 Mar. 1323.

(4) Quitclaim of Simon de Sibthorp to Thomas [etc.] of his suit to Simon's court at Hawksworth every three weeks for the lands bought from John son of John le Campion and Robert le Campion of Hawksworth; also of a customary rent for them due to Simon, scutage, relief, homage and all other services from these and other lands in Sibthorpe owed by the said Thomas and William le Mareschal, notwithstanding the statute of Mortmain. Witnesses; John de Mounteneye, kt., Richard de Watton, Henry Musters, John de Skyrington, clerk, Geoffrey atte Lane of Sibthorpe. Sibthorpe, 1 Dec. 1323.

(5) Letters patent of Edward II.[69] Licence for alienation in mortmain [Fo.357; N.F.432] to his clerk, Thomas de Sibethorp, to grant two messuages, a toft, 60 acres of land and ten of meadow in Hawksworth and Aslockton (*Aslokton*) to a chaplain celebrating for Thomas and his soul after death, and the souls of his parents, brothers, sisters, ancestors and heirs, and of Simon de Sibthorp and his sons William and Reginald, Geoffrey le Clerk, his wife Alice, and all the faithful departed, in a chapel Thomas has built in honour of Saints Mary, John the Baptist and Thomas the Martyr at the north end of St. Peter's church, Sibthorpe; also to grant the reversion of a messuage, twelve acres of land and three of meadow in Sibthorpe and Syerston held (by grant of Thomas) by Thomas son of Geoffrey le Clerk of Sibthorpe for his life. Cippenham, 23 Oct. 1325.

(6) Charter of Thomas de Sibthorp, clerk, founder of [the above] chapel, in devotion to Saints Mary, John and Thomas, and for the safety of his soul and the souls of his parents William and Maud, his brothers [etc. as in (5), adding John de Sibthorp, clerk], granting by royal licence to John Notebroun, chaplain, keeper of the altar of St. Mary and of the chantry in the said chapel, two messuages [etc. as in (5) above], for the perpetual support of John and his successors celebrating daily at this altar according to ordinances to be made by William, archbishop of York; grant also of books, ornaments and lights for the masses, with houses, tofts, gardens, rents, services, etc. of tenants, and of [the above] reversion. Witnesses: M. Henry de Clif', William de Clif', Thomas de Bamburgh, Simon de Sibthorp, Robert de Skridelington, Robert le Graunt, John de Cougham, William de Orston of Hawksworth, his sons John and Robert, William son of Geoffrey le Clerk, Geoffrey atte Lane of Sibthorpe. London, 1 Nov. 1325.

The archbishop considers that Thomas's purpose will encourage popular devotion and relieve souls. An inquest has valued the chantry's endowment. He

[69] As in *CPR 1324–7*, 182.

has received submissions to accept his decree for the chantry or chantries to be founded; quoting letters patent of Thomas de Sibthorp, rector of Beckingham (dioc. Lincoln), dated London, 1 May 1326; William de Aslacby, rector [Fo.357v; N.F.432v] of Sibthorpe, which was also sealed with the seal of office of Hugh, vicar of Rolleston (*Roldeston*), dean of Newark, at Newark, 3 May 1326; and John Notebroun, chaplain, dated Newark, 1 May 1326.

Decree that there shall be a chantry at the altar of St. Mary in the said chapel. Its chaplain shall be presented by Thomas and, after his death, by the chapter of Southwell, to the archbishop, his successors or keepers of the spirituality, and instituted within fifteen days of a vacancy; or else presented by the prior and convent of Thurgarton within the same time, or otherwise by the archbishop [etc.], saving the rights of patrons at subsequent vacancies.

At his institution, the chaplain shall swear to carry out his office in accordance with the following ordinances, and not to prejudice the revenues and rights of Sibthorpe church. If he refuses to take the oath, he will lose his presentation and another chaplain willing to take it be presented. The archbishop [etc.] shall remove an unworthy chaplain admitted, without legal process (*sine strepitu judiciali*), and admit another who is suitable. If a chaplain becomes incapable by age or bodily infirmity, he shall employ a chaplain as coadjutor at his own cost within two months; otherwise the archbishop [etc.] shall do so at the cantarist's expense, for which the coadjutor may distrain him after fifteen days, if he is unpaid. John [Notebroun] is named keeper of the chantry.[70]

Every keeper shall daily say mattins, vespers and other hours, in the church with or without its rector or parish priest, as they choose. Keepers shall have free access to the chapel and a key to its door. They shall daily celebrate mass at its altar, *viz.* on Sundays, of the day; on Saturdays, of Our Lady; and on double feasts as appropriate; and on weekdays, for the dead; with a collect for the welfare of Thomas, the king, Hugh le Despenser, junior, and Robert de Bardelby, while they live, and afterwards for their souls, and for the souls of the archbishop, Thomas's parents [etc. as in (5)]. On high days, mass may not be said or sung before the offertory at the parochial high mass, save by licence of the rector or parish chaplain.

Keepers shall take care of houses, the chalice, books, ornaments and other things assigned by Thomas, leaving all in good condition to their successors. Rectors or keepers shall not alienate any lands or [the above] goods.

[Fo.358; N.F.433] Thomas granted John [Notebroun], to engage another chaplain perpetually celebrating daily at the said altar, three messuages, three bovates and 50 acres of land, twenty of meadow and 10s. rent in Sibthorpe, Syerston, Elston, Aslackton and Thoroton, as in the following evidences:

(7) Final concord made in the king's court at Westminster, 12 Nov. 1325, before William de Bereford, John de Mitford, William de Herle, John de Stonore and John de Bousser, justices, between Thomas de Sybthorp, clerk, plaintiff, and William son of Geoffrey le Clerc of Sibthorpe, his brothers Henry and Thomas, Hugh son of John Alisaundre of Sibthorpe and Marjory his wife, defendants, concerning two messuages, three bovates and twelve acres of land,

[70] His letters of institution were also dated at Westminster, 26 May 1326 (Reg. Melton, fo.571; N.F.711).

fifteen of meadow and 3s. rent in Sibthorpe, Syerston and Aslockton, in a plea of covenant. They conceded the same to Thomas for £20.

(8) Charter of Simon de Sybthorp granting Thomas his meadow in *Le Bradmere* in Sibthorpe and half a bovate of land, except for the meadow of that bovate in Sibthorpe which [Simon] recently bought from Geoffrey son of William de Staunton and is called *Le Mille land*. Witnesses: William de Ayremynne, William de Everdon and Thomas de Banburgh, clerks, Benedict de Normanton, Robert de Kelm, Robert de Scritelington, Thomas son of Geoffrey de Sybthorp. York, 28 June 1323.

(9) Letters patent of Edward II.[71] Licence for alienation in mortmain to his clerk, Thomas de Sybthorp, to grant three messuages, three bovates [etc. as in (7) above] to John Notebroun and his successors celebrating [as in (5), adding William, Henry, Thomas and Marjory, children of Geoffrey and Alice le Clerc]. Cippenham, 23 Oct. 1325.

(10) Indented charter of Thomas [etc. as in (6), with commemorated persons as in (5) and (9) above] granting three messuages [etc. as in (7) above] to John Notebroune, keeper of the chantry, in order to provide food and clothing for another chaplain celebrating at the altar in accordance with the archbishop's ordinances. After obtaining seisin, John is to grant the property to Thomas for his life; it shall revert to the chantry after his death. Sealed by both [Thomas and John]. Witnesses [as in (6) adding Hugh de Bardelby]. Sibthorpe, 8 Mar. 1326.

(11) Letters patent of Edward II[72] confirming Thomas's grants to John Notebroune of five messuages, a toft, three bovates and 100 acres of land, 30 of meadow and 30s. rent in Sibthorpe, Hawksworth, Syerston, Elston, Aslackton and Thoroton. [Fo.358v; N.F.433v] Westminster, 28 Nov. 1325

[Repetition of the provision of life interest to Thomas, as in (10) above]. Following reversion to the keeper, he will engage a chaplain celebrating daily at [St. Mary's] altar or at that of Saints Nicholas and Catherine in [Sibthorpe] church.

[The archbishop] ordains that within fifteen days of the reversion, a suitable chaplain of Sibthorpe parish, or one born there, to be named the second chaplain of the chantry, shall be nominated by the rector of Sibthorpe for admission by the archbishop or keepers of the spirituality, when he will take an oath like the keeper's. Later secondary chaplains will be similarly appointed, the archbishop [etc.] nominating if the rector is negligent. On his admission, he shall be accepted as a colleague by the keeper, and live with him and have food and drink, and 33s. 4d. *p.a.* at Whitsun and Martinmas for clothing and necessary expenses.

The secondary shall say mattins and other hours with the keeper and celebrate mass of the day on Sundays, of the Transubstantiation of Corpus Christi on Thursdays and of the dead on other days, save on double feasts as then appropriate, always making special mention of Thomas and the named souls.

[71] As in *CPR 1324–7*, 182, save that the licence is there said to be also granted to William le Mareschal of Sibthorpe.

[72] As in ibid., 196.

The secondary shall obey the keeper's lawful commands. The archbishop [etc.] may remove and replace unsuitable and useless secondaries without process. Neither keeper or secondary shall alienate the chantry's belongings. Every keeper of the chantry shall leave to his successor six oxen or four horses for ploughing.

Reservation to the archbishop to amend this ordinance at will, with Thomas's consent, without opposition from John or other keepers. Their and the secondaries' consciences are charged to obey all the foregoing. Four copies have been made and sealed, to remain with keepers of the chantry, the chapter of Southwell, the prior and convent [of Thurgarton] and the archbishop. Westminster, 26 May 1326.

429 [*Order to Shelford priory to admit John de Foxoles, sometime prior of Newburgh, enjoining penances.*[73]]

PRIORI ET CONVENTUI DE SHELFORD QUOD ADMITTANT FRATREM JOHANNEM DE FOXOLES NUPER PRIOREM DE NOVOBURGO. Willelmus etc. dilectis filiis . . priori et conventui monasterii de Shelford nostre diocesis salutem [*etc.*]. Quia plerumque visum est quod loci et societatis mutacio mores mutat hominum ac conditiones, ex hac et aliis de causis legitimis fratrem Johannem de Foxoles dudum domus de Novoburgo ordinis vestri dicte nostre diocesis priorem ad vos et domum vestram predictam inibi inter vos moraturum[74] dicte domus de Novoburgo sumptibus et expensis, quos pro primo anno ad octo marcas sterlingorum secundum vero ad novem et tercio et sic deinceps ad x marcas dumtamen bene et honeste sicut decet se habuerit pro omnibus suis necessariis taxamus,[75] et[76] secundum ordinis vestri disciplinam et observancias regulares duximus transmittendum, penitenciam infrascriptam inter cetera eidem injungentes: videlicet quod septa monasterii vestri non exeat seu litteras emittat vel recipiat, nisi in prioris seu custodis ordinis vestri presencia; et quod singulis sextis feriis ab esu piscium et quartis feriis ab esu [. . .?] se abstineat, et eisdem sextis feriis pane[77] et debili servicia omnino sit contentus, et eisdem sextis feriis unum a manibus vestris, vos prior, recipiat disciplinam humiliter et devote, sequaturque conventum continue nisi impedimento honesto fuerit prepeditus. Quocirca vobis in virtute sancte obediencie firmiter injungendo mandamus quatenus prefatum fratrem Johannem inter vos modo premisso benigne admittatis, ipsum regulari ac fraternali affectione in sinu caritatis debite pertractantes, eundemque ad dictam penitenciam peragendam secundum regule vestre disciplinam donec in hac parte aliud juxta ipsius gesta duxerimus ordinandum vice nostra debite cohercentes. Et nos de omni eo quod feceritis in premissis et qualiter prefatus frater Johannes prefatam penitenciam subierit et peregerit

[73] He resigned, with a bad record, in 1318 (*Reg. Melton,* II.7, 16–17, 23–5, 43–7, nos. 19, 36, 50, 86).

[74] Interlined.

[75] The following clause in the lower margin was possibly to be inserted here: 'Ita quod vos pro esculentis et poculentis et aliis ejusdem necessariis minutis recipiatis annuatim quinque marcas dumtaxat, et residuum dicto fratri Johanni per vos priorem pro aliis necessariis suis vicissim liberetur prout videritis expedire'

[76] Interlined.

[77] MS. *pano*

reddere tempore oportuno curetis debite cerciores distincte et aperte per vestras patentes litteras harum seriem continentes. Valete. [Bishopthorpe, 19 July 1327.]

430 [*John de Heriz, lord of Gonalston, (in a witnessed letter dated 7 Oct. 1326) informs the archbishop of his undertaking to present masters of Broadbusk hospital*[78] *for institution, with regulations for a chantry of three chaplains, including the master, who will appoint the chaplains after John's death; with the master's and a brother's assent (8 Oct.) and the archbishop's approval (9 Oct.).*]

[Fo.359; N.F.434] ORDINACIO PERPETUE CANTARIE HOSPITALIS BEATE MARIE MAGDALENE DE BRADEBUSK'. Venerabili in Christo patri domino Willelmo dei gracia Ebor' archiepiscopo Anglie primati suus Johannes de Heriz filius domini Johannis de Heriz dominus de Gonalston' ac patronus hospitalis de Bradbusk' salutem in domino. Quia magistri hospitalis beate Marie Magdalene de Bradbusk' per me nec per antecessores meos ad archiepiscopum Ebor' loci diocesanum hucusque non fuerant presentati nec per ipsum admissi nec instituti, volo et concedo quantum in me est et ad me pertinet pro me heredibus meis et successoribus universis quod ipse nunc magister et alii magistri perpetuo successuri per me et successores meos ad loci diocesanum tanquam magistri presententur et per ipsum [archi]episcopum qui pro tempore fuerit sede plena et ipsa vacante per decanum et capitulum ecclesie Ebor' sint admissi ad custodiam dicti hospitalis sancte Marie Magdalene de Bradbusk' [et] canonice instituti, et post mortem magistri qui nunc est et successorum suorum seu ad quamlibet vacacionem cessionem seu resignacionem eorundem successores sui magistri in ordine sacerdotali constituti ad loci archiepiscopum et successores suos per me et dominos manerii de Gonaldeston post mortem meam modo consimili imperpetuum presententur et a dicto archiepiscopo et successoribus suis ac decano et capitulo distinctis temporibus de quibus premittitur in forma predicta admittantur et instituantur. Et si ego vel domini manerii predicti de Gonaldeston post mortem meam infra mensem postquam dictam custodiam quocienscumque ex quacumque causa imperpetuum vacare contigerit in forma predicta non presentavero vel non presentaverint, volo et concedo pro me heredibus et successoribus meis universis quod archiepiscopus Ebor' qui pro tempore fuerit illam custodiam conferat capellano idoneo jure suo, salvo tamen mihi et dominis manerii de Gonaldeston et heredibus suis ad dictam custodiam quatenus ad eos pertinet cum alia vice vacaverit pleno jure ut premittitur presentandi. Eodem vero modo conservetur forma presentandi seu conferendi custodiam predictam imperpetuum quocienscumque et quamcumque ipsam vicariam[79] vacare contigerit quovis modo. Adhuc volo et concedo quod magister qui nunc est et successores sui universi antequam sint per vos ad custodiam dicti hospitalis admissi et in eadem instituti, coram vobis sint juramento seu sacramento astricti quod ordinaciones et constituciones subscriptas tempore Roberti de Gayteford quondam dicti[80] hospitalis magistri defuncti ordinatas et factas observabunt imperpetuum.

In primis volo et concedo quantum in me est et ad me pertinet pro me heredibus et successoribus universis quod magister qui pro tempore fuerit post mortem meam et successores sui eligant sibi unum vel duos capellanos in

[78] Its site is now Spital Farm (*EPNS Notts.*, 166). See also *VCH Nottingham*, II.166.
[79] *Sic*. Gonalston church was a rectory (see **169**).
[80] Interlined.

confratres divina celebrantes in ecclesia de Gonaldeston et in capella de Bradebusk' vel loco competenti pro anima mea et animabus antecessorum et successorum meorum imperpetuum, ita quod magister qui pro tempore fuerit sit tercius celebrans capellanus; set si unus eorum qui fuerit perpetuus[81] egritudinis langore fuerit impeditus quod non poterit celebrare divina, non teneatur ipso vivente magister antedictus capellanum alium perpetuum admittere nec pro tempore ad celebrandum conducere. Et cum in dicta domo hospitalis de Bradebusk' tres capellani fuerint admissi, sumptibus dicte domus vivant in communi. Volo et concedo quod magister et socii sui et eorum successores imperpetuum quando ad dictum hospitale admissi fuerint de bonis et catallis dicte domus inter se fidelem faciant indenturam, cujus indenture pars una penes magistrum et altera penes socios suos in salva custodia remaneant, et quod idem magister semel vel bis in anno de bonis dicti hospitalis sociis suis oretenus vel in scriptis compotum reddere teneatur. Volo et concedo quod magister dicti hospitalis nulla faciat convivia nec convocaciones amicorum nec vendiciones magnas bonorum dicti hospitalis nisi ex consensu socii vel sociorum pariter et assensu. Cohabitacio mulierum sit eis omnino interdicta in illo hospitali. Volo et concedo quod sigillum dicti hospitalis commune sub clavibus singulorum magistri socii vel sociorum suorum custodiatur et servetur. Volo et concedo quod magister et socii sui aliquas terras et tenementa alicui dandi alienandi vendendi aut corrodia seu pensiones in oneracionem dicte domus concedendi nullam decetero habeant potestatem. Liceat tamen magistro et confratribus suis pro domus neccessariis ut in victualibus et com[m]odacionibus per suum sigillum commune securitates facere et contractus componere, ita quod iidem contractus sint moderati secundum quod domus mobilia habita sustentacione ejusdem poterint sufficere. Item volo et concedo quod nullus capellanus ibidem perpetuo admittatur nisi ille qui admittendus est in dicto hospitali moram fecerit per annum per quam ejus conversacio melius experiri poterit.

Item ad hec volo et concedo pro me et expresse inhibeo heredibus et successoribus meis universis ne liceat michi vel ipsis seu alicui eorum aliquid de bonis et catallis ejusdem hospitalis neque pro magistro vel fratre ibidem presentando sive statuendo vel eciam in tempore vacacionis magistri vel aliqua alia de causa seu alio aliquo tempore capere dilapidare vel extorquere, nec eosdem magistros vel fratres ad compotum bonorum dicti hospitalis in aliquo tempore reddendum compellere nec in curiis nostris fatigare nec dictum hospitale aliqua persona ecclesiastica vel laica pro victu seu vestitu exceptis magistro et duobus sociis suis decetero onerare. Item volo et ordino quantum in me est et ad me pertinet in hoc casu quod nec dictus magister qui pro tempore fuerit nec aliquis fratrum ejusdem a tempore quo habuerunt factum dicte domus pro sua mora perpetua inibi facienda ab eadem initi quomodolibet amoveantur, nisi ex talibus causis pro quibus rectores ecclesiarum et perpetui vicarii de suis beneficiis de jure fuerint amovendi. In cujus rei testimonium presentibus sigillum meum est appensum. Datum apud Gonaldeston die Martis proximo ante festum sancti Wilfridi episcopi anno domini MCCCXXVI. Hiis testibus: Ricardo de Watton, Thoma de Goushull, Johanne Bret, militibus, Sampsone de Strellei, Roberto de Couland, Alexandro de Gonaldeston, Nicholao de Wynfeld tunc ballivo de Gonaldeston, et aliis.

[81] Interlined over *perpetuis*, cancelled.

Et nos Willelmus de Gonaldeston sacerdos magister dicti hospitalis et Thomas de Lenton in eodem hospitali frater et sacerdos omnia et singula premissa prout suprascribuntur quantum in nobis est et ad nos pertinet acceptantes et approbantes, eisdemque consensus nostros expressius adhibentes, sigillum nostrum commune hospitalis predicti presentibus duximus appendum hujus sigilli nostri communis apud Gonaldeston die Mercurii proximo ante festum sancti Wilfridi episcopi anno predicto.

Et nos Willelmus permissione divina etc. omnia et singula premissa de quibus premittitur prout supra in serie plenius continentur, omnibus debite ponderatis ac maturius recensitis, de consensu communi quorum interest auctoritate nostra pontificali ordinamus statuimus et in suo robore perpetuo permansura fore decrevimus pronunciamus ac eciam diffinimus expressius in hiis scriptis, jure jurisdictione statu privilegio ac libertatibus et dignitate nostris successorum nostrorum et ecclesie nostre Ebor' in omnibus semper salvis. In cujus rei testimonium has presentes litteras sigilli nostri impressione fecimus communiri. Datum hujusmodi communicacionis et appensionis sigilli nostri predicti apud Suwell' die Jovis proximo ante dictum festum sancti Wilfridi anno domini supradicto et pontificatus nostri decimo.

431 Institution and mandate for induction of William de Gonaldeston, chaplain, to the custody of the perpetual chantry of Broadbusk hospital, in accordance with the above ordinance; presented by John de Hers, kt. Southwell, 10 Oct. 1326.

432 Note of licence for Alan de Rothewell, rector of Sutton Bonington, to be absent for one year in the service of Lady de Segrave. Tottenham (*Totenhale*) near London, 15 Feb. 1327.[82]

433 CONDEMPCIO HENRICI DE WYNKBURN. Note that Henry de Wynkburn was appointed curator of his daughter Amicia to receive on her behalf a bequest of ten marks from the executors of the lady of Gamston; he swore on the gospels to honour this payment. Southwell, 17 Apr. 1327.

434 [*Commission to the elected penitentiary of Nottingham deanery.*]
[Fo.359ᵛ; N.F.434ᵛ] CREACIO PENITENCIARII IN DECANATU NOT'. Willelmus etc. dilecto filio domino Johanni de Muston capellano parochiali ecclesie beate Marie Notingh' nostre diocesis salutem [*etc.*]. Cum reverendus pater dominus Otto dudum sedis apostolice in Anglia legatus proinde duxerit statuendum quod per quoslibet decanatus constituantur per episcopum confessores quibus rectores vicarii et minores clerici confiteri valeant, statutum etiam synodale ecclesie nostre Ebor' precepit quod in singulis decanatibus per ipsorum capitula eligantur presbiteri moribus et sciencia prediti qui confessiones audiant sacerdotum,[83] te in capitulo decanatus Notingh' ad hoc ut accepimus alias electum de cujus consciencie puritate confidimus in ipso decanatu Notingh' nostrum preficimus penitenciarium, tibique penitenciarie officium ad audiendum con-

[82] Other letters are dated at Tottenham from 15 Jan. to 11 Feb. (Reg. Melton, ff.575–7; N.F.715–16, 719), the time of Edward II's last and Edward III's first parliament.
[83] See *Councils and Synods* II, part II, p.487 (no.11).

fessiones personarum hujusmodi de quibus premittitur ac etiam aliorum parochianorum nostrorum dicti decanatus tibi confiteri volencium, qui adeo sunt senio confracti paupertate[84] seu adversa valitudine detenti quod si in casus nobis a jure reservatos inciderint ad nos vel ad penitenciarium nostrum Ebor' vel Suwell' pro absolucione obtinenda accedere nequeunt quovismodo, eosque absolvendos necnon injungendum eisdem pro modo culparum suarum penitencias salutares etiam in casibus a jure nobis reservatis quos haberi volumus singillatim pro expressis, parcorum nostrorum fractoribus seu in eis vel eorum aliquo contra voluntatem nostram vel custodum eorundem feras vel feram capientibus ac sanctimoniales rapientibus aut cum eis carnaliter commiscentibus dumtaxat exceptis, committimus per presentes pro nostra voluntate duraturas quas in proximo capitulo inibi celebrando precipimus solempniter pupplicari. Vale. [Cawood, 10 Mar. 1327.]

435 Note of similar commissions to Elias, parish chaplain of Shelford, for Bingham deanery; Simon, parish chaplain of West Retford, for Retford deanery; and Robert de Muskham and Roger, chaplains of Newark and Hawton (*Houghton*) churches, for Newark deanery. Same date.

436 Monition to Bro. Rocelinus, vicar of Newark, not to leave without the archbishop's licence, as he is bound to personal residence by his oath and a legatine constitution. Southwell, 24 Feb. 1327.

437 Dispensation to Joan Luterel, lady of Gamston, weakened by age and infirmity, to eat any kind of vegetable and meat during Lent until she has recovered [see **433**]. Same date.

438 Commission to the archdeacon's official and the dean of Nottingham to receive the purgation of William Tusard of Bathley (*Bathelay*), clerk, on 8 May, after proclaiming in St. Mary's, Nottingham, that objectors should appear there and then; he has been accused before the king's justices of burgling the house of Robert the carpenter of Southwell, and is imprisoned in the archbishop's prison at Nottingham. Southwell, 17 Apr. 1327.

439 Note of licence to study for three years at a *studium generale* to Henry de Stanford, rector of a mediety of Gedling,[85] which he may farm. Southwell, 26 Apr. 1327.

440 Institution (in the person of his proctor Robert de Ravenfeld, clerk) and mandate for induction of M. Robert de Nova Villa, clerk, to Flintham (*Flyntham*) church; presented by the abbot and convent of Welbeck in an exchange of benefices from the canonry and prebend of Oxton and Cropwell (*Crophill*) in Southwell collegiate church with Henry de Edenestowe, the last rector. Durham, 13 May 1327.

[84] MS. *paupertatis*

[85] Instituted 14 Jan. 1326; presented by Thomas Bardolf, kt., in exchange from Clayton, Sussex, with Alexander Chaggele (Reg. Melton, fo.566^v; N.F.703^v).

441 LICENCIA PRO MAGISTRO R. DE NOVA VILLA IN FORMA CONSTITUCIONIS. Note of licence to study at a *studium generale* for one year from the date of his (above) institution. Bishopthorpe, 12 June 1327.

442 Note [interlined] of letters dimissory to the same. Bishopthorpe, 18 June 1327.

443 Note of licence to study (*in scholis*) for one year to John [de Clifton], rector of Clifton. Same date [as **441**].

444 Note [interlined] of similar licence to John for a year from the end of the last, with extra condition that he rebuilds the house of the rectory; at the instance of R. de Stanford, kt. Saxilby,[86] 22 Sept. 1327.

445 Institution (in the person of his proctor Richard de Gedelyng) and mandate for induction of M. Richard de Kirkeby, priest, to a mediety of Trowell church, vacant by the resignation of John de Trowell; presented by the prior and convent of Sempringham. Bishopthorpe, 5 July 1327.

446 Institution (in the person of his proctor Robert de Lameley, clerk) and mandate for induction of Roger de Lameley, acolyte, to Lambley church, vacant by the resignation of William de Skerington; presented by Ralph de Crumbwell, kt. St. Mary's abbey, York, 6 July 1327.

447 [*Acceptance of Cotham church by Richard le Boteler, a poor clerk provided by John XXII.*]
[Fo.360; N.F.435] ACCEPTATIO RICARDI LE BOTELER DE SANDALE DE ECCLESIA DE COTUM IN FORMA PAUPERUM. In dei nomine amen. Ego Ricardus le Boteler de Sandale Ebor' diocesis pauper clericus, cui sanctissimus in Christo pater et dominus dominus Johannes digna dei providencia pape xxii in forma qua pro pauperibus clericis beneficiandis curia Romana scribere consueverat nuper graciam concessit de beneficio ecclesiastico spectante communiter vel divisim ad collationem vel presentationem religiosorum virorum . . prioris et conventus prioratus de Thurgarton ordinis sancti Augustini dicte Ebor' diocesis, audiens et intelligens quod ecclesia de Cotum dicte Ebor' diocesis spectans ad presentationem prioris et conventus de Thurgarton predictorum vacat[87] ad presens, ipsam ecclesiam secundum vim formam et effectum litterarum apostolicarum michi in hac parte concessarum et processus per vos venerabilem in Christo patrem et dominum dominum Willelmum dei gracia Ebor' archiepiscopum Anglie primatem executorem dicte gracie mee habiti super eis si et quatenus mihi debetur existens infra mensem a tempore noticie vacacionis ecclesie antedicte accepto; protestans quod si contingat et appareat in eventum dictam ecclesiam mihi non deberi virtute gracie supradicte, extunc liceat mihi aliud beneficium ecclesiasticum ad dictorum religiosorum collationem seu presentationem spectans mihi debitum cum vacaverit acceptare et illud vi et virtute dicte gracie mee consequi cum effectu. [n.d.]

[86] MS. *Saxelby*. Saxilby, Lincs., is 6 miles from Laneham, where other letters were dated 22 Sept. (*Reg. Melton*, I.89, no.279). See also **455–6**, **460–1**.
[87] MS. *vacant*

448 [*Collation by the archbishop as executor of the provision.*]
COLLATIO FACTA EIDEM RICARDO POST HUJUSMODI ACCEPTATIONEM DE EADEM ECCLESIA DE COTUM. Willelmus etc. dilecto filio Ricardo le Boteler de Sandale pauperi clerico nostre diocesis salutem [*etc.*]. Litteras sanctissimi [*etc.*]. vera bulla plumbea et filo canapis bullata pro te nobis directas recepimus sub infrascripto tenore: Johannes episcopus servus servorum dei etc. Nos igitur de vita et conversacione tua et aliis articulis debitis inquisicione prehabita diligenti nulloque canonico obsistente quod provisionem tibi auctoritate apostolica in hac parte faciendam possit aut debeat quomodolibet impedire, ecclesiam parochialem de Cotum nostre diocesis vacantem et ad presentacionem religiosorum virorum prioris et conventus de Thurgarton ordinis sancti Augustini ejusdem nostre diocesis spectantem et per te acceptatam tibi si et quatenus vi et virtute gracie et acceptacionis predictarum tibi deberi poterit auctoritate apostolica conferimus cum suis juribus et pertinenciis universis et de ea providimus, investientes te canonice de eadem ac decernentes te fore in corporalem possessionem ejusdem ecclesie inducendum, jure cujuscumque semper salvo cui non intendimus per aliqua facta seu facienda aliqualiter prejudicare. Vale. [Bishopthorpe, 21 June 1327.]

449 [*Mandate to induct the provisor.*]
INDUCTIO EJUSDEM. Willelmus etc. executor ad infrascripta a sede apostolica specialiter deputatus dilectis filiis magistris Willelmo de Barneby canonico Suwellen' et Willelmo de Hundon rectori ecclesie de Barneburgh ac domino Johanni de Sewale perpetuo vicario ecclesie de Colston Basset salutem et mandatis nostris immo verius apostolicis firmiter obedire. Cum auctoritate apostolica nobis in hac parte commissa ecclesiam de Cotum nostre diocesis ut dicitur vacantem et ad presentationem religiosorum virorum prioris et conventus prioratus de Thurgarton dicte nostre diocesis spectantem per Ricardum le Boteler de Sandale pauperem clericum virtute cujusdam provisionis sedis apostolice sibi facte et concesse in forma pauperum coram nobis acceptatam eidem Ricardo si et quatenus sibi debeatur et non aliter virtute provisionis et gracie memorate contulerimus et eidem providerimus de eadem, ipsum de ea presencialiter investientes; vobis auctoritate qua fungimur in hac parte committimus et mandamus vobis nichilominus in virtute obediencie et sub pena excommunicationis majoris, quam vos et quemlibet vestrum incurrere volumus ipso facto si presens mandatum nostrum immo verius apostolicum neglexeritis aut aliquis vestrum neglexerit adimplere, firmiter injungentes quatinus vos vel duo aut unus vestrum quos vel quem per dictum Ricardum vel procuratorem suum super hoc requiri contigerit ad dictam ecclesiam de Cotum personaliter et sine more dispendio accedentes vel accedens, predictum Ricardum vel procuratorem suum ejus nomine in corporalem possessionem dicte ecclesie de Cotum cum suis juribus et pertinenciis universis auctoritate nostra immo verius apostolica inducatis vel inducat unus vestrum ac defendatis et defendat inductum, contradictores et rebelles quoscumque per censuras ecclesiasticas auctoritate simili compescendo. Valete. [Bishopthorpe, 21 June 1327.]

450 [*The provisor gives up his title to Cotham church.*]
RENUNCIACIO SEU RESIGNACIO JURIS DICTI RICARDI LE BOTILLER QUOAD DICTAM ECCLESIAM DE COTUM. Noverint universi quod ego Ricardus le Botiller

de Sandale omni jure si quod michi ad ecclesiam de Cotum juxta Newerk' Ebor' diocesis ad presentacionem religiosorum virorum . . prioris et conventus de Thurgarton ejusdem diocesis spectantem ratione cujuscumque gracie et provisionis de beneficio ecclesiastico quocumque ad eorundem religiosorum presentacionem pertinente in forma pauperum seu alia forma quacumque a sede apostolica qualitercumque concesse competiit seu competat quovismodo, acceptacioni per me et ex parte mea ac collationi cuicumque de eodem beneficio michi factis, gracie etiam predicte ac omni processui ejus auctoritate factis et concessis, renuncio pure sponte simpliciter et absolute et ab eis totaliter recedo. Et fateor me nullum jus habere nec aliquo tempore habuisse ad ecclesiam antedictam quovismodo. In cujus rei testimonium sigillum decani Doncastr' presentibus appendi procuravi. [Doncaster, 28 July 1327.]

451 Commission to the commissary-general of the official of York to admit, institute and induct M. Ralph de Yarewell, clerk, to Cotham church, on the presentation of the prior and convent of Thurgarton, receiving his oath of obedience. Bishopthorpe, 2 Aug. 1327.

452 Certificate of the commissary-general that he has executed this commission. York, 5 Aug. 1327.

453 Memorandum of oath of obedience sworn to the archbishop (*exhabundanti*) by M. Ralph de Yarewell. Bishopthorpe, 5 Aug. 1327.

454 Letter of the commissary-general to M. Ralph instituting him as rector of Cotham by authority of the above commission. York, 3 Aug. 1327.

455 Institution and mandate (to the archdeacon etc.) for the induction of William de Wyllesthorp, chaplain, to Beeston vicarage; presented by the subprior and convent of Lenton, the prior being in distant places. Saxilby,[88] 20 Sept. 1327.

456 Note of mandate to the sequestrator and other ministers in the archdeaconry to stay execution until further instruction of the fine of £10 imposed on the prior and convent of St. Katherine [outside Lincoln], rector of Newark. Laneham, 23 Sept. 1327.

457 [Fo.360v; N.F.435v] Mandate of John XXII requiring the archbishop to enquire whether banns were called for the marriage of William son of Geoffrey le Clerk of Sibthorpe and Alina daughter of Roger de Botelsford (dioc. York), as claimed in their petition; if so, they are to be dispensed to remain married, despite being related in the fourth degree, and their issue declared legitimate. Avignon, 14 July 1326.[89]

[88] See note to **444**.
[89] See *CPL*, II.252; also **458**, **482**.

458 [*Commission to enquire about this marriage.*]
LITTERA AD INQUIRENDUM SUPER SUGGESTIS IN DICTA BULLA. Willelmus etc. ad infrascripta judex vel executor unicus a sede apostolica deputatus discretis viris magistris Thoma de Luda thesaurario et Johanni de Sutton canonico ecclesie Linc' salutem et mandatis apostolicis firmiter obedire. Litteras apostolicas vera bulla plumbea filo canapis pendente ad modum Romane curie bullatas non cancellatas non rasas et non abolitas integras nulla sui parte corruptas seu viciatas, quas vobis transmittimus originales inspiciendas latori presencium ilico retradendas, dispensacionem super impedimento matrimonii inter Willelmum natum Galfridi le Clerc de Sibthorp laicum et Alinam Rogeri de Botelesford mulierem nostre diocesis in Linc' diocesi contracti contingentes recipimus non est diu, quarum auctoritate litterarum vobis conjunctim et divisim et cuilibet vestrum per se etiam in solidum[90] committimus et mandamus quatinus super omnibus et singulis articulis et eorum circumstanciis in dictis litteris apostolicis contentis super quibus fuerit inquirendum per viros fidedignos juratos et in forma juris receptos et examinatos hujus rei noticiam optinentes inquiratis diligencius per omnia veritatem. Et quicquid feceritis et inveneritis in hac parte una cum processu vestro nobis debite constare faciatis distincte pariter et aperte per vestras litteras patentes harum seriem continentes, quibus deposiciones testium in hac parte productorum receptorum et examinatorum in quadam cedula in scriptis plenius redactas clausas et sigillis vestris consignatas annecti volumus et mandamus. Valete. [Bishopthorpe, 8 Aug. 1327.]

459 [Exchequer] writ of Edward III (tested by W[alter] de Norwico) ordering the archbishop to certify the treasurer and barons, by 13 October, whether Marnham church, in Newark deanery, was appropriated to the prior of St. John of Jerusalem in England when Pope John XXII imposed a biennial tenth on the clergy; he is to suspend any demand to the prior for this tenth or any sequestration of his ecclesiastical goods. Westminster, 14 July 1327.

Return [undated]. The archbishop has full information on Marnham's appropriation to the former Templars 27 years ago.[91] After their dissolution, the church was occupied by many temporal lords until the Hospitallers entered by papal grant and licence of Edward II;[92] they have been in occupation for at least eight years.

460 [*Appointment of official during the vacancy of the archdeaconry.*]
CREACIO OFFICIALIS IN ARCHIDIACONATU NOT' IPSO VACANTE. Willelmus etc. dilecto filio magistro Roberto de Clareburgh curie nostre Ebor' advocato salutem [*etc.*]. De vestris fidelitate et industria plenius confidentes, vos officialem nostrum in archidiaconatu Not' ipso archidiaconatu per consecracionem discreti viri domini Johannis de Grandisono nuper archidiaconi dicti archidiaconatus in episcopum Exon'[93] vacante preficimus et creamus per presentes, dantes et concedentes vobis potestatem ipsius vacacione durante omnia et singula faciendi exercendi et expediendi que ad dictum officium pertinent seu pertinere poterunt

[90] Interlined from *conjunctim*
[91] See *CPL*, I.587 (dated 1300).
[92] See *CPL*, I.198 (dated 1320); cf. **468**.
[93] This was premature: see **470**, **477**.

de consuetudine vel de jure cum cujuslibet cohercionis canonice potestate. Omnibus et singulis subditis et parochianis nostris per dictum archidiaconatum Not' constitutis injungimus firmiter et mandamus quatenus vobis in hiis que ad dictum pertinent officium pareant ut convenit humiliter et intendant. In cujus rei testimonium litteras nostras vobis fieri fecimus has patentes. Valete. [Laneham, 24 Sept. 1327.]

Item tunc scriptum fuit magistro Johanni de la Launde rectori ecclesie de Arnale nuper officiali dicti archidiaconatus ad liberandum predicto magistro Roberto rotulos et munimenta dictum officium tangentia per indenturam ac etiam sigillum ipsius officialitatis.[94]

461 Note of licence to study for three years at a *studium generale* to M. Gilbert de Pontefracto, rector of Rempstone. [Laneham, 24 Sept. 1327.]

462 The like for one year to M. Hugh de Wylughby, rector of Willoughby on the Wolds. Bishopthorpe, 2 Oct. 1327.

463 Note of licence to M. Adam de Amundesham, rector of Barton in Fabis, to be absent for one year. Bishopthorpe, 11 Oct. 1327.

464 Note of licence to study at a *studium generale* for one year from 19 September last to Roger de Whatton, rector of Elton. Bishopthorpe, 12 Oct. 1327.

465 Commission[95] to Matthew de Halifax, keeper of the hospital of St. John the Baptist by Nottingham, and John Cosyn, vicar of St. Mary's, Nottingham, to claim and receive into safe custody clerks charged before the king's justices of gaol delivery and imprisoned at Nottingham. Bishopthorpe, 16 Oct. 1327.

Memorandum quod ista commissio est duplicata ita quod una remaneat penes unum eorum et alia penes alium de precepto domini.

466 Institution and mandate for induction (to the official of the vacant archdeaconry) of William de Gonaldeston, priest, to Kneeton church, vacant by the death of John de Clatford; presented by the abbot and convent of Newbo. Bishopthorpe, 19 Oct. 1327.

467 The like of William de Lameley, acolyte, to Cromwell church, vacant by the death of Robert de Swyligton; presented by Ralph de Crumbwell, kt. Bishopthorpe, 23 Oct. 1327.

468 [N.F.436] Report[96] of the commissary-general of the official of York, quoting a mandate of the archbishop (dated in his inn by Westminster, 9 Nov. 1325) to execute a writ of Edward II (tested by R[oger] Beler at Westminster, 6 Nov. 1325) about the appropriation of Marnham church to the

[94] This note was interlined.
[95] The formula varies from **92** in the final clause, adding after *receperitis* 'seu alter vestrum receperit sub salva servatis seu salvet alter vestrum custodia donec . . .'
[96] Apparently the original; facing fo.360ᵛ it measures 23 cms. wide by 11 cms.

Hospitallers [similar to **459**, requiring return by 14 Jan. 1326]. An enquiry found that the church was appropriated to the Templars 26 years ago [etc., as in **459**]. York, 4 Jan. 1326.

[dorse] A much corrected draft of the archbishop's return to the Exchequer, similar to **459**, adding that he has suspended proceedings against the prior and his brothers and released his sequestration, as required by the writ.[97]

469 [*Copy of process in the court of the verge (of the king's household) on 17 Oct. 1327 against Robert le Serjeaunt of Wilford and Richard de Wygemor, whom Robert as approver accused (on 8 Oct.) of robbery at Adbolton on 5 Oct.; also against Walter de Webbeley*[98] and Richard le Bakere of Stratford (Essex) *charged with highway robbery at 'Morkel' bridge (between Newark and Farndon)*[99] *on 7 Oct. All were delivered as clerks to the archbishop's commissary.*]

[N.F.437[1]] Saluz. Je vous envoy le record et le proces tochaunz Robert le Serjaunt de Wilford appellour Richard de Wygemor Wautier de Webbeley et Richard le Bakere de Stratford, qe furent chalangez et demandez come clers par Matheu de Halifex ordinar' devant le seneschal et mareschaux le roi et a ly liverez come ateynz.

Robert le Serjaunt de Wilford captus apud Adbolton in presencia domini regis et infra virgam etc. et per constabularium ejusdem ville prisone mareschalli domini regis ductus et ibidem liberatus pro quodam roberia facta in dicta villa de Adbolton in presencia domini regis etc., qui quidem Robertus juratus et examinatus coram Simone Croyser coronatore hospicii dicti domini regis die Jovis proximo post octabas sancti Michaelis anno regni regis Edwardi nunc primo, quo die idem Robertus liberatus fuit prisone predicte, devenit probator. Et appellavit Ricardum de Wygemor de eo quod ipsi adinvicem simul cum aliis latronibus die Lune proximo post festum sancti Michaelis anno supradicto felonice noctanter depredaverunt quemdam Ricardum Anketyn de Adbolton de bonis et catallis suis, videlicet de pannis lineis et laneis tapetis et lintheamentis et aliis bonis et catallis suis ad valenciam xx solidorum, in presencia domini regis etc., unde quilibet eorum habuit partem etc. Et predictus Ricardus de Wygemor per appellum predictum captus per mareschallum etc. et dicte prisone mareschalli liberatus etc.

Et predictus Robertus le Serjaunt probator simul cum predicto Ricardo in custode mareschalli venit coram senescallo et mareschallis hospicii domini regis etc. et in curia etc., videlicet die Sabbati proximo ante festum sancti Luce Ewangeliste anno supradicto. Et predictus Robertus requisitus si appellum suum predictum versus predictum Ricardum prosseciturus voluerit necne, dicit quod clericus est et membrum sancte ecclesie etc. et quod non tenetur[2] respondere sine ordinario etc. Et super hoc venit quidam Matheus de Halifex custos hospitalis sancti Johannis Baptiste juxta Notingham et profert litteras domini W. archiepiscopi Ebor' in hec verba: Willelmus permissione divina etc.[3]

97 See *Calendar of Memoranda Rolls, 1326–1327* (H.M.S.O., 1969), 153 (no.966).
98 See **488** for his purgation.
99 Now Devon Bridge (*EPNS Notts.*, 214).
1 This membrane interleaved facing fo.360v is 24 cms. wide and 30 deep. The writing is a law-court hand, different from the scripts of the register.
2 MS. *teneatur*
3 See **356**, **465**.

Pretextu cujus littere predictus Robertus per predictum Matheum ordinarium in plena curia examinatus et tanquam clericum per eundem ordinarium ibidem extitit calumpniatus. Et sic predictus Robertus in curia predicta quasi convictus per recognicionem suam coram predicto coronatore factam etc. et prout in appello predicto plenius est expressatum etc. eidem ordinario secundum legem et consuetudinem regni etc. deliberatus fuit etc. ad salvo et secure custodiendum etc. sub pena etc.

Et predictus Ricardus ad sectam domini regis allocutus qualiter de roberia predicta unde appellatus est se velit acquietare etc., dicit quod clericus est et membrum sancte ecclesie etc. et quod non tenetur respondere sine ordinario etc. Et ut sciatur pro quali deliberari debeat etc., venit inde inquisicio etc. ibidem in curia etc. Juratores dicunt super sacramentum suum quod predictus Ricardus culpabilis est de roberia predicta. Idcirco consideratum est quod predictus Ricardus liberetur predicto ordinario prisone predicti archiepiscopi liberandus ad salvo et secure custodiendum etc. sub pena etc.

Walterus de Webbeley et Ricardus le Bakere de Stratford in comitatu Essex venerunt in custodia mareschalli in curia domini regis coram senescallo et mareschallis etc. hic ad hunc diem etc., videlicet die Sabbati proximo ante festum sancti Luce Ewangeliste anno regni regis Edwardi nunc primo. Et allocuti de eo quod indictati sunt coram predictis senescallo et mareschallis, quod die Mercurii proximo post octabas sancti Michaelis anno supradicto tenuerunt passum apud Morkelbrigg' in regia via inter Newerk et Farndon simul cum quodam Willelmo in the Hale et ibidem felonice depredaverunt quemdam Willelmum Hugh de Geynesburgh de v solidis in denariis numeratis et alios mercatores extraneos de bonis et catallis suis, videlicet de pannis lineis et laneis et aliis bonis et catallis ad valenciam xx solidorum etc. in presencia domini regis et infra virgam etc.

Et predicti Walterus et Ricardus ad sectam domini regis ibidem requisiti qualiter de predictis feloniis et roberiis se velint acquietare, dicunt quod ipsi sunt clerici et membra sancte ecclesie et quod non tenentur respondere sine ordinario etc. Et ut sciatur pro quibus deliberari debeant, venit inde inquisicio etc. ad sectam domini regis etc. de visnetu de Morkelbrig' etc. Juratores dicunt super sacramentum suum quod predicti Walterus et Ricardus culpabiles sunt de feloniis et roberiis predictis. Idcirco consideratum est quod predicti Walterus et Ricardus liberentur predicto ordinario prisone predicti archiepiscopi liberandi ad salvo et secure custodiendum etc. sub pena etc.

470 [*Order to return the seal and receipts of the archdeacon's official pending John de Grandisson's consecration as bishop of Exeter.*[4]]

[Fo.361; N.F.438] MAGISTRO ROBERTO DE CLAREBURG' OFFICIALI ARCHIDIACONATUS NOT' PER DOMINUM DEPUTATO AD LIBERANDUM SIGILLUM OFFICIALITATIS OFFICIALI ARCHIDIACONI. Willelmus etc. dilecto filio magistro Johanni de la Launde rectori ecclesie de Arnale nostre diocesis . . archidiaconi Not' officiali salutem [*etc.*]. Quia intelleximus quod magister Johannes de Grandisono dominus vester nondum est in episcopum Exon' consecratus, scribimus magistro Roberto de Clareburg quod ipse sigillum officialitatis predicti archidiaco-

[4] See **460**. It was apparently not yet known that Grandisson had been consecrated at Avignon on 18 October.

natus una cum omnibus perceptis a tempore quo idem magister Robertus dictum sigillum in sua custodia habuit, que quidem percepta ad ipsum archidiaconatum pertinent de consuetudine vel de jure, vobis liberet indilate nam sequestrum alias in hac parte interpositum fecimus relaxari; volentes ut officium officialis dicti archidiaconatus non obstantibus prius factis exercere libere valeatis. Adhuc volumus quod de hiis que ad archidiaconum in ultimo synodo apud Suwell' celebrata pertinere poterunt cum receptore nostro Ebor' plenarie computetis, et quod justum fuerit recipiatis ad usum vestri domini de eisdem. Valete. [Bishopthorpe, 4 Nov. 1327.]

Memorandum quod eisdem die et loco scriptum fuit prefato magistro Roberto de Clar' ad liberandum dicto magistro J. sigillum officialitatis in forma predicta.

471 Mandate to M. William de Hundon, rector of Barnburgh, and Thomas de Radeclif, bailiff of Southwell, to receive from Matthew de Halifax, keeper of the hospital of St. John the Baptist by Nottingham, and John [Cosyn], vicar of St. Mary's, Nottingham, the clerks delivered to either or both of them by the king's justices and imprisoned at Nottingham. They will receive them at Doncaster, if it can be done safely by land, otherwise at Newark, and sent thence by water to York, as swiftly, secretly and securely as can be done. They are to report their expected arrival at Doncaster or York to the archbishop so that arrangements can be made. William de Hokerton, receiver at Southwell, has been ordered to pay their expenses. Cawood, 8 Nov. 1327.

472 Order to William de Hokerton, receiver at Southwell, to pay John Cosyn, vicar of St. Mary's, Nottingham, the bearer, 27s. 9d. for his expenses with the delivery and custody of clerks imprisoned at Nottingham. Also to pay William de Hundon and Thomas de Radeclyf their expenses in conducting the clerks to York by water or to Doncaster by land, at their discretion. He is to show these letters and indentures with John, William and Thomas when making his account. Same date.

473 [Cancelled] mandate to M. Robert de Clareburgh, sequestrator in the archdeaconry[5], to deliver the sequestration of John de Kirkebrid's goods to M. Henry de Clif, canon of York [see **475**]. Cawood, 10 Nov. 1327.

474 Commission to the prior of Holy Trinity, York, Walter de Yarewell, canon of York, and M. Thomas de Nevill, D.C.L., rector of Gisburn (*Gysburn*), or two of them, to hear and determine the cause begun before the official of York and his commissary-general (or one of them) between the abbot and convent of Selby, plaintiffs, and Robert de Sutton, rector of Averham (*Ergum*), concerning an annual pension of 40s. and arrears claimed from the rector and Averham church. Cawood, 13 Nov. 1327.

[5] His commission was dated at Scrooby, 25 Sept. 1326; it is like **297** as amended (Reg. Melton, fo.574; N.F.714).

475 [*Citation of creditors of John de Kirkebrid, kt., deceased.*]
Willelmus etc. dilecto filio magistro Roberto de Clareburgh sequestratori nostro in archidiaconatu Not' salutem [*etc.*]. Volumus quatinus recepta de magistro Henrico de Clif ' canonico ecclesie nostre beati Petri Ebor' vera estimacione bonorum que fuerant domini Johannis de Kirkebrid militis nuper defuncti tempore mortis sue, faciatis proclamare per fora et ecclesias prout de jure fuerit facienda quod si qui sint creditores quibus dictus Johannes dum vixerat tenebatur coram vobis certis die et loco seu certis diebus et locis prout justum fuerit compareant, acciones quas adversus dictum defunctum ejusdemve testamenti executores aut bonorum suorum administratores quoscumque sibi pretendunt competere in forma juris ostensuri easque et debita sua probaturi, facturi et recepturi quod in hac parte convenerit canonicis institutis et justicia suadebit; proviso quod illis creditoribus dicti defuncti qui sua debita de quibus premittitur legitime probaverint, habita ratione ad legem falcidiam de dictis bonis satisfacere curetis in forma juris, recipientes acquietancias sufficientes de creditoribus antedictis quibus aliquas pecunie summas occasione premissa solvere vos continget. Et quid in premissis feceritis nos per vestras litteras patentes harum seriem continentes distincte et aperte ac debite tempore oportuno curetis reddere certiores. Valete. [Cawood, 22 Nov. 1327.]

476 Appointment of M. Robert de Clareburgh as official in the archdeaconry during its vacancy.[6] Bishopthorpe, 15 Dec. 1327.

477 LITTERA OFFICIALI ARCHIDIACONI NOT' AD LIBERANDUM OFFICIALI DOMINI SIGILLUM PERQUISITA ET MEMORANDA OFFICIALITATIS.[7] Mandate to M. John de la Launde, rector of Arnold. As John de Grandisson was consecrated bishop of Exeter on 18 October, he is to deliver to M. Robert de Clareburgh, on the archbishop's behalf, all the receipts and revenues of the archdeaconry since that date, together with its seal, rolls and memoranda. Same date.

478 Licence during pleasure for Lady Marjory de Bevercotes to hear divine service in an oratory in Bevercotes manor, provided the parish church suffers no injury. Southwell, 15 Nov. 1329.

479 [*Assessors of a lay subsidy are urged to exempt Broadbusk hospital as an ecclesiastical benefice.*]
[Fo.361^{v}; N.F.438^{v}] TAXATORIBUS VICESIMI DENARII BONORUM TEMPORALIUM IN COMITATU NOT' DOMINO REGI CONCESSI NE TAXENT INTER TEMPORALIA CAPELLAM SEU HOSPITALE DE BRADEBUSK'. Willelmus permissione etc. taxatoribus vel subtaxatoribus xx denarii bonorum temporalium domino regi concessi[8] in comitatu Not' salutem [*etc.*]. Ad nostrum jam deduxit auditum relatio fidedigna quod licet capella seu hospitale de Bradbusk' in dicto comitatu sit beneficium ecclesiasticum merito reputandum vel saltem sacer locus et religio-

[6] Identical to **460**; and see **470**.
[7] There is a semi-circular hole in the right-hand margin, 10 cms. deep and 3.5 cms. wide at its centre. This heading is written in the body of the text.
[8] Interlined from *bonorum*

sus deo dedicatus, in quo magister seu custos existit nostra auctoritate pontificali canonice institutus,[9] tanquam in re spirituali cui quecumque bona annexa ecclesiastico debent privilegio gaudere et eidem juri censeri, videlicet ne inter bona laica taxantur cum de jure a laicis exactionibus sint exempta; vos tamen vel saltem aliquis vestrum ut accepimus intromisistis seu intromisit inter alia bona laica manus vestras ad dicte capelle seu hospitalis predicti bona spiritualia vel saltem spiritualibus annexa illicite extendere et ea inter alia mere temporalia sic taxare in ecclesiastice libertatis prejudicium dicteque capelle seu hospitalis predicti ejusdemque magistri seu custodis dampnum non modicum et gravamen animarum vestrarumque grande periculum et aliorum Christi fidelium perniciosum exemplum. Quocirca devocionem vestram filialem in domino exhortamur, vos nihilominus rogantes quatinus ob reverenciam Jesu Christi et ecclesie sue sancte cujus estis fideles filii reputati, et ne in promptum et presens ea occasione animarum periculum insidatis, ad taxacionem bonorum dicte capelle seu hospitalis de quibus premittitur amovere velitis si libeat manus vestras, ea in pace libera et quieta sicut extiterant singulis temporibus retrolapsis penitus dimittentes, ut digni ecclesie filii valeatis merito nuncupari et ne nos in eventu quod absit contrario pro defensione libertatis ecclesiastice necesse habeamus in vestri defectum penes majores querelam deponere graviorem et nihilominus eo pretextu contra vos prout justum fuerit per mucronis acrimoniam procedere spiritualis. Valete. [Cawood, 4 Jan. 1328.]

480 Commission to the official of York, his commissary-general and Richard de Grymston, precentor of St. John's, Beverley (or two of them). After receiving from M. Henry de Clif' (by the hands of the sequestrator) an estimate in an inventory of the goods of John de Kyrkebride, kt., who died intestate, they are to proclaim that his creditors [as in **475**[10]]. Cawood, 3 Jan. 1328.

481 Institution and mandate for induction (to the dean of Retford) of Gilbert de Blida, chaplain, to Gringley on the Hill (*Gryngeley*) vicarage; presented by the prior and convent of Worksop. Cawood, 13 Jan. 1328.

482 Dispensation to William le Clerk and Alina de Botelsford in accordance with papal letters [i.e. **457**, but fully repeated here]; an enquiry found that banns were called. Bishopthorpe, 27 Jan. 1328.

Subscription by Richard de Snoweshull, clerk (dioc. Worcester), notary and the archbishop's scribe; witnessed by M. Adam de Haselbech and Richard de Melton, clerks.

483 Note of licence to study at a *studium generale* for one year from Easter to William de Aslakby, rector of Sibthorpe. Bishopthorpe, 18 Feb. 1328.

484 Institution and mandate for induction (to the official of the vacant archdeaconry) of John de Hoghton, chaplain, to a mediety of Eakring (*Aykering*) church, vacant by the death of Robert de Souchirche; presented by John de Ros, kt., the king's steward. Bishopthorpe, 21 Feb. 1328.

[9] See **430–1**.

[10] Omitting *ejusdemve testamenti executores* and *habita ratione ad legem falcidiam*, and inserting after *vos contingет* a clause giving powers to complete the business.

485 [*Letters patent announcing the purgation of the rector of Misterton from an accusation of repeated incontinence.*]
PURGACIO MAGISTRI THOME RECTORIS ECCLESIE DE MISTERTON SUPER INCONTINENCIA. Universis Christi fidelibus pateat per presentes quod cum magister Thomas de Sancto Albano rector ecclesie de Misterton nostre diocesis fuisset coram nobis Willelmo permissione divina etc. super vicio incontinencie et recidivo cum Isabella filia Walteri Berdeles de Misterton[11] parochiana sua graviter diffamatus, et personaliter citatus et ad racionem judicialiter positus proximo die juridico post festum sancti Matthie apostoli anno gracie MCCCXXVIII apud Cawode predictum vicium cum prefata Isabella a tempore correctionis sue per nos dudum facte constanter negaverit, cui purgationem suam in hac parte faciendam cum manu sua xii rectorum et vicariorum ad secundum diem juridicum proximo post festum sancti Luce Evangeliste proximo futurum ubicumque tunc fuerimus in nostra diocesi duxerimus indicendum; quo die apud Northcave personaliter comparens cum dominis Willelmo Thoma Laurencio Willelmo Radulpho Johanne et Edmundo ecclesiarum de Babworth de Fledburgh de Ordesale de Misne de Sandeby de Grove et de Rosington nostre diocesis rectoribus necnon Johanne Jacobo Thoma Roberto et Waltero ecclesiarum de Hedon de Lanum de Wheteley de Bekigham et de Walcringham ejusdem nostre diocesis vicariis canonice se purgavit, unde prefatum magistrum Thomam pristine sue fame quatenus potuimus restituimus per decretum. In cujus rei testimonium sigillum nostrum presentibus est appensum. [North Cave, 20 Oct. 1328].

486 [Fo.362; N.F.439] Licence to Richard de Wylughby, kt., and Adam Brome, clerk, royal justices, to take during Lent and Passion Week assizes arraigned by the prior of Worksop against Thomas de Furnivall, senior, concerning a free tenement and common pasture in Worksop, and against Richard le Parker and Thomas le Parker concerning common pasture in Worksop. Bishopthorpe, 5 Mar. 1328.

487 The like to the same for all assizes in the archdeaconry of Nottingham. Bishopthorpe, 12 Mar. 1328.

488 Commission to John de Wodhous, commissary-general of the official of York, Thomas de Nova Villa, D.C.L., Philip de Nassington, advocate of the court of York, and Richard de Grymeston, precentor of St. John's, Beverley (or three or two of them), to receive the purgation of Walter de Webbeley, clerk, on 18 April, after proclaiming in York Minster that objectors should appear there and then; he has been accused before the king's justices of robbing Hugh de Gaynesburgh between Newark and Farndon (*Farneburn*) and is in the archbishop's prison [see **469**]. Bishopthorpe, 25 Mar. 1328.

489 Institution[12] and mandate for induction (to the official of the vacant archdeaconry) of Thomas Cok' of Ravenser, deacon, to West Markham (*Parva*

[11] Cf.**620**.
[12] *B* in the margin indicates that this should follow **490**, which is marked with *A*.

Markham) vicarage, now vacant; presented by M. John de Arundell, keeper of Tickhill chapel [see **713**]. Bishopthorpe, 19 Mar. 1328.

490 SENTENCIA DIFFINITIVA SUPER PRIVACIONE RICARDI DE HOTON A VICARIA DE WESTMARKHAM. To the archbishop from John de Wodehous, commissary-general of the official of York, deputed to act in the cause about the vicarage of West Markham between Richard de Hareworth, claiming to have been presented, and Richard de Hoton, in possession [see **98**]. He has pronounced the vicarage to be vacant and judicially (*sentencialiter*) removed Hoton as having no right to it. York, 18 Dec. 1327.

491 Letter of Denis Avenell, archdeacon of the East Riding, to Ingram de Mathersay, priest, quoting the archbishop's commission (dated Bishopthorpe, 14 Apr. 1328) to examine Ingram's presentation to Elton church by the prior and convent of Blyth; also to enquire about his person and, if there were no canonical obstacle, institute him as rector, reserving his obedience and induction to the archbishop. The archdeacon has accordingly carried out the institution. York, 15 Apr. 1328.

492 Memorandum that Ingram took the customary oath of obedience; also that the official of the vacant archdeaconry was ordered to induct him. Cawood, 16 Apr. 1328.

493 Note [interlined] of licence to Ingram for study for two years at a *studium generale*; he paid 40s. to the receiver of York. Bishopthorpe, 28 Oct. 1329.

494 Note of licence to study (*standi in scolis*) for one year to M. Robert de Nevill, rector of Flintham, subdeacon. Cawood, 1 June 1328.

495 Notes of mandates to the prior of Bolton to receive Hugh de Notingham and the prior of Drax Robert de Ebor', both canons of Thurgarton, at its costs assessed by the archbishop at 5½ marks for food and other necessaries; also to the prior of Thurgarton to send the canons to Bolton and Drax, where they are not to leave the precincts unless accompanied by the priors. Bishopthorpe, 7 June 1328.

[Added] note that the mandate to the prior of Drax was revoked and Kirkham substituted. Bishop Wilton, 21 Aug. 1328.

496 [Fo.362v; N.F.439v] To William de Brokelesby, rector of Wilford, quoting letters of M. Thomas de Nova Villa, D.C.L., the archbishop's familiar clerk (dated Bishopthorpe, 4 June 1328), reporting execution of the archbishop's commission (quoted; dated Bishopthorpe, 3 June) to institute and induct William, a chaplain, to Wilford, provided there is no obstacle, in accordance with the report of an enquiry into his presentation (which was enclosed), reserving his obedience to the archbishop; he was presented by Gervase son of Robert de Clyfton and Margaret his wife after the resignation of the previous rector. The archbishop confirms his commissary's proceedings. Bishopthorpe, 8 June 1328.

497 Mandate to M. William de Stanes, official of the court of York, to remit by special grace the fine incurred by the prior and convent of St. Katherine outside Lincoln, as rector of their appropriated church of Newark, pronounced contumacious for not appearing on citation at the recent synod celebrated by the official at Southwell,[13] saving the rights [etc.] of the churches of York and Southwell. Ripon, 11 July 1328.

498 [*Threat to depose the prior of Shelford if he allows John de Foxholes to continue his excursions* (see **429**).]
PRIORI DE SHELFORD PRO FRATRE JOHANNE DE FOXHOLES CANONICO DE NOVO BURGO. Willelmus permissione divina etc. dilecto filio . . priori de Shelford nostre diocesis salutem [*etc.*]. Audivimus et merito conturbamur quod vos ut oberrans filius paterna monita perinpendens fratrem Johannem de Foxholes canonicum de Neuburgh dicte nostre diocesis, ad agendam[14] injunctam sibi per nos pro quibusdam suis excessibus penitenciam salubrem juxta mandatum nostrum vobis directum alias pro eodem in vestro monasterio commorari, extra septa dicti vestri monasterii pro sue temeritatis libito vagari permittitis et morari in sinistrum plebis obloquium scandalum ordinis ac nostri et regule vestre contemptum notorium et offensam, qui sub vestro laxo regimine vitam ducit ut dicitur dissolutam loca sibi suspecta utpote Linc' ubi prius deliquisse dinoscitur attrita fronte publice visitando, qui etiam nuper ad ostendendam perverse adinventionis sue nequitiam accedens ad insulam de Haxholm' . . dominum de Moubray fundatorem dicte domus de Neuburgh ad irruendum in priorem ipsius ac in subversionem domus nequiter ut potuit excitavit. Quocirca vobis in virtute sancte obediencie ac sub pena deposicionis injungimus firmiter et mandamus quatinus eundem juxta primarum nostrarum continenciam litterarum ad agendam injunctam sibi penitenciam debite compellentes, omnem sibi adimatis vagandi et discurrendi extra vestrum monasterium facultatem sicque sibi opportunitates et occasiones malignandi excludere satagatis, ut lucrum deo de ipsius anima faciatis et ut preteritam vestram negligenciam redimere valeat futura ferventis obediencie promptitudo; scientes quod si decetero in execucione premissorum negligentes fueritis vel remissi, sic vestram curabimus insolenciam urgentis ultionis acrimonia procellere quod pena vestra aliis cedet in terrorem. Valete. [Ripon, 11 July 1328.]

499 Commission to M. Robert de Bridelyngton, canon of Lincoln, steward of the archbishop's lands, to examine accounts of the obedientiaries (*officiariorum intrinsecorum*) of Thurgarton priory, enquire concerning attached articles, and act further as necessary, with powers of canonical coercion, reporting by letters patent. Ripon, 19 July 1328.

ARTICULI SUPER QUIBUS AUDIRE DOMUS COMPOTUM PREDICTUM. Articuli de quibus premittitur sunt isti videlicet.[15] In primis queratur in quo statu domus de Thurgarton fuit tempore quo prior qui nunc est constitutus fuit et prefectus. Item que debita tunc temporis imminebant in eadem. Item que imminent in

[13] A sixteenth-century hand noted, in the margin, 'Synodus Southwellen' auctoritate domini celebratus', and underlined relevant words in the text.
[14] *Sic*, as twice again below.
[15] Underlined from *Articuli de*, probably by a hand contemporary with the ms.

presenti. Item an aliquibus oneribus dicta domus temporibus prioris nunc existentis sit exonerata et relevata. Item de cellerario nunc ibidem existente Ricardo de Sibthorp et Thoma de Barkeby suis in eodem officio immediate predecessoribus, et an Ricardus de Thurgarton nunc in eodem officio existens dicte domui in officium suum contingentibus melius aut[16] de minori faciat deserviri quam Ricardus de Sibthorp et Thomas predicti pro tempore suo fecerunt. Et de hiis supervideantur compotis eorum tam in maneriis quam aliis ipsum officium qualitercumque contingentibus.

500 [N.F.440[17]] Writ of Edward III (tested by R[ichard] de Wylughbi). In an assize of mort d'ancestor at Nottingham before Wylughbi and his fellows, justices of assize in Nottinghamshire, William son of John de Oscynton sued Richard de Sutton of Walesby and Marjory his wife concerning a messuage and a bovate of land in Kirton (*Kirketon juxta Walesbi*) of the seisin of his father John. They claimed William was not John's heir but a bastard, which he denied. The archbishop is to enquire into the truth of this matter. Nottingham, 26 May 1328.
[Interleaved N.F.441 is an identical writ *de bastardia*.]

501 [Fo.363; N.F.442] Grant during pleasure to Bartholomew de Bourne, clerk, of custody of the sequestrated revenues of Farndon (*Farendon*) prebendal church, now vacant, in the church of Lincoln. Bishopthorpe, 3 Aug. 1328.
[margin] Note that Bartholomew's proctor, M. Hugh de Walmesford, took the usual oath of fealty and obedience on the same date.

502 PRESENTACIO AD PREDICTAM PREBENDAM PER LITTERAS PATENTES SUBDECANI ET CAPITULI ECCLESIE LINC'. From the subdean and chapter of Lincoln, the dean being absent, announcing that Henry [Burghersh], bishop of Lincoln, had conferred the vacant prebend of Farndon in Lincoln church and York diocese on their fellow canon, Bartholomew de Bourn,[18] and they had duly assigned him a stall in the choir and a place in the chapter. The archbishop is asked to do what is needful on his part. Lincoln, 8 Aug. 1328.

503 Commission to M. William de Alberwyk, precentor of York, and M. Robert de Bridelyngton, canon of Lincoln, to induct Bourn or his proctor to Farndon prebendal church if it is vacant and not lawfully due to another and reserved to papal collation.[19] Bishopthorpe, 11 Aug. 1328.

504 Note of licence to study for two years from 29 September to John de Sibthorp, rector of North Collingham; he may farm the church and need not personally attend synods if sufficiently represented. Same date.

505 The like for one year from 9 Aug. 1328 while at the university of Cambridge to Adam de Preston, rector of Hickling.[20] Bishopthorpe, [date omitted].

16 MS. *et*
17 Interleaved facing fo.362^{v}, a writ measuring 24 by 8 cms.
18 See *Fasti*, I.56, 65, 76; *BRUO*, I.232–3.
19 The same conditional phrase appears in **506**; and see also **540**.
20 Not traced in *BRUC*.

506 [*Commission to confer the archdeaconry of Nottingham, if its collation is not reserved, on M. Gilbert de Alberwyk.*[21]]
COLLATIO ARCHIDIACONATUS NOTINGHAM.[22] Willelmus permissione divina etc. dilecto filio magistro Willelmo de Alberwyk' ecclesie nostri beati Petri Ebor' precentori salutem [*etc.*]. De vestre circumspeccionis industria plenius confidentes, ad conferendum magistro Gilberto de Alberwyk' clerico, quem mores et merita multipliciter reddunt com[m]endabilem donaque sciencie et virtutum efferunt et exornant, archidiaconatum Notinghamie in ecclesia nostra Ebor' ad nostram collationem spectantem cum suis juribus et pertinenciis universis, si vacet et nulli alii de jure debeatur ac auctoritate sedis apostolice domini nostri pape collationi seu dispositioni nullatenus reservetur, et ad inducendum seu induci faciendum per vos alium seu alios eundem magistrum Gilbertum seu procuratorem ejus nomine suo in corporalem possessionem dicti archidiaconatus cum suis juribus de quibus premittitur et pertinenciis universis, necnon ad faciendum eidem magistro Gilberto stallum in choro et locum in capitulo . . archidiacono Not' debitis in dicta ecclesia nostra Ebor' absque juris alieni prejudicio ut convenit assignari, et ad compescendum contradictores et rebelles in hac parte, vobis vices nostras [committimus] cum cohercionis canonice potestate. Valete. [Ripon, 12 July 1328.]

507 Letter of William de Alberwyk' to Gilbert conferring the archdeaconry in accordance with the archbishop's commission (quoted) and ordering that he or his proctor be inducted and installed. Bishopthorpe, 2 Aug. 1328.

Subscription by John de Thoresby, clerk (dioc. Lincoln), notary by papal authority, present at this time and place with M. Adam de Haselbech and Richard de Melton, rectors of Lythe and Bootle (*Botill'*; dioc. York); he inspected the archbishop's letter and its pendant seal and certifies that they appeared *prima facie* in no part suspect.

508 Letter of William de Alberwyk' to the dean and chapter of York, quoting the above commission. By its authority [Fo.363^v; N.F.442^v] he has conferred the archdeaconry on Gilbert if no other has a right to it and it has not been reserved to the pope's collation, and orders them to carry out their part in this matter. Bishopthorpe, 4 Aug. 1328.

Note of subscription by John de Thoresby 'etc. as appears on another part of this folio'.

509 Institution and mandate for induction (to the archbishop's official in the vacant archdeaconry) of William de Buttercrombe, chaplain, to a mediety of Eakring church, vacant by the resignation of Henry de Sibthorp; presented by John de Ros, kt. Bishopthorpe, 16 Sept. 1328.

510 The like of John de Mekesburgh, priest, to Barton in Fabis church, vacant by the death of M. Adam de Hamundesham; presented by the subprior and convent of Lenton, the prior being abroad. Cawood, 18 Sept. 1328.

[21] See *BRUO,* I.17; and cf. **591** and continuing notices of the archdeaconry's vacancy.
[22] Supplied by a sixteenth-century hand, with a bracket for **506–8**, none of which have contemporary marginal descriptions.

511 [*Appointment of Ralph de Toto, monk of Sainte-Cathérine-du-Mont, Rouen, as prior of Blyth, on the nomination of his abbot.*[23]]
PREFECTIO FRATRIS RADULPHI DE TOTO IN PRIOREM DOMUS DE BLIDA.[24] In dei nomine amen. Nos Willemus etc. ad nominacionem et missionem religiosi viri fratris G[uillelmi] abbatis monasterii sancte Katerine juxta Rothomagum ordinis sancti Benedicti te fratrem Radulphum de Toto dicti monasterii monachum et professum, de cujus meritis et virtutibus sinceram fiduciam in domino obtinemus, in priorem prioratus de Blida nostre diocesis per mortem fratris Roberti de Clivilla ultimi prioris ejusdem vacantis prefecimus et eidem fratri Roberto substituimus in priorem dicte domus et pastorem, curam et administracionem dicti prioratus de Blida quantum ad nos attinet tibi in spiritualibus et temporalibus committentes. [n.d.]

512 [*Mandate to the monks of Blyth to obey Ralph as their prior.*]
LITTERA SUBPRIORI ET CONVENTUI DE BLIDA QUOD PAREANT ET OBEDIANT FRATRI RADULPHO DE TOTO UT PRIORI EJUSDEM DOMUS. Willelmus permissione etc. dilectis filiis . . subpriori et conventui monasterii de Blida nostre diocesis salutem [*etc.*]. Quia fratrem Radulphum de Toto monachum vestri ordinis et professum ad nominacionem et missionem religiosi viri fratris G[uillelmi] abbatis monasterii sancte Katerine juxta Rothomagum ordinis sancti Benedicti in priorem vestre domus vacantis per mortem fratris Roberti de Clivilla ultimi prioris ejusdem[25] prefecimus, curam et administracionem dicti prioratus quantum ad nos pertinet eidem fratri Radulpho in spiritualibus et temporalibus committentes, vobis omnibus et singulis in virtute sancte obediencie et sub pena districtionis canonice mandamus firmiter injungendo quatinus eundem fratrem Radulphum de Toto in priorem vestrum humiliter admittentes, eidem pareatis decetero et obediatis reverenter in omnibus que regule vestre et sancte religionis conveniunt honestati. Valete. [Bishopthorpe, 30 Sept. 1328.]

513 Mandate to the archbishop's official in the vacant archdeaconry to install Ralph as prior. Same date.

514 Letters patent appointing Ralph prior [as in **511**]. Same date.

515 [*Nomination of Ralph as prior by the abbot of Sainte-Cathérine-du-Mont, Rouen.*]
NOMINACIO ABBATIS MONASTERII SANCTE KATERINE JUXTA ROTHOMAGUM DE FRATRE RADULPHO DE TOTO IN PRIOREM DE BLIDA PREFICIENDUM.[26] Reverendo in Christo patri ac domino suo carissimo domino W[illelmo] dei gracia Ebor' archiepiscopo primati Anglie frater G. dei paciencia humilis abbas monasterii sancte Katerine juxta Rothomagum ordinis sancti Benedicti reverenciam et honorem tanto patri ac domino debitas cum prompto obsequio et humili famulatu. Cum intellex[er]imus et verum sit quod dilectus filius noster frater Robertus prior prioratus nostri de Blida vestre diocesis viam universe carnis sit ingressus et per mortem ipsius dictum prioratum vacavisse et etiam vacare;

[23] Shown as Ralf de Tête in list of priors in *Blyth Cartulary* (see **227**), I.li.
[24] *B* in the margin indicates that this entry should follow **515**.
[25] Interlined.
[26] A capital *A* in the margin indicates that this entry should precede **511**.

tandem nos, deliberacione prehabita diligenti prout potuimus cum peritis et cum majoribus de conventu nostro, per nostras litteras patentes nominavimus[27] et nominamus juxta laudum nostrum et consilium gratiosum dilectum filium nostrum fratrem Radulphum de Toto hominem bene probatum providum et honestum in temporalibus et spiritualibus circumspectum ac religiosa conversatione pollentem in priorem dicti nostri prioratus de Blida substituendum. Vestre reverende paternitati quantum possumus supplicamus humiliter et devote quatinus ad promocionem dicti negocii sine nostro et nostri monasterii ac prioratus ejusdem dispendio dignemini favorabiliter intendere, dictosque priorem et locum recommendatos habere prout vestri gracia consuevistis hucusque. Feliciter et diu valeat in domino Jesu Christo vestra reverenda paternitas que nobis precipiat quicquid placet. In cujus rei testimonium sigillum nostrum presentibus litteris duximus apponendum. Datum anno domini MCCCXXVIII decimo die Septembris.

516 [*Letter to the abbot of Sainte-Cathérine urging him, in view of Blyth's poverty, to assist its payment of a debt to Cardinal John Gaetani.*]
[Fo.364; N.F.443] LITTERA DOMINI TRANSMISSA ABBATI SANCTE KATERINE JUXTA ROTHOMAGUM UT MONASTERIO SUO DE BLIDA SUBVENIAT PENES JOHANNEM DEI GRACIA SANCTI THEODORII DIACONUM CARDINALEM. Venerande religionis viro domino abbati sancte Katerine juxta Rotomagum Willelmus permissione divina etc. salutem cum dei benedictione et gracia salvatoris. Preces nostras a vobis eo credimus liberalius exaudiri quo per eas religionis vestre decorem ac vestrorum prosequimur interesse. Convertentes igitur nostre consideracionis intuitus ad statum miserabilem monasterii de Blida nostre diocesis, quod pre multis incomodis jam a diu sibi notorie nimis novercantibus sic facultatibus quod dolenter referimus est collapsum quod vix adiciet ut resurgat, nisi divine affluencia largitatis vobis mediantibus illud gratius consoletur, devocionem vestram digne duximus deprecandum quatinus dictum monasterium corporis vestri membrum debile quodammodo et infirmum resolidare satagentes erga dominum Johannem dei gracia sancti Theodorii diaconum cardinalem pro pecunia sibi debita, prout ex litteris prioris et conventus de Blida vobis plenius liquere poterit, eisdem in tante necessitatis articulo manum gratiosi juvaminis dignemini prorogare, ne dominus vobis impropet per prophetam quod illud quod crassum est assumitis et quod erat debile abjecistis. Absit etenim quod confratres vestros et ipsorum monasterium suspensionis excommunicationis et interdicti sentenciis ligari paciamini vel involvi si per solutionem tante quantitatis pecunie eorum possetis indigencie subvenire. Crescat semper vestra religio in unigenito dei patris. [York, 12 Aug. (1328).]

517 [*Appointment by the abbot of his proctor to present the prior-designate.*]
PROCURATORIUM FRATRIS WILLELMI COUPEL AD PRESENTANDUM FRATREM RADULPHUM DE TOTO DOMINO IN PRIOREM DOMUS DE BLIDA NOMINATUM. Reverendo in Christo patri ac domino domino G[uillelmo] dei gracia archiepiscopo Ebor' primati Anglie frater Guillelmus permissione divina humilis abbas monasterii sancte Katerine de monte juxta Rothomagum salutem cum omni reverencia et honore. Noveritis quod nos dilectum filium nostrum fratrem

[27] MS. *nominaverimus*

Willelmum Coupel conmonachum nostrum latorem presencium nostrum facimus constituimus et ordinamus procuratorem et nuncium specialem ad presentandum vobis cum reverencia qua decet fratrem Radulphum de Toto conmonachum nostrum a nobis nominatum in priorem prioratus nostri de Blida vestre diocesis modo debito substituendum, et ad suppliendum et petendum et vobis et nobis que super hiis supplicandum fuerint, et petendum et ad faciendum et peragendum omnia alia et singula que circa premissa fuerint oportuna et que faceremus si presentes affuerimus, ratum habituri et gratum quicquid idem procurator in premissis duxerit faciendum, quod paternitati vestre reverende que diu et bene valeat in omnibus quorum interest presencium significamus. Datum anno domini MCCCXXVIII decimo die Septembris.

518 [*The abbot thanks the archbishop for his letters about the state of Blyth and recommends Ralph as prior-designate.*]
LITTERA CLAUSA PREDICTI ABBATIS DOMINO DIRECTA AD REGRACIANDUM SIBI ETC. Reverendo in Christo patri ac domino suo carissimo domino G[uillelmo] divina providencia Ebor' archiepiscopo primati Anglie frater G[uillelmus] permissione divina humilis abbas monasterii sancte Katerine juxta Rothomagum cum sui recommendacione devota reverenciam et honorem debitas tanto patri. Vestre paternitatis litteras recepimus facientes mencionem super statu nostri prioratus de Blida vestre diocesis, ad cujus reformacionem et consolacionem tanquam pastor sollicitus et pius pater gracia vigilare placuit et placet, ipsum gerens in visceribus caritatis, unde vestre paternitati reverende plusquam sciamus exprimere per litteras assurgimus ad graciarum uberes acciones. Ad quem siquidem prioratum et ejus regimen carissimum conmonachum et confratrem nostrum fratrem Radulphum de Toto virum religiosum providum et honestum per cujus circumspectionem et diligenciam favente deo dictus prioratus ab oppressionibus et incommodis relevari poterit et laudabiliter gubernari cum litteris nostris destinamus, supplicantes humiliter et devote quatinus ipsum ad dictum prioratum et custodiam seu regimen ejusdem favorabiliter admittatis ipsumque recom[m]endatum habere velitis intuitu pietatis. Valeat vestra reverenda paternitas in domino feliciter in dierum longitudine cum successivum votivorum augmento que nobis precipiat quicquid placet. Scriptum apud sanctam Katerinam anno domini MCCCXXVIII decimo die Septembris.

519 Institution and mandate for induction (to the archbishop's official) of William de Douseby, priest, to Kirton (*Kirketon*) church, vacant by the death of Henry de Athelastr'; presented by Nicholas de Cantilupo, kt. Bishopthorpe, 5 Oct. 1328.

520 Note of licence to William de Lameley, rector of Cromwell (*Crombewell*), to be absent for one year. Eastrington (*Estrington*), 16 Oct. 1328.

521 Note of commendation of M. Robert de Bridelington to Clayworth church 'in same form as in quire for first year' [*i.e.* **15**]. Hunmanby (*Hundmanby*), 11 Nov. 1328.

522 Note of licence at the request of Lady Maud de Holand to Adam de Preston, rector of Hickling, to be absent until 11 June 1329. Bishopthorpe, 3 Dec. 1328.

523 Collation and mandate for induction (to M. Robert de Clareburgh, official in the vacant archdeaconry) of William de Langeley, priest, to Carlton in Lindrick church in an exchange from Acaster Malbis church with William de Feriby. Bishopthorpe, 13 Dec. 1328.

524 [Fo.364v; N.F.443v.] PROHIBICIO REGIS PRO ECCLESIA DE STRETTON IN THE CLAY. [Chancery] writ *ne admittatis* forbidding the archbishop to admit a parson to Sturton le Steeple church, now vacant, while its advowson is disputed in the king's court between Thomas Prat of Sturton and the abbot of St. Mary's, York. Wallingford, 9 Nov. 1328.

525 RECUPERACIO JURIS PATRONATUS PREDICTE ECCLESIE. [Common Pleas] writ *admittatis non obstante reclamacione* ordering the archbishop to admit a suitable presentee of the abbot of St.Mary's to Sturton church because he has recovered the presentation in the king's court at York against Thomas Prat by default. Tested by W[illiam] de Herle, York, 28 Nov. 1328.

526 Institution[28] and mandate for induction (to the archbishop's official) of M. Adam de Haselbech, priest, to Sturton le Steeple church, vacant by the death of Geoffrey Golias; presented by the abbot and convent of St. Mary's, York. Cawood, 23 Dec. 1328.

Memorandum that Adam immediately resigned Lythe church, in accordance with the constitution *Execrabilis*, before M. John de Barneby, notary, M. John de Shoteswell, D.Cn.L., and Richard de Melton, clerk. Same date.

527 [*Citation before the archbishop of those who took trees from Clayworth churchyard, to show why they should not be excommunicated unless they make restitution within ten days.*]

CONTRA AMPUTANTES ET ASPORTANTES ARBORES CRESCENTES IN CIMITERIO ECCLESIE DE CLAWORTH. Willelmus etc. dilecto filio . . decano nostro de Retford salutem [*etc.*]. Cum laicis quamvis religiosis disponendi de rebus ecclesie nulla sit attributa potestas quos obsequendi monet necessitas non auctoritas imperandi, dolemus in quibusdam ex illis sic refrigescere caritatem quod immunitacionem[29] ecclesiastice libertatis, quam non tamen sancti patres set etiam principes seculares multis privilegiis munierunt, suis subdolis machinacionibus et usurpacionibus perversis ipsam non formidant atrociter impugnare. Sane ad nostrum deduxit auditum relatio fidedigna quod quidam ingratitudinis filii ad vetita manus illicitas extendentes, arbores grossas et in altum se dum creverunt plurimum dirigentes nuper in cimiterio ecclesie de Claworth nostre diocesis crescentes que ipsam ecclesiam a procellis et ventorum turbinibus multipliciter protegant et ipsius dictum cimiterium non modicum decorarunt, propria temeritate absque licencia nostra seu cujuscumque alterius ipsius ecclesie custodiam tunc temporis obtinentis amputarunt asportarunt et de eisdem disposuerunt pro sue libito voluntatis, in divine magestatis offensam dicte ecclesie nostreque jurisdiccionis prejudicium vilipendium et contemptum ac multorum Christi fidelium perniciosum exemplum. Quocirca tibi mandamus

[28] Marginal note: *dupplicatur*

[29] MS. *in immutacionem*

firmiter injungentes quatinus omnes et singulos dicti excessus presumptores fautores et auctores in dicta ecclesia de Claworth tribus diebus dominicis et festivis intra missarum solempnia moneas et efficaciter inducas quod de dicta transgressione prefate ecclesie ejusdemque custodi infra decem dies satisfaciant competenter. Alioquin omnes hujusmodi rei patratores et actores, dumtamen eorum nomina et persone ignorentur, monicionibus licitis premissis servato ordine juris qui in hac parte requiritur totidem aliis diebus dominicis et festivis intra missarum solempnia cum major aderit populi multitudo, pulsatis campanis candelis accensis et extinctis ac cruce erecta, cum ea solempnitate qua decet in dicta ecclesia de Claworth et aliis evicinis de quibus videris expedire in genere excommunices et excommunicari facias ac sic excommunicatos publice nunciari quousque de tanta injuria deo et ecclesie satisfecerint et beneficium absolutionis in forma juris meruerint obtinere. Inquirens nihilominus de nominibus eorundem de quibus cum tibi constiterit, ipsos cites peremptorie quod compareant coram nobis aliquo certo die tuo arbitrio statuendo ubicumque tunc fuerimus in nostra diocesi, causam rationabilem si quam habeant et quicquid juris sibi competere crediderint quare in sentenciam majoris excommunicationis de qua premittitur in genere latam specialiter et nominatim occasione predicta incidisse et excommunicatos esse minime debeant pronunciari ostensuri propposituri facturi et recepturi in premissis et circa ea quod secundum eorum qualitatem et naturam justum fuerit et consonum rationi. De die vero recepcionis presencium et citacionis tue et nominibus in hac parte citatorum et ad quem diem ipsos citaveris ac de toto processu tuo ac omni eo quod feceris in hac parte, nos tempore oportuno distincte et aperte ac plenius certifices per tuas litteras patentes harum seriem continentes. Vale. [Cawood, 30 Dec. 1328.]

528 Writ of prohibition [similar to **524**] in respect of Clayworth church pending a plea between William Daubenay of Clayworth and M. Henry de Mammesfeld, dean of Lincoln. York, 3 Aug. 1328.

529 Writ *admittatis* [similar to **525**] in favour of M. Henry, who has recovered the presentation to Clayworth by William's default. York, 28 Nov. 1328.

530 Institution (in the person of M. Adam de Haselbech, rector of Sturton le Steeple, as proctor) and mandate for induction (to the archbishop's official) of M. Robert de Bridelington, priest, to Clayworth church, vacant by the death of M. John de Notingham; presented by M. Henry de Mammesfeld, dean of Lincoln. Cawood, 6 Feb. 1329.

531 Note of licence to Robert Norreys, rector of West Retford,[30] to be absent for one year in the service of Sir John Marmyon. Bishopthorpe, 24 Feb. 1329.

532 Note of licence to Olive Darcy to have divine service celebrated in her oratory or chapel at Fenton in Sturton le Steeple parish. Same date.

533 [Fo.365; N.F.444] Institution and mandate for induction (to the archbishop's official) of William de Hanay, priest, canon of Worksop, to Worksop

[30] Instituted 13 Mar. 1326, presented by Hugh de Hercy (Reg. Melton, fo.587; N.F.729).

vicarage, vacant by the death of Bro. Robert de Beverley. Bishopthorpe, 16 Feb.1329.

534 [*Mandate to the bailiff of Southwell to receive two prisoners delivered by the king's justices at Nottingham.*]
William par la soeffrance de Dieu etc. a Thomas de Radclyf' nostre baillyf de Suwell salutz ove la beniceon de Dieu et la nostre. Pur ce que noz commissaries de Notingham, qui sont deputez par nostre commission de receivre les prisons a nostre garde des justices nostre seignur le roy [en] celes parties, se pleynent que deux prisons qui sont liverez a meismes noz commissaires et a nostre perille y demoerent en autri prisone a noz grefs coustages; vous mandoms que vous receivez meismes les prisones et les facez sauvement et mayntenant mener de Notyngham a nostre prisone Deverwyk. Et quele houre que tieux prisones serront agardez a nostre prisone, soiez meismes a la deliverance et sanz delay les facez sur sauve garde mener a nostre dite prisone Deverwyk as noz custages. Et voloms que les custages que noz ditz commissaires ount mis en le mener Thomas Amour tanque a Everwyk, leur seient paiez par nostre receivour de Suwell ensemblement ove les custages que ils ount mis sur la sauve garde [Richard] de Kymberworth et Johan de Allastre prisones a Notyngham come est avantdit a nostre prisone liverez. Adieu. Done a Thorp pres Deverwyk le darrayn jour de Feverer, lan de nostre sacre douzisme.[28 Feb. 1329.]

535 [*Warrant to the receiver of Southwell to pay the above expenses.*]
Willelmus etc. dilecto filio domino Willelmo de Hokerton receptori nostro Suwell' salutem [*etc.*]. Tibi mandamus quatinus expense que fuerint et stent circa salvam custodiam Thome Amour Ricardi de Kymberworth et Johannis Allastre prisonum apud Not' commissariis nostris liberatorum ipsis commissariis nostris et Thome de Radclif', tam pro hujusmodi custodia quam pro salvo conductu eorum apud Ebor', statim visis presentibus solvere non omittas, quas quidem expensas rationabiles tibi super tuo compoto volumus allocari. Vale. [Bishopthorpe, 28 Feb. 1329.]

536 Commission to William de Wylughby, rector of St. Peter's, Nottingham, and John Cosyn, vicar of St. Mary's, Nottingham, to claim John de Trusseleye, clerk, who is accused of various felonies and imprisoned at Nottingham; he has been sent to the archbishop's prison by Sir John le Bourser, lately justice of gaol delivery. They are to keep him securely until otherwise ordered. Same date.

537 Request to the prior and convent of Blyth to grant an annual pension to Matthew de Burwode, the archbishop's messenger, for his life, claimed according to diocesan custom on the appointment of abbots and priors.[31] Bishopthorpe, 7 Mar. 1329.

[31] As in *Reg. Melton*, II.33, no.67, omitting its first sentence, to *pariter et accepta*, then continuing: 'taliter vos in hac parte habentes si placet ut eo favorabiliores vos inveniat dictus Mattheus quo nobis insidet magis cordi ac vobis et vestro monasterio in vestris agendis arcius decetero teneamur. Et nos de eo quod in premissis duxeritis faciendum nobis velle vestrum plenius rescribatis presencium per latorem.' And cf. **651**.

538 [*Provision by papal authority of John son of Thomas of Sherburn (Y.E.R.), a poor clerk, to Rempstone church.*]
REMPSTON ECCLESIE INSTITUTIO.[32] Willelmus etc. executor seu provisor gracie vel provisionis Johanni Thome de Shirbourn in Hertfordlyth pauperi clerico de beneficio ecclesiastico certi valoris spectante communiter vel divisim ad collationem vel presentationem religiosorum virorum prioris et conventus de Lenton ordinis Cluniacensis nostre Ebor' diocesis sub forma qua pro pauperibus clericis beneficiandis summus pontifex interdum scribere consuevit concesse a sede apostolica specialiter deputatus tibi Johanni Thome de Shirburn in Hertfordlith nostre Ebor' diocesis salutem [*etc.*]. Ecclesiam parochialem de Rempston dicte nostre diocesis per mortem magistri Gilberti de Pontefracto ultimi[33] rectoris ejusdem notorie ad presens vacantem ad presentacionem dictorum religiosorum virorum communiter vel divisim spectantem per te sub certis forma et modo acceptatam, et taxacionem gracie tue nullatenus excedentem secundum vim formam et effectum hujusmodi gracie vel provisionis tibi ab apostolica sede concesse et processuum inde per reverendum[34] religiosum virum . . priorem sancti Andree juxta Ebor', cui in hac parte commisimus vices nostras donec eas ad nos duxerimus revocandas, rite habitorum et factorum et acceptacionis tue predicte auctoritate apostolica nobis in hac parte commissa conferimus cum suis juribus et pertinenciis universis et tibi providemus canonice de eadem ac te nihilominus per nostrum anulum de ea presencialiter investimus, salvis tibi tuis protestacionibus in acceptacione tua predicta factis quibus prejudicare non intendimus quovis modo. In cujus rei testimonium has litteras nostras sigilli nostri appensione facimus communiri. [Bishopthorpe, 10 Mar. 1329.]

539 [*Mandate for his induction.*]
Willelmus etc. ut supra usque deputatus, et tunc . . decano nostro de Byngham salutem et mandatis apostolicis firmiter obedire. Quia ecclesiam parochialem de Rempston [as in **538** *mutatis mutandis*–investivimus[35]]; tibi eadem auctoritate firmiter injungendo committimus et in virtute obediencie qua sedi teneris apostolice supradicte mandamus quatinus prefatum Johannem pauperem clericum in corporalem possessionem ecclesie de Rempston sibi per nos ut premittitur collate cum suis juribus et pertinenciis universis auctoritate nostra immo verius apostolica actualiter inducas et inductum defendas, ac facias sibi de universis fructibus redditibus et proventibus eidem qualitercumque spectantibus integraliter responderi. Vale. [Same date.]

540 [*Mandate to induct Francis son of Neapoleo Orsini, a provisor admitted by the bishop of Lincoln to the prebend of Farndon cum Balderton* (cf. **501–3**).]
[Fo.365v; N.F.444v] INDUCTIO PREBENDE DE FARNDON ET BALDERSTON PER DOMINUM PAPAM COLLATE. Willelmus permissione etc. dilecto filio . . officiali nostro in archidiaconatu Not' ipso vacante salutem [*etc.*]. Quia dominus Henricus episcopus Linc' secundum formam gracie domino Francisco nato

[32] Supplied in a sixteenth-century hand.
[33] MS. *ultimo*
[34] MS. *reverende*
[35] Omitting *per reverendum . . . revocandas*

nobilis viri domini Neapolionis militis de filiis Ursi de Urbe per sanctissimum in Christo patrem et dominum nostrum dominum Johannem divina providencia papam XXII de canonicatu et prebenda de Farndon et Balderston, quos dominus Pandulphus nuper dicti domini nostri pape notarius obtinuit dum vixit, in ecclesia Linc' infra nostram diocesim constitutos facte et processus super ea habiti prefatum dominum Franciscum in personam magistri Mathei Thomaxii de Cortanello Sabinen' diocesis procuratoris sui ad hoc specialiter constituti ad predictos canonicatum et prebendam admisit, prout per quoddam instrumentum publicum manu et signo Willelmi dicti le Peyntur de Derby clerici Coventr' et Lych' diocesis publici auctoritate apostolica notarii inde ut nobis apparuit confectum ac nobis ostensum constare poterit cuilibet intuenti; vobis mandamus quatinus prefatum dominum Franciscum vel procuratorem suum ejus nomine in corporalem possessionem dicte prebende de Farndon et Balderston inducatis vel faciatis induci. [Bishopthorpe, 18 Mar. 1329.]

541 (i) Institution of Robert de Dernesford, priest, to Fiskerton church (dioc. Lincoln), quoting a commission of Henry [Burghersh], bishop of Lincoln (dated London, 12 Mar. 1329), for an exchange of benefices between Robert, rector of Bunny, and John de Houton, rector of Fiskerton, forwarding the report of an enquiry by the archdeacon of Lincoln's official into the causes of the exchange; presented by the abbot and convent of Peterborough. (ii) Note of mandate for induction to the same official. (iii) Certificate to the bishop of Lincoln [here describing Robert as chaplain]. (iv) Institution of John, chaplain, to Bunny in the person of William de Northewelle, rector of a mediety of Eckington (*Ekynton*), his proctor; presented by Sir Robert de Wodhous. (v) Note of mandate for his induction to the archbishop's official in the vacant archdeaconry of Nottingham. Bishopthorpe, 26 Mar. 1329.

542 Institution and mandate for induction (to the archbishop's official) of John de Loudham, priest, to Bingham church, vacant by the death of M. Alan de Neusom; presented by Alice, lady of Bingham. Bishopthorpe, 14 Apr. 1329.

543 TERTIA VISITATIO DOMUS DE BLIDA. Mandate to the prior and convent of Blyth for their visitation on Saturday 20 May; absent brethren are to be recalled. To prove receipt and compliance, these letters are to be shown to the archbishop or his commissaries, with the names of all brethren and others cited, with their seal pendant. Cawood, 25 Apr. 1329.

Notes of similar mandates to Thurgarton, for Saturday 3 June, and Shelford, for Monday 26 June. [Same date.]

544 [*Transfer of three monks from Blyth priory, which is unable to support them, to Sainte-Cathérine-du-Mont, Rouen.*]

[Fo.366; N.F.445] LITTERA DIRECTA ABBATI MONASTERII BEATE KATERINE IN MONTE JUXTA ROTOMAGUM PRO PRIORATU DE BLIDA. Willelmus etc. venerande religioso viro domino . . abbati monasterii beate Katerine in monte juxta Rotomagum salutem cum benediccione dextere salvatoris. Quia nuper depressionem et statum miserabilem prioratus vestri de Blida nostre diocesis debite compassionis oculis intuentes, ad relevandum membri vestri tam depressi manifestam inopiam litteratorie vestri excitavimus manum juvaminis precum instancia cordiali,[36] cujus hactenus non curastis ut intelleximus indigencie subvenire, sicque dictus prioratus ere alieno graviter oneratus lapsusque facultatibus est ut veraciter asseritur sic depressus quod proventus ejusdem ad sustentacionem monachorum ibidem jam existencium sufficere nequeunt, donec ipsius excreverint que adhuc non suppetunt facultates; propter quod tres monachos dicti prioratus quos prior ejusdem prioratus viderit expedire ad vos ordinavimus remittendos, cum plures ibi morari non debeant quam de ipsius facultatibus poterunt comode sustentari quod etiam tam propter honestatem ordinis quam officii nostri debitum non poterimus sana consciencia tolerare, per quod juribus vestris non intendimus in aliquo derogare. Fratres igitur vestros et monachos ex hac causa et non ex alia ad vestrum monasterium ut ad matris gremium redeuntes benigne admittatis[37] et ipsos affectu paterno si placuerit pertractetis. Crescat feliciter vestra religio dierum longitudine in obsequiis Jesu Christi. [Bossall, 30 Apr. 1329.]

545 [*Mandate to three monks of Blyth to obey the order for their transfer to Rouen.*] MISSIO TRIUM MONACHORUM DE BLIDA AD MONASTERIUM SANCTE KATERINE JUXTA ROTHOMAGUM. Willelmus etc. dilectis filiis fratribus Willelmo Burel dicto le Spicer Galfrido Filiole et Johanne de Cane dicto de Rothom' monachis de Blida salutem [*etc.*]. Cum nuper abbati vestro monasterii sancte Katerine in monte juxta Rothom' ad recipiendum tres vestrum de quibus videretur priori vestro pocius expedire pro inevitabilibus domus vestre necessitatibus ad presens imminentibus saltim in aliquo relevandis litteras nostras duxerimus transmittendas, quarum copiam vestro misimus monasterio quibuscumque vestrum volentibus intuendis, idemque prior vester vos tres elegerit et nominaverit ad prefatum monasterium sancte Katerine occasione premissa hac vice prout convenit transituros; vobis et cuilibet vestrum injungimus et mandamus quatenus hujusmodi prioris vestri dispositioni humiliter parentes quod vobis in hac parte per eundem injungitur quantum ad vos actum peragere non tardetis promptitudine filiali, alioquin alias censuras quas dictus prior in vos ob vestram intulerit rebellionem et offensam faciemus inviolabiliter observari. Valete. [Topcliffe (*Topclif'*), 4 May 1329.]

546 Institution and mandate for induction (to the archbishop's official) of M. Hugh de Wylughby, priest, to Ruddington church, vacant by the resignation of John de Loudham;[38] presented by Lady Alice de Byngham. Pontefract, 12 May 1329.

547 The like of M. Simon de Staunton, acolyte, to Staunton church, vacant by the resignation of Robert [de Staunton[39]]; presented by Geoffrey de Staunton. Also notes of licence to study for two years (*in forma constitutionis*)[40] and letters dimissory. St. Oswald's priory, Nostell, 12 May 1329.

[36] See **516**.
[37] MS. *quos admittatis*
[38] Cf. **340**, **542**.
[39] Instituted 1311 (*Reg. Greenfield*, IV.115–16, no.1914).
[40] See *BRUO*, III.1769.

548 Institution and mandate for induction (to the archdeacon of York or his official) of Nicholas de Scaleton, acolyte, to Laxton church, vacant by the death of Ralph de Langethwayt; presented by Adam de Everyngham, kt. Southwell, 28 May 1329.

549 Institution and mandate for induction (to the archbishop's official) of M. Richard de Melton, priest, to All Saints church, Willoughby on the Wolds, vacant by the resignation freely made into the archbishop's hands, and accepted, of M. Hugh de Wylughby; presented by the prior and convent of Worksop. Finningley (*Fyningley*), 20 May 1329.

550 [*Commission to investigate a petition of the dean and chapter of Lincoln that two convicted clerks escaped from Newark castle to Southwell, seeking sanctuary, and to restore them if it is true.*]
COMMISSIO AD LIBERANDUM CLERICOS AD ECCLESIAM SUWELL' FUGIENTES PRIORI CUSTODIE CARCERIS DE NEUWERK'. Willelmus etc. dilectis filiis magistris Symoni de Courtmaiour canonico nostre ecclesie Suwell' et Willelmo de Hundon rectori ecclesie de Barnburgh nostre diocesis salutem [*etc.*]. Humilis amicorum nostrorum Henrici decani et capituli ecclesie Linc' oblata petitio continebat quod cum Johannes filius Andree Hod de Stikeney et Radulphus atte Abbotes de Linc' clerici variis criminibus capitalibus irretiti et propter hec capti ac coram justiciariis domini regis in foro seculari adducti et convicti, subsequenterque tamquam clerici venerabili patri domino dei gracia Linc' episcopo canonice judicandi sub periculo quod de consuetudine regni Anglie in talibus iminet liberati qui eos per aliqua tempora in castro suo de Neuwerk' detinuit et carcerali custodie mancipavit, eandem custodiam jam subdole evaserint ad ecclesiam nostram de Suwell fugientes et maliciose sub immunitate ecclesie se tenentes ibidem, hiis qui ad custodiam eorumdem extiterant deputati dictos confugas liberari absque more diffugio in juris subsidium faceremus. Verum quia dictorum clericorum restitucio et in priorem locum retrusio si preces porrecte veritatem minime continerent in grave tenderent prejudicium ecclesiastice libertatis, vobis in virtute obediencie firmiter injungendo committimus et mandamus quatenus per viros fidedignos juratos clericos et laicos habentes noticiam pleniorem premissorum omnium inquiratis diligentius veritatem, et si per inquisicionem eandem ad plenum et delucide vobis constiterit premissa nobis suggesta veritatem in sua serie continere, predictos confugas ministris Linc' episcopi memorati qui ad recipiendum et admittendum eosdem ab ipso episcopo mandatum litteratorie exhibuerint specialem priori mancipandos custodie liberetis et ilico assignetis, proviso quod ipsis confugis nova afflictio non addatur nec fuge vel evasionis pretextu inhumaniter futuris temporibus pertractentur sed tamen ad immunitatem ecclesiasticam primitus acceptatam et in priorem custodiam reducantur. Et super eo quod inveneritis et feceritis in hac parte nobis constare faciatis tempore oportuno litteris vestris patentibus habentibus hunc tenorem. [Filey (*Fyvelay*), 12 Nov. 1328.]

551 Dispensation to Thomas [son] of Richard Hotoht, clerk (dioc. York), to hold a benefice with cure of souls, despite his illegitimate birth, provided that he takes orders at statutory times and resides; quoting letters of Gaucelin, cardinal bishop of Albano, papal penitentiary [Fo.366v; N.F.445v] (dated at Avignon, 24 Sept. 1328). Southwell, 31 May 1329.

552 [*Undertaking (in triplicate, dated 15 May 1326) by the prior and convent of St. Katherine outside Lincoln that they will provide in perpetuity for a chaplain celebrating at St. James's altar in Newark church for William and Isabel Durant, with a manse (described) and £4 p.a.; with regulations for the presentation of chaplains, their offices and obligations, and provision against arrears in payments. Confirmed by the master of the order of Sempringham and the archbishop (8 June 1326).*[41]]

ORDINACIO PERPETUE CANTARIE AD ALTARE SANCTI JACOBI IN ECCLESIA DE NEUWERK' PRO WILLELMO DURANT ETC. Universis Christi fidelibus ad quos presens scriptum pervenerit frater Gilbertus prior sancte Katerine extra Lincoln' et ejusdem loci conventus ecclesiam parochialem de Newerk' Ebor' diocesis in proprios usus canonice obtinentes salutem in domino sempiternam. Bonorum munificenciam que dilectus noster et specialis Willelmus Durant de Newerk' parochianus noster hactenus liberaliter contulit intime recolentes, unanimi assensu et voluntate pro nobis et successoribus nostris concedimus et presenti scripto confirmamus quod nos inveniemus nostris sumptibus modo infrascripto unum capellanum secularem pro ipso Willelmo et Isabella uxore ejus dum vixerint et animabus patrum et matrum dictorum Willelmi et Isabelle ac aliorum antecessorum suorum et omnium fidelium defunctorum et post mortem eorumdem Willelmi et Isabelle pro eorum animabus et animabus omnium prius nominatorum ad altare sancti Jacobi in ecclesia nostra parochiali de Newerk' predicta missam singulis diebus quibus congruit et absque impedimento corporali congrue poterit celebraturum modo qui sequitur sustentandi nominandi seu presentandi et admittendi perpetuis temporibus in futurum; concedentes eidem capellano pro manso suo illam partem mesuagii in Kirkegate de Newerk' versus occidentem quam Ricardus de Bekyngham quondam de nobis tenuit cum omnibus domibus in eadem parte dicti mesuagii constructis cum columbari cum libero introitu et exitu, salva nobis et successoribus nostris tota illa domo que quondam fuit lanaria dicti Willelmi Durant cum illa parte domus ad gablum australe ejusdem lanarie sicut eadem domus lanaria ex parte orientali se extendit linialiter usque ad mansum Ricardi de Gretton versus austrum et usque ad mansum Walteri de Landeford versus boriam cum stillicidio, ad quas domus cooperiandas emendandas et reedificandas licebit nobis et successoribus nostris habere liberum introitum et exitum quociens indigeruit reparari absque impedimento seu contradictione dicti capellani seu successorum suorum vel alterius cujuscumque.

Omnes vero domos eidem capellano concessas, videlicet aulam cum solario et celariis ad gablum orientale aule et solarium cum celariis eidem aule annexum quod se extendit versus boriam et abuttat super cameram quam Radulphus Cocus de nobis tenet et illam partem domus ex parte occidentali aule que se extendit versus occidentem usque ad dictam domum que fuit lanaria cum columbari ibidem constructo, idem capellanus qui pro tempore fuerit suis

[41] On this last date, at Westminster, John de Thornhagh, presented by William Durant, was instituted as chaplain of the chantry (Reg. Melton, fo.571v; N.F.711v). For Newark's chantries, see A.H. Thompson, *The English Clergy*, 134, 138, and his articles in *Transactions of the Thoroton Society*, 17 (1914), 68–88, and 18 (1915), 138–49.

sumptibus propriis in omni eventu perpetuis temporibus reparabit et reedificabit. Et pro sustentatione sua et pro omnibus aliis oneribus sibi et cantarie predicte incumbentibus sex marcas argenti una cum domibus ei concessis a nobis per manus vicarii nostri ibidem qui pro tempore fuerit vel alterius procuratoris domus nostre annuatim percipiendas in festis sancti Michaelis et Pasche per equales porciones; ita quod solutio cujuslibet termini se referat ad tempus sequens sic videlicet quod si contingat capellano qui pro tempore fuerit in aliquo predictorum terminorum plenarie satisfieri ac ipsum ante terminum proximum sequentem solucionis faciende ut premittitur decedere, successori suo qui pro tempore fuerit de bonis ejusdem defuncti pro rata temporis satisfaciat competenter.

Dictus vero Willelmus Durant dum vixerit quociens dicta cantaria vacaverit dictum capellanum idoneum nominabit et archiepiscopo Ebor' presentabit, qui quidem archiepiscopus ipsum in forma juris admittat ad eandem. Post decessum vero dicti Willelmi Durant cum dictam cantariam qualitercumque vacare contigerit, vicarius noster qui pro tempore fuerit ibidem statim in periculo anime sue assumet sibi quatuor viros ejusdem parochie nomine ipsius parochie suo judicio fidedigniores, qui de consensu majoris et sanioris partis eorumdem aliquem capellanum idoneum de dicta villa de Newerk' oriundum et maxime de consanguinitate ipsius Willelmi si talis aliquis poterit reperiri omnibus aliis extraoriundis preferendum;[42] alioquin de extraoriundis nominabunt et archiepiscopo ut premittitur presentabunt admittendum per eundem. Et si vicarius noster et quatuor viri per ipsum assumpti ut premittitur inter se dissenserint, quod absit, ita quod infra xv dies a tempore vacacionis dicte cantarie capellanum idoneum ut premissum est neglexerint seu non curaverint nominare et presentare, extunc nominacio et presentacio capellani pro[43] predicta cantaria ad nos et successores nostros illa vice pertinebunt. Et si forte nos et successores nostri post lapsum dictorum xv dierum infra alios xv dies immediate sequentes a tempore dissensionis hujusmodi nobis note eidem cantarie idoneum capellanum non nominaverimus et presentaverimus ad eandem, extunc potestas providendi eidem cantarie et ipsam conferendi illa vice ad archiepiscopum Ebor' sede plena vel ad decanum et capitulum sede vacante absque prejudicio cujuslibet pro illo tempore devolvatur.

Predicti vero capellani sic successive assumendi et admittendi pro Willelmo et Isabella predictis et animabus supranominatis celebraturi dicent singulis diebus pro mortuis, videlicet Commendacionem Placebo et Dirige, et in festis principalibus[44] missam celebrabunt de die, videlicet de sanctis quorum festa aguntur, et in diebus dominicis similiter de die vel de sancta Trinitate prout devocio eorum melior fuerit et semel in septimana de beata Maria; ita tamen quod memoriam et orationem pro defunctis faciant speciales. Dictus vero capellanus missis matutinis et aliis horis canonicis cotidie intererit nisi legitima causa rationabili et honesta fuerit impeditus. Et eidem Willelmo Durant dum vixerit in hiis que ad cultum divinum pertinent cum licencia vicarii nostri intendet et ministrabit.

[42] MS. *preferendis*
[43] Interlined.
[44] Preceded by *dupplicibus*, struck through.

Et idem capellanus statim in admissione sua coram archiepiscopo juramentum ad sancta dei ewangelia, ipsis visis et tactis, prestabit residenciam personalem ibidem se facturum et omnia onera premissa sibi et cantarie predicte incumbencia sine fraude et fictione aliqua pro suis viribus impleturum. Vicario insuper nostro easdem faciet seu facient observancias sicut secundum consuetudines ejusdem ecclesie facere consueverant sacerdotes inibi communiter celebrantes. Et si forte dictus capellanus in premissis faciendis vel exequendis negligens vel remissus fuerit repertus vel contra juramentum suum venerit, et super hiis vel aliis excessibus notabilibus legitime fuerit convictus et incorrigibilis inventus, ipso pro suis demeritis amoto, confestim alius [Fo.367; N.F.446] capellanus idoneus ad dictam cantariam in forma premissa nominetur et presentetur ac etiam preficiatur.

Et sciendum quod pro oneribus sustentacionis capellani predicti et cantarie predicte subeundis predictus Willelmus Durant dedit nobis tria mesuagia in Newerk' et tres acras terre in Newerk' Northgate et Houton juxta Newerk'.[45] Ad quam quidem solucionem dictarum sex marcarum capellano predicto qui pro tempore fuerit terminis predictis fideliter faciendam obligamus nos et successores nostros et nedum dicta tria mesuagia et tres acras terre que habemus ex dono dicti Willelmi Durant pro onere sustentacionis dicti capellani set etiam omnia alia terras et tenementa que habemus in Newerk' et Northgate juxta Newerk' et etiam omnia bona nostra temporalia in Newerk' predicta; concedentes pro nobis et successoribus nostris quod quandocumque et quociens predicta pecunia ultra terminos statutos suprascriptos per culpam nostram aretro fuerit non soluta, liceat predicto capellano in terris et tenementis predictis ubique et locis singulis eorumdem pro toto eo quod debetur distringere per quecumque inveniendum in eisdem et districtiones fugare amovere et retinere quousque de universo eo quod debetur unacum dampnis et expensis si que forsan incurrerit vel fecerit eidem fuerit plenarie satisfactum.

In quorum omnium testimonium presenti scripto quod pro majori securitate tripplicari fecimus, quorum unus penes nos retinuimus pro memoria premissorum perpetuo habenda, et aliud penes capellanum predictum qui pro tempore fuerit, videlicet in ecclesia de Newerk' predicta in aliquo coffino ad hoc specialiter ordinato et in loco securo ponendo, et tercium penes dictum Willelmum heredes et executores suos volumus perpetuis temporibus remanere, sigillum nostrum commune videlicet cuilibet scripto predictorum de voluntate unanimi et consensu apponi fecimus et appendi. Et nos frater Philippus magister ordinis de Sempingham omnia et singula premissa quantum in nobis est confirmamus ratificamus et etiam approbamus et presentibus sigillum nostrum apposuimus in fidem et testimonium premissorum. Nos vero Willelmus permissione divina Ebor' archiepiscopus Anglie primas de consensu omnium quorum interest omnia et singula premissa prout in serie suprascribuntur auctoritate nostra pontificali ordinamus et ea in suo robore perpetuo duratura et in omni parte sui fideliter observanda pronunciamus et decernimus in hiis scriptis. In cujus rei testimonium sigillum nostrum presentibus duximus apponendumve appendendum. Datum in capitulo nostro Idus Maii anno domini MCCCXXVI.[46] Datum quoad nos Willelmum Ebor' archiepiscopum

[45] By licence dated 4 Aug. 1321 (*CPR 1321–4*, 13).
[46] This sentence appears misplaced.

Anglie primatem apud Westmonasterium VI idus Junii anno domini supradicto et pontificatus nostri nono.

553 [*Transfer of Robert of York, a quarrelsome canon of Thurgarton, to Bridlington priory. Richard de Sibthorpe is to be cellarer, and Hugh de Notingham may stay under penance.*]
MISSIO FRATRIS ROBERTI DE EBOR' CANONICI DE THURG' AD MONASTERIUM DE BRIDEL'. Willelmus etc. dilecto filio . . priori de Thurgarton nostre diocesis salutem [*etc.*]. Considerantes dampnosa dispendia que vestro monasterio attulit in preterito et afferret verisimiliter in futuro si duraret tumultuosa contentio inter fratres, fratrem Robertum de Ebor' quem hujusmodi dissensioni prebuisse comperimus occasionem non modicam et fomentum a vestro monasterio sicut alias ex hoc et aliis causis legitimis ordinavimus emittendum, et ad monasterium de Bridelyngton fore vestris sumptibus transmittendum et etiam moraturum quousque aliud super hoc duxerimus disponendum. Vobis igitur injungimus firmiter et mandamus quatinus dictum fratrem Robertum ad predictum monasterium de Bridelyngton, pro cujus admissione et benigna pertractacione priori et conventui dicti monasterii nostras fieri fecimus litteras speciales quas vobis transmittimus per vos ulterius destinandas, honeste juxta religionis decenciam transmittatis, facientes pro eodem tam expensas moderatas itineris quam pro mora sua quas ad quinque marcas annuas taxavimus congrue ministrari; et si dictus frater Robertus vobis parere renuerit in premissis, ipsum sevientis virga discipline ac per censuras ecclesiasticas ad hoc vice nostra canonice compellatis. Volumus etiam quod fratrem Ricardum de Sibthorp concanonicum domus vestre juxta asserciónem et testimonium majoris et sanioris partis conventus vestri virum providum et honestum et ad officium celerarii magis aptum, illi officio proponatis quod vestro monasterio credimus non mediocriter proficturum. Fratri Hugoni de Notingham sub spe gestus quiescioris ad tempus inter vos morari concedimus, ita tamen quod stallum inter juniores canonicos sacerdotes et silencium ubique teneat ac claustrum non exeat nisi ex speciali licencia presidentis. Valete. [Laneham, 10 June 1329.]

554 [*Mandate to Bridlington priory to admit Robert, detailing penances.*]
PRIORI ET CONVENTUI DE BRID' QUOD ADMITTANT DICTUM FRATREM ROBERTUM. Willelmus etc. dilectis filiis . . priori et conventui de Bridelyngton nostre diocesis salutem [*etc.*]. Quia ex causis certis et legitimis nuper in visitacione nostra quam in monasterio de Thurgarton exercuimus compertis fratrem Robertum de Ebor' canonicum monasterii de Thurgarton a dicto monasterio ordinavimus exigente justicia emittendum et seorsum ad tempus moraturum, sperantes in domino quod locorum mutacio ac inter exteros conversacio ipsius animum reformabunt in melius ac lese rediment dispendia caritatis; ipsum Robertum ex causis premissis ad vestrum monasterium transmittimus inter vos sumptibus dicte domus de Thurgarton, quos ad quinque marcas taxavimus annuatim, sub vestris habitu et regulari observancia moraturum, cui penitenciam injungimus infrascriptam, ut singulis sextis feriis ab esu piscium abstineat et eisdem diebus unam a presidente in vestro capitulo recipiat disciplinam. Vobis igitur injungimus firmiter et mandamus quatinus eundem quem ordinis et habitus ydemptitas vobis merito recomendant inter vos in vestro monasterio recipientes ut premittitur moraturum, ipsum affeccione fraternali in omnibus ut

convenit amicabiliter pertractetis quousque aliud a nobis receperitis in mandatis; proviso quod cum viris secularibus nisi audiente aliquo concanonico domus vestre non loquatur, nec litteras mittat vel recipiat nisi per vos priorem visas primitus atque lectas. Feliciter in domino valeatis. [Laneham, 10 June 1329.]

555 Note of licence to be absent to study (*in studio*) from 29 Sept. for two years to Peter de Bekeryng, rector of Tuxford. Laneham, 11 June 1329.
He paid two marks for the licence at Cawood.

556 COMMISSIO SUPER QUIBUSDAM OBLATIONIBUS PROVENIENTIBUS AD CAPELLAM BEATE MARGARETE DE GRIVES IN PAROCHIA DE OXTON. Commission to the official of the vacant archdeaconry and Gregory [Fairfax], rector of Headon, to hear and conclude (*summarie et de plano sine strepitu et figura judicii*) a cause between William [de Beckford], vicar of Oxton, and the prior and convent of Worksop concerning offerings at the chapel of St. Margaret the Virgin at Greaves[47] in Oxton parish, which the priory received and the vicar claims. Eastwood by Rotherham (*Estwode juxta Roderham*), 10 July 1329.

557 Note of licence for Alan de Rothewell, rector of Sutton Bonington, to be absent for one year in the service of Lady Christine de Segrave. Southwell, 4 Aug. 1329.

558 Note of dispensation for illegitimacy to Robert son of Hugh de Beston; he has letters with the tenor of a bull. Willoughby on the Wolds, 18 July 1329.

559 Note of licence to study for two years at a *studium generale* to John de Clifton, rector of Clifton. Cawood, 23 Aug. 1329.

560 The like to M. John [de Scarborourgh], rector of Grove.[48] Worksop, 9 Nov. 1329.

561 [*Certificate of the prior of Newstead that he has executed the archbishop's commission to examine and confirm the election of John de Kyrkeby as prior of Felley.*] [Fo.367v; N.F.446v] COMMISSIO AD EXAMINANDUM ELECTIONEM ELECTI IN PRIOREM DE FELLEYA ET AD CASSANDUM EANDEM ETC. UNA CUM CERTIFICATORIO PRIORIS DE NOVO LOCO IN HAC PARTE. Venerabili in Christo patri ac domino domino Willelmo dei gracia Ebor' archiepiscopo etc. suus humilis et devotus prior de Novo Loco in Shirwode obedienciam reverenciam et honorem debitas tanto patri. Mandatum vestrum reverendum recepimus sub eo qui sequitur tenore:

Willelmus permissione divina Ebor' archiepiscopo etc. dilecto filio priori monasterii de Novo Loco in Shirwode nostre diocesis salutem [*etc.*]. Quia vacante ut accepimus prioratu de Felleya ejusdem nostre diocesis per mortem fratris Elye ultimi[49] prioris ejusdem, conventus ipsius fratrem Johannem de Kyrkeby suum concanonicum in ipsius priorem futurum per ipsos ut dicitur

[47] Cf. Greaves Lane (*EPNS Notts.*, 161.).
[48] Instituted 1315 (*Reg. Greenfield*, IV.174, no.2041).
[49] MS. *ultimo*

electum nobis per suas litteras patentes presentarunt per nos ut convenit confirmandum; nos variis negotiis occupati dicto negotio intendere non valentes ac volentes ipsorum laboribus parcere et expensis, necnon de vestris fidelitate et circumspectione plenam in domino fiduciam obtinentes, ad proponendum per vos vel alium in ecclesia conventuali prioratus de Felleya predicti et alibi ubi expedire videritis publicum proclamationis et citacionis edictum ut si quis sit qui contra predictam electionem vel electionis formam seu electi personam quicquam canonicum pro se habuerit et proponere voluerit quare ad confirmationem predicte electionis quatenus justum fuerit minime procedi debeat propositurus in forma juris et legitime ostensurus coram vobis certis die et loco quos adhoc duxeritis assignandos compareat, ulteriusque facturus et recepturus quod secundum qualitatem ipsius negocii justicia suadebit; quo die adveniente ac ullo contradictore seu oppositore in hac parte comparente, ad cassandum predictam electionem tamquam contra formam constitutionis edite in hoc casu celebratam, necnon ad preficiendum vice et auctoritate nostra prefatum fratrem Johannem de Kyrkeby in priorem predicti prioratus de Felleya si nichilominus obviet de canonicis institutis, et ad installandum eundem et ad committendum eidem administracionem ipsius prioratus tam in spiritualibus quam in temporalibus, et ad injungendum suppriori et conventui ejusdem prioratus ac aliis quibus fuerit injungendis quod eidem tanquam priori pareant ut tenentur, necnon ad cognoscendum procedendum statuendum diffiniendum et exequendum super objectis seu objiciendis si que emerserint in hoc casu, ac alia omnia et singula facienda et expedienda que in premissis et circa ea necessaria fuerint vel oportuna, vobis vices nostras committimus cum coercionis canonice potestate, ipsius prioris obediencia canonica nobis specialiter reservata. Et nos de omni eo quod feceritis in premissis expedito negocio reddatis plenius certiores distincte et aperte per vestras litteras patentes harum seriem continentes. Valete. [Bishop Burton, 25 Nov. 1328.]

Cujus auctoritate mandati publicum proclamacionis et citacionis edictum in ecclesiis de Annesley Papelwyk' et Greseley ac in aliis locis evicinis fieri fecimus si qui contra electionem predictam vel electionis formam seu electi personam quicquam canonicum pro se habuerint et proponere voluerint quare ad confirmacionem electionis de predicto fratre Johanne de Kyrkeby canonico de Felleya factam procedere non deberemus, quod comparerent coram nobis in ecclesia conventuali de Felleya die Mercurii proximo post festum sancte Lucie virginis proximo sequenti proposituri in forma juris et legitime ostensuri, ulteriusque facturi et recepturi quod secundum qualitatem ipsius negocii justicia suaderet. Quo die iterum publico proclamacionis edicto ut premittitur facto nulloque comparente nec se aliqualiter opponente, procurator prioratus de Felleya coram nobis comparuit et confirmacionem electionis de predicto fratre Johanne facte[50] peciit cum effectu. Et nos auctoritate mandati vestri reverendi nobis inde directi predictam confirmavimus electionem, et ipsum fratrem Johannem in priorem prefati prioratus prefecimus ipsumque installavimus in eundem ac administracionem ipsius prioratus tam in spiritualibus quam in temporalibus assignavimus, et[51] suppriori et conventui ejusdem prioratus et aliis quibus fuerat injungendis injunximus quod eidem fratri Johanni tanquam priori

[50] MS. *factam*
[51] MS. *ut*

obedirent ut tenentur, obediencia canonica vobis specialiter reservata. Et sic mandatum vestrum reverendum in omnibus et singulis suis articulis prout tenemur reverenter sumus executi. Datum apud Felley die dominica post festum sancte Lucie virginis anno domini MCCCXXVIII [18 Dec. 1328].

562 Licence to Thomas de Whatton in Stoke Bardolph (*Stokbardolf'*) to have services celebrated in an oratory or chapel in his house there, for three years, without prejudice to the parish church. Southwell, 15 July 1329.

563 [*Penances ordered for canons of Thurgarton* (see **553–4**).]
PRO FRATRIBUS ROBERTO DE EBOR' ET HUGONE DE NOT' CANONICIS DE THURGARTON. Willelmus etc. dilectis filiis priori et conventui monasterii de Thurg' nostre diocesis salutem [*etc.*]. Permittimus quod cum pro fratre Roberto de Ebor' domus vestre concanonico apud Bridel' commorante mittere volueritis penitenciam infrascriptam in domo vestro peragendam prout convenit mittatis, videlicet quod stallum teneat inter sacerdotes juniores in capitulo, in collocutorio nisi a presidente fuerit requisitus silencium teneat, necnon in claustro et alibi locis et horis debitis sicut novicii silencium teneat, claustrum non exeat nisi de licencia presidentis, qualibet septimana unum dicat psalterium. Permittimus etiamque vos penitenciam fratri Hugoni de Not' vestro concanonico per nos alias injunctam juxta ipsius gesta merita vel demerita mitigare et ipsum in pristinum statum reducere possitis quociens et quando videritis expedire, potestate nostra ordinaria semper salva. [Southwell, 4 Aug. 1329.]

Note of mandate to the prior and convent of Bridlington to send Robert to Thurgarton when his prior and convent send for him. Same date.

564 [*Commission to order the executors of the last rector of Laxton to pay his successor £20 for dilapidations.*]
COMMISSIO SUPER DEFECTIBUS CANCELLI ET DOMORUM ECCLESIE DE LAXTON. Willelmus etc. dilectis filiis dominis Gregorio rectori ecclesie de Hedon et Willelmo perpetuo vicario ecclesie de Estmarkham[52] nostre diocesis salutem [*etc.*]. Cum super defectibus domorum cancelli librorum et aliorum ornamentorum ecclesie de Laxton de tempore quo dominus Radulphus de Langthwayt defunctus rector extitit ejusdem iminentibus et aliis articulis in hac parte consuetis per viros fidedignos tam clericos quam laicos evicinos juratos inquiri mandaverimus in forma juris, qui jurati hujusmodi defectus ad triginta marcas taxaverint, et nos bona dicti defuncti ad valenciam hujusmodi taxacionis per vos vicarium predictum mandaverimus sequestrari; vobis mandamus firmiter injungentes quatinus moneatis et efficaciter inducatis executores testamenti dicti defuncti quod de dicta pecunie summa domino Nicholao de Scaleton nunc predicte ecclesie rectori infra certum tempus per vos eisdem ad hoc assignandum ad emendacionem defectuum predictorum satisfaciant competenter, alioquin extunc dictis executoribus coram vobis evocatis ipsam pecunie summam de predictis bonis sequestratis prout justum fuerit levari celeriter faciatis et prefato domino Nicholao ad effectum predictum plenarie liberari, ad que omnia et singula facienda exercenda et expedienda vobis cum cohercionis canonice potestate vices nostras committimus per presentes, aliis litteris nostris

[52] William de Corringham, instituted 1314 (*Reg. Greenfield*, IV.136, no.2578).

in contrarium editis vobis seu aliis in hac parte prius directis nullatenus obsistentibus, quas tenore presencium duximus revocandas. Et nos de omni eo quod feceritis in premissis tempore oportuno reddatis plenius certiores distincte et aperte per vestras litteras patentes harum seriem continentes. Valete. [Laneham, 5 Aug. 1329.]

565 Note of dispensation for illegitimacy and for receiving minor orders secretly (*furtive*) to John son of Adam de Heselley, acolyte, by authority of letters of Gaucelin [cardinal] bishop of Albano, the papal penitentiary. Ripon, 22 Sept. 1329.

566 Institution and mandate for induction (to the archbishop's official) of Jolanus son of Jolanus de Nevill, kt., acolyte, to Barnby in the Willows (*Barneby super Wythum juxta Newerk'*) church, vacant by the death of Hervey [de Sutton]; presented by Jolanus de Nevill, kt. Bishopthorpe, 3 Oct. 1329.

567 Notes [interlined] of licence to study for one year to Jolanus, and of letters dimissory. Southwell, 20 Nov. and 23 Dec. 1329.

568 Dispensation to Walter de Burgeys of Ragnall (*Ragenell*), acolyte (dioc. York), to hold a benefice with cure of souls, despite his illegitimate birth, provided that he takes orders and resides, by authority of letters of John XXII. Laneham, 12 June 1329.

569 Note of commission to M. John de Not', rector of Elkesley, and M. Ralph de Yarwell, rector of Cotham, to correct *comperta* in the deaneries of Newark and Southwell and in Southwell church; they are to report. Bishopthorpe, 8 Oct. 1329.

570 [Fo.368; N.F.447] Commission to Gilbert [de Otterington], rector of St. Nicholas', Nottingham, Adam [de Lansill], rector of Broxtowe (*Brokelstowe*), Richard [de Mowes], vicar of Radford (*Radeford*), and John [Cosyn], vicar of St. Mary's, Nottingham, to claim and receive into safe custody clerks accused of crimes and tried at Nottingham before Sir William de Herle and his fellow justices itinerant or other justices and ministers appointed to deliver Nottingham gaol. Burton Joyce (*Burton Jorz*), 14 Nov. 1329.

571 [*Mandate to Shelford priory to readmit a former apostate.*]
PRO FRATRE ROGERO DE MAR QUOD READMITTATUR IN MONASTERIUM DE SHELFORD. Willelmus etc. dilectis filiis priori et conventui monasterii de Shelford nostre diocesis salutem [*etc.*]. Cum ovis que erravit sit pastoris humeris ad ovile de quo exierat reportanda, ad vos fratrem Rogerum de Mar dudum inter vos professum ordinem et habitum regularem a sentencia excommunicationis majoris quam incurrerat eo quod habitu regulari prorsus abjecto in seculo per aliqua tempora vitam ducens dissolutam est in religionis et sui ordinis grave scandalum non sine apostasie crimine conversatus mittimus absolutum, cui pro modo excessus hujusmodi secundum vestre regule observanciam et ordinis vestri disciplinam injungatis vice nostra prout anime sue videritis expedire

penitenciam salutarem ipsumque sincera et fraterna in domino caritate in omnibus pertractetis. Valete. [Southwell, 15 Nov. 1329.]

572 Institution and mandate for induction (to the archbishop's official) of Gilbert de Otrington, chaplain, to the church of St. Nicholas, Nottingham, in an exchange from Blackwell (*Blakwell*) church (dioc. Coventry and Lichfield) with Geoffrey [de Wilford]; presented by the prior and convent of Lenton. Bishopthorpe, 27 Oct. 1329.

573 The like of Thomas de Stowe, priest, to Marnham vicarage, vacant by the resignation of Nicholas [de Sixtenby]; presented by Thomas Larthier, prior of the hospital of St. John of Jerusalem in England. Wollaton, 11 Nov. 1329.

574 Memorandum of the oath of obedience to the archbishop by M. Anthony de Beek, dean of Lincoln, for his churches in York diocese. In the Carmelite church, Nottingham, 13 Nov. 1329.

575 [*Testimonial that Stephen and Henry de Thorp had been canonically purged of homicide, as Archbishop Greenfield's register testifies.*[53]]
LITTERA TESTIMONIALIS SUPER PURGACIONE STEPHANI DE THORP ET HENRICI FRATRIS SUI CLERICORUM ETC. Universis sancte matris ecclesie filiis in quorum noticiam presentes littere pervenerint Willelmus etc. salutem in auctore salutis. Noveritis quod cum Stephanus de Thorp et Henricus frater suus de eadem clerici super crimine homicidii de morte videlicet Willelmi de Westwode dudum ut dicebatur interfecti in foro seculari diffamati fuissent, carceralique custodie bone memorie domini Willelmi Ebor' archiepiscopi predecessoris nostri immediati per justiciarios domini regis apud Notingham juxta libertatem ecclesiasticam et[54] laudabilem regni Anglie consuetudinem pacifice observatam ut clerici et membra ecclesie[55] liberati, iidem Stephanus et Henricus coram magistro Symone de Curta Majori tunc canonico Suwell' ac domino Thoma Torkard tunc vicario ecclesie de Hokenal commissariis a dicto predecessore nostro ad hoc specialiter deputatis de prefato crimine homicidii eis imposito in ecclesia nostra Suwell' canonice se purgarunt, prout tam per inspectionem registri predecessoris nostri predicti quam per probationes alias legitimas dilucide nobis constat. In cujus rei testimonium litteras nostras dictis Stephano et Henrico fieri fecimus has patentes. [Southwell, 17 Nov. 1329.]

576 Institution and mandate for induction (to the archbishop's official) of Thomas de Brampton, canon of Worksop, priest, to Normanton [on Trent] vicarage, vacant by the resignation of Richard de Langold; presented by the prior and convent of Worksop. Southwell, 19 Nov. 1329.

577 Licence to Thomas Bekering, kt., for the celebration of services until Easter in an oratory in his manor of Laxton by a suitable chaplain assigned to celebrate for his forebears in a chapel of Laxton church. Same date.

[53] A commission ordered the purgation on 27 June 1306, but there is no surviving notice of its outcome (*Reg. Greenfield*, IV.1, no.1673).
[54] Interlined from *libertatem*
[55] Interlined from *et*

578 Mandate[56] to the archbishop's official in the vacant archdeaconry to order John de Malton, rector of a mediety of Treswell, to resume residence within a month or appear before the archbishop. Southwell, 22 Nov. 1329.

579 [Fo.368v; N.F.447v] (i) Institution of Peter Barry, chaplain, to Foston church (dioc. Lincoln), quoting a commission of Henry [Burghersh], bishop of Lincoln (dated Warwick (*Warewyk'*), 21 Nov. 1329) for an exchange of benefices between Peter, rector of Tollerton (*Torlaston*), and John de Leyc', rector of Foston, forwarding the report of an enquiry by the archdeacon of Leicester's official into Foston's vacancy; presented by the prior and convent of Lenton. (ii) Mandate for Peter's induction to the archdeacon of Leicester. (iii) Institution of John, priest, to Tollerton; presented by John [de Aslockton?[57]], kt. (iv) Mandate for his induction to the archbishop's official. (v) Certificate to the bishop of Lincoln. Southwell, 26 Nov. 1329.

580 Note of licence to the said John de Leyc', rector of Tollerton, to study for one year. Same date.

581 Note of licence to John de Hoghton, rector of a mediety of Eakring, to stay away in a decent place until the following Lent. Southwell, 23 Nov. 1329.

582 Note of licence to John de Aslocton, kt., to have services celebrated in his oratory at Tollerton, for two years. Widmerpool, 11 Dec. 1329.

583 [*Following receipt of a recognisance for £300, Thomas de Radeclif,*[58] *a clerk imprisoned for abducting a woman, is to be kept in Southwell manor.*]
PRO THOMA DE RADECLIF' CLERICO SUPER RAPINA CUJUSDAM MULIERIS PER JUSTICIARIOS DAMPNATO INFRA MANERIUM SUWELL' MORATURO. Willelmus etc. dilecto filio Thome de Radeclif' ballivo nostro Suwell' salutem [*etc.*]. Ad instantem requisicionem quorumdam amicorum nostrorum excitati volumus et tibi mandamus quatenus si dominus Johannes de Brette dominus Thomas de Goushill et dominus Phillippus de Caltoftes milites nobis fecerint litteras suas obligatorias de CCCtis libris in quibus fateantur nobis ex causa mutui se teneri, tunc illa[s] littera[s] obligatorias nobis transmittere non tardes et unacum ipsis litteris ordines notam unius barre sub tali forma, videlicet quod si Thomas filius Thome de Radeclif' qui nuper propter rapinam cujusdam mulieris nostro apud Not' extitit carceri liberatus evadat de carcere nostro aliquomodo nobis invitis, tunc dicte littere obligatorie in suo robore maneant et effectu; quod si forsan contingat dictum Thomam filium Thome a dicte crimine rapine coram nobis aut commissariis nostris canonice se purgare vel in carcere nostro decedere, tunc volumus in eo eventu dictas litteras obligatorias viribus carere penitus et effectu. Quibus omnibus sic peractis ac prius receptis per nos dictis litteris obligatoriis, volumus unam cameram predicto Thome loco carceris in manerio nostro Suwell' ordinari etiam et parari, quam non exeat nisi causa spatiendi et tunc nullo modo ipsum manerium nostrum egrediatur nisi tamen ad ecclesiam

[56] Similar in form to no.90, *Reg. Melton,* II.51–2; omitting *et edificia sue rectorie corruere permittendo.*
[57] See **582**. Cf. Thoroton, *Nottinghamshire* (cited under **410**), I.171–2.
[58] See **613–15**; and note 60 below.

nostram Suwell' pro sua missa tantummodo audienda, qua audita ad dictam cameram suam ilice revertatur, ne quod absit videatur ab aliquo evagari. Et quod in premissis feceris nos distincte et aperte certifices tempore oportuno. Vale. [Southwell, 13 Dec. 1329.]

584 [*Transfer of prisoners from Nottingham to York.*]
ROBERTO DE SKAKELTHORP CUSTODI CARCERIS DOMINI APUD EBOR' AD RECIPIENDUM PRISONES VENIENTES DE NOTYNGHAM USQUE EBOR'. Willelmus etc. dilecto filio Roberto de Scakelthorp custodi carceris nostri Ebor' salutem [*etc.*]. Volumus et tibi mandamus quatinus Thomam Baseley[59] Johannem de Radeclif'[60] Walterum de Bughton[61] dominum Thomam de Bulcotes capellanum Willelmum Tusard de Notingham[62] Johannem Michel de Leek Thomam de Creyk' et Johannem Spede prisones nostros apud Notingham nobis liberatos, quos Rogerus de Beltoft Thomas de Haldenby Ricardus de Warwyk' et Johannes Dring' valetti nostri vel eorum aliquis tibi liberabunt seu liberabit, recipias et salvo custodiatis sicut decet et sub periculo quod incumbit, ministrans eis sicut aliis hujusmodi prisonibus est hactenus fieri consuetum. Vale. [Scrooby, 15 Dec. 1329.]

585 Licence to William de Herle, Robert de Malberthorp and other justices itinerant at Nottingham to take during Advent the assize sued by the prior of Worksop against Sir Thomas de Furnivall the elder, Sir Henry de Fauconberge, or Robert Ingram or any others in Nottinghamshire. Leicester (*Leycestr'*), 3 Dec. 1329.

586 Note of licence to study (*insistere scolasticis disciplinis*) for one year to M. Hugh de Wylughby, rector of Ruddington. Bishopthorpe, 22 Jan. 1330.

587 [Fo.369; N.F.448] Collation and mandate for induction (to the archbishop's official) of M. John de Lambok of Nottingham, clerk, to the custody of the hospital of St. John the Baptist, Nottingham, vacant by the death of Matthew de Halifax. Cawood, 9 Feb. 1330.

588 Note of licence to study for one year in a place of his choice to Robert Noreys, rector of West Retford. Bishopthorpe, 20 Feb. 1330.

589 The like to William de Douseby, rector of Kirton. Bishopthorpe, 22 Feb. 1330.

[59] See **699**.
[60] Like Thomas (**583**), John was a son of Thomas de Radeclif (**622**), who may have been the bailiff of Southwell. They were named with, among others, Baseley and Bughton (above) and Robert Jorz (**667**) as members of the Folville gang, in an order for their arrest dated 22 July 1327 (*CCR 1327–30*, 213; and see E.L.G. Stones, 'The Folvilles of Ashby-Folville, Leicestershire, and their associates in crime', *Transactions of the Royal Historical Society*, 5th ser.7 (1957), 117–36).
[61] See **622**.
[62] See **622**.

590 Note of licence to study for one year at a *studium generale* to William de Hasclakby, rector of Sibthorpe. Bishopthorpe, 17 Mar. 1330.

591 [*Mandate to the dean and chapter of York to do their part for M. Manuel de Fieschi, provided by John XXII to the archdeaconry of Nottingham and admitted, with reservations, by the archbishop.*[63]]
LITTERA DIRECTA DECANO ET CAPITULO ECCLESIE EBOR' GRACIE ADMISSIONE MAGISTRI MANUELIS DE FLISCO IN ARCHIDIACONATUM NOTYNGH' PER DOMINUM PAPAM SIBI COLLATUM QUOD IPSI ULTERIUS FACIANT QUOD AD IPSOS PERTINET IN HOC CASU. Willelmus etc. dilectis filiis . . decano et capitulo ecclesie nostre beati Petri Ebor' salutem [*etc.*]. Cum secundum formam litterarum gracie per sanctissimum in Christo patrem et dominum nostrum dominum Johannem divina providencia papam XXII magistro Manueli de Flisco de archidiaconatu Not' in eadem[64] ecclesia nostra per consecracionem magistri Johannis de Grandissono ultimi archidiaconi ejusdem in Exon' episcopum vacante concesse et processus habiti super ea, eundem magistrum Manuelem in personam magistri Johannis de Munkegate procuratoris sui substituti nomine ejusdem domini sui[65] ad archidiaconatum predictum et in ipsius archidiaconatus archidiaconum quatenus de jure ac virtute gracie sedis apostolice et processus predictorum tenebamur, salvis nobis et successoribus nostris et ecclesie nostre predicte excepcionibus et defensionibus quibuscumque tam nullitatum quam aliarum quarumcumque materiarum tam contra personam dicti magistri Manuelis quam litteras et processus habitos et habendos in hac parte qualitercumque competentibus et competituris, salva etiam nobis potestate conferendi predictum archidiaconatum ac alias dignitates canonicatus et prebendatus ceteraque officia et beneficia ecclesie nostre predicte cum vacaverint qui et que prefato magistro Manueli debiti et debite non fuerint virtute gracie et processus predictorum, admiserimus; vobis mandamus quatinus in premissis circa predictum magistrum Manuelem vel procuratorem suum in hac parte ulterius exequamini quod est vestrum. Valete. [Bishopthorpe, 27 Mar. 1330.]

592 Mandate to the abbots, priors, clergy and people of the archdeaconry of Nottingham to obey M. Manuel and his official as archdeacon.[66] Bishopthorpe, 25 Mar. 1330.

593 Note of letter to M. Robert de Clareburgh, official in the archdeaconry's vacancy, to deliver the seal of the officiality to M. Manuel or his proctor. Same date.

594 (i) Certificate to Henry [Burghersh], bishop of Lincoln, that the archbishop has executed his commission (quoted; dated Winchester, 14 Mar. 1330) for an exchange of benefices [as follows], forwarding the report of an enquiry by

[63] Cf. **506–8**; *Fasti*, VI.24.
[64] Interlined.
[65] See note to **592**.
[66] Repeating **591** to *competituris*; replacing *nomine ejusdem domini sui* with *magistri Thome de Luco procuratoris principalis ejusdem magistri Manuelis*; and omitting *tam nullitatum . . . materiarum*. Note that **592–3** are dated two days earlier than **591**.

the archdeacon of Bedford's official. (ii) Institution of Roger de Lamelaye, priest, to Northill (*Northyevele*) church (dioc. Lincoln), vacant by the resignation of Thomas Trayly; presented by Walter Trayli. (iii) Mandate for his induction to the archdeacon of Bedford. [Fo.369v; N.F.418v] (iv) Institution of Thomas Trayly, priest, to Lambley church, vacant by Roger's resignation; presented by Ralph de Croumwell, kt. (v) Mandate for his induction to the official of the vacant archdeaconry of Nottingham. Bishopthorpe, 25 Mar. 1330.

595 Testimonial for Stephen Pavely of Ruddington, clerk. He was defamed of the homicide of Richard Pavele, kt.,[67] and delivered by the justices at York[68] to the dean and chapter of York, keepers of the spiritualities after the death of Thomas de Corbrigg'. He purged himself in York Minster before M. John Fraunceys, the keepers' commissary, of which there is sufficient proof. Southwell, 6 May 1330.

596 Institution and mandate for induction (to the archdeacon or his official) of Roger de Stowe, priest, to the vicarage of the prebendal church of Clifton, vacant by the death of M. William de Wykyngby; presented by the rector, M. Thomas Beek. Colston Basset, 17 Apr. 1330.

597 Note of licence to study for two years to Robert [de Brunnesleye[69]], rector of a mediety of Trowell, which he may farm. Southwell, 5 May 1330.

598 Institution [etc.] of William Lyouns, priest, to Egmanton vicarage, now vacant; presented by the prior and convent of Newstead. Cawood, 23 May 1330.

599 [*Licence by authority of papal letters (dated 29 Sept. 1327)*[70] *for Newstead priory to appropriate Egmanton church, with assignment of land and receipts for the vicar's portion. Newstead is to build his dwelling, repair the chancel, and pay the archbishop (or dean and chapter) an annual pension at Southwell synods.*]
APPROPRIACIO ECCLESIE DE EGMANTON. Willelmus etc. dilectis in Christo filiis . . priori et . . conventui prioratus de Novo Loco in Shirwode ordinis sancti Augustini nostre diocesis salutem [*etc.*]. Litteras sanctissimi in Christo patris et domini nostri domini Johannis divina providencia pape XXII non cancellatas non abolitas nec in aliqua sui parte viciatas sed sanas et integras ad modum sacrosancte Romane curie vera bulla plumbea filo canapis pendente bullatas et omni suspicione carentes nobis ex parte vestra dudum presentatas recepimus eo qui sequitur sub tenore:

Johannes episcopus servus servorum dei venerabili fratri archiepiscopo Ebor' salutem et apostolicam benedictionem. Apostolice sedis providencia circumspecta devotorum laudabiles actiones intenta consideracione discuciens illos non merito amplioris gracia favoris attolit in quibus uberioris devocionis studia

[67] For another Paveley appealed of this crime, see *CPR 1301–7*, 537. There is no information about it in the register for the vacancy of 1304–6 (*Reg. Corbridge*, II.165–80).
[68] Named in **600** as Ralph de Ingham and Peter Malure, justices of Edward I (*celebris memorie*), to deliver York gaol.
[69] Instituted 1310 (*Reg. Greenfield*, IV.86, no.1861).
[70] See *CPL*, II.254. A royal licence was granted in 1315 (*CPR 1313–17*, 398).

contemplatur. Exhibita siquidem nobis pro parte dilectorum filiorum prioris et conventus prioratus de Novo Loco in Shirwode ordinis sancte Augustini tue diocesis peticio continebat quod prioratus ipse in nemore juxta viam publicam situatus propter distanciam villarum undequaque hospitalitate tam divitum quam pauperum ultra vires possessionum suarum, que notorie sunt tenues et exiles, adeo graviter et continue onerantur quod ea que pro cotidiano victu parata existunt oportet hospitibus ad prioratum ipsum subito advenientibus communiter ministrari, unde et debitus numerus canonicorum abolim ibidem ordinatus non prout propter oppressiones multiplices comode sustentari potissime cum illa regio novis cotidie tribulacionibus emergentibus plus solito atteratur, ecclesiamque ipsorum que ruinosa evidenter apparet ex causis predictis nequeunt reparare. Quare pro parte dictorum prioris et conventus nobis extitit humiliter supplicatum ut eis pio super hiis compacientes affectu, ne in eodem prioratu cultus divinus quoad dictum numerum canonicorum ipsorum aut hospitalitas minuatur aut eorum ecclesia ruine subiciatur prefate, parochialem ecclesiam de Egmanton dicte diocesis in qua iidem prior et conventus ut asserunt jus obtinent patronatus, cujusque fructus decem librarum sterlingorum secundum taxacionem decime summam annuam non excedunt, eis in usus proprios in supportacionem predictorum onerum concedere et unire imperpetuum de benignitate sedis apostolice dignaremur. Nos igitur de premissis noticiam non habentes, gerentes quoque de tue circumspectionis industria in hiis et aliis fiduciam in domino specialem ac volentes eisdem priori et conventui paterna solicitudine providere, fraternitati tue per apostolica scripta committimus et mandamus quatinus si est ita prefatam parochialem ecclesiam cum omnibus juribus et pertinenciis suis eidem prioratui auctoritate apostolica perpetuo concedas unias et annectas, sic quod post concessionem unionem et annexionem hujusmodi cedente vel decedente ipsius parochialis ecclesie rectore prefati prior et conventus auctoritate propria per se vel alium seu alios ejusdem ecclesie possessionem libere apprehendere et tenere fructusque ipsius in usus proprios convertere possint, tua vel cujuscumque alterius licencia minime requisita; reservata tamen et assignata primitus de ipsius parochialis ecclesie proventibus perpetuo vicario instituendo canonice in eadem porcione congrua ex qua idem vicarius comode sustentari valeat et episcopalia jura solvere aliaque sibi incumbencia onera supportare; non obstantibus si aliqui super provisionibus sibi faciendis de hujusmodi parochialibus ecclesiis vel aliis beneficiis ecclesiasticis in illis partibus speciales vel generales dicte sedis vel legatorum ejus litteras impetrarunt, eciam si per eas ad inhibicionem reservacionem et decretum vel alias quomodolibet sit processum, quas litteras et processus habitos per eosdem ad prefatam parochialem ecclesiam si inveneris ut premittitur ita esse et per te contingat auctoritate predicta hujusmodi fieri unionem volumus non extendi set nullum per hoc eis quoad assecucionem ecclesiarum et beneficiorum aliorum prejudicium generari, seu quibuslibet litteris et indulgenciis apostolicis generalibus vel specialibus quorumcumque tenorum existant per que effectus presencium impediri valeat quomodolibet vel differri et de quibus quorumque totis tenoribus habenda sit in nostris litteris mencio specialis, contradictores per censuram ecclesiasticam appellacione postposita compescendo. Nos enim irritum decrevimus et inane si secus super hoc a quoquam quavis auctoritate scienter vel ignoranter contigerit attemptari. Datum Avinion' III kalendas Octobris pontificatus nostri anno XI.

Quarum litterarum ac commissionis et mandati de quibus in eisdem fit mencio auctoritate magistro Thoma de Sancto Leonardo nunc rectore ecclesie de Egmanton antedicte specialiter et nominatim, archidiacono Notinghamie ac ipsius ecclesie parochianis et aliis in genere quorum intererunt [Fo.370; N.F.449] si qui fuerant ad certos diem et locum peremptorie citatis ad proponendum quicquid canonicum haberent ac proponere vellent quare predictam ecclesiam de Egmanton cujus jus obtinetis patronatus vobis ac vestro prioratui in usus vestros proprios auctoritate apostolica concedere unire et annectere minime deberemus, et nullo oppositorum comparente nec quicquam in hac parte proponente, productisque testibus ex parte vestra ad probandum veritatem contentorum in suggestione vestra et ipsam suggestionem receptis in forma juris juratis et diligenter examinatis et eorum dictis seu attestacionibus in scriptis redactis ac eciam publicatis, dictisque archidiacono rectore et aliis predictis ex habundanti ad dicendum in testes et eorum dicta et subsequenter ad proponendum omnia in facto consistencia si quid proponere vellent in premissis peremptorie citatis et nullo modo comparentibus nec quicquam aliqualiter proponentibus, processu eciam per nos ac juris ordine qui in hoc casu quatenus juxta canonica instituta et formam litterarum apostolicarum predictarum ac qualitatem hujus negocii requirebantur in omnibus observatis; quia invenimus contenta in dicta vestra suggestione vera esse et sufficienter probata, prefatam ecclesiam de Egmanton cujus fructus decem librarum sterlingorum secundum taxacionem decime summam annuam non excedunt cum omnibus juribus et pertinenciis suis vobis priori et conventui ac vestro prioratui memoratis in usus vestros proprios in supportacionem onerum de quibus in dictis litteris apostolicis fit mencio prefata auctoritate apostolica perpetuo concedimus unimus et annectimus, sic quod cedente vel decedente prefato ipsius ecclesie rectore qui nunc est, vos prior et conventus auctoritate propria per vos alium seu alios ejusdem ecclesie possessionem libere apprehendere et tenere fructusque ipsius in usus vestros proprios convertere possitis, nostra seu cujuscumque alterius licencia minime requisita; reservata tamen et assignata primitus de ipsius ecclesie parochialis proventibus perpetuo vicario instituendo canonice in eadem porcione congrua ex qua idem vicarius[71] comode sustentari valeat et episcopalia jura solvere aliaque sibi incumbencia onera supportare, videlicet duobus toftis melioribus et propinquioribus ecclesie in quorum uno vos prior et conventus unam aulam cameram et[72] unam coquinam competentes pro habitacione dicti vicarii vestris sumptibus construatis, viginti acris terre arabilis, tribus acris prati, de quibus ac eciam ovibus et aliis animalibus suis quibuscumque nullam omnino decimam solvere teneatur, mortuariis vivis et mortuis ac aliis minutis decimis et oblacionibus quibuscumque tam in pecunia quam in aliis rebus et speciebus predicte ecclesie qualitercumque per totum annum provenientibus cum toto alteragio excepta lana, que omnia dicto vicario specialiter reservamus, quibus omnibus sic reservatis dictus vicarius pro porcione congrua totaliter contentetur.

Volumus et eciam ordinamus quod vos prior et conventus ut rectores ecclesie predicte cancellum ejusdem quociens opus fuerit de novo construatis cooperiatis et reficiatis vestris sumptibus competenter. Jura vero episcopalia vicarius qui pro

[71] Margin: *Egmaunton vicarie taxatio* in sixteenth-century hand.
[72] Interlined.

tempore fuerit solvat insolidum. Cetera vero onera ordinaria et extraordinaria dicte ecclesie qualitercumque incumbencia vos prior et conventus pro duabus partibus et vicarius pro tercia parte agnoscatis et agnoscat. Salvo tamen nobis jure dictam porcionem vicarii, si et quandocumque nimis diminuta fuerit vel exilis, juxta juris exigenciam et prefati domini nostri pape intencionem summarie et de plano absque strepitu et figura judicii de fructibus redditibus et proventibus ecclesie predicte augmentandi. Omnibus et singulis jure jurisdictione ac dignitate nostris et ecclesie nostre Ebor' nobis et eidem ecclesie nostre nostrisque successoribus semper salvis, quibus aut juri archidiaconi loci per premissa non intendimus aliqualiter derogare. In recompensacionem vero lesionis juris ecclesie nostre Ebor' nobis et successoribus nostris sede plena ac decano et capitulo ecclesie nostre predicte sede archiepiscopali vacante sex solidos et octo denarios nomine annue pensionis per vos priorem et conventum predictos de fructibus et proventibus ecclesie predicte in sinodis de Suwell post festa sancti Michaelis et Pasche per equales porciones annuatim solvendos tenore presencium reservantes. In quorum omnium testimonium sigilli nostri impressione presentes litteras mandavimus communiri. [Ripon, 22 June 1329.]

600 To Edward III [repeating **595**]. Request that, according to custom, the sheriff of Nottingham be instructed to restore Stephen Pavely's goods and chattels.[73] Laneham, 19 June 1330.

601 Note of licence for study for one year from 29 Sept. 1330 to John de Sibethorp, rector of North Collingham, which he may farm. Hawton by Newark, n.d.

602 [Fo.370v; N.F.449v] Appointment of Lady Alice de Compton, widow of Nicholas de Widmerpole, as curatrix of their children Reginald and Maud, with administration of their goods. Granby, 7 July 1330.

603 Note of licence to Adam [de Preston], rector of Hickling, to farm his church for two years and be absent for one. Worksop, 22 July 1330.

604 Note[74] that the king's writs about John and William sons of John de Oscynton, registered in [the section for] the archdeaconry of York under the year 1330, should be registered here.

605 Note of mandate [recipients not named] for the visitation of churches and places of Newark deanery not yet visited, as follows: on Monday 2 July in [South] Scarle church; on Tuesday 3 July in Newark church; and on Wednesday 4[75] July in Sibthorpe church. Laneham, 27 June 1330.

606 TERCIA VISITATIO DECANATUS DE BYNGHAM. Mandate[76] to the archdeacon or his official to cite the clergy (including religious claiming appropriated churches, etc.) and four or six men from each vill in Bingham deanery to

[73] Ordered 26 June 1330 (*CCR 1330–3*, 40–1).
[74] In large lettering with marginal drawing of pointing hand and face, suggestive of cocking a snook.
[75] MS. *tercio*
[76] As for third visitation of Cleveland in 1332 (*Reg. Melton*, III.148, no.393).

attend visitation by the archbishop or his commissaries as follows: on Thursday 5 July in Kneeton church; on Friday 6 July in Aslockton chapel; on Monday 9 July in Stanton on the Wolds (*Staynton*) church; on Tuesday 10 July in East Leake (*Magna Leyk'*) church; and on Wednesday 11 July in West Leake (*Parva Leyk'*) church. Laneham, 16 June 1330.

607 Note of similar mandate for Nottingham deanery, for attendance on Saturday 14 July in Stoke Bardolph chapel; Monday 16 July in St. Mary's, Nottingham; Tuesday 17 July in Nuthall (*Notehale*) church; and Friday 20 July in Mansfield church. Laneham, 27 June 1330.

608 Mandate [similar to **543**] to the prior and convent of Shelford for their visitation on Thursday 12 July. Laneham, 18 June 1330.

609 Note of similar mandate to the prior and convent of Worksop for their visitation on Saturday 21 July. Laneham, 27 June 1330.

610 [Fo.371; N.F.450] Certificate of M. Richard de Cestria, canon of York, and the commissary general of the official of York that they have executed the archbishop's commission (quoted[77]; dated Bishopthorpe, 30 July 1330) to receive in York Minster, on the last juridical day before 1 August, the purgation of Thomas de Beltoft', junior, clerk (dioc. York), defamed before justices itinerant at Nottingham[78] for receiving in his houses at Clayworth and Hayton Ralph son of Thomas de Beltoft', senior, outlawed for the death of John de Bekyngham and other crimes; he had been delivered to the archbishop's prison.[79] On 31 July, Thomas appeared before them in chains. Their commission was read. An enquiry about his life and character was made, also a proclamation by the dean of Retford as ordered by the archbishop. There being no objection, Thomas was purged by the oaths of William del Byry, Thomas de Thirnir, Hugh Bacour, William de Hamerton and Adam de Boulton, chaplains, and William de Loncastr', John de Tadecastr', Nicholas called Mazoun, Robert Urry, William de Nassyngton, John Whyte, John Akentoth and Roger de Wakefeld, clerks. York, 1 Aug. 1330.

611 ALIA SUPER EODEM. [Shorter version of the above, omitting the commission.] Same date.

612 Mandate [similar to **543** and **608**] to the prior and convent of Newstead for their visitation on Wednesday 18 July. Laneham, 27 June 1330.

613 To Edward III. Request that the sheriff of Nottingham be instructed to restore Thomas de Radeclyf's lands, tenements, goods and chattels, following his purgation [with details as in **614**]. Bishopthorpe, 13 Aug. 1330.

[77] Its form is similar to no.289 in *Reg. Melton*, II.113–14, without its final clause.
[78] Named as Robert de Malberthorp and Robert de Scorburgh in an order for the restitution of Thomas's lands, etc., dated 18 Aug. 1330 (*CCR 1330–3*, 59).
[79] At York, according to **611**.

614 Certificate of the prior of Thurgarton, M. William de Hundon, rector of Barnburgh, and William de Hokerton, penitentiary of Southwell, that they have executed the archbishop's commission (quoted; [Fo.371v; N.F.451v] dated Radcliffe on Trent, 13 July 1330) to receive in Southwell Minster, on 30 July, the purgation of Thomas de Radclif', son of Thomas de Radclif' super Trentam, clerk. He was defamed before justices itinerant at Nottingham[80] of the crime of seizing Alice de Rughford against her will at Carlton by Nottingham and abducting her to Radcliffe on Trent;[81] he had been delivered to the archbishop's prison. [The certificate is as follows:]

Quarum auctoritate litterarum coram nobis . . priore Willelmo et Willelmo protribunali sedentibus in ecclesia Suwellens' die Lune proximo ante festum sancti Petri ad vincula ultimo preteritum[82] predictus Thomas filius Thome de Radclif' super Trentam clericus in medium productus est admodum incarcerati, in cujus presencia ac cleri et populi multitudine copiosa commissionem vestram nobis factam ac litteras certificatorias discreti viri . . decani Notingh' publice legi fecimus. Quibus lectis trino edi[c]to publice proclamari fecimus coram nobis et in portis ecclesie Suwell' preconizari quod si quis vel qui essent qui aliquid proponere aut opponere vellet seu vellent quominus dictus Thomas suam non possit aut non debeat facere purgacionem coram nobis de crimine raptus cujusdam Alicie de Rughford apud Carleton juxta Not' sibi inposito, protestantes solempniter et expresse quod si quis compareret oppositorum vel contradictorum unus vel plures, parati eramus et erimus domini nostri . . archiepiscopi [auctoritate?] ei vel eis omnibus et singulis secundum qualitatem negocii exhibere et facere cum effectu justicie complementum. Set cum nullus appareret oppositorum vel contradictorum nec manus armata quam vidimus propter quam timere deberet aliquis se opponere, iterato publice coram nobis in ecclesia predicta et ante fores ecclesie fecimus preconizari trino edicto et proclamari sicut prius. Et cum nullus quoquomodo appareret oppositorum nec contradictorum aliquantulum exspectati, ipsius Thome purgacionem recepimus de crimine raptus supradicto in forma juris debita et consueta cum duodecima manu presbiterorum et clericorum honestorum prout gestu et habitu apparebat et assistencium multitudo testabatur (videlicet cum dominis Roberto de Barnby, Willelmo de Hedon, Johanne le Taverner de Not', Simone de Halum, Willelmo filio Nicholai et Willelmo de Thurgarton, capellanis, et Roberto Pepircorn, Henrico Austyn de Suwell', Roberto filio Henrici, Henrico Fraunceys, Roberto de Hyford et Ada Sewall', clericis) pronunciantes ipsum Thomam de crimine predicto legitime se purgasse ac fame sue bone quatenus nos attingit restituentes. Et sic mandatum vestrum reverendum in omnibus sumus reverenter executi. In quorum omnium testimonium sigilla nostra sunt appensa. Valeat reverenda vestra paternitas per tempora prospera et longeva. [Southwell, 30 July 1330.]

615 Letters patent testifying the above purgation of Thomas Radeclif. He was pronounced guiltless of the said crime and his good name restored. Bishopthorpe, 13 Aug. 1330.

[80] Named in **613** and **615** as Robert de Malberthorp and Robert de Scorburgh.

[81] See also **622**.

[82] MS. *preterito*

616 To Edward III. Request for restitution of the lands, tenements, goods and chattels of Stephen de Misterton, clerk.[83] He had been defamed before Robert de Malberthorp and Robert de Scorburgh, justices itinerant at Nottingham, of the crime of stealing two cartloads of beans from the rector of Misterton and Robert de Welton and other men of Misterton, valued at five shillings, and twenty cartloads of peat from John son of Gilbert and Beatrice Freman, valued at twenty pence; and also of being a common thief. The justices delivered him to the archbishop. He has now purged himself, his good name is restored, and he is innocent of these crimes. Cawood, 18 Aug. 1330.

617 Letters patent testifying that Stephen de Misterton's purgation from the above charge took place in York Minster (*in loco consistorii*) on 17 August. Same date.

618 Certificate of M. Richard de Cestr', canon of York, the commissary-general of the official of York and M. John de Notingham, rector of Elkesley, that they have executed the archbishop's commission (quoted; [Fo.372; N.F.451] dated Bishopthorpe, 3 Aug. 1330) to receive Stephen de Misterton's purgation in York Minster on 17 Aug.; he was defamed [as in **616**]. These letters were read publicly, as were the report of an enquiry about his manner of life (*conversacione*) and a proclamation by the dean of Retford. No objectors appeared, and Stephen purged himself by suitable honest persons named in a schedule. York, 17 Aug. 1330.

619 Institution and mandate for induction of M. Thomas de Waldeby, priest, to the vicarage of East Stoke prebendal church, now vacant;[84] presented by [John de Northwode] the prebendary. Bishop Burton, 31 Aug. 1330.

620 [*Abjuration of his mistress by the rector of Misterton, under pain of deprivation; with sentence by the auditor of causes that he pay 100 marks despite the season.*]
CONDEMPNACIO MAGISTRI THOME DE SANCTO ALBANO. Memorandum quod xxv die mensis Augusti anno domini supradicto apud Thorp juxta Ebor' magister Thomas de Sancto Albano rector ecclesie de Misterton et prebendarius prebende de Dunham abjuravit Aliciam Berdeles de Misterton[85] sub pena privacionis ab utroque beneficio si ipsum contigerit convinci quod eam in futurum carnaliter cognoverit. Et juravit solvere domino archiepiscopo centum marcas in festis subscriptis, videlicet:[86] Et fuit in dicta pecunia sentencialiter condempnatus, presentibus magistro Ricardo de Snoweshull notario publico Roberto de Wycumbe rectore ecclesie de Botyl' et Gilberto de Maunfeld clerico etc. etc. JTDBSD.[87]

[83] Ordered 30 Aug. 1330 (*CCR 1330–3,* 58).
[84] Cf. **621**.
[85] Cf. **485**.
[86] Followed by 5.5 cms. blank.
[87] Enclosed in oblong; identified by Professor David Smith as the initials of Johannes Thome de Barneby super Done, a notary whose sign and eschatocol (dated 1336) are reproduced (from Reg. Melton) in J.S. Purvis, *Notarial Signs* (St. Anthony's Press, London and York, 1957), plate 18. See also **526**.

In dei nomine amen. Nos auditor causarum venerabilis patris domini Willelmi [*etc.*] te magistrum Thomam de Sancto Albano canonicum ecclesie Suwell' in centum marcis sterlingorum ex causa certa et legitima dicto domino archiepiscopo vel ejus receptori Suwell' apud Suwell' in terminis in litteris tuis obligatoriis inde confectis et secundum earundem vim formam et effectum plenius contentis non obstante instanti tempore messium et vindemiarum de consensu tuo expresso per precepti sentenciam condempnamus in hiis scriptis. [Bishopthorpe, 25 Aug. 1330.]

621 [*Award of pension from East Stoke vicarage to John de Arsent, who was its incumbent when M. Thomas de Waldeby was presented.*[88]]
ORDINACIO DOMINI ARCHIEPISCOPI INTER PRESENTATUM AD VICARIAM ECCLESIE DE STOKE ET INCUMBENTEM POSSESSIONI EJUSDEM. Universis sancte matris ecclesie filiis presentes litteras inspecturis Willelmus permissione divina etc. salutem in omnium salvatore. Cum dilectus filius dominus Johannes de Northwode prebendarius ecclesie prebendalis de Stoke nostre diocesis magistrum Thomam de Waldeby presbiterum ad vicariam de Stoke quam vacantem asseruit nobis presentasset, fuissetque auctoritate nostra de vacacione dicte vicarie ac jure et possessione presentantis et ceteris solitis articulis ut moris est legitime inquisitum, compertumque fuisset per hujusmodi inquisicionem quod dictus dominus Johannes fuit et est dicte vicarie verus patronus habetque jus presentandi ad eandem ac quod dicta vicaria tunc extitit plena et consulta de domino Johanne de Arsent possessioni ejusdem incumbente; et quamquam ex parte dicti presentati fuisset a nobis petitum quod ipsum ad dictam vicariam admitteremus et vicarium institueremus canonice in eadem, dictoque domino Johanne asserente dictam vicariam de se plenam ut premittitur et consultam propter quod dictus magister Thomas ad eam admitti non debuit presentatus; tandem tamen tam dictus dominus Johannes vicarie predicte possessioni incumbens quam dictus magister Thomas ad ipsam vicariam ut premittitur presentatus in nostra presencia personaliter constituti, ut litium[89] amfractus evitarent pro bono pacis et quietis et ut hic inde parceretur laboribus et expensis, dictus tamen Johannes quoad totum jus quod sibi competit seu quomodolibet competiit in vicaria predicta prefatusque magister Thomas ad vicariam predictam ut predicitur presentatus totum jus quod habet habuit seu habere potuit sibi competens ad vicariam predictam occasione dicte presentacionis sibi facte de eadem nostris ordinacioni arbitrio laudo et decreto alte et basse sponte pure simpliciter et absolute singillatim legitime submiserunt. Et quamquam ante quamcumque ordinacionem dictus dominus Johannes dictam vicariam cum suis juribus et pertinenciis universis pure sponte simpliciter et absolute in nostris manibus resignasset, prefatusque magister Thomas ad eam postea legitime admissus fuisset et vicarius perpetuus institutus canonice in eadem; idem tamen magister Thomas ad ordinandum de eadem vicaria pro sustentacione dicti domini Johannis qui dum vicarius extitit tenuit et habuit statum honestum, ne in obprobrium et oblocucionem plurium victum et vestitum non haberet competentes, se et eandem vicariam suam nostris ordinacioni laudo et decreto per omnia se submisit, eo qui sequitur sub tenore:

[88] See **619**. Arsent presumably succeeded as vicar after John de Coates (**253**).
[89] MS. *licium*

Noverint universi quod ego Thomas de Waldeby perpetuus vicarius ecclesie prebendalis de Stoke prope Neuwerk' Ebor' diocesis super eo quod venerabilis pater et dominus dominus Willelmus dei gracia Ebor' archiepiscopus Anglie primas assignare ordinare et constituere poterit domino Johanni Arsent [Fo.372v; N.F.451v] nuper vicario ecclesie de Stoke predicte de eadem vicaria mea annuam pensionem de qua, ne in obprobium cleri et populi victum et vestitum non habeat futuris temporibus competentes qualitercumque, percipiendam in vicaria mea predicta seu de ea ad terminum vite dicti domini Johannis ordinacioni et decreto et laudo dicti venerabilis patris in omnibus et per omnia me et vicariam meam predictam submitto, ratum semper habiturus et firmum quicquid dictus venerabilis pater ordinandum laudandum decernendum et constituendum duxerit in premissis et quolibet premissorum. In cujus rei testimonium presentibus sigillum meum apposui. Datum apud Burton prope Beverl' Kalendas Septembris anno gracie MCCCXXX.

Et subsequenter a nobis fuerat instanter petitum ex parte eorum qui se ut premittitur submiserunt quatinus ad aliquam ordinacionem prout nobis expedire videretur procederemus. Unde nos habita deliberacione aliquali ad honorem dei et utilitatem ipsius vicarie et animarum salutem ac eciam pietate moti ad statumque predicti domini Johannis qui in diebus suis non modicum processit debite intuitum convertentes, et presertim advertentes quod in dicta vicaria diu profecit ejusque utilitatem hactenus promovit et pro viribus procuravit multaque fecerat in eadem, cum non habeat sufficienter aliunde unde valeat ut dicitur sustentari ne sui victus necessarius processu temporis quod absit destitui videatur.

In dei nomine amen. Nos Willelmus archiepiscopus Ebor' supradictus ordinamus et decernimus quod idem dominus Johannes de vicaria predicta ac de magistro Thoma vicario ejusdem et ejusdem vicariis qui pro temporibus fuerint quibuscumque ad totam vitam suam pensionem annuam viginti marcarum in festis Nativitatis Domini Pasche Nativitatis beati Johannis Baptiste et sancti Michaelis per porciones equales singulis annis percipiat sibi in dicta vicaria absque dilatione ulteriori fideliter persolvendam, ad quam quidem pensionem prefato domino Johanni dictis terminis singulis annis quoad vixerit fideliter persolvendam oneramus predictam vicariam et ejusdem vicarios omnes et singulos qui pro temporibus fuerint intuitu caritatis, causisque supradictis et aliis moti causis sufficientibus in hoc casu si necesse fuerit declarandis. Injungimus insuper dicto magistro Thoma et quibuscumque vicariis dicte ecclesie futuris qui pro tempore fuerint si et quatenus de jure poterimus sub pena excommunicationis majoris quod dictam pensionem agnoscant et prefato domino Johanni persolvant et eorum quilibet pro tempore suo persolvat terminis et loco assignatis fideliter ut est dictum.

Et nihilominus ad instantem peticionem dicti domini Johannis eundem magistrum Thomam predictam pensionem agnoscentem et confitentem eam ipsi domino Johanni deberi a se et vicaria sua predicta, volentemque tempore messium non obstante nostram condempnacionem in hac parte subire, in dicta pensione annua prefato domino Johanni prout in ordinacione nostra superius continetur premissam ejus confessionem sicuti sentencialiter et diffinitive per precepti nostri sentenciam condempnamus ac predictam pensionem prefato domino Johanni ut premittitur deberi ad totam vitam suam declaramus in hiis scriptis. In quorum omnium testimonium presentem ordinacionem nostram sigilli nostri appensione fecimus communiri. [Bishop Burton, 1 Sept. 1330.]

622 Memorandum that John de Radeclif' son of Thomas de Radeclif' and Walter de Bucton, clerks, purged themselves in York Minster on 7 September before M. Richard de Cestr', canon of York, the official of York's commissary-general, John de Notingham, rector of Elkesley, and Adam de Spyriden, rector of St. Saviour's, York, the archbishop's commissaries. They had been defamed before William de Herle and other justices itinerant in Nottingham of seizing Alice de Rughford at Carlton and abducting her to Radcliffe on Trent (see **614**); they were delivered to the archbishop's prison.

Also that William Tussard of Nottingham, clerk,[90] purged himself in York Minster on 5 September before M. John de Wodehous, commissary-general of the official of York, Adam de Spiriden, rector of St. Saviour's, York, and William de Jafford, the archbishop's penitentiary. He had been defamed before Robert de Malberthorp and Robert de Schorburgh, justices itinerant in Nottingham, of stealing twenty sheep at Spalford, valued at eighteen pence each, from Nigel de Spaldeford, and two bullocks at South Muskham, valued at twenty shillings, from Henry son of William de Southmuskham; he was delivered to the archbishop's prison.

Note that the king was asked for the restitution of their goods and chattels,[91] and that they had letters testimonial about their purgation. [n.d.]

623 Institution [etc.] of Stephen le Eyr, priest, to Wilford church, vacant by the resignation of William de Brokelesby; presented by Gervase de Clifton and his wife Margaret. Bishopthorpe, 16 Sept. 1330.

624 Note of licence to William de Walkyngham, rector of Greasley, to be absent for two years in a decent place. Bishopthorpe, 22 Sept. 1330.

625 Institution [etc.] of Richard de Foston, priest, to Radford vicarage, vacant by the death of Richard de Foston;[92] presented by the prior and convent of Lenton. Cawood, 3 Oct. 1330.

626 Institution (in the person of John de Wirkesop, clerk, as proctor) and mandate for induction of Thomas de Fairfax, priest, to Walkeringham vicarage, vacant by the resignation of Walter de Carleton; presented by the prior and convent of Worksop. Cawood, 7 Oct. 1330.

627 [Fo.373; N.F.452] Certificate of Henry [Burghersh], bishop of Lincoln, that he has executed the archbishop's commission (quoted; dated Bishop Burton, 2 Sept. 1330) for an exchange of benefices between Henry de Staunford, rector of a mediety of Gedling, and John de Glaston, rector of Easton on the Hill (*Eston juxta Staunford*; dioc. Lincoln); forwarding the report of an enquiry by the

[90] A recidivist (see **438**)?

[91] Ordered for Walter (only), 16 Sept. 1330 (*CCR 1330–3*, 59).

[92] In error for Richard de Mowes, instituted 1312 (*Reg. Greenfield*, IV.121, no.1929).

archdeacon of Nottingham's official. John was instituted to Gedling.[93] Lenton, 16 Oct. 1330.

628 Mandate for John de Glaston's induction to Gedling. Southwell, 19 Oct. 1330.

629 Note of licence to William de Lameley, rector of Cromwell, to be absent for one year to study (*in scolis*) and farm his church. Southwell, 19 Oct. 1330.

630 [*Order to enforce William del Clay's payment of alimony for illegitimate children.*] CONDEMPNACIO ALIMENTORUM. Willelmus etc. dilecto filio decano nostro de Retford salutem [*etc.*]. Quia Willelmum del Clay de Markham ad dandum et solvendum Beatrici filie Johannis le Spenser de Upton singulis annis per triennium proximo sequentem pro sustentacione et alimentacione prolis quam suscitavit ex ea quinque solidos sterlingorum eidem Beatrici ex causa predicta liberandos annuatim in festis sancti Martini et Pasche in equales porciones, incipiente primo termino in instanti festo sancti Martini, vel quod predictus Willelmus dictam suam prolem penes se recipiat alendam et eam alat competenter per tempus supradictum, condempnavimus justicia exigente; tibi mandamus quatinus prefatum Willelmum ad hec si id non fecerit per quascumque censuras ecclesiasticas compellas canonice vice nostra. Vale. [Southwell, 20 Oct. 1330.]

631 (i) Institution (in the person of Roger de Twyford, his proctor) of John de la Bourne, priest, to Screveton[94] church in [the following] exchange; presented by William Bozon of Screveton, clerk. (ii) Mandate for his induction. (iii) Collation[95] (in the person of Gilbert de Mammesfeld, rector of Wickersley, substitute of the principal proctor, M. Ralph de Yarwell, rector of Cotham) to M. John de Nassington, the archbishop's dear clerk, of Shobrooke (*Shokbrok'*) church (dioc. Exeter) by authority of a commission of John [Grandisson], bishop of Exeter (quoted; dated Bampton, 15 July 1330) for an exchange of benefices between [Nassington] rector of Screveton and John de la Bourne, rector of Shobrooke. [Fo.373v; N.F.452v] (iv) Certificate to the bishop of Exeter. Southwell, 27 Oct. 1330.

632 Note of licence to be absent until 1 Aug. 1331 to William de Buttercromb, rector of a mediety of Eakring, provided that he inspects it in Advent, Lent, and other times. Southwell, 30 Oct. 1330.

633 [*In return for Maud Sausmere's benefactions, Wellow abbey undertakes to pay a chantry priest at the altar of St. Lawrence in Newark church, with provisions for presenting his successors, and their duties and conduct, and conceding them means to remedy any delay*

[93] Presented by the king as Thomas Bardolf's lands were in his hands (*CPR 1327–30*, 550).
[94] MS. *Kirketon*: see note to **410**.
[95] Described in margin as *Certificatorium dicte permutacionis.*

in paying their pension, despite the abbey's privileges; its ordinance in triplicate was sealed on 7 Nov. 1330 and confirmed by the archbishop.[96]]

ORDINACIO CANTARIE IN ECCLESIA DE NEWERK' PRO ANIMABUS WILLELMI DE SAUSMER ET MATILDIS UXORIS EJUSDEM AD ALTARE SANCTI LAWRENTII.[97]

Universis Christi fidelibus in quorum noticiam presentes littere pervenerint frater Thomas permissione divina abbas monasterii sancti Augustini de Welhou juxta Grymmesby et ejusdem loci conventus Lincoln' diocesis salutem in domino sempiternam. Pias bonorum collaciones et domui nostre proficuas munificencias quas dilecta nobis in Christo Matilda Sausemer de Neuwerk' nobis ad utilitatem domus nostre fecit contulit liberaliter et donavit pia et religiosa consideracione memorie commendantes, unanimi assensu et spontanea voluntate pro nobis et successoribus nostris concedimus et promittimus per presentes, quod nos abbas et conventus antedicti sustentabimus unum capellanum secularem pro ipsa Matilde Sausemer dum vixerit et pro anima Willelmi Sausemer mariti ejusdem et pro animabus patrum et matrum ipsorum et pro animabus omnium fidelium defunctorum, et post mortem ejus pro anima ipsius et pro animabus omnium prenotatorum, missam ad altare sancti Laurencii in ecclesia parochiali de Neuwerk' singulis diebus, impedimento cessante legitimo, modo quo sequitur celebraturum sustentandum nominandum presentandum et admittendum perpetuis temporibus in futurum.

Pro cujus quidem capellani perpetui et successorum suorum capellanorum in cantaria predicta sustentacione et pro omnibus aliis oneribus sibi et cantarie predicte qualitercumque incumbentibus damus et concedimus quemdam annuum redditum sex marcarum sex solidorum et octo denariorum argenti de monasterio nostro predicto de Welhou, et solvendum a nobis et successoribus nostris per manus thesaurarii nostri qui pro tempore fuerit vel alterius procuratoris domus nostre generalis vel specialis sumptibus et periculo nostris capellano apud Neuwerk' annuatim in festis videlicet sancti Michaelis et Pasche per equales portiones; ita videlicet quod solucio cujuscumque termini se referat ad sequendum tempus sic videlicet, quod si contingat capellanum qui pro tempore fuerit in aliquo predictorum terminorum pro rata plenarie satisfieri ac ipsum ante terminum proximo sequentis solucionis faciende ut premittitur decedere, successori suo capellano qui pro tempore fuerit satisfiat pro rata temporis competenter de bonis et catallis dicti capellani predecessoris sui.

Dicta vero Matilda dum vixerit quociens antedicta cantaria vacaverit capellanum ydoneum ad dictam cantariam domino archiepiscopo Ebor' libere presentabit, qui quidem dominus archiepiscopus ut premittitur nominatum et presentatum in forma juris et ordinacionis predicte ad ipsam cantariam admittat et canonice instituat in eadem. Post vero decessum dicte Matildis cum dicta cantaria qualitercumque vacaverit, vicarius qui pro tempore fuerit in ecclesia de Newerk' deum habens pre oculis assumptis sibi sex viris suo judicio fidedignioribus ejusdem parochie et de ipsorum consilio aliquem capellanum nominet idoneum moribus et sciencia commendatum per ipsum vicarium et assumptos

[96] For an inspeximus (and ample English summary) of this document dated 10 Feb. 1347, see *CPR 1345–8*, 251–2. The ordinance founding this chantry was approved by the archbishop at Laneham, 27 Sept. 1326; next day he instituted Robert de Athelington as its chaplain, presented by William Sausemer (Reg. Melton, ff.573^{v}–4; N.F.713^{v}–14). See also first note to **552**.

[97] The last four words are in a sixteenth-century hand.

predictos domino archiepiscopo ut premittitur presentandum, et si sint aliqui sufficientes de parentela dictorum Matildis et Willelmi ceteris omnibus in nominacione et presentacione ut convenerit preferantur. Quod si forsan in nominacione dicti septem dissenserint, nominatus a majori parte numeri[98] domino archiepiscopo presentetur. Si vero eodem tempore vacent vicaria et cantaria predicte, capellanus parochialis ejusdem ecclesie tempore vacacionis ebdomodarius cum predictis viris in forma premissa nominet et presentet. Et si, quod absit, dictus vicarius et viri sibi assumpti dissenserint ita quod infra quindecim dies a tempore vacacionis dicte cantarie capellanum ydoneum neglexerint seu non curaverint vel distulerint nominare et presentare, extunc potestas providendi eidem cantarie et ipsam conferendi illa vice ad archiepiscopum Ebor' sede plena et capitulo Ebor' sede vacante absque prejudicio futuri temporis devolvatur.

Predicti vero capellani successive assumendi et admittendi pro predicta Matilde et pro superius nominatis[99] ut est premissum celebraturi singulis diebus plenum servicium mortuorum, videlicet Commendacionem Placebo et Dirige, dicere teneantur et dicant, ac onera dicte cantarie incumbencia supportare.

Quilibet eciam capellanus qui pro tempore fuerit in cantaria predicta statim in admissione sua coram archiepiscopo ad sancta dei ewangelia juramentum prestet corporale personalem residenciam se facturum, qui etiam et unus alius capellanus admissus vel admittendus in futurum ad cantariam illam, quam Willelmus Sausemer quondam maritus ejusdem Matildis pia mente ordinavit in ecclesia supradicta, in divinis teneantur adinvicem se juvare et omnia premissa pro viribus suis adimplere. Dictusque capellanus qui pro tempore fuerit vicario predicte ecclesie de Neuwerk' easdem faciet observancias quas secundum consuetudines ejusdem ecclesie facere consueverant sacerdotes inibi celebrantes, ac insuper dictam Matildem dum vixerit in celebratione divinorum expectabit. Et si forte predictus capellanus in premissis faciendis vel exequendis negligens repertus fuerit vel remissus et super hiis et aliis excessibus notabilibus legitime convincatur, ipso pro suis excessibus notoriis rite amoto, confestim alius capellanus ydoneus ad dictam cantariam in forma predicta nominetur et domino archiepiscopo ut premittitur presentetur.

Pro oneribus vero sustentacionis predicti capellani et predicte cantarie sue subeundis predicta Matilda dedit nobis quamdam pecunie summam quam in usus nostros et in utilitatem domus nostre seu monasterii nostri nos convertimus et convertisse firmiter profitemur. Ad quem quidem annuum redditum sex marcarum sex solidorum et octo denariorum singulis annis terminis statutis imperpetuum de domo nostra predicta modo et forma predictis percipiendum et solvendum tam pro tempore vacacionis abbathie nostre quam aliis temporibus obligamus nos et successores nostros ac domum nostram predictam et omnes terras et omnia tenementa nostra et omnia bona nostra temporalia ad eandem domum nostram tam infra comitatum Lincoln' quam extra ubicumque fuerint, sive penes nos retineantur sive ad firmam dimittantur, districcioni predicti capellani et successorum suorum capellanorum in cantaria predicta; ita videlicet quod quandocumque contigerit, quod absit, nos vel successores nostros in

[98] MS. *numero*

[99] Followed by *ut superius*, cancelled.

solucione dicti annui redditus in aliquo termino pro rata termini deficere vel cessare per quindecim dies, quod libere et sine contradiccione nostra quacumque liceat predicto capellano et successoribus suis[1] capellanis predictis in omnibus terris et tenementis nostris supradictis ubicumque pro voluntate sua distringere et districciones capere et abducere et retinere quousque eidem capellano de arreragiis dicti annui redditus si que fuerint ac eciam de dampnis et expensis si quas fecerit ea occasione vel sustinerint plenarie fuerit satisfactum. Volumus insuper et concedimus pro nobis et successoribus nostris quod quocienscumque et quandocumque predicta pecunia ultra terminos predictos per culpam nostram aretro fuerit per quindecim dies non soluta, quod quicumque ordinarius diocesis Lincoln' quem elegerit sacerdos qui pro tempore fuerit possit fructus nostros quandocumque et qualitercumque apud Thorgramby inventos libere sequestrare, et de bonis sic sequestratis sine reclamacione nostra et absque omni strepitu judiciali dictam pecuniam non solutam levare et dicto capellano liberare, et ita fructus nostros predictos sub sequestro retinere quousque predicta pecunia non soluta fuerit eidem capellano soluta. Si vero post sequestrum dicto capellano infra viginti dies in parte vel in solidum post aliquem terminum transactum non fuerit satisfactum, volumus et concedimus pro nobis et successoribus nostris nos teneri domino episcopo Linc' sede plena vel decano et capitulo Lincoln' sede vacante in quadraginta solidis et archidiacono Linc' in [Fo.374; N.F.453] viginti solidis eisdem nomine pene et eidem capellano satisfacere de dampnis et expensis, que seu quas propter tales dilacionem et fatigacionem sustinuisse vel fecisse coram episcopo vel archidiacono predictis vel alio ordinario ab eodem capellano ut premittitur electo juramento suo ad sancta dei ewangelia idem capellanus asseveret sine quocumque alio genere probationis, sub pena superius annotata et eciam sub aliis penis excommunicationis suspensionis et interdicti et censuris ecclesiasticis quibuscumque in nos et dictum monasterium nostrum de consensu nostro expresse per dominum episcopum Linc' qui pro tempore fuerit simpliciter et de plano sine strepitu et figura judicii canonice promulgandis tociens quociens in solucione hujusmodi statutis terminis defecerimus in parte vel in toto; renunciantes in[2] premissis omni provocationi appellationi excepcioni defensioni regie prohibicioni ac prosecucioni ejusdem, sive ex parte domini regis sive alterius cujuscumque fuerit impetrata seu porrecta, privilegiis statutis consuetudinibus nostris quibuscumque a sede apostolica vel aliis ordinariis seu ex originali fundamento domus nostre provenientibus repugnantibus premissis vel alicui premissorum qualitercumque optinentibus vel in futuris modis quibuslibet obtinendis ac omni alii juris remedio que seu quod nobis contra premissa in premissorum prorogacionem seu derogationem possint seu possit competere quovismodo. Hoc per omnia et singula premissorum semper supposito et intellecto in omni eventu quod quandocumque predicta pecunia sex marcarum sex solidorum et octo denariorum predictorum predicto capellano qui pro tempore fuerit sub qualicumque forma prenotata fuerit in parte vel in toto uno quocumque modo vel via soluta, quod ex illa solucione preclusi sint omnino capellano predicto omnis alius modus et via ad petendum vel recipiendum ulterius per alios quoscumque modum et viam pro rata porcionis solute.

[1] Interlined over *nostris*, cancelled.
[2] Interlined.

In quorum omnium testimonium presenti scripto quod ad perpetuam rei memoriam necnon pro majori securitate fecimus triplicari, quorum unus penes nos retinuimus pro habenda memoria premissorum, et aliud penes capellanum predictum qui pro tempore fuerit in ecclesia de Neuwerk' predicta in aliquo cophino specialiter ad hoc deputato et in loco securo ponendo, et tercium[3] penes dictam Matildem heredes et executores suos volumus perpetuis temporibus remanere, sigillum nostrum commune de nostris voluntate unanimi et assensu apponi fecimus et appendi. Datum in capitulo nostro VII idus Novembris anno gracie MCCCXXX.

Nos vero Willelmus [*etc.*] attentis clementer pio desiderio dilecte filie Matildis Sausemer predicte divini cultus augmento et aliis considerandis in hac parte, vocatis omnibus quorum interest, omnia et singula premissa prout in serie suprascribuntur ordinamus quatenus ad nos attinet acceptamus roboramus ratificamus approbamus et ea in suo robore perpetuo duratura et in omni sui parte fideliter observanda confirmamus, statu dignitate jure et jursidiccione nostris et nostre Ebor' ecclesie ac jure cujuscumque alterius per omnia semper salvis. Datum quoad nos archiepiscopum supradictum [Southwell, 8 Nov. 1330].

634 COMMISSIO AD CORRIGENDUM COMPERTA TERTIE VISITATIONIS DECANATUUM DE NOT' NEUWERK' ET BINGHAM. Commission to M. John de la Launde, D.C.L., rector of Arnold, M. William de Hundon, rector of Barnburgh, and Gregory de Beverl' [*alias* Fairfax], rector of Headon, (or two of them) to correct crimes etc. discovered during the archbishop's visitation of the deaneries of Nottingham and Newark [*sic*] as contained in attached rolls, reporting by letters patent with these rolls and records of their proceedings. Southwell, 10 Nov. 1330.

635 Institution and mandate for induction of Roger de Muston, priest, as perpetual chaplain of the perpetual chantry newly established in Newark church; presented by Maud Saucemer according to its ordinance [**633**]. Southwell, 14 Nov. 1330.

636 Appointment of Henry Asselyn of Halam, chaplain, as coadjutor to Ralph [de Hertford], rector of Hockerton, who is old, totally blind and physically incapable; he is to make an inventory of the rector's goods and render an account when asked. Southwell, 12 Nov. 1330.

637 Commission to the prior of Thurgarton, M. Robert de Clareburgh, sequestrator in the archdeaconry of Nottingham, M. William de Hundon, rector of Barnburgh, and William de Hokerton (or three or two of them, including the sequestrator) to audit the account of the executors of the will of John de Hercy, kt., granting an acquittance if satisfied; their report by letters patent and close, with rolls of administration attached, is to be sent to M. John de Not', receiver of York. Southwell, 13 Nov. 1330.[4]

638 Note of licence for William de Aslagby, rector of Sibthorpe, to be absent for two years in the service of Luke de Flisco [Fieschi], cardinal deacon of S.

[3] MS. *terciam*

[4] The following break in the record coincides with Melton's second term as treasurer of England, from 1 Dec. 1330 to 1 Apr. 1331 (*HBC*, 105); see note to **418**.

Maria in Via Lata, excusing him from personal appearance at synods. Southwell, 26 Apr. 1331.

639 Note of licence to study (*in forma constitutionis Cum ex eo*) for two years to M. Simon [de Staunton], rector of Staunton. Southwell, 24 Apr. 1331.

640 Note of licence to John [de Clifton], rector of Clifton, to be absent for two years from 1 May last, to go on pilgrimage and for other lawful causes. Bishopthorpe, 27 May 1331.

641 Certificate of the commissary-general of the official of York and M. John de Not', receiver of York, [Fo.374^v; N.F.453^v] that they have executed the archbishop's commission (quoted; addressed also to the official of York; dated Southwell, 6 Nov. 1330) to receive the purgation of Thomas de Bulcote, chaplain, in York Minster on 13 November; he had been defamed before Robert de Malberthorp and Robert de Scorburgh, justices itinerant at Nottingham, of the death of John de Meryng' in his house at Meering (*Mering'*), and delivered to the archbishop's prison. There being no objection, he purged himself by the oaths of Adam de Boulton, William de Faldington, chaplains, Richard de Gedeling', Robert Urry, John de Blida, clerks, William de Wauld, Richard Cook (*Coco*), Richard de Laycestr', Thomas de Hoton, John de Burgh, Roger de Ravenglasse, Martin le Taillour and Thomas de Strensale. York, 14 Nov. 1331.

642 Note of licence to William de Langeley, rector of Carlton in Lindrick, to be absent for one year in a decent place. [Bishopthorpe][5] 1 June 1331.

643 [*Commission to settle a dispute between the rectors of Rampton and Treswell concerning tithe from sixty selions of arable land called 'Theveswelhill'*.]
COMMISSIO SUPER DISSENSIONE INTER DOMINUM WILLELMUM DE BEVERCOTES PREBENDARIUM PREBENDE DE RAMPTON IN ECCLESIA SUWELL' ET MAGISTRUM JOHANNEM DE MALTON RECTOREM MEDIETATIS ECCLESIE DE TYRESWELL OCCASIONE PERCEPCIONIS DECIMARUM ORTA. Willelmus etc. dilectis filiis magistro Johanni de la Launde juris civilis professori ac magistro Henrico de Wylton ecclesiarum de Arnall et de Gamelston nostre diocesis rectoribus salutem [*etc.*]. Orta dudum dissencionis materia inter dominum Willelmum de Bevercotes prebendarium prebende de Rampton in ecclesia Suwell' et magistrum Johannem de Malton rectorem medietatis ecclesie de Tyrswell super perceptione decimarum proveniencium de sexaginta selionibus jacentibus in cultura quadam Theveswelhill nuncupata, utraque parte pretendente nomine ecclesie sue sibi jus competere percipiendi eas, post varios[6] processus super hiis inter eos habitos amicis communibus mediantibus demum in vestras personas consenserunt et concordarunt in forma subscripta: ut vos ad partes illas personaliter accedentes et locum ipsum vestris ecclesiis subicientes, viros bonos et fidedignos de parochiis de Rampton et Tyrswell et aliis locis evicinis neutri parti suspectos nec partes ipsas procurandos seu producendos[7] sed quos videritis magis ydoneos

[5] See *Reg. Melton*, II.143–4.
[6] MS. *varias*
[7] Corrected from *procedendos*

et pro veritate melius eruenda duxeritis assumendos in testimonium admittatis, et super jure et possessione utriusque partis diligenter et prudenter examinetis, et secundum probata et testificata causam ipsam summarie et de plano absque strepitu judiciali citra festum sancti Petri ad vincula proximo futurum juxta predictum consensum partium predictarum fine debito decidatis, alioquin dictam causam cum omni informacione per vos habita in eadem remitti volumus et mandamus. Nos igitur condictum et consensum suum hujusmodi quantum ad nos pertinet approbantes et de vestra cicumspectione et industria plenius confidentes, ad convocandum coram vobis partes predictas diebus et locis quibus videritis expedire et compellendum testes si opus fuerit et premissa omnia et singula et ea contingencia fideliter peragenda, vobis vices nostras cum cohercionis canonice potestate committimus et mandamus, vobis firmiter injungentes quatinus in forma predicta deum pre oculis habentes negocium ipsum infra terminum antedictum inquisita plena veritate terminetis, ne forte per vestram negligenciam seu desidiam quod absit partes predicte ad nos redeant negocio minime terminato. Valete. [Bishopthorpe, 11 June 1331.]

644 Dispensation to John Shireve of West Thorpe (*Westhorpe*), acolyte (dioc. York), to hold a benefice with cure of souls despite his illegitimate birth, provided that he takes higher orders at statutory times and resides; quoting letters of John XXII (dated Avignon, 5 May 1331). Bishopthorpe, 27 June 1331.

645 Note of similar dispensations to John de Stoke and John de Kirtelington, clerks. Same date.

646 Note of licence to be absent for one year to John de Emeldon, rector of Burton Joyce, farming his church and selling tithes as he sees fit. Bishopthorpe, 1 July 1331.

647 Collation and mandate for induction of Robert de Crumwell, priest, to the vicarage of a mediety of Gedling, vacant by the death of Hugh de Kerkolston; the archbishop acting as executor of a papal provision *in forma pauperis* to a benefice [of unstated value] in the patronage of the prior and convent of Shelford.[8] [Fo.375; N.F.454] Cawood, 4 Aug. 1331.

648 Institution [etc.] of John de la Gore, priest, to Sutton cum Lound (*Sutton in Hattefeld juxta Retteford*) vicarage, vacant by the death of John de Waltham; presented by M. John Busse, sacrist of the chapel of St. Mary and the Holy Angels, York. Doncaster, 18 Sept. 1331.

649 To the subprior and convent of Thurgarton. Their election of Robert de Hatherne, canon of the house, as prior was defective. Right having devolved, the archbishop subsequently provided him as prior and committed its administration to him, whom they are to obey. Southwell, 24 Sept. 1331.

650 Letter to Robert de Hatherne providing him as prior of Thurgarton; the archbishop was mindful of the convent's unanimous consent to his election after the resignation of John de Hicling. Southwell, 23 Sept. 1331.

[8] Same form as **538**, with investment *per nostrum birretum*.

651 [*Request to Thurgarton priory to grant a pension to the archbishop's poor kinsman, John de Brungelflet.*]
LITTERA MISSA PRIORI ET CONVENTUI DE THURGARTON QUOD ASSIGNENT ANNUAM PENSIONEM RACIONE CREACIONIS NOVI PRIORIS. Willelmus [*etc.*] dilectis filiis . . priori et conventui monasterii de Thurgarton nostre diocesis salutem [*etc.*]. Cum a nostris predecessoribus a multis retroactis temporibus provide sit obtentum et a tempore cujus non extat memoria inconcusse laudabili consuetudine observatum, ut in prefectione . . abbatum et priorum nostre diocesis per eosdem et eorum conventus constituende sint personis bene meritis per prelatum nominandis certe pensiones annue, ut prelatus qui juxta credite sibi dispensacionis officium voluntarios multociens amplectitur pro ipsorum honore comodis et quiete labores eorum suffragio assequatur per quod aliis se reddere valeat graciosum; devocionem vestram rogamus monemus attencius et hortamur quatinus dilecto consanguineo nostro Johanni de Brungelflet', cujus indigencie vellemus prospicere et mederi, quem ad hoc vobis specialiter duximus pre certis nominandum juxta premissam ecclesie nostre consuetudinem constituatis et per vestras eciam patentes litteras concedatis quoad vixerit unam pensionem a vobis et vestro monasterio predicto annuatim percipiendam, que secundum facultates dicti vestri monasterii et dantes deceat et recipienti utilis ac fructuosa existat, nobisque merito grata esse debeat pariter et accepta, taliter vos habentes in hac parte si placet ut eo favorabilius vos inveniat dictus Johannes carus noster consanguineus operis per effectum que nobis insidet magis cordi ac vobis et[9]

652 [Fo.375^v; N.F.454^v] Institution (in the person of William de Radeclyf, clerk, as proctor) and mandate for induction of John Gerarde, acolyte, to Ratcliffe of Soar church, vacant by the death of Walter de Alleslond; presented by the prior and convent of Norton (dioc. Coventry and Lichfield). Caldbeck (*Caldebek'*), 25 Oct. 1331.[10]

653 Writ of Edward III permitting the archbishop to accept the presentation by the prior of Norton of his clerk, John Gerard, to Ratcliffe on Soar church, notwithstanding the prohibition (*ne admittatis*) issued because Ebulo Lestraunge presented his clerk, Walter de Wetewang', to the same church; Ebulo renounced his right in Chancery. Westminster, 10 Oct. 1331.[11]

654 Institution and mandate for induction of John de Swyn, priest, to Hawton church, vacant by the death of Robert de Helpeston; presented by Robert de Compton, lord of Hawton. Bishopthorpe, 15 Nov. 1331.

655 The like of M. William Odmel of Harby (*Herdeby*; dioc. Lincoln), priest, to Kilvington church, vacant by the resignation of M. Ralph de Holbech; presented by Isabel de Staunton, widow of William de Staunton, kt. Bishopthorpe, 18 Nov. 1331.

[9] Ending here. Cf. note to **537**.
[10] Following the visitation of south-west Cumberland (see *Reg. Melton*, I.55); and see ibid., II.145 (no.374, dated Appleby, 27 Oct. 1331); both were in Carlisle diocese.
[11] As in *CCR 1330–3*, 355; and see ibid., 10, for a debt acknowledged by Gerard on the same day.

656 The like of Adam de Lonsill, priest, to a mediety of Trowell church, vacant by the resignation of Richard de Kirkeby; presented by John, prior, and the convent of Sempringham. Bishopthorpe, 20 Nov. 1331.

657 Mandate to the dean and chapter of York to do their part for Anibaldus [Gaetani de Ceccano], cardinal priest of S. Laurentius in Lucina, who has been provided by John XXII to the archdeaconry of Nottingham following its resignation by M. Manuel de Flisco into the hands of Peter, bishop of Palestrina, in an exchange for the canonry and prebend of Milton [Manor] in Lincoln cathedral; the archbishop has accordingly admitted Anibaldus in the person of his proctor, Fulco de Vichio, clerk. Bishopthorpe, 23 Nov. 1331.[12]

658 Mandate to the clergy and people of Nottingham archdeaconry, referring to the admission of Anibaldus [incomplete].[13]

659 Note of licence to John Gerard, rector of Ratcliffe on Soar, to be absent for one year in a decent place. 25 Nov. 1331.

660 Note of similar licence for absence until 1 Aug. 1332 to John de Swyn, rector of Hawton. 26 Nov. 1331.

661 [*Release of the sequestration of Ratcliffe on Soar following payments due to the pope and archbishop.*]
RELAXACIO SEQUESTRI FRUCTUUM DE RADCLIF' SUPER SORE. Willelmus etc. dilecto filio decano nostro de Bingham salutem [*etc.*]. Quia de fructibus ecclesie de Raddeclif super Sore nostre diocesis de ultimo autumpno[14] per magistrum Willelmum de Gotham rectorem ecclesie de Althorp Linc' diocesis Johannem Ward de Kynston et Henricum de Aderley nobis pro domino nostro papa et pro nobis est ut convenit satisfactum, propter quod sequestrum nostrum alias in eisdem fructibus interpositum duximus relaxandum; tibi mandamus quatinus dictis magistro Willelmo Johanni et Henrico dictos fructus integre liberes seu visis presentibus statim facias liberari, ut de eisdem disponant pro sue libito voluntatis. Vale. [Bishopthorpe, 3 Dec. 1331.]

662 [Fo.376; N.F.455] Institution [etc.] of William Bernak, clerk, to Gonalston church, vacant by the death of M. Thomas de la Forde; presented by Richard de la Rivere, kt. Bishopthorpe, 5 Dec. 1331.

663 Memorandum. Richard de Brehill, clerk, was defamed of the theft of two silver dishes in the king's court at Nottingham and delivered to the archbishop's custody by Hugh de Turpynton, then the king's steward.[15] On 23 Sept. 1331, he

[12] There are no reservations, as in **591**. See also *CPL*, II.359; *Fasti*, VI.24.
[13] Followed by space 2 cms. deep; cf. **592**.
[14] Under this entry, in the lower margin, is this half line: *o .. videlicet anno instanti infrascripto quos emimus de*. There are also two dots in the outer margin, to the left of *de ultimo autumpno*, suggesting this is an omission after those three words.
[15] He was steward of the king's household from August 1330 and killed when Roger Mortimer was arrested in Nottingham castle on 19 Oct. following (*HBC*, 76; *CPR 1330–4*, 53, 172).

appeared in Ripon[16] collegiate church before M. Robert de Ripon, canon of Ripon, M. William de Wandesford and Alan son of Iditha, commissaries *ad hoc*. There being no objection, he purged himself, as is more fully shown in letters certificatory in the registrar's keeping. Richard has letters testimonial in customary form.

664 Institution [etc.] of Hugh de Trouwell, priest, to Broxstowe church, vacant by the resignation of Adam de Lansill; presented by the prior and convent of Sempringham. Bishopthorpe, 12 Dec. 1331.

665 Letters patent testifying that William de Aslakby, rector of Sibthorpe, defamed for incontinence with Isabel de Flyntham, had purged himself in the archbishop's presence. Bishopthorpe, 13 Dec. 1331.

666 Memorandum of dispensation to William Gange, acolyte, to receive all orders and hold a benefice with cure of souls, despite his illegitimate birth, provided that he resides, etc., by authority of letters of Gaucelin, bishop of Albano, the pope's penitentiary; with ratification of minor orders received without letters dimissory. Bishopthorpe, 20 Dec. 1331.

667 (i) Letters testimonial that Robert Jorz, clerk (dioc. York), purged himself in Southwell minster on 18 Dec. 1331; he had been defamed of the homicide of William de Pykeworth at Gedling before Richard de Gray and other justices of oyer and terminer at Nottingham, and delivered to the archbishop's prison. (ii) Request to the king for the restitution of his lands, etc.[17] Cawood, 3 Jan. 1332.

668 [*Decree accepting the resignation by Thomas Wylford, clerk, of his claim to Wilford church, which he had unlawfully occupied.*[18]]
RENUNCIACIO THOME DE WYLFORD DE ECCLESIA DE WYLFORD. In dei nomine amen. Intellecto nuper quod Thomas filius Radulphi de Wilford clericus tunc malo ductus consilio dominum Stephanum le Eyr verum rectorem et canonicum possessorem ecclesie de Wilford nostre diocesis dicta ecclesia sua spoliavit et se intrusit temere in eadem, fructus et bona in rectoria dicte ecclesie quam aliquamdiu detinuit per vim et potenciam laicalem reperta dissipando alienando et perperam consumendo, in ipsius domini Stephani rectoris prefati dampnum non modicum et gravamen et aliorum perniciosum exemplum; qui postmodum ad cor reversus dimissa dicta ecclesia ac domino Stephano pacificam possessionem ejusdem adepto in nostra presencia constitutus, quandam confessionem et renunciacionem fecit sub hac forma:

Venerabili [*etc.*] suus humilis et devotus Thomas filius Radulphi de Wylford clericus nuper rector ecclesie de Wylford Ebor' diocesis omnimodam reverenciam tanto patri debitam cum honore. Pater reverende, ego Thomas antedictus in presencia vestra personaliter constitutus confiteor me in dicta ecclesia nullum

[16] Corrected from 'Southwell'.
[17] Ordered 22 Jan. 1332 (*CCR 1330–3*, 429). See also second note to **584**.
[18] See **48**, **496** and **623** for institutions to Wilford; also *CPR 1330–4*, 129, for a commission (dated 10 Feb. 1332) issued on Stephen's complaint.

jus omnino habere, et si aliquod jus in eadem ecclesia vel ad eam mihi aliqualiter competat, eidem ac omni juri michi in ipsa vel ad eam qualitercumque competenti pure sponte simpliciter et absolute et ex certa sciencia in nullo circumventus totaliter renuncio per presentes.

Nos Willelmus [*etc.*] ipsius Thome confessionem acceptantes et renunciacionem juris si quod sibi compeciit admittentes, ipsum in dicta ecclesia et ejus cura absolvimus et sibi de ea perpetuum silencium imponimus per decretum. Inhibemus eciam eidem Thome de Wylford et eum monemus unica monicione pro omnibus cum id facti necessitas et negocii qualitas sic suadeat moderandum, ne dictum dominum Stephanum rectorem ecclesie de Wylford vel suos de cetero de dicta ecclesia spoliet amoveat spoliari amoverive procuret, ne ipsum vel suos in possessione ejusdem ecclesie seu percepcione rerum fructuum seu reddituum ejusdem molestet vel perturbet dampnumve inferat per se vel alios clam vel palam directe vel indirecte sub pena excommunicacionis majoris, quam exnunc prout extunc hujusmodi canonica monicione premissa in personam suam si in aliquo contrafecerit et monicionibus nostris non paruerit cum effectu ipsius culpa mora delicte seu offensa precedentibus et id poscentibus proferimus in hiis scriptis. In cujus rei etc. Data et acta[19] [Cawood, 15 Sept. 1331].

669 [Fo.376v; N.F.455v] Note of licence to William de Langeley, rector of Carlton in Lindrick, to be absent for one year and farm his church. Cawood, 28 Jan. 1332.

670 Institution [etc.] of Adam de Graneby, chaplain, to Lenton vicarage, vacant by the death of John Berd; presented by the prior and convent of Lenton. Cawood, 29 Jan. 1332.

671 The like of John de Muston, chaplain, as perpetual chaplain of the chantry of St. Helen in Stapleford church, vacant by the death of Richard Anneys; presented by Alice le Palmer of Nottingham. Cawood, 1 Feb. 1332.

672 Note of licence to M. John de Notingham, rector of Elkesley, to be absent for three years, wherever he pleases, farm his church and be represented by proxy at synods. Bishopthorpe, 20 Feb. 1332.

673 Institution (in the person of Roger de Twiford as proctor) and mandate for induction of John son of John son of Peter de Newerk', chaplain, as perpetual chaplain of the chantry in the chapel of St. Nicholas in Newark church, celebrating for the soul of Robert de Bosco; presented by Henry Mous, Robert Stuffyn, Walter le Tavernere and others of the community of the town of Newark. Bishopthorpe, 28 Feb. 1332.

674 The like of Robert de Edenstowe, clerk (dioc. York), to Warsop church, now vacant; presented by John de Ros, kt. Bishopthorpe, 1 Mar. 1332.

675 ADMISSIO DOMINI ROBERTI DE LAFELDE DE HEMELHAMSTEDE IN CANONICATU ECCLESIE SUWELL'. Mandate to the chapter of Southwell to do its part for

[19] *et acta* interlined.

Robert de la Felde of Hemel Hempstead, clerk, provided by John XXII to a canonry and prebend in Southwell.[20] The archbishop accordingly admitted him in the person of his proctor, John de Kirketon, clerk, with reservations:

Salvis nobis et ecclesie nostre supradicte excepcionibus et defensionibus omnibus competentibus et competituris tam contra personam quam graciam et executionem omnem in hac parte habitam et habendam; salva eciam nobis potestate conferendi canonicatus et prebendas quoscumque qui et que predicto Roberto deberi seu debite non fuerint virtute gracie memorate. [Bishopthorpe, 4 Mar. 1332.]

676 Institution and mandate for induction[21] of Robert de Brustewik', chaplain, to Lambley church; presented by Ralph de Crumbewell, kt., in an exchange from Ribchester (*Rykestre*) church with Thomas Trayly.[22] Ripon, 15 Mar. 1332.

677 Note of licence to Robert de Brustewyk, rector of Lambley, to stay in another place of his choice until Whit Sunday [7 June]. Ripon, 16 Mar. 1332.

678 [*Inspeximus of the dean of Lincoln's appointment (dated 7 March 1332) of M. Thomas Beek as vicar-general in Derby collegiate church and the deanery.*]
Noverint universi quorum interest seu poterit interesse quod nos Willelmus etc. quasdam litteras reverendi et discreti viri magistri Antonii Beek[23] decani ecclesie cathedralis Lincoln' in nulla sui parte viciatas ac omni suspicione carentes quod[dam] sigillo rubeo pendente nomine dicti magistri Antonii Beek circumscripto inspeximus sigillatas sub infrascripta tenore:

Antonius Beek decanus ecclesie cathedralis Lincoln' discreto viro magistro Thome Beek juris canonici professori salutem in eo qui est omnium vera salus. Ad cognoscendum statuendum et diffiniendum visitandum et corrigendum quorumcumque subditorum excessus et omnimoda jurisdictione nobis in ecclesia collegiata Derbeie cum suis juribus et pertinenciis universis tam in temporalibus quam in spiritualibus nobis qualitercumque competentibus seu competuris excercendum, et specialiter ad conferendum quascumque prebendas in dicta ecclesia collegiata et ad presentandum ad quecumque beneficia alia quorum collacio vel presentacio ad nos seu dignitatem nostram decanalem pertinere dinoscitur cum vacaverint vel vacaverit aliquod eorundem, necnon ad omnia alia et singula facienda et exercenda que nobis competunt in premissis vel circa ea jure communi vel speciali, vobis vices nostras committimus cum cohercionis canonice potestate necnon vicarium nostrum generalem in premissis et quibuscumque aliis nos[24] seu decanatum nostrum contingentibus in absencia nostra seu nobis in remotis agentibus ordinamus facimus et constituimus per presentes. In cujus rei testimonium sigillum quo utimur duximus apponendum. Datum Lincoln' septimo die mensis Marcii anno domini MCCCXXXI.

In cujus inspectionis testimonium sigillum nostrum presentibus duximus apponendum. Datum hujusmodi inspectionis [Bishopthorpe, 4 Apr. 1332].

[20] By letters dated 11 Mar. 1331 (*CPL*, II.332).
[21] The latter mistakenly names the church as Warsop (cf. **674**).
[22] See *Reg. Melton*, I.56, no.157.
[23] Interlined. See *BRUO*, I.152–3.
[24] Interlined.

679 Institution [etc.] of Adam de Ingoldeby, priest, as perpetual chaplain of the chantry founded for the soul of Queen Eleanor in the chapel of Harby (*Herdeby*); presented by the subdean and chapter of Lincoln, the dean being absent. Bishop Burton, 14 Apr. 1332.

680 [Fo.377; N.F.456] The like of William de Trowell, chaplain, to Bilborough church, vacant by the death of William de Strelley; presented by Robert son of Robert de Strelley, kt. Middlesbrough (*Middlesburgh*), 9 May 1332.[25]

681 The like of Simon de Wrangel, priest, to South Leverton vicarage, vacant by the death of Robert [de Allerton]; presented by M. Thomas Beek, vicar-general of the dean of Lincoln. Bishop Burton, 14 Apr. 1332.

682 [*Release of sentences against Robert de Nevill, rector of Flintham, provided that he indemnifies the archbishop in respect of a summons before the king's justices.*]
PRO RECTORE DE FLYNTHAM. Willelmus etc.dilecto filio . . officiali curie nostre Ebor' vel ejus . . commissario generali salutem [*etc.*]. Si Robertus de Nevill rector ecclesie de Flyntham nostre diocesis caucionem juratoris[26] et sub pena privacionis beneficii sui penalem vobis vel alteri vestrum prestiterit de conservando nos et ministros nostros indempnes occasione cujusdam regii brevis contra ipsum ad instanciam Henrici de Nevill impetratum, virtute cujus demandatum est vicecomiti Noting' quod ponat nos per vadia et salvos plegios ita quod habeamus dictum rectorem coram justiciariis domini regis apud Westm' in crastino sancti Johannis Baptiste extunc, suspensionis et excommunicationis sentencias si quas tulistis in eundem relaxetis et relaxatas denuncietis, sequestracionem in bonis ecclesiasticis prefati rectoris ex causa premissa interpositam relaxantes et relaxatam publice nunciantes. Valete. [Bishopthorpe, 5 June 1332.]

683 Certificate of Roger [Northburgh], bishop of Coventry and Lichfield, that he has executed the archbishop's commission (quoted; dated Bubwith, 18 June 1332) for an exchange of benefices between Ralph de Benyngholme, rector of Ashton (*Assheton*; dioc. Lichfield), and Gregory de Neuton, vicar of Blyth; forwarding a report by the archdeacon of Nottingham's official into Blyth's vacancy, the reputation of the presentee, etc. Ralph was instituted to Blyth; presented by the prior and convent of Blyth. Beaudesert (*Bellum Desertum*), 28 June 1332.

684 Note of the archbishop's mandate for Ralph's induction to Blyth. 3 July 1332.

685 [*Dispensation to a priest of illegitimate birth.*]
DISPENSACIO ROBERTI FILII WILLELMI DE HOLM. Memorandum quod ij Nonas Augusti anno gracie etc. xxxij apud Thorp juxta Ebor' auctoritate litterarum domini Gaucelini dei gracia Albanen' episcopi dominus dispensavit cum Roberto filio Willelmi de Holm super defectu natalium et super eo quod non

[25] The day appointed for the archbishop's visitation at Acklam, now in Middlesbrough (*Reg. Melton*, II.148).
[26] MS. *jurator'*

obstante hujusmodi defectu ad omnes ordines se fecit promoveri et in eisdem ministravit dispensa[tione] legitima super hoc non obtenta, injuncta sibi pro modo culpe penitencia salutari et eo a dicto reatu prius per dictum dominum in forma juris absoluto, ita tamen quod idem presbiter prout requiret onus beneficii quod eum post dispensacionem hujusmodi obtinere contigerit personaliter resideat in eodem. [Bishopthorpe, 4 Aug. 1332.]

686 Note of licence during pleasure to Edmund de Wasteneys, kt., for the celebration of services in an oratory in his manse at Headon (*Hedon*). 17 Sept. 1332.

687 Note of licence to the prior and convent of Shelford to demise a mediety of North Muskham church for three years. Laneham, 18 Sept. 1332.

688 [*Oath of obedience by the archdeacon's official.*]
Memorandum quod magister Radulphus de Yarwell officialis archidiaconi Notinghamie decimotertio die mensis Septembris apud Lanum Ebor' diocesis in camera venerabilis patris domini Willelmi [*etc.*] coram eodem patre personaliter comparuit ac eidem patri, tactis sacrosanctis dei evangeliis, ratione officii sui predicti obedienciam juravit sub hiis verbis:

Ego Radulphus de Yarwell officialis archidiaconi Notinghamie vobis patri vestrisque successoribus canonice intrantibus officialibus et ministris in canonicis mandatis ero obediens.[27] Sic deus me adjuvet et hec sancta.

Presentibus magistris R[oberto] de Nassington utriusque juris professore Ada de Haselbech rectore ecclesie de Streton et me W[illelmo] de Carleton notario publico testibus etc. Indictione quintadecima. [Laneham, 13 Sept. 1332.]

689 [Fo.377^{v}; N.F.456^{v}] Institution [etc.] of Robert of the Bail of Lincoln (*de Ballio Lincoln'*), chaplain, to South Leverton vicarage; presented by M. Thomas Beek, canon of Lincoln and vicar-general of M. Anthony Beek, dean of Lincoln. Laneham, 25 Sept. 1332.

690 Licence (at the request of Sir Ralph de Nova Villa) to Peter [le Roy], rector of Weston (*Weston in le Clay*), to be absent for three years, demising his church at farm to Simon de Sener, clerk; with provision for appearing by proxy at synods, visitations and other convocations (*aliis convocacionibus nostris*). Bishopthorpe, 15 Oct. 1332.

691 Institution [etc.] of John de Schupton, chaplain, as vicar of the prebendal church of Farndon and Balderton (*Balderdon*), now vacant; presented by Francis son of Neapoleo [Orsini] kt., prebendary of [the same] in Lincoln cathedral. Bishopthorpe, 19 Oct. 1332.

692 Note of licence to Adam [de Preston], rector of Hickling, to be absent for one year to stay at Garendon (*Gernedon*) abbey; with provision for appearing by proxy at synods celebrated at Southwell. 2 Nov. 1332.

[27] Cf. **405**.

693 [*Licence to rebury the remains of Simon de Sibethorp's parents in his new chapel in Sibthorpe church.*]
TRANSLATIO CORPORUM SEPULTORUM IN CIMITERIO ECCLESIE DE SIBTHORP USQUE IN CAPELLAM DE NOVO CONSTRUCTAM IN EADEM. Willelmus [*etc.*] dilecto filio officiali archidiaconi nostri Notynghamie salutem [*etc.*]. De vestris fidelitate et circumspecta industria plenius confidentes, ad movendum ossa Willelmi Le Lorde de Sibethorp nostre diocesis et Margarete quondam uxoris Simonis de eadem antecessorum et parentum ipsorum, que in cimiterio ecclesie de Sibethorp predicta[28] infra spacium viginti pedum ex capite orientali capelle in honore beate Anne per ipsum Simonem de novo constructe ut dicitur quiescunt humata, et ea de ipso cimiterio in dictam capellam ut inibi reponantur transferenda, si vobis per inquisicionem juratam a viris fidedignis premissorum noticiam habentibus pleniorem constiterit ipsorum corpora fuisse et esse intemerata et ossa a tegumento carnis plenius excussa eaque inibi tumulanda et auctoritatem premissa faciendi imparcienda, vobis vices nostras committimus et licenciam specialem concedimus per presentes. Valete. [Bishopthorpe, 2 Nov. 1332.]

694 Institution [etc.] of M. Robert de Wyvill, clerk, to Bulwell (*Bolewell*) church, vacant by the resignation of Bartholomew de Bradden;[29] presented by Edward III. Bishopthorpe, [day and month omitted] 1332.[30]

695 [*Mandate to publish the excommunication and interdict by the archbishop's commissaries of the master and others of the hospital (of St. Leonard) by Newark for opposing their visitation.*]
LITTERA MISSA DECANO DE NEWERK' AD DENUNCIANDUM MAGISTRUM HOSPITALIS DE NEWERK' ET ALIOS IN LITTERA CONTENTOS EXCOMMUNICATOS. Willelmus etc. dilecto filio decano nostro de Newerk' salutem [*etc.*]. Quia dilecti filii dominus Johannes de Sandale canonicus ecclesie nostre collegiate Suwell' magistri Johannes de Landa juris civilis professor officialis archidiaconi nostri Noting' et Willelmus de Hundon decanus noster Suwell', commissarii nostri una cum priore de Schelforde ad visitandum hospitale juxta Newerk' situatum nostre diocesis magistrum et fratres ejusdem et alios in eodem habitantes cum potestate cohercendi contradictores et rebelles specialiter deputati, dominum Robertum de Stanford[31] magistrum hospitalis predicti, dominos Johannem de Bredon Robertum de Calveton capellanos et Adam de Gretton fratres ejusdem, dominum Johannem de Uffynton, Galfridum servientem magistri Willelmi Jolle clericum, Ricardum Fayrman et Amiciam ancillam ejusdem hospitalis, ad subeundum hujusmodi visitacionem in capella dicti hospitalis certo die ac moniciones et injuncta canonica recipienda legitime evocatos et visitacionem hujusmodi subire contumaciter recusantes, propter suas multiplicatas contumacias pariter et offensas manifestas residencias rebelliones contradictiones et impedimenta contra nos et jurisdictionem nostram notorie factas et ausu

[28] MS. *predicte*
[29] Presented by the king in 1326; he had attempted to leave Bulwell by exchange in 1331 (*CPR 1324–7*, 260; *1330–4*, 173).
[30] The presentation was dated 30 Sept. 1332 (*ibid.*, 341).
[31] Not recorded in *VCH Nottingham*, II.168.

temerario perpetratas nostra auctoritate monicionibus premissis canonicis ac juris ordine in omnibus observato majoris excommunicationis sentencia innodarunt, dictumque hospitale capellam et omnia loca ejusdem supposuerunt ecclesiastico interdicto, sicut in processu per eos inde habito plenius vidimus contineri; nos volentes sentencias per dictos commissarios proinde et rite latas pro conservacione jurisdictionis et juris ecclesie nostre execucioni debite demandare, tibi [Fo.378; N.F.457] in virtute obediencie nobis jurate districte precipiendo mandamus quatinus dictos dominos Robertum de Stanford magistrum hospitalis predicti Johannem de Bredon Robertum de Calveton Adam de Gretton Johannem de Uffynton Galfridum servientem magistri Willelmi Jolle clericum Ricardum Fayrman et Amiciam ancillam ejusdem hospitalis in ecclesia parochiali de Newerk' singulis diebus et in omnibus aliis ecclesiis tui decanatus diebus dominicis et festivis intra missarum solempnia, cum in eis major fuerit populi multitudo, pulsatis campanis candelis accensis et prout moris est extinctis ac cruce erecta, sic excommunicatos fuisse et esse nominatim et in specie ac dictum hospitale capellam et omnia loca ejusdem que nobis subsunt interdicta esse publice et solempniter denuncies et per alios facias nunciari, a denunciacione et publicacione hujusmodi non cessando quousque aliud a nobis receperis in mandatis. De nominibus eciam divina officia celebrancium in hospitali capella seu locis que nobis subsunt aliis eorumdem nostra auctoritate rite ut premittitur suppositis interdicto et qui post hujusmodi interdictum inibi celebrarunt inquiras nihilominus diligenter de quibus cum tibi constiterit de eisdem, ac de omni eo quod feceris in hac parte nos citra festum Purificationis beate Marie Virginis proximo futurum distincte et aperte certifices per tuas litteras patentes harum seriem continentes. Vale. [Bishopthorpe, 3 Dec. 1332.]

696 Certificate of M. William de Hundon, rector of Barnburgh, and John de Stanton, rector of Colwick, that they have executed the archbishop's commission to them and the prior of Thurgarton (quoted; dated Bishopthorpe, 4 Nov. 1332) to receive the purgation of Nicholas Froward of Wirksworth (*Wirkesworth*), clerk, on 4 December in St. Mary's, Nottingham. He was defamed before Richard de Gray and other royal justices at Nottingham for the maintenance and harbouring of James Coterell, Roger Sauvage, Walter servant of James Coterell, Thomas de Buckestans, his brother William, and John Coterell,[32] knowing that they were outlawed for divers felonies committed in Nottinghamshire; he had been delivered to the archbishop's prison. After the commission and certificates of the deans of Nottingham and Ashbourne (dioc. Coventry and Lichfield) had been read, it was proclaimed [etc., as in **614**, *mutatis mutandis*, but omitting the names of the compurgators]. Nottingham, 4 Dec. 1332.

697 (i) LITTERA TESTIMONIALIS SUPER PURGATIONE NICHOLAI FROWARD. Letters patent [in the same form as **699**]. [Fo.378^v; N.F.457^v] (ii) Request to the king for the restitution of his lands, etc.[33] Bishopthorpe, 16 Dec. 1332.

[32] See J.G. Bellamy, 'The Coterel Gang: an Anatomy of a Band of Fourteenth-century Criminals', *English Historical Review*, LXXIX (1964), 698–717.
[33] Ordered, at York, 15 Dec. 1332 (*CCR 1330–3*, 508–9).

698 Note of licence to Adam [de Preston], rector of Hickling, to be absent for three years from 2 Nov. 1332, farm his church and appear by proxy at synods. Bishopthorpe, 18 Dec. 1332.

699 [*Testimonial of the purgation on 8 January 1333 of Thomas Basily, a clerk appealed of complicity in a burglary.*[34]]
LITTERA TESTIMONIALIS SUPER PURGATIONE THOME BASILY. Universis sancte matris ecclesie filiis presentes littere inspecturis Willelmus permissione etc. salutem in auctore salutis. Noverit universitas vestra quod cum Thomas Basily de Raddeclyf' super Trentam nostre diocesis clericus nuper in foro seculari coram domino Willelmo de Herle et sociis suis justiciariis domini nostri regis itinerantibus apud Notyngham super eo quod idem Thomas appellatus per Nicholaum de Spaldyng' probatorem suspensum de precepto et assensu burgarie domus Roberti Race apud Saxindale in wappentachio de Byngham per ipsum probatorem et alios latrones facte et bonorum et catallorum (videlicet unius robe precii x s., unius supertunice precii v s., quadraginta ulnarum panni linei precii dimidie marce, viii lyntheaminum precii viii s., quatuor tapetarum precii viii s. et de ii s. argenti) ibidem furtive depredatorum, unde idem Thomas habuit ad partem suam predictas robam supertunicam et xx ulnas de predicto panno lineo sex lyntheamina quatuor tapetas et ii s., et eciam de eo quod eundem Nicholaum probatorem et alios latrones apud Radeclif' in wappentachio predicto post predictam roberiam factam receptavit, sciens ipsum Nicholaum et alios esse latrones, graviter diffamatus fuisset nostreque carcerali custodie juxta libertatem ecclesiasticam et[35] consuetudinem regni Anglie ut clericus et membrum ecclesie per predictos justiciarios liberatus; idem Thomas die Veneris proxima post festum Epiphanie domini ultimo jam preteritum videlicet anno domini MCCCXXXII in ecclesia nostra cathedrali beati Petri Ebor' personaliter comparens, premissis omnibus et singulis que de jure requirebantur in hoc casu auctoritate nostra super criminibus burgarie furti et receptacione predictis legitime se purgavit, propter quod ipse ab impositis sibi criminibus inculpabilis pronunciatus fuerit et immunis tunc ibidem ac bone fame sue pristine restitutus exigente justicia per decretum. [Bishopthorpe, 8 Jan. 1333.]

700 [*Confirmation of an ordinance (dated 13 January 1333) by the master and brethren of the hospital of St. Leonard, East Stoke, providing for the celebration of sixty masses annually.*]
NOTA DE HOSPITALI SANCTI LEONARDI JUXTA STOKE.[36] Universis sancte matris ecclesie filiis ad quos presentes littere pervenerint Willelmus etc. salutem in auctore salutis. Noveritis nos litteras Johannis Chanson magistri hospitalis sancti Leonardi de Stok' juxta Newerk' nostre diocesis et Roberti de Wilbourgh Roberti de Donham capellanorum et Simonis de Botelesford clerici confratrum dicti hospitalis sigillo communi dicti hospitalis ut prima facie apparebat sigillatas inspexisse sub eo qui sequitur tenore:

Noverint universi quorum interest hoc scriptum inspicere vel audire quod cum sit justum ac consonum racioni ut illis sancte consideracionis ecclesie filiis

[34] See **584**. For restitution of his goods, etc., see *CCR 1330–3*, 522; *1333–7*, 8–9.
[35] Interlined from *libertatem*
[36] Supplied in sixteenth-century hand.

beneficia perpetua impendantur per quos cultus dei augetur, pauperes aluntur, hospitalitas sustinetur, loca pia salubrius reformantur, variisque largicionibus et auxiliis muniuntur; hiis igitur attentis, nos Johannes Chanson magister hospitalis sancti Leonardi de Stok' juxta Newerk' Ebor' diocesis et Robertus de Wilbourgh' Robertus de Donham' capellani et Simon de Botelesford clericus confratres dicti hospitalis quadraginta acras terre et triginta solidos annui redditus nostris laboribus adquisitos cum providencia diligenti et auxilio amicorum inferius subscriptorum in evidentem utilitatem dicti hospitalis et usus perpetuos convertimus pia mente. Ex hoc ergo nos predicti magister et confratres unanimi assensu proinde statuimus ac eciam ordinamus et concedimus pro nobis et successoribus nostris quod magister dicti hospitalis qui fuerit in eodem pro eisdem Johanne Roberto Roberto Simone ac pro venerabili patre domino Willelmo dei gracia Ebor' archiepiscopo Anglie primate et pro viro discreto magistro [Ada] de Heselebech ac eciam pro domino Willelmo de Calverton Johanne de Cotom Waltero de Santon Alicia de Thorp et pro Agnete atte Wryg' de Wynigton et pro magistris et fratribus, qui pro tempore erunt in eodem, sexaginta missas celebrabit seu per confratres suos vel per alios capellanos faciet devotione qua convenit celebrari modo qui sequitur singulis annis perpetuis temporibus in futurum (videlicet tres missas infra octabas festorum inferius expressorum cum collectis quarum prima sic incipit *Deus qui es nostra redempcio*, scilicet Annunciacionis beate Marie, Pasche, Ascencionis, Pentecostes, Trinitatis, Assumpcionis beate Marie, Nativitatis ejusdem, Natale domini,[37] Epiphanie, Purificationis beate Marie) et alias triginta missas diebus quadragesimalibus singulis annis continue a die Cinerum celebrandas.

Magister vero dicti hospitalis qui predictas missas ut predicitur celebrabit vel alius quem idem magister faciet celebrare singulis annis percipiet in recompensacione[38] sui laboris quinque solidos de redditu cujusdam tenementi cum pertinenciis in villa de Stok' quod fuit quondam Willelmi Freman de WyninGton. Et si quis redditus vel terras sive tenementa aliqua dicto hospitali caritative conferre et approbare voluerit ad recompensandum uberius labores magistrorum dicti hospitalis qui pro tempore fuerint dictas sexaginta missas celebraturorum[39] ut superius est ostensum, liceat dictis magistris ipsos redditus sive [Fo.379; N.F.458] profectus de ipsis terris et tenementis provenientes una cum redditu quinque solidorum predictorum libere et pacifice retinere suis usibus profituros.

Ad hec autem ut ista ordinacio et concessio inviolabiliter perpetuis temporibus observetur, volumus faciamus et concedimus pro nobis et successoribus nostris quod quicumque assumendus vel recipiendus est in magistrum dicti hospitalis vel in fratrem, tempore assumpcionis vel recepcionis hujusmodi omni excusacione cessante juret tactis sacrosanctis dei ewangeliis si capellanus fuerit quod diligenciam quam poterit exhibebit ut dicte sexaginta misse pro personis prenominatis ac aliis ut premittitur suo tempore celebrantur, et si quis forsan attemptaverit aliquibus premissorum temere contraire, ipsum impediet eique resistet modo debito prout consonum fuerit racioni; et si laicus receptus fuerit, curabit quod premissa erit penes se rata habiturus et grata nec ea impediet

[37] *domini* interlined.
[38] MS. *recompensacioni*
[39] MS. *celebraturi*

quovismodo. Quod si forsan predicti assumendi vel recipiendi in magistros et in fratres prefatos prestare recusaverint juramenta, eo ipso assumpcio et confirmacio dicti magistri et fratrum recepto suspendatur, quousque in forma premissa prestiterint juramentum. Et ne predicti magister et fratres ignoranciam pretendere valeant in premissis, volumus et ordinamus quod in recepcione quorumcumque fratrum hoc presens scriptum distinctim legatur, et singulis annis in capella sancti Leonardi convocatis fratribus et omnibus quorum interest publicetur. Et si quod absit idem celebrare cessaverit predictas missas vel eas per alium non procuraverit celebrari, preter offensam dei quam non inmerito poterit formidare ab exactione predicti annui redditus quinque solidorum per biennium sit exclusus et in utilitatem dicti hospitalis celeriter convertatur. Et nos predicti magister et fratres huic salubri ordinacioni nostre sigillum nostrum commune apposuimus in perpetuam memoriam premissorum. Datum apud Stok' die sancti Hillarii anno domini MCCCXXXII.

Nos igitur Willelmus permissione etc. supradicta premissa omnia et singula auctoritate nostra pontificali quatenus ad nos attinet, salvis jure jurisdiccione honore et dignitate nostris et ecclesie nostre Ebor', confirmamus approbamus ratificamus et eciam acceptamus. In cujus rei testimonium sigillum nostrum presentibus est appensum. [Bishopthorpe, 28 Jan. 1333.]

701 [*Confirmation of a charter of Sir Richard de Wilughby (dated 12 March 1332) granting rents from properties (described) in Nottingham to endow a chantry in the church of Willoughby on the Wolds, with detailed regulations; also quoting the licence of Edward II granted in 1324.*[40]]

ORDINACIO PERPETUE CANTARIE IN ECCLESIA PAROCHIALI DE WYLUGHBY. Universis sancte matris ecclesie filiis ad quos presentes littere pervenerint Willelmus etc. salutem in sinceris amplexibus salvatoris. Illius devocionem sinceram convenit pia mentis intencione fovere qui ad divini cultus augmentum et multiplicandum numerum ministrorum in ecclesia sancta dei ac ad instituendum missarum celebracionem perpetuam porcionem congruam de suis possessionibus et facultatibus libertate cupit graciam ita elargiri. Cum itaque cartam dilecti filii domini Ricardi de Wilughby militis ac ordinacionem ipsius factam super quadam cantaria in ecclesia parochiali de Wilughby predicta ad divini laudem nominis sui cultus augmentum et pro salute animarum perpetuis temporibus facienda sigillo ejusdem domini Ricardi signatam inspeximus in hec verba:

Omnibus Christi fidelibus presens scriptum visuris vel audituris Ricardus de Wilughby miles filius domini Ricardi de Whilughby militis salutem in domino. Noveritis me dedisse et hoc presenti scripto meo confirmasse domino Waltero de Wilughby capellano divina celebraturo in ecclesia omnium sanctorum de Wilughby ad altare beate Marie, ubi corpus domini Ricardi patris mei quiescit humatum, et successoribus capellanis in ipsa ecclesia pro animabus domini Ricardi de Wilughby patris mei et domine Juliane uxoris ejus matris mei et pro anima mea et Isabelle uxoris mee et pro animabus omnium antecessorum et heredum meorum ac parentum et benefactorum meorum et omnium fidelium

[40] It may be noted that Sir Richard, a justice of King's Bench, founded the chantry shortly after his capture and ransom by the Folville gang in January 1332 (Stones, art. cit. (under **584**), 122).

defunctorum divina sub forma et modo infrascriptis imperpetuum celebraturis quinque marcatas redditus cum pertinenciis in Notingham percipiendis de tenementis subscriptis (videlicet quinque solidos de uno curtilagio jacente inter Orgerlane et curtilagium Willelmi de Batheley, et quatuor solidos et sex denarios de Alicia le Palmere exeuntes de Asselingholm, et sex solidos et sex denarios exeuntes de uno mesuagio jacente inter venellam que vocatur le Berkergate et tenementum Willelmi de Stowe, et viginti solidos de uno mesuagio jacente inter tenementum Ricardi Samoun et tenementum Willelmi de Spondon, et quindecim solidos exeuntes de uno tenemento jacente inter tenementum Ricardi de Bingham et tenementum domini Johannis de Grantham, et octo solidos et sex denarios de uno mesuagio jacente inter tenementum Legge Dinnyng ex parte occidentali et tenementum Andree Loterell ex parte orientali, et septem solidos et duos denarios exeuntes de uno mesuagio jacente inter mesuagium Willelmi Scotor ex parte orientali et tenementum Willelmi de Amyas ex parte occidentali, et totum servicium tenementorum illorum que tenementa tamen illa unde redditus ille provenit tenent), habenda et tenenda eidem Waltero capellano et successoribus suis capellanis divina in ecclesia predicta celebraturis tota vita cujuscumque illorum successive de me et heredibus meis sive assignatis in perpetuam elemosinam; faciendo inde cantariam subscriptam in predicta ecclesia, videlicet celebrando matutinas horas missam vesperas et completorium quolibet die in septimana et qualibet septimana per totum annum et quolibet anno sub hiis forma et modo (videlicet quolibet majori festo dupplici de ipso festo, et singulis diebus dominicis de dominica, et qualibet ebdomada semel de domina, et reliquis diebus pro animabus predicti domini Ricardi patris et Juliane uxoris ejus matris mee et pro anima mea et Isabelle uxoris mee et pro animabus omnium antecessorum et heredum meorum ac parentum et benefactorum ac omnium fidelium defunctorum ut supradictum est imperpetuum) sine aliquo servicio vel aprovamento servicio inde michi et heredibus meis sive assignatis quoquo faciendo exceptis cantaria in forma predicta et superius dicenda, proviso quod quando de dupplici festo dominica vel de domina ut premittitur celebratur quod in missa de animabus predictis specialis memoria habeatur ac collecte et oraciones specialiter pro eis dicantur.

Et volo quod predictus capellanus et successores sui in predicta ecclesia ut predicitur celebraturi per me et heredes meos archiepiscopo Ebor' loci diocesano qui pro tempore fuerit sede archiepiscopali plena et ea vacante custodi spiritualitatis ejusdem archiepiscopatus presententur, et ad premissa proficienda per ipsum recipiantur ac admittantur et instituantur in cantaria predicta. Et si forsan contingat quod absit eorum aliquem super inhonesta conversacione vel super aliquo excessu defectu seu crimine notabili diffamari, vel ipsum capellanum in celebracione serviciorum predictorum necgligenter cessare et defectum celebracionis serviciorum esse propter ipsius necligenciam sive culpam, et super hujusmodi excessu defectu crimine vel cessacione celebracionis serviciorum predictorum culpa ipsius mediante ut prefertur coram ordinario judicio canonice convincatur ac privetur et amoveatur per eundem, ad presentacionem meam heredum meorum vel custodis heredum meorum si infra etatem fuerint a predicto archiepiscopo sede Ebor' plena et ea vacante custode spiritualitatis ejusdem archiepiscopatus Ebor' loco illius capellani amoti alius capellanus idoneus ad dictam cantariam admittatur et instituatur in eadem. Et quandocumque ego predictus et heredes mei vel custodes heredum meorum dum infra etatem fuerint post noticiam mortis vel amocionis alicujus capellani in dicta ecclesia divina celebrantis ut predictum est infra tres septimanas proximo sequentes alium non presentaverimus, ita quod noticia mortis vel amocionis ejusdem capellani infra tempus predictum ad nos vel heredes nostros vel custodes heredum nostrorum dum infra etatem fuerint comode pervenire poterit, volo et concedo quod archiepiscopus Ebor' sede plena et ea vacante custos spiritualitatis ejusdem archiepiscopatus qui pro tempore fuerit de idoneo provideat capellano ea vice quo defuncto vel amoto ut supradictum est. Ego Ricardus et heredes mei et custodes heredum meorum dum infra etatem fuerint alium capellanum jure nostro ad cantariam predictam prefato archiepiscopo vel ejus locum tenenti presentabimus quociens necesse fuerit ut supradictum est imperpetuum.

Predictus vero Walterus de Wilughby concedit pro se et successoribus suis quod ipse et successores sui et quilibet eorum successores imperpetuum omnia necessaria ad predictam cantariam facienda et sustinenda spectancia sibi provideant secundum quod melius viderint expedire imperpetuum, proviso quod quicquid oblatum fuerit ad missarum celebracionem in ecclesia predicta [cui?: Fo.379ᵛ; N.F.458ᵛ] in nullo volumus prejudicare prejudicium inferatur quiete remaneat imperpetuum ecclesie parochiali de Wilughby et ejusdem rectori, ac ipsi rectori ecclesie de Wilughby qui fuerit pro tempore integre solvatur ac fideliter liberetur. Et quod quilibet capellanus et[41] successorum eorum successive tactis sacrosanctis evangeliis prestent eidem Ricardo vel heredibus vel custodibus heredum suorum dum infra etatem fuerint corporale sacramentum ad predictam cantariam continue sine diminucione fraude vel negligencia pro posse suo ut predictum est suo perpetuo faciendi antequam ad predictam cantariam recipiantur. Et ego predictus Ricardus et heredes mei totum predictum redditum ut supradictum predicto Waltero de Wilughby capellano et successoribus suis capellanis divina celebraturis ut supradictum est warantizabimus imperpetuum. In cujus rei testimonium partes hiis scriptis indentatis alternatim sigilla sua apposuerunt. Hiis testibus Laurencio le Spicer tunc majore Notingham, Roberto de Morewode et Willelmo de Cropphall' tunc ballivis, Willelmo de Amyas de Not', Johanne le Colyer de Not', Johanne Bully de Not', Radulpho le Taverner de Not' et aliis. Datum apud Notingham die Jovis in festo sancti Gregorii pape anno domini MCCCXXXI et anno regni regis Edwardi tercii a conquestu sexto.

[Letters patent of Edward II.[42] On 16 November last, he granted Richard de Wylughby, now deceased, licence to give five marks of rent in Nottingham to a chaplain celebrating at the altar of the Blessed Virgin Mary in the church of Willoughby on the Wolds, notwithstanding the statute of Mortmain. Richard died before he could assign the rent. His son and heir Richard, desiring to fulfil his father's purpose (*voluntatem*), asked for the licence to be extended to himself, as the king now does. Cippenham, 22 Oct. 1325.[43]]

Omnia et singula supradicta prout continentur in serie acceptantes, ipsa sic fieri debere et esse ac imperpetuum inviolabiliter observari, dumtamen patron-

[41] MS. *eorum et*

[42] This text follows immediately, without any indication that it came from another document.

[43] See *CPR 1324–7*, 51, 186.

orum dicte ecclesie et rectoris ejusdem et aliorum quorum interest si qui sint voluntas intervenerit et consensus quibus prejudicare non intendimus quoquomodo, ordinamus decernimus confirmamus ratificamus pronunciamus et eciam diffinimus expressius in hiis scriptis, jure jurisdiccione statu privilegio libertate et dignitate nostris successorum nostrorum et nostre Ebor' ecclesie et cujuslibet alterius semper salvis. In cujus rei testimonium sigillum nostrum fecimus hiis apponi. [Bishopthorpe, 13 Feb. 1333.]

702 Note of licence to study (*stare in scolis*) for two years to [Thomas de Casterton] rector of a mediety of Cotgrave. Bishopthorpe, 16 Apr. 1333.

703 Institution [etc.] of William de Clyve, clerk, to Epperstone (*Epreston*) church, now vacant; presented by Edward III, by reason of the minority and wardship of the son and heir of Sir Payn de Tybetoft.[44] Bishopthorpe, 10 May 1333.

704 Certificate of M. William de Leicestr', canon of Lichfield, M. John de la Launde, rector of Arnold, and John de Staunton, rector of Colwick, dean of Nottingham, that they have executed the archbishop's commission to them and M. Richard de Havering', canon of York (quoted; dated Bishopthorpe, 20 Feb. 1333) to receive the purgation of M. Robert Bernard, lately vicar of Bakewell (*Baukewell*; dioc. Coventry and Lichfield), on the second juridical day after [Friday] 12 March in St. Mary's, Nottingham. He was defamed before Richard de Grey and other justices at Nottingham of the maintenance and harbouring of James Coterell [as in **696**–'prison'].
[*The certificate (dated 16 March 1333) records an objection to the purgation by Roger Wyne and Walter de Neuton, vicar of Bakewell.*[45]]

Quarum auctoritate litterarum dicto die Lune ad ecclesiam beate Marie Notyngh' personaliter accedentes, facta primitus proclamacione in forma litterarum vestrarum inde directarum prout per certificatoria nobis transmissa et super hoc confecta recepimus, et ad plenum juxta vim et effectum dicte vestre commissionis in forma juris procedentes, proclamari sepius et palam fecimus tunc ibidem quod si quis vel qui quicquam racionabile vel justum proponere voluerit vel voluerint quare ad purgacionem dicti magistri Roberti Bernard minime procedi debeat, dictis die et loco comparens vel comparentes coram nobis cum plenitudine justicie audietur et audientur juxta canonicas sancciones; demum comparentibus coram nobis domino Rogero Wyne et Waltero de Neuton qui se gerit pro vicario de Baukewell, nulloque eorum aliquid racionabile in forma juris coram nobis proponente quare inpedire poterat aut debuerat admissionem purgacionis antedicte sed ut videbatur pocius ex odii semite quam zelo justicie eorum quilibet se opposuit, nullo alio oppositore tunc ibidem legitime se opponente, post varias et iteratas protestaciones nostras palam et publice factas de audiendo quemcumque legitimum oppositorem et de justicia sibi exhibenda, tandem astante populi multitudine copiosa tunc ibidem nos ex officio nostro obiecimus Roberto Bernard memorato manutentacionem et

[44] *CPR 1330–4*, 428.
[45] For his expulsion by the Coterells, see Bellamy, art. cit. (under **696**), 699, 701; also *CPL*, II.271.

receptacionem Jacobi Coterell Rogeri Sauvage et aliorum in litteris vestris nominatorum. [Fo.380; N.F.459] Idemque Robertus famam et factum per nos sibi objectum statim expresse negavit et de purgando suam innocenciam in premissis optulit se paratum, unde nos de expresso consensu Walteri de Neuton antedicti purgacionem eidem Roberto induximus cum duodecima manu hominum ordinis sui approbatorum, qui quidem Robertus eandem purgacionem admittens per duodecim rectores vicarios et capellanos vite laudabilis conversacionisque honeste approbatos presente domino Waltero statim se purgavit tunc ibidem. Unde nos pronunciavimus ipsum Robertum legitime fore purgatum super premissis ipsumque restituimus bone fame sue et a vinculo carceralis custodie eundem absolvimus justicia mediante, que omnia paternitati vestre innotescimus per presentes. In cujus rei testimonium presentibus sigilla nostra apposuimus. Datum apud Notingham die Martis post festum sancti Gregorii pape anno domini supradicto. Valeat et crescat vestra sanctissima paternitas reverenda ad regimen ecclesie sancte per tempora feliciter longiora.[46]

705 Institution [etc.] of Reginald de Sibthorp, chaplain, to Bilborough church, now vacant; presented by Robert de Strelleye, son of Robert de Strelleye kt. Bishopthorpe, 27 May 1333.

706 The like of Richard Tenerey, acolyte, to Kneesall church, vacant by the death of William de Thorntoft; presented by the prior and convent of Norton (dioc. Coventry and Lichfield) [see **711–12**]. Also licence for Richard to study at a *studium generale* for one year. Bishopthorpe, 27 May 1333.

707 The like of Oliver de Wermondesworth, chaplain, to Strelley church, now vacant; presented by Robert de Strelleye, son of Robert de Strelleye kt. Also note of licence to be absent for one year. Bishopthorpe, 18 June 1333.

708 Note that after the archbishop confirmed the first tonsure received by John de Hemsel of Nottingham without any dispensation, he dispensed him by papal authority to receive all orders and hold a benefice despite his illegitimacy, provided that he takes orders and resides. Bishopthorpe, 29 June 1333.

709 Institution [etc.] of William son of Hugh Sewale of Southwell, deacon, to Colston Bassett vicarage, vacant by the resignation of John Sewall; presented by the prior and convent of Laund (*Landa*). Bishopthorpe, 2 July 1333.

710 [*Note (dated 2 July 1333) of a bond by Thomas Cok, vicar of West Markham, dated 13 March 1330, to pay Richard de Hareworth five marks p.a.* (see **713**).] [Fo.380v; N.F.459v] OBLIGATIO THOME COK'. Memorandum quod secundo die mensis Julii anno domini MCCCXXXIII indiccione prima apud Thorp juxta Ebor' dominus Thomas Cok' perpetuus vicarius ecclesie de West Markham nostre diocesis, recitata coram nobis littera quadam sigillo ejusdem Thome et decani de Retteford signata, cujus tenor sequitur in hec verba:

[46] Followed by space 2 cms. deep, possibly intended for notes of letters testimonial and petition for restitution of lands, etc. For issue of the latter, dated 18 Mar. 1333, see *CCR 1333–7*, 43.

Noverint universi per presentes me Thomam Cok' perpetuum vicarium ecclesie de Westmarkham teneri et per presentes obligari Ricardo de Hareworth de Tikhull clerico in quinque marcis sterlingorum bone et legalis monete de vicaria mea predicta quamdiu in pacifica possessione ejusdem permansero annuatim ad terminos, videlicet Pentecostes et sancti Martini in yeme, per equales porciones fideliter percipiendas quousque beneficium ecclesiasticum fuerit assecutus,[47] ad quam quidem solucionem predictis terminis faciendam obligo me et omnia[48] bona mea mobilia et immobilia cohercioni et districtioni cujuscumque ballivi vel judicis ecclesiastici vel secularis. In cujus rei testimonium sigillum meum presentibus apposui. Et quia sigillum meum pluribus[49] sigillum decanatus de Retford presentibus apponi procuravi. Scriptum apud Retford in crastino sancti Gregorii pape anno domini MCCCXXIX.

711 PROHIBICIO DE KNESALE. Writ *ne admittatis* of Edward III prohibiting the admission of a parson to Kneesall church while the advowson is disputed in the king's court between William de Bohun and the prior of Norton. Pontefract, 20 Mar. 1333.

712 RELAXACIO EJUSDEM. Writ of Edward III allowing the archbishop to proceed with the presentation by the prior of Norton of his clerk, Richard Teverey [see **706**], notwithstanding the [above] prohibition as William de Bohun has recognised before the king that the presentation does not belong to him *ista vice*. Tweedmouth (*Twedemouth*), 21 May 1333.

713 [*Decree settling the dispute about West Markham vicarage in favour of Thomas Cok', who is to pay Richard de Hareworth a pension* (as in **710**)*; with the consent of the patron, M. John de Arundell, warden of Tickhill chapel, dated 1330 (only).*]
CONCORDIA RICARDI DE HAREWORTH ET THOME COK' SUPER VICARIA ECCLESIE DE PARVA MARKHAM. Universis sancte matris ecclesie filiis presentes litteras inspecturis Willelmus etc. salutem in auctore salutis. Dudum inter Ricardum de Harewrth clericum ad vicariam ecclesie de Parva Marcham nostre diocesis per Bonefacium de Saluciis tunc custodem capelle regie de Tikhill ipsiusque vicarie patronum presentatum ex parte una, et dominum Ricardum de Hoton possessioni ipsius vicarie incumbentem ex altera, super dicta vicaria et ejus occasione orta materia questionis et coram officiali curie nostre Ebor' et ejus commissario generali diucius agitatis, demumque ipso domino Ricardo ad instanciam et prosecucionem dicti Ricardi de Harewrth clerici presentati ab ipsa ecclesia et ejus possessioni judicialiter amoto,[50] cum ipso presentatus a nobis ad dictam vicariam peteret se admitti et vicarium institui in eadem; quidam dominus Thomas Koc' clericus per magistrum Johannem de Arundell tunc custodem capelle regie et vicarie predicte patronum ad eandem vicariam vacantem nobis presentatus ipsi Ricardo de Harewrth se opposuit, et ejus presentacionem satagens multipliciter inpugnare petiit ipsum ad prefatam vicariam admitti et vicarium perpetuum institui in eadem. Tandem altercacione dissensione et briga

[47] Interlined from *quousque*
[48] Interlined.
[49] Omitting 'is unknown'.
[50] See **490**.

diutina habitis[51] in hoc casu, ambe partes decima octava die mensis Aprilis anno domini Millesimo CCC^mo vicesimo septimo[52] apud Thorp juxta Ebor' in nostra presencia personaliter constitute ut litium[53] amfractus et jurgia evitarent pro bono pacis et quietis et ut hinc inde parceretur laboribus et expensis, se ac jura eis et cuilibet ipsorum ad dictam vicariam vel in ea qualitercumque competencia nostris ordinacioni arbitrio laudo et decreto alte et basse sponte pure simpliciter absolute singillatim et legitime submiserunt et pars utraque se submisit, petentes humiliter ut super hoc pro ipsorum quiete ordinare misericorditer dignaremur. Nos igitur Willelmus archiepiscopus supradictus super premissis deliberacione habita pleniori dictorum Ricardi de Harwrth et Thome Kok' submissiones in nos factas admisimus, et ad honorem dei utilitatem ipsius vicarie [et] animarum salutem de assensu magistri Johannis de Arundell patroni vicarie predicte se ordinacioni nostre hujusmodi submittentis sub hac forma:

Venerabili in Christo patri domino suo reverendo domino Willelmo dei gracia Ebor' archiepiscopo Anglie primati suus humilis et devotus Johannes Arundell custos capelle regie de Tikhill ac patronus vicarie ecclesie de Parva Markham vestre diocesis obedienciam reverenciam et honorem debitos tanto patri. Reverende pater, litteras vestras mihi nuper transmissas si placet intellexi quod Ricardus de Harwrth clericus ad vicariam predictam per Bonefacium de Saluciis predecessorem meum ac patronum ejusdem vicarie nuper presentatus et Thomas Koc' per me nunc verum patronum ejusdem vicarie ad eandem presentatus[54] super jure ipsius vicarie qualitercumque ipsos contingente vestris ordinacioni laudo et decreto dicto seu arbitrio se pure sponte simpliciter et absolute submiserunt. Paternitati vestre reverende significo per presentes quod dictas submissiones quantum ad me attinet approbo et eisdem conficio necnon me laudo ordinacioni decreto dicto seu arbitrio vestro submitto penitus per presentes. In cujus rei testimonium presentibus sigillum meum apposui. Datum apud Longstawe juxta Huntington anno gracie MCCCXXX.

Et ex causis aliis legitimis ad id nos moventibus de consilio jurisperitorum nobis assistencium ordinamus diffinimus et laudamus quod Thomas Cok' vicarius ecclesie de Parva Markham predicte per nos nuper vi et virtute presentacionis de ipso facte hujusmodi admissus et vicarius in ea perpetuus institutus, ipsam vicariam cum suis juribus et pertinenciis universis habeat et teneat pacifice et quiete. Ordinamus etiam decernimus et laudamus quod Ricardus de Harwrth predictus de vicaria ecclesie de Parva Markham et de Thoma Cok' vicario ejusdem ecclesie [et] de quibuscumque ipsius ecclesie vicariis qui pro temporibus fuerint pensionem annuam quinque marcarum sterlingorum ad festa Pentecostes et sancti Martini in yeme per porciones equales singulis annis sibi in dicta vicaria absque [Fo.381; N.F.460] dilacione ulteriori fideliter persolvendas percipiat et habeat ad totam vitam suam, nisi interim ad aliquod beneficium ecclesiasticum promotus fuerit a cujus promocionis tempore cesset dumtaxat pensio memorata, quam quidem pensionem de fructibus dicte vicarie in forma loco et terminis fideliter persolvendam dicto Thome Cok' et successoribus suis vicariis dicte ecclesie qui pro tempore fuerint

[51] MS. *habita*
[52] An error, because Cok was instituted in March 1328 (**489**).
[53] MS. *licium*
[54] MS. *est presentatus*

ac ipsi vicarie vi et virtute submissionum predictarum ac presentis ordinacionis nostre realiter quantum de jure possumus cum effectu imponimus, ac ipsum Thomam successores suos ac vicariam predictam de dicta pensione modo quo pretangitur efficaciter oneramus et ipsos ut premissa fideliter perficiant sub pena excommunicacionis majoris quam in personam dicti Thome Cok' vicarii predicti et successorum pretactorum si in solucione dicte pensionis vel alicujus partis ejusdem loco terminis prenotatis seu eorum aliquo defecerit seu defecerint canonica monicione premissa, quem et quos exnunc monemus ferimus in hiis scriptis sententialiter condempnamus ordinamus etiam et ordinando decernimus quod ad dictas soluciones in forma qua premittitur faciendas, quibus vicario ecclesie de Parva Markham exnunc in ipsa ecclesia futuro corporale ad sancta dei ewangelia in admissione et institucione sua ad dicte ecclesie vicariam prestet et faciat juramentum. Ut autem hec nostra ordinacio in omnibus suis articulis rata et stabilis perseveret, sigillum nostrum eidem apponi fecimus in testimonium premissorum. [Bishop Burton, 4 Sept. 1330.]

714 BREVIA TANGENCIA PATRONATUM ECCLESIE DE STANTON. Three writs *admittatis* of Edward III ordering the archbishop to admit the presentee of Thomas de Widmerpole to the church of Stanton on the Wolds because he has recovered the presentation: (i) by judgment of the court, against Simon de Sibethorp (tested by William de Herle and dated Westminster, 18 June 1333); (ii) against Simon and his wife Cecily, by their default (tested by the king and dated Westminster, 12 July 1333); and (iii) likewise against Simon [alone, as in (ii)].

715 Institution [etc.] of John Martel, clerk, to Stanton on the Wolds church, vacant by the death of John Seman; presented by Thomas de Widmerpole. Newcastle upon Tyne, 20 July 1333.

716 The like of Richard de Glatton, chaplain, to Fledborough (*Fledeburgh*) church, vacant by the death of Thomas [de Buckden]; presented by John de Leyseus, kt. York, 14 Aug. 1333.

717 Note of licence to [Ingram de Mattersey] rector of Elton to be absent for one year and sell the fruits, etc. York, 24 Sept. 1333.

718 Institution [etc.] of M. William de Hundon to Car Colston (*KIRCOLSTON, Kyrkelston*) church, now vacant; presented by the prior and convent of Worksop. York, 25 Sept. 1333.

719 (i) Institution of William de Sutton, chaplain, to Sutton [cum Lound] vicarage in [the following] exchange; presented by Thomas de la Mare, sacrist of the chapel of St. Mary and the Holy Angels, York. (ii) Mandate for his induction to the dean of Laneham. [Fo.381^{v}; N.F.460^{v}] (iii) Institution of John de la Gore, chaplain, to the church of St. Mary, Willingham (*Wylingham*; dioc. Norwich) by authority of a commission of William [Ayermine], bishop of Norwich (quoted; dated South Elmham (*Suthelmham*), 10 Sept. 1333) for an exchange of benefices between [John] vicar of Sutton [cum Lound] and William de Sutton, rector of Willingham; forwarding the report of an enquiry by the archdeacon of Sudbury's (*Subir'*) official. (iv) Certificate to the bishop of Norwich. York, 5 Oct. 1333.

720 Institution [etc.] of Bro. Robert de Aslakton to Norton Cuckney (*Cukenay*) vicarage, vacant by the resignation of Bro. John de Neubold; presented by the abbot and convent of Welbeck. York, 6 Oct. 1333.

721 Certificate of the official of York and his commissary-general that they have executed the archbishop's commission (quoted; dated Bishopthorpe, 18 Apr. 1333) to receive in York Minster, on the first juridical day after Ascension [13 May], the purgation of Simon le Litster of Rotherham, clerk, who was defamed before the king's justices[55] of receiving Thomas Kene, Richard Drugg', Walter Innsand and William Stork', approvers of hanged thieves; he was delivered to the archbishop's prison. No objector appeared, and Simon purged himself by the oaths of Peter Frost, William Blaunkamy, John de Houeden, John de Derlington, Peter de Grymeston, and William de Derlington, chaplains, Richard de Grauenhowe, Robert le Yung' of Rotherham, William Lamberd of Sheffield, Richard son of Stephen de Roderham, Thomas de Atterclif', William de Bradeley, John de Schefeld, Paul de Hauvill and Richard le Lang', clerks. York, 14 Oct. 1333.

722 [Fo.382; N.F.461] (i) Request to the king to order the sheriff of Nottingham to restore Simon's lands, etc. (ii) Letters patent testifying the above purgation.[56] York, 14 Oct. 1333.

723 (i) Memorandum that Nicholas de Holm purged himself in York Minster on 25 October before M. Richard de Snoweshull and M. William de Jafford; he had been defamed of the theft of two oxen at Hoveringham. (ii) Letters patent testifying that Nicholas de Holm, clerk (York dioc.), defamed [as above] before Richard de Grey and other justices, had purged himself, 'etc., as in the letters for Simon Litster'. York, 27 Oct. 1333.[57]

724 Institution [etc.] of William de Lee of Blyth, priest, to Weston (*juxta Tukesford*) church, vacant by the death of Peter le Roy; presented by the prior and convent of Blyth. York, 29 Oct. 1333.

725 Note of licence to study for one year at a *studium generale* to Robert de Brustewik', rector of Lambley, excusing him from personal appearance at synods. 2 Nov. 1333.

726 The like to Nicholas de Skaleton, rector of Laxton (*in le Clay*). 10 Jan. 1334.

727 [*Dispensation to Geoffrey Luterell, kt., and his wife Agnes, daughter of Richard de Sutton, kt., to remain married despite their possible consanguinity, by authority of letters of John XXII dated 19 Oct. 1331; witnesses were unaware of their previous kinship.*[58]]

[55] Named as Henry de Percy and his fellows in **722** (ii), justices of oyer and terminer in the West Riding according to the order for restitution (28 Nov. 1333; *CCR 1333–7*, 162).
[56] Giving its date as ordered in **721**.
[57] Also the date of the king's order for restitution (*CCR 1333–7*, 147).
[58] See *CPL*, II.368. They were probably married by 1310 (*Complete Peerage*, by G.E.C., 1910–59, VIII.286–7).

DISPENSACIO DOMINI GALFRIDI LUTERELL ET AGNETIS UXORIS EJUSDEM. Willelmus etc. dilectis filiis nobis in Christo domino Galfrido Luterell militi et Agneti quondam Ricardi de Sutton militis nate salutem [*etc.*]. Litteras sanctissimi in Christo patris et domini domini Johannis divina providencia pape XXII vera ipsius bulla more Romane curie bullatas non abolitas seu viciatas set omni prorsus ut prima facie apparuit suspicione carentes pro vobis nuper presentatas[59] recepimus, quarum tenor sequitur in hec verba:

Johannes episcopus servus servorum dei venerabili fratri archiepiscopo Ebor' salutem et apostolicam benedictionem. Ex oblate nobis pro parte dilecti filii Galfridi Luterell militis et dilecte in Christo filie Agnetis quondam Ricardi de Sutton militis nate tue diocesis peticionis tenore collegimus quod olim dicti Galfridus et Agnes in domo paterna existentes, de voluntate patris ipsius Agnetis bannis ut moris et juris est in facie ecclesie solempniter editis per verba de presenti ante publicationem constitutionis a felice recordationis Clemente papa V predecessore nostro edite, qua inter cetera cavetur quod qui scienter in gradibus consanguinitatis constitucione canonica interdictis matrimonia contrahunt excommunicationis sentencie subjaceant ipso facto matrimonium insimul contraxerunt, Agnete prefata impedimentum inter eos fore aliquod quo nequirent matrimonialiter copulari penitus ignorante, ac deinde ipsi numerosam prolem in hujusmodi matrimonio procrearunt. Tandem vero ad noticiam Agnetis predicte pervenit quod ipsi Galfridus et Agnes tercio et quarto consanguinitatis gradu se adinvicem contingebant. Quare nobis pro parte dictorum Galfridi et Agnetis fuit humiliter supplicatum ut cum si fieret matrimonii prefati divorcium, grave posset oriri scandalum presertim cum ipsi sint nobiles et potentes et hujusmodi numerosa proles ut premittitur procreata existeret desolata, providere ipsis in hac parte de oportune dispensationis gracia ex benignitate apostolica dignaremur. Nos igitur qui cunctorum Christi fidelium salutem summis desideriis affectamus et libenter pacis et quietis comoda procuramus, eisdem viam quibuslibet scandalum quantum nobis desuper conceditur precludere intendentes ac volentes super hoc de apostolice sedis clemencia salubriter provideri hujusmodi supplicacionibus inclinati, fraternitati tue per apostolica scripta [Fo.382^v; N.F.461^v] committimus et mandamus quatinus si premissa repereris ita esse, cum predictis Galfrido et Agnete ut impedimento consanguinitatis hujusmodi non obstante possint in dicto matrimonio licite remanere auctoritate nostra dispenses, dictam prolem susceptam et suscipiendam inantea ex dicto matrimonio legitimam nunciando. Datum Avinion' xiiii kalendas Novembris pontificatus nostri anno xvi.

Quarum auctoritate litterarum quia per inquisicionem in forma juris factam reperimus omnia et singula superius in litteris apostolicis expressa et suggesta continere per omnia in facti serie veritatem, hoc excepto quod in nullo gradu consanguinitatis vos adinvicem attingitis quod testes ipsi per quos fuit inquisitum sciebant nec aliquo tempore impedimentum consanguinitatis audiverunt subesse, vobiscum ut impedimento consanguinitatis hujusmodi si quod fuerit non obstante possitis in dicto matrimonio licite remanere tenore presencium dispensamus, dictamque prolem susceptam et suscipiendam inantea ex dicto matrimonio legitimam nunciamus et decernimus auctoritate apostolica supradicta. Valete. [York, 18 Jan. 1334.]

[59] MS. *presentatos*

728 Institution [etc.] of Edward de Stapilford, chaplain, to a mediety of Trowell church, vacant by the death of Adam [de Lansill]; presented by the prior and convent of Sempringham. York, 28 Jan. 1334.

729 Note of licence to M. William de Langeleye, rector of Carlton in Lindrick, to be absent for two years, farm his church and not attend synods in person. Bishopthorpe, 11 Feb. 1334.

730 Certificate of Henry [Burghersh], bishop of Lincoln, that he has executed the archbishop's commission (quoted; dated Bishopthorpe, 2 Feb. 1334) for an exchange of benefices between William de Risle, rector of Misson, and John de Sculthorp, vicar of Gainsborough (*Geynesburgh*; dioc. Lincoln), forwarding the report of an enquiry by the archdeacon of Nottingham's official.[60] Liddington (*Lidington*), 14 Feb. 1334.

731 Note of the archbishop's mandate for John's induction to Misson. Bishopthorpe, 20 Feb. 1334.

732 Institution (in the person of William de Beckeford, vicar of Oxton, as proctor) and mandate for induction of William de Ambaldeston, chaplain, as perpetual chaplain of the second chantry (*alteram cantariam*) of St. Mary de Hethebeth by Nottingham, previously held by Edward de Stapelford, chaplain; presented by the prior and convent of Newstead. Bishopthorpe, 26 Feb. 1334.

733 [*Mandate to publish the release of sentences imposed on the hospital of St. Leonard outside Newark* (see **695**).]
[Fo.383; N.F.462] RELAXACIO SEQUESTRI INTERPOSITI IN CAPELLA HOSPITALIS SANCTI LEONARDI EXTRA NEUWERK'. Willelmus etc. dilecto filio . . decano nostro de Neuwerk' salutem [*etc.*]. Quia interdictum nuper propter contumacias et offensas magistri et fratrum et aliarum personarum degencium in hospitali sancti Leonardi juxta Neuwerk' nostre diocesis visitacionem nostram tunc subire nolencium in capella ipsius hospitalis auctoritate nostra interpositum ac[61] censuras alias ecclesiasticas in singulares personas ejusdem qualitercumque promulgatas relaxavimus, justicia mediante, tibi mandamus quatinus id omnibus[62] quorum interest cum inde requisitus fueris publice intimes vice nostra. Vale. [Bishopthorpe, 27 Feb. 1334.]

734 Note of licence to [M. Robert de Neville] rector of Flintham to be absent for one year from 14 Oct. 1333 and farm his church. Bishopthorpe, 2 Mar. 1334.

735 The like to [John de Sculthorpe] rector of Misson for two years. Bishopthorpe, 3 Mar. 1334.

736 Note of letter instructing the auditors of accounts to allow M. R[ichard] de Snoweshull, receiver at York, for £20 paid by him to Sir Fulk FitzWaryn, and for

[60] The patron of Misson is not named (cf. **214**).
[61] Interlined.
[62] Interlined.

the delivery of a cup valued at £7 8s. 7d. and a gold episcopal ring valued at 100s. to Sir William de Feriby, as he has acknowledged. 9 Mar. 1334.

737 Note of licence to study (*stare in scolis*) for one year from 29 Sept. 1334 to John [de Sherburn], rector of Rempstone (*Rampstone*). Southwell, 21 Apr. 1334.

738 [*Monition against the exaction of tolls on clergy of Newark deanery bringing produce into Newark.*]

LITTERA NE EXIGATUR TOLNETUM PANAGII VEL GUYDAGII AB ECCLESIASTICIS PERSONIS. Willelmus etc. dilecto filio . . decano nostro de Neuwerk' salutem [*etc.*]. Cum ecclesie ecclesiasticeque persone ac res ipsarum non solum jure humano quinimmo et divino a secularium personarum exaccionibus sint immunes, nec contraria consuetudine quorumcumque que dicenda est coruptela verius non obstante liceat collegio nec universitati nec alicui singulari persone cujuscumque sit dignitatis condicionis aut status ab ecclesiis aut personis ecclesiasticis[63] pro personis ipsis aut rebus predictis talia exigere vel extorquere per se vel per alium suo nomine vel eciam alieno aut eas ad pedagiorum guidagiorum tolneti panagii seu cujuscumque alterius exaccionis onera compellere persolvenda, et hii qui contra fecerint si persone fuerint singulares excommunicacionis si autem collegium vel universitas civitatis castri seu loci eciam alterius cujuscumque ipsa civitas castrum vel locus interdicti sentencias incurrerint ipso facto, nec ab excommunicacione hujusmodi absolucionem vel interdicti relaxacionem obtinere potuerint donec exacta plenarie restituerint et de transgressione hujusmodi satisfecerint competenter; tibi in virtute obediencie firmiter injungendo mandamus quatinus moneas et efficaciter inducas prout tociens et quando fueris requisitus constabularium castri de Neuwerk' et ejus ministros ac ville de Neuwerk' ballivos et servientes quocumque nomine censeantur, ne decetero de ecclesiarum de Averham de Shelton de Kelom aut aliarum ecclesiarum tui decanatus rectoribus seu personis aliis ecclesiasticis quibuscumque guidagium pedagium panagium tolnetum seu exaccionem aliam quamcumque pro pecoribus bladis seu aliis rebus suis propriis venalibus quibuscumque, quas ad vendendum seu distrahendum et non causa negociandi deferunt vel deferri faciunt seu deferri transmittunt, petant exegant vel extorqueant quoquomodo. Et si contrarium fecerint monicionibusque tuis non paruerint in hac parte, ipsos et eorum singulos in dictam excommunicacionis sentenciam contra hujusmodi petitores exactores et extortores a canone proinde latam incidisse et ea occasione dampnabiliter involutos esse in ecclesia parochiali de Neuwerk' et aliis ecclesiis parochialibus et locis tui decanatus quibus videbitur expedire, cum in ipsis ecclesiis ad audiendum divina major affuerit populi multitudo, pulsatis campanis candelis accensis et extinctis cruceque erecta, juris tamen ordine qui requiritur in hoc casu ac canonica monicione premissis, publice et solempniter denuncies et per alios facias nunciari, a publicacione et denunciacione hujusmodi non cessans quousque reatus hujusmodi transgressores exacta hujusmodi restituerint, de offensa satisfecerint et alias absolucionis beneficium in forma juris meruerint obtinere. Vale. [Southwell, 24 Apr. 1334.]

[63] Interlined.

739 [*Faculty to the inhabitants of West Stockwith, in Misterton parish, to have services in their new chapel.*]
LICENCIA CELEBRANDI DIVINA IN CAPELLA DE STOKWITH. Willelmus etc. universis incolis et inhabitatoribus villule de Stokhyth parochianis ecclesie de Misterton nostre diocesis salutem [*etc.*]. Ad distanciam ejusdem villule de Stokhyth a dicta ecclesia sua parochiali aliqualiter distante[64] ac viarum discrimina aliaque pericula et impedimenta, quominus dicti incole et inhabitatores ad ipsam ecclesiam parochialem comode poterint accedere pro divinis audiendis obsequiis ut incumbint, paterne compassionis intuitum debite convertentes, ut in capella beate Marie in dicta villula de Stokhyth de novo constructa per sacerdotem ydoneum missas et alias horas canonicas celebrari facere valeatis, ita per hoc prejudicium ecclesie parochiali minime generetur nec in suis proinde proventibus detrahatur, quodque in majoribus festis in canone comprehensis dictam ecclesiam vestram personaliter visitetis legitimo impedimento cessante, de consensu ejusdem ecclesie rectoris expresso vobis et sacerdoti hujusmodi cuicumque ydoneo tenore presencium liberam deinceps in domino concedimus facultatem. Valete. [Southwell, 21 Apr. 1334.]

740 Note of licence to William de Walkyngham,[65] rector of Greasley, to be absent for one year from 29 Sept. 1334. Lenton priory, 28 Apr. 1334.

741 The like to William de London, rector of South Collingham, for two years. Same date.

742 Note of licence to Robert Jorz, kt., to have divine service celebrated in a chapel or oratory in his manor of Burton Joyce. Southwell, 1 May 1334.

743 The like to John de Boolyngbrok in his manor of Leverton (*Lyverton*). Same date.

744 Note of licence to M. William de Hundon, rector of Car Colston, to be absent for two years. Same date.

745 [Fo.383v; N.F.462v] Note of licence to [Robert de Burstwick] rector of Lambley to be absent for two years, farm his church and be exempt from personal appearance in synods at Southwell. Bishopthorpe, 22 May 1334.

746 The like for three years to [Ralph de Hertford] rector of Hockerton. Cawood, 26 July 1334.

747 [*Commission to the rector of Willoughby on the Wolds to order its ministers to obey him and absolve parishioners who had assaulted clergy.*]
LICENCIA AD AMMOVENDUM ET COHERCENDUM MINISTROS ECCLESIE ET ABSOLVENDUM PAROCHIANOS. Willelmus etc. dilecto filio domino Ricardo de Melton rectori ecclesie de Wylighby nostre diocesis salutem [*etc.*]. Cum disposicio et ordinacio posicio et deposicio necnon amocio ministrorum ecclesie

[64] Interlined from *aliqualiter*
[65] MS. *Walkyngton* (cf. **361**, **624**, **763**).

vestre in eadem qualitercumque ministrancium seu ministrare volencium ad nos de jure dinoscantur pertinere, vobis ad monendum et cohercendum eosdem omnes et singulos in genere et nominatim in specie ut vobis pareant et canonice intendant in licitis et canonicis mandatis vices nostras committimus cum cohercionis canonice potestate. Ad absolvendum insuper omnes et singulos parochianos vestros a quibuscumque suspensionis seu excommunicacionis sententiis quas incurrerint seu incurrere contigerit occasione injectionis manuum violenter in clericos seu personas ecclesiasticas in casibus in quibus de jure possumus et ad injungendum eisdem et eorum singulis penitenciam salutarem, vobis tenore presencium committimus vices nostras, quibus sigillum nostrum apponi fecimus in testimonium premissorum. Valete. [Cawood, 31 July 1334.]

748 Institution [etc.] of William de Gonaldeston, acolyte, to Elton church, vacant by the death of Ingram [de Mattersey]; presented by the prior and convent of Blyth. Cawood, 10 Aug. 1334.

749 Collation [etc.] of M. Thomas Sampson, D.C.L., to Misterton church, vacant by the death of M. Thomas de Sancto Albano. Bishop Burton, 27 Aug. 1334.

750 Note of licence to Richard de Glatton, rector of Fledborough, to be absent until 24 June 1335 to go on pilgrimage to St. James [of Compostella]. 16 Sept. 1334.

751 The like to William de Flyntham, rector of Cromwell, for one year, with exemption from personal appearance in synods. Laneham, 21 Sept. 1334.

752 ORDINACIO PERPETUE CANTARIE IN ECCLESIA DE TUXEFORD PRO ANIMA DOMINI THOME DE LONGEVILERS. Inspeximus by the archbishop of the following charter of Thomas de Longevilers, kt.: by licence of Edward III (quoted; dated Raby (*Rabi*), 23 June 1334)[66] he has granted to Ralph de Laxton, chaplain, and his successors celebrating [Fo.384; N.F.463] in perpetuity in Tuxford church for his soul and the souls of his ancestors and all faithful departed, a piece of land (measuring 100 by 55 feet) in the western part of his manor of Tuxford and five marks of annual rent from the manor, at Martinmas and Whitsun. Ralph and his successors are to celebrate daily before sunrise at the altar of St. Mary Magdalene in the north part of the church, in honour of the Blessed Virgin Mary and for the said souls. They are to reside in that land. In vacancies Thomas and his heirs shall present chaplains to the diocesan for institution and induction. Thomas intends to provide the chaplain with a chalice, books, vestments and other necessities for the celebration of masses, and charges his heirs to provide them in perpetuity. If the chantry remains vacant for two months by [the patron's] fault, the archbishop of York shall provide a chaplain for that turn. Chaplains may distrain on the manor if the rent is not fully paid at any term; with warranty clause. This writing is an indenture, sealed alternately by Thomas and Ralph (in his name and that of his successors). Witnessed by Hugh de Hercy, John de Lisours, knights, William de Bevercotes, Richard de Sutton of

[66] See *CPR 1330–4*, 562.

Walesby, John de Marcham, Nicholas Petyd, Thomas Dayvill of Egmanton, and others. Haughton, 18 Sept. 1334.

The archbishop, wishing to cherish Thomas's devotion,[67] approves of all the contents of the ordinance and orders their full observation forever, saving his right etc. and that of his church. Laneham, 26 Sept. 1334.

753 Memorandum that Baldwin [de Cockfield], rector of Langar, took the customary oath of obedience to the archbishop in his chapel at Laneham, 27 Sept. 1334.

754 Note of licence to William de Buttercambe, rector of a mediety of Eakring, to be absent for one year. Laneham, 28 Sept. 1334.

755 Note of licence for study (*in forma constitutionis*) for one year to Baldwin de Cokefeld, rector of Langar; he also had letters dimissory for all holy orders. Same date.

756 Institution and mandate for induction of Ralph de Laxton, chaplain, as perpetual chaplain of the newly founded chantry in Tuxford church; presented by Thomas de Longvilers, kt. Laneham, 26 Sept. 1334.

757 Note of licence to William de Aslakby, rector of Sibthorpe, to be absent for two years in the service of Manuel de Flisco. Cawood, 28 Oct. 1334.

758 Commission[68] to Masters William de Alberwik', D.D., Gilbert de Alberwik', rector of Langton (*Langeton),* William de Langeleye, rector of Carlton in Lindrick and Simon de Courtmaiour, rector of Clayworth (or two or three of them including William de Alberwik), to visit Blyth priory, with power to receive the resignations of the prior and other obedientiaries or remove them from office, reporting by letters patent. Cawood, 28 Oct. 1334.

759 [Fo.384v; N.F.463v] Memorandum of mandate to the sequestrator in the archdeaconry of Cleveland to induct 'the said' Innocent [de Fieschi] or his proctor into the archdeaconry of Cleveland and to sequestrate its fruits from the time of its vacancy. [Cawood, 28 Oct. 1334.][69]

760 [*Monition to the prior of Worksop to enforce the injunctions in a decree drawn up after the archbishop's second visitation of the priory and found at the next visitation not to have been observed.*[70]]

INJUNCTIONES FACTE PRIORI ET CONVENTUI DE WYRKESOP'. Willelmus etc. dilecto filio . . priori monasterii de Wirkesop' nostre diocesis salutem [*etc.*]. Sicut

[67] This clause is also written at the bottom edge of fo.383v.

[68] Similar to no.303 in *Reg. Melton,* II.125–6, with the addition for obedientiaries (*officiciarii*) and without provision for the election, etc., of a new head (*et ad concedendam–recipiendum*) and the order to obey the commissaries (*Predicte priorisse–intendant*).

[69] The occurrence of *dictum*, etc., in this notice suggests that Innocent's admission was the preceding entry; in fact it is in the *Capitula* section of the register, dated 28 Oct. 1334 (see *Fasti*, VI.19).

[70] For the second visitation, in 1325, see **403** (and note to **398**); subsequent injunctions are not in this register. For the third visitation, in 1330, see **609**; also **825**.

cure congruit boni medici ibi acriora medicine antidota adhibere ubi levia proficere non prospicit, sic pastoris officio convenit ubi subditos monicionem suavem verborumque comminacionem non avertere nec timere comperit ne effrenis delinquendi audacia invalescat, penas adicere[71] et infligere ac inflectas crescente protervia aggravare ut sic quos ad obediendum lac dulcedinis non emollit, severitas coherceat discipline. Sane visitationis nostre officium in monasterio vestro secunda vice exercentes personaliter, quedam ad animarum salutem religionis augmentum vestrique utilitatem monasterii perpetuam ordinavimus et a vobis inviolabiliter perpetuo observari injunximus per decretum, quod in pluribus articulis ejusdem in subsecuta proxima visitatione nostra quam inibi exercuimus comperimus non servatum; propter quod injunxiones novas fecimus mencionem de prioribus non servatis expressius facientes, quas sicuti nec primas curastis ut in pluribus non absque inobediencie nota hactenus observare in monasterio vestri quod prosperiora cupimus grave dampnum. Cum igitur nil inobediencia prodesse videretur humilibus si contemptus contumacibus non obesset, vos monemus primo secundo et tercio ac peremptorio vobisque in virtute obediencie districte precipiendo mandamus quatinus articulos primi decreti nostri et contenta in ipsis articulis, qui cum quadam addicione quam post primum articulum pro prima interpretacione[72] seu declaracione ejusdem inseruimus sequ[u]ntur per ordinem in hec verba:

(Item injungimus vobis . . priori et ceteris officiatis domus in virtute obediencie et sub pena amocionis eorumdem ab officiis suis ut compotus omnium officiatorum annis singulis semel reddatur ac bis supervideatur coram . . priore et senioribus de conventu, necnon compotus administracionis . . prioris coram senioribus et sanioribus domus ejusdem, ac post compoti tocius ostendatur publice omnibus et singulis de conventu ac status domus annis singulis omnibus et singulis expressius innotescat. Seniores vero et saniores quoad auditionem[73] compoti officiatorum domus ac binam supervisionem ejusdem unacum . . priore, si velit personaliter interesse, ac compoti administracionis . . prioris dominos Rogerum de Walkringham suppriorem Robertum de Leverton elemosinarium Willelmum de Hanay sacristam . . Petrum de Deneby et duos bursarios, qui pro tempore fuerint canonicos dicte domus dumtamen per totum conventum vel majorem partem ejusdem ad id deputati vel assignati fuerint, reputamus et ut seniores et saniores admitti volumus et mandamus, et unius vel plurium ipsorum hujusmodi actus expedicioni vacare seu intendere non valencium vel nolencium loco alius seu alii per . . priorem et conventum proinde deputentur.

Item injungimus omnibus et singulis de conventu sub pena districtionis canonice quod nullus de cetero elomosinam emittat vel distribuat quoquomodo absque licencia presidentis, elemosinario dumtaxat excepto, qui totam elemosinam fideliter et diligenter colligat et pauperibus erroget prout sanctius viderit faciendum, super quo ejus conscienciam oneramus.

Item precepimus et eciam ordinamus quod decetero duo sint bursarii in domo ad quorum manus omnis pecunia de bonis domus qualitercumque proveniens integraliter perveniat, excepta pecunia officiatis pro suis officiis

[71] MS. *aditere*
[72] *articulum pro* interlined over this word.
[73] MS. *audiacionem*

assignata, et per ipsos bursarios . . priori ac ceteris officiatis pro negociis domus expediendis secundum ordinacionem . . prioris prout expediens visum fuerit liberetur, ita quod domi venerint statim eisdem compotum reddant de eadem.

Item ordinamus quod canonici licenciati ex causa necessaria et probabili ad visitandum amicos vecturas expensas moderatas de bursario habeant prout domus suppetere poterunt facultates.)

servetis[74] de cetero juxta ipsorum posteriorum injunctionum nostrarum de ipsis monicionem facientium exigenciam et tenorem, et faciatis ab officiatis et aliis monasterii vestri prout ipsos concernunt districtius inviolabiliter custodiri.

Quodque Walterum de Hull in pistrina et Johannem de Carleton in aula hospitum dudum servientes et ab ipsis officiis ipsorum exigentibus demeritis de mandato nostro amotos et nunc per vos et custodes grangiarum domus vestre prefectos, sic quod dissipandi[75] et contractandi bona vestra ipsis liberior est attributa facultas, a suis officiis amoveatis penitus infra sex dies a die recepcionis presentium continue numerandos, ipsos ad dicta officia seu alia in dicto monasterio seu extra imposterum nullatenus admittentes sub pena excommunicationis majoris, quam dicta canonica amonicione premissa nisi mandatis nostris omnibus et singulis parueritis cum effectu in personam vestram culpa vestra mora et delicto precedentibus et id poscentibus ferimus in hiis scriptis.

Item cum operarii sua digni sint mercede que si solucio ejusdem tardetur tempore inmoratur, vobis injungimus quod servientibus stipendiariis et mercenariis vestris pro ipsorum ministerio et labore de tempore preterito satisfaciatis absque more diffugio competenter, et quod futuris temporibus ipsorum mercedem stipendium et salarium postquam[76] dies solucionis ejusdem evenerit solvere non tardetis.

Item precipimus quod ad curam et custodiam instauri ovium dirigendas unus de domo canonicus eligatur qui oves debiles morbidas et infectas extrahat atque vendat, quorum loco alios bidentes sanos et utiles submittat, ac de extantibus bidentibus extractis et venditis et de lana pellibusque lanutis ac exitibus ipsorum singulis annis compotum plenum reddat sicut in domo vestra retroactis temporibus est fieri consuetum, nec in hiis de cetero preter superiores curam vobis aliquid usurpetis ut sic vestre parcatur fame pariter et honori.

Item volumus et mandamus quod molendinum de Denynby de quo in decreto vestro[77] fit mencio reficiatur plene et debite infra annum; et quod noviciis vestris ad ordines accedentibus vecture expense prout facultates domus suppetunt faciatis congrue ministrari. Valete. [Cawood, 14 Nov. 1334.]

761 Note of licence in accordance with the constitution *Cum ex eo* to Robert de Wyvill, rector of Bulwell, for five years. Cawood, 23 Nov. 1334.

762 Institution [etc.] of John son of Simon de Southleverton, chaplain, to South Leverton vicarage, vacant by the resignation of Robert de Ballio; presented by M. Anthony Beek, dean of Lincoln. Cawood, 25 Nov. 1334.

[74] Continuing from before the articles enclosed in round brackets.
[75] Interlined over *dispensandi*, cancelled.
[76] Repeated in MS.
[77] *Sic.*

763 [Fo.385; N.F.464] The like of John de Monte, chaplain, to Greasley (*Grisley*) church, vacant by the death of William de Walkyngham; presented by Nicholas de Cantilupo, kt. Cawood, 10 Mar. 1335.

764 The like of William de Loscow, chaplain, to Selston church, vacant by the resignation of John de Kendale; presented by Nicholas de Cantilupo, kt. Cawood, 16 Mar. 1335.

765 (i) Letters patent testifying that the archbishop has appointed and provided Peter Meslier, monk of Sainte-Cathérine-du-Mont, Rouen, as prior of Blyth, vacant by the cession of Ralph de Toto; presented by the abbot and convent of the said mother house. (ii) Mandate for his installation to the archdeacon or his official [as in **513**]. (iii) Appointment of Peter as prior [as in **511**], with his oath of obedience. (iv) Mandate to the subprior and convent to obey him [as in **512**]. Cawood, 5 Apr. 1335.

766 [*Letter of the abbot and convent of Sainte-Cathérine thanking the archbishop for his interest in Blyth, including a visitation which revealed disorders (attributed to Satan); they agree to the recall of Ralph de Toto, who had resigned to commissaries* (see **758**), *and four other monks named by the archbishop, and to send a suitable replacement as prior and two monks considered able to adapt to life at Blyth.*]
LITTERA CLAUSA . . ABBATIS ET CONVENTUS MONASTERII BEATE KATERINE JUXTA ROTHOM' PRO EODEM PRIORE. Reverentissimo in Christo patri ac domino domino Willelmo dei gracia Ebor' archiepiscopo Anglie primati sui humiles ac devoti J[ohannes] permissione divina abbas sancte Trinitatis in monte sancte Katerine prope Rothomagum ejusdemque loci conventus reverenciam cum honore et beatitudinis eterne pro premio laboris in hac vita solacium obtinere. Visis litteris caritatis vestre quibus satis perpenditur quanto studio placuit paternitati vestre pro nostro prioratu de Blida in visitando et corrigendo exhibere non modice gavisi fuimus [et] sumus ut debemus. Addidit eciam reverencia vestra inter priorem et monachos dicti loci lites rixas sedicionem invidiam non modicam esse ortam, quodque regularis disciplina pretermittitur, non fit ibidem correctio et quod multa ymo pocius infinita in spiritualibus et temporalibus dispendia dictus prioratus nunc sustinet et speratur majora, nisi sibi subveniatur in brevi sustinere; quod cum sit dictus prioratus competenter dotatus ex instigacione versuti hostis credimus obvenire, habet enim nocendi mille modos nec ignoramus astuciam ejus conatur namque a principio ruine sue unitatem ecclesie rescindere, caritatem vulnerare,[78] sanctorum operum dulcedinem invidie felle inficere et omnibus modis humanum genus evertere et perturbare, dolet enim satis et erubescit caritatem quam in celo nequivit habere homines constantes ex lutea materia in terra tenere; unde oportet quantum fragilitati nostre conceditur ut omnis aditus nocendi ejus versucie minuamus ne mors ingrediatur portas nostras. Paternitatem ac dominacionem vestram non in quantum debemus set in quantum possumus regraciamur de cura et solicitudine per vos seu gentes vestras in reformacione dicti prioratus inpensis, ut in litteris vestris vestri gracia nobis missis vidimus contineri. Recensentes in vobis esse impletum quod scribitur clemens si tanquam omnibus preesse volueris singulos

[78] MS. *wlnerare*

prout poteris et singulos releva, quia et singulorum onus et solicitudinem portas nomen merito episcopi portans quod magis est operis quam honoris quia fieri intendit in subditos, idcirco omnibus consideratis exortacioni seu consilio vestro laudabili parere intendimus in quantum poterimus. Et cum nobis intimaverit quod prior de Blida per gentes vestras inductus renunciavit prioratui et juri quod in eodem sibi competebat, timens ne turpius inde sibi eveniret, quam renunciacionem gentes vestre duxerunt admittendam et quod ibidem alium ydoneum mitteremus et quod litteratorie quatuor de sociis revocaremus; sciat paternitas vestra nos consensu tocius conventus nostri priorem utilem et ydoneum prout dominacioni vestre dei gracia apparebit elegisse, et duos alios monachos qui sunt bone vite et habiles persone et quos non credimus mores suos mutare propter mutacionem suam, quia sepe evenit quod mutatio loci distancia amicorum et eorum qui timentur et post esse terribiles talia multociens sunt causa mutandi mores [Fo.385v; N.F.464v] bonos in pejoribus. Insuper miseritur litteris dictum prioratum tam in reparacione maneriorum quam in defectu victualium inopia laborare et mole debitorum undiquaque esse obpressum, licet fuerimus et simus in pluribus gravati, tamen quia de novo in officio nostro assumpti, tamen de decimis et in multis aliis quia dies mali sunt ut quibus experitur, verumtamen in eis in quibus poterimus et in quantum intendimus cum vestro consilio et auxilio in reformacione dicti prioratus vigilare; de statu fratris Radulphi de Toto cum ad nos redierit unacum aliis quatuor litteris vestris nominatis quos litteratorie proponimus revocare, tantum facere intendimus per dei graciam quod vos eritis de nobis contenti et ipse non habebit de vobis materiam conquerendi. Valeat vestra reverentissima paternitas cum incremento gracie et bonorum. Datum in monasterio nostro xiii die mensis Marcii anno domini MCCCXXXIV. [13 Mar. 1335.]

767 [*Request to the abbot and convent of Sainte-Cathérine to make provision for Ralph de Toto, as was promised by the archbishop's commissaries when he renounced his office at Blyth, where he will stay pending a reply; Peter Meslier has been appointed prior in his place.*]

ABBATI ET CONVENTUI MONASTERII SANCTE KATERINE DE MONTE JUXTA ROTHOM' PRO FRATRE RADULPHO DE [TOTO] NUPER PRIORE DE BLIDA. Venerande religionis viris fratri Johanni dei gracia abbati monasterii sancte Trinitatis in monte beate Katerine juxta Rothomagum et ejusdem loci conventui Willelmus etc. salutem et sincere dilectionis continuum incrementum cum benediccione et gracia salvatoris. In offensam dei cleri scandalum et nostri verecundiam amici carissimi cederet sicut scitis si frater Radulphus de Toto nuper prior monasterii de Blida, qui officio suo sponte cedens ordinacioni nostre se submisit, competenti sustentacione defraudaretur et se illusum ex pulcris promissis et circumventum sentiret, ex quibus graciam multiformem et bonam fidem que in personis ecclesiasticis exuberare debet se credidit reportasse. Hiis igitur et aliis que nuper in litteris nostris expressimus vobis missis cum maturitate pensatis que petimus per vos memoraliter recenseri, attencius sicut alias vos rogamus quatinus ne ipsi fratri Radulpho de nobis vel nostris clericis detur materia conquerendi, qui sibi post cessionem suam hujusmodi fiducialiter promiserunt se velle et debere efficaciter laborare et penes nos cum instancia procurare ut eidem sustentacionem de proventibus domus de Blida vel alibi faceremus ad terminum vite sue congruam ministrari;

velitis eidem fratri Radulpho unum ex tribus prioratibus ditioribus[79] partium vestrarum in quibus priores preficitis pleno jure conferre caritatis et nostri rogaminis interventu et ipsum in personam fratris sui seu alterius procuratoris ejusdem in corporalem possessionem hujusmodi prioratus inducere cum suis juribus et pertinenciis universis, litteras collacionis hujusmodi prefato fratri Radulpho per procuratorem suum predictum si libeat transmittentes quas cum receperit eundi ad partes vestras cum festinancia arripiet iter suum. In monasterio tamen de Blida medio tempore moram trahet ut si preces nostre iteratis vicibus vobis facte quod absit transeant sine fructu, de proventibus domus de Blida sibi attento statu suo providere possumus et id forsitan processu temporis vobis videbitur magis grave, decet enim quod pulcris promissis facta condigna corespondeant et verba blanda opera utilia subsequantur. Ad presentacionem vero vestram fratrem Petrum Meslier in priorem monasterii de Blida prefecimus die confectionis presencium, sibi liberam administracionem in spiritualibus et temporalibus prout moris est et alia necessaria committentes. Si que facere poterimus vobis grata, ac id quod nostre contemplacione persone pro statu dicti fratris Radulphi duxeritis concedendum, nobis rescribere velitis presencium per latorem. Ad impendendum sibi devotum sub regulari observancia famulatum, diu faciat altissimus vos valere. [Cawood, 5 Apr. 1335.]

768 [*Presentation by the abbot and convent of Sainte-Cathérine of Peter Meslier, whom they have unanimously nominated to be prior of Blyth.*]
NOMINACIO EORUMDEM ABBATIS ET CONVENTUS DE FRATRE PETRO MESLIER IN PRIOREM DOMUS DE BLIDA PREFICIENDUM. Reverendissimo in Christo patri ac domino domino Willelmo etc. seu venerabili vicario ejusdem domini sui devoti et humiles frater J[ohannes] miseracione divina abbas sancte Trinitatis in monte sancte Katerine prope Rothomagum totusque ejusdem loci conventus reverenciam et honorem debitas tanto patri. Cum dominacioni vestre placuerit nobis intimare nostrum prioratum de Blida ad presens vacare per resignacionem seu renunciacionem fratris Radulphi de Toto nuper et ultimo ejusdem loci prioris, quam renunciationem vos vel gentes vestre vestri gracia gratanter receperunt, nos predicta scientes et attendentes cicius quam comode potuerimus omnes qui in electione . . prioris de Blida vobis mittendi interesse poterant et debebant, certo die in . . capitulo nostro . . pro dicto priore eligendo congregati post aliquas prolocutiones inter nos agitatas tandem convenimus et consensum nostrum unanimiter, nullo contradicente set omnibus et singulis expresse consencientibus, prebuimus in unum de fratribus nostris quem elegimus vobis presentandum et mittendum. Iccirco paternitati vestre supplicamus ut ad dictum prioratum de Blida nunc vacantem per resignationem seu renunciacionem fratris Radulphi de Toto fratrem Petrum Meslier, quem concorditer elegimus virum utique religiosum de legitimo matrimonio procreatum in omnibus sacris ordinibus constitutum ordinem regularem beati Benedicti expresse professum in legitima etate constitutum moribus et sciencia ornatum vita laudabili et honesta conversacione fulgentem et quamplurimis aliis virtutibus circumspectum, ad vestram presentacionem et quem vobis presentamus nostri interventu admittatis sibique dictum prioratum intuitu caritatis conferatis cum omnibus

[79] MS. *dicioribus*

juribus spiritualibus et temporalibus, curamque ejusdem committatis et in dicto prioratu preficiatis et instituatis seu prefici et institui faciatis et in corporalem possessionem omnium predictorum solempnitatibus consuetis intervenientibus et adhibitis eundem inducatis seu induci faciatis, et ipsum sic inductum protegatis et eciam defendatis. In quorum premissorum testimonium sigilla nostra quibus utimur ac uti consuevimus presentibus litteris duximus apponenda. Datum in monasterio nostro xiii die mensis Marcii anno domini MCCCXXXIV. [13 Mar. 1335.]

769 [*Appointment by the same of three monks elected as proctors to present the prior-designate.*]
PROCURATORIUM ILLORUM QUI DICTUM FRATREM PETRUM DOMINO PRESENTARUNT. Universis presentes litteras inspecturis frater J[ohannes] miseracione divina humilis abbas[80] sancte Trinitatis [in monte] sancte Katerine prope Rothomagum totusque ejusdem loci conventus salutem in domino. Noveritis nos omnes unanimes in nostro capitulo propter hoc specialiter congregati fecimus constituimus et ordinavimus nostros procuratores seu nuncios speciales et quemlibet eorum in solidum, ita quod non sit melior condicio occupantis sed quod unus eorum inceperit alter prosequi valeat et finire, videlicet dominos Ricardum Hemery Guillelmum Fauquet alias Denibat ac Simonem Ascii fratres ac commonachos nostros, ad presentandum fratrem Petrum Meslier per nos electum concorditer in priorem de Blida reverendissimo in Christo patri ac domino domino Willelmo dei gracia archiepiscopo Ebor' primati Anglie seu venerabili vicario ejusdem domini, et dicto domino supplicandum ut paternitati sue placeat dictum fratrem Petrum ad dictum prioratum ad presentacionem nostram admittere, sibique intuitu caritatis dictum prioratum cum omnibus juribus suis spiritualibus et temporalibus ac dependenciis eorumdem conferre et in possessionem omnium predictorum inducere seu induci facere cum optato effectu, dantes et concedentes eisdem procuratoribus nostris et cuilibet eorum in solidum plenariam potestatem et mandatum speciale premissa et omnia alia et singula faciendi que circa premissa et eorum tangencia fuerint necessaria seu eciam oportuna, ratum et gratum habentes et habituri quicquid per dictos procuratores nostros seu eorum quemlibet actum gestumve fuerit in premissis seu quolibet premissorum sub obligacione rerum nostrarum ac monasterii nostri. In quorum premissorum omnium testimonium sigilla nostra quibus in talibus et aliis utimur ac uti consuevimus presentibus litteris duximus apponenda. Datum in monasterio nostro terciadecima die mensis Marcii anno domini MCCCXXXIV.

770 [*Citation of objectors to the election to Blyth to appear before the archbishop on 5 April.*]
LITTERA PROCLAMACIONIS PRO DICTO ELECTO. Willelmus etc. dilecto filio . . perpetuo vicario ecclesie de Blida nostre diocesis salutem [*etc.*]. Presentata nobis nuper electione facta in capitulo monasterii sancte Trinitatis in monte sancte Katerine prope Rothom' ut dicitur de fratre Petro Meslier monacho ejusdem monasterii in priorem monasterii de Blida presentato[81], ex parte . . abbatis et

[80] Interlined.
[81] Interlined.

conventus dicti monasterii sancte Trinitatis a nobis extitit humiliter supplicatum ut electionem hujusmodi confirmare canonice curaremus. Nos igitur volentes in ipsius electionis negocio statuta canonica sicut convenit observare, tibi committimus et mandamus quatinus receptis presentibus coelectum [Fo.386; N.F.465] et competitorem si sit et oppositorem si quis appareat nominatim ac nihilominus in ecclesia conventuali de Blida predicta proposito publice monicionis et vocacionis edicto si qui sint qui electioni predicte se opponere voluerint quovis modo moneas ac peremptorie cites eosdem quod die Mercurii proximo post datum presencium, quem diem eisdem et eorum cuilibet pro termino preciso et peremptorio assignamus et per te volumus assignari, coram nobis compareant et compareat ubicumque tunc fuerimus in nostra diocesi propposituri objecturi ac eciam ostensuri quicquam canonicum habuerit seu habuerint quod proponere objicere et ostendere voluerit aut voluerint contra electi seu eligencium personas vel electionis formam quare non debeamus electionem hujusmodi prout ad nos pertinet confirmare decernere statuere et exequi ulterius quod est justum, facturi ulterius et recepturi quod justicia suadebit et secundum qualitatem et naturam ipsius negocii consonum fuerit racioni. Citacionem vero et terminum de quibus premittitur ad evitacionem periculi animarum et ne dicta domus de Blida ex ipsius diutina vacacione paciatur in temporalibus incomoda et jacturas, et ut dilapidacionis excessus caucius evitetur qui forsitan ex diffusiori termino immineret, ac ex causis aliis si necesse fuerit oportunis loco et tempore exprimendum sic duximus moderandum. Et nos de omni eo etc. [Cawood, 1 Apr. 1335.]

771 Note of order to the official of the court of York, his commissary, and the receiver there, not to molest John de Emeldon, rector of Burton Joyce (*Jorce*), for non-residence during the last two years, and to relax any fine for this cause on sight of this letter. Cawood, 11 Apr. 1335.

772 [*Mandate to the archdeacon's official not to implement letters of the official of York concerning accusations made in the synod of Southwell; the archbishop has revoked them, as interested parties are to be told.*]

REVOCACIO CENSURARUM FACTARUM PER . . OFFICIALEM CURIE NOSTRE EBOR' PRO SINODO SUWELL'. Willelmus [*etc.*]. dilecto filio . . officiali . . archidiaconi nostri Notinghamie salutem [*etc.*]. Licet officialis curie nostre Ebor' decanis rectoribus et vicariis ac aliis ecclesiarum prelatis dicti archidiaconatus litteratorie nuper dederit in mandatis quod ipsi excessus crimina et defectus quorumcumque subditorum dicti archidiaconatus in sinodo Suwell' nunc proximo celebranda et extunc de sinodo in sinodo eidem . . officiali nostro seu aliis ministris nostris eisdem sinodis presidentibus[82] nunciarent et eciam revelarent ac alia facerent que ipsis litteris continentur; volumus tamen et vobis mandamus quatinus litteris ipsius . . officialis nostri predictis in hac parte minime pareatis, quia ipsas litteras et effectum ipsarum ex certis causis nos moventibus revocamus et subducimus, et hujusmodi revocacionem et subductionem ad omnium et singulorum quorum interest noticiam deducimus per presentes et vos eciam sicut expedit deducatis. Valete. [Cawood, 19 Apr. 1335.]

[82] Underlined from *ministris*, possibly by the same sixteenth-century hand which wrote in the margin here *Nota pro synodo Southwellen'*.

773 INSTITUTIO VICARIE ECCLESIE DE EDENESTOWE PER LAPSUM TEMPORIS. Collation (by lapse) and mandate for induction of Thomas son of Henry de Edenestowe, priest, to Edwinstowe vicarage, vacant by the death of John de Friston. Cawood, 1 May 1335.

774 COMMISSIO IN NEGOTIO PROVISIONIS WALTERI HARDY DE MISTERTON.[83] Commission to M. Richard de Eryom, canon of York, and M. Thomas Samson, canon of Beverley, sending them a papal grace addressed to the archbishop for Walter son of Walter Hardy of Misterton, a poor clerk (York dioc.); they are to examine him, and if he is of good repute, not beneficed nor otherwise canonically barred, provide him to a benefice in the diocese in the gift of the prior and brethren of the Hospital of St. John of Jerusalem in England. Bishopthorpe, 30 May 1335.

775 Note of a similar commission to the abbots of Welbeck and Rufford, [prior of] Worksop and M. Richard de Eryom, canon of York, to provide Andrew Durdaunt of Newark, a poor clerk, to a benefice in the gift of the abbot and convent of Whitby. Same date.

776 Note of licence for absence for one year (*in forma constitucionis Cum ex eo*) to Jollanus de Nevill, rector of Barnby in the Willows, excusing him from personal appearance at synods. Bishopthorpe, 31 May 1335.

777 Commission to the abbots of Welbeck and Rufford to provide Thomas son of Henry de Clippston in Schirwode, a poor priest, to a benefice in the gift of the prior and convent of Nostell. Bishopthorpe, 9 June 1335.

778 [*Commission to determine a suit between Robert de Silkeston, kt., and the executors or administrators of Robert Mayre of Pontefract.*]
[Fo.386^{v}; N.F.465^{v}] COMMISSIO SUPER ADMINISTRACIONE BONORUM ROBERTI MAYRE DE PONT'. Willelmus etc. dilectis filiis magistris Ricardo de Snoweshull rectori ecclesie de Huntington nostre diocesis et Willelmo de Jafford decano nostro Christianitatis Ebor' salutem [*etc.*]. De vestris circumspectione et industria plenam fiduciam reportantes, ad cognoscendum procedendum statuendum diffiniendum et exequendum in omnibus et singulis causis et negociis inter dominum Robertum de Silkeston militem actorem ex parte una motis seu movendis et executores seu administratores bonorum Roberti Mayre de Pont' defuncti ex altera cum potestate sequestrandi et sequestrum in dictis bonis interpositum seu interponendum relaxandi, creditoribus et legatariis quibuscumque dicti defuncti super peticionibus suis et aliorum contra eos coram vobis proponendis cognoscendi procedendi et diffiniendi et plenam justiciam exhibendi, executores seu administratores si qui de administracione sua suspecti inveniantur amovendi et alios ydoneos locis eorum subrogandi, et omnia alia faciendi et expediendi que secundum naturam et qualitatem premissorum fuerint necessaria seu eciam oportuna, vobis vices nostras committimus cum cohercionis canonice potestate. Valete. [Bishopthorpe, 1 June 1335.]

[83] In same form as no.442 (dated 17 June 1335) in *Reg. Melton*, II.170.

779 Commission to M. William de Alburwyk, D.D., chancellor of York, and M. Richard de Erium, D.Cn.& C.L., canon of York, to provide John de Roeston, a poor clerk (dioc. York) to a benefice in the gift of the abbot and convent of Welbeck. Bishopthorpe, 17 June 1335.

780 Note of the like to Masters Richard de Havering, Richard de Eriom and John de Warenna, canons of York, to provide John Stayngate of Thorne, a poor clerk, to a benefice in the gift of the abbot and convent of Whitby. 28 June 1335.

781 [*Mandate to induct Margaret de Thorp juxta Loude (Acthorpe near Louth) as an anchoress in a new house near St. Nicholas church, Nottingham; the right to present future anchorites will alternate between the prior of Lenton and the see of York.*]
ADMISSIO CUJUSDAM ANACHORITE.[84] Willelmus etc. dilecto filio decano nostro Notingh' salutem [*etc.*]. Quia Margaretam de Thorp juxta Loude caste et honeste vivere proponentem in anachoritam admisimus in quadam domo juxta ecclesiam sancti Nicholai Notinghamie de novo pro manso ejusdem constructa perpetuo recludendam, ipsam in anachoritam et reclusam instituimus in dicta domo pro manso suo ut premittitur ordinata, tibi firmiter injungimus et mandamus quatinus ipsam Margaretam in dicta domo cum ex parte ejusdem fueris congrue requisitus inducas ut moris est actualiter vice nostra; jure presentandi personam ydoneam in anachoritam dicte domus quociens ipsam vacare contigerit priori de Lenton et nobis ac successoribus nostris sede Ebor' plena, et ipsa vacante decano et capitulo ejusdem ecclesie, admissione et institucione hujusmodi persone presentate in omnibus semper salvis. Et super eo quod feceris in hac parte nos expedito negocio distincte et aperte certifices per tuas litteras patentes harum seriem continentes. Vale. [Bishopthorpe, 4 July 1335.]

782 Commission to the abbot of Rufford, prior of Newstead, and M. Alan de Conyngesburgh, canon of York, to provide Robert Jolani de Neuton, a poor clerk (dioc. York), to a benefice in the gift of the prior and convent of Lenton. Bishopthorpe, 5 July 1335.

783 Note of the like to the priors of Thurgarton and Newstead to provide William Fraunceys of Halam, a poor priest, to a benefice in the gift of the prior and convent of Lenton. 6 July 1335.

784 The like to the abbot of Rufford and prior of Thurgarton to provide William son of Robert de Staunford of Southwell,[85] a poor priest, to a benefice in the gift of the abbot and convent of Welbeck. 7 July 1335.

785 Commission to the rectors of Clayworth [Simon de Courtmaiour] and Headon [Gregory Fairfax] to hear the account of the executors of the will of Roger de Lanum and to grant final acquittance. Bishopthorpe, 8 July 1335.

[84] Followed by note in another hand: *ista littera non valet.*
[85] Named William *de Suwell* in margin.

786 Note of commission to the abbot of Roche and prior of Worksop to provide Adam son of William Barbour of Blyth, a poor priest, to a benefice in the gift of the prior and convent of Blyth. Bishopthorpe, 10 June 1335.

787 Note of the like to the priors of Thurgarton and Shelford to provide William le Heye of Hawton to a benefice in the gift of the provost of Beverley. 12 Aug. 1335.

788 [*Oath and blessing of William de Aslaghton as abbot of Welbeck.*]
[N.F. 466[86]] Ego frater Willelmus de Aslaghton abbas monasterii de Welbek' Ebor' diocesis promitto subjectionem reverenciam et obedienciam a sanctis patribus patribus constitutam secundum regulam sancti Augustini vobis pater domine Willelme Ebor' archiepiscope vestrisque successoribus canonice substituendis et sancte Eboracen' ecclesie ac sancte sedi apostolice, salvo ordine meo, perpetuo me exhibiturum. Et hoc propria manu subscribo.

Memorandum quod idem frater Willelmus fecit professionem suam suprascriptam et subscripsit eidem, et archiepiscopus supradictus sibi munus benedictionis impendebat in capella sua de Cawode xix Kalendas Januarii anno domini MCCCXXXV et pontificatus sui xix, presentibus magistris Willelmo de la Mare Hamone de Cessay Ada de Haselbech Johanne de Barreby, dominis Willelmo de Popilton Willelmo de Feriby Johanne de Castelford et pluribus aliis. [Cawood, 14 Dec. 1335.]

789 [Fo.387; N.F.467] Note of commission to M. Thomas Sampson, official of York, and M. Richard de Eriom, D.Cn.& C.L., canon of York, to provide Walter de Tokotes to a benefice in the gift of the prior and convent of Blyth. Bishopthorpe, 15 Aug. 1335.

790 Licence to study for three years at a *studium generale* to John Martel, rector of Stanton on the Wolds, subdeacon, dispensing him from proceeding to further orders and from personal residence and attendance of synods, [etc.]. Cawood, 23 Aug. 1335.

791 Note of licence for absence for two years from 2 Feb. 1336 to John de Swyna, rector of Hawton, with provision for appearing by proxy at synods. Cawood, 5 Nov. 1335.

792 Note of commission to the prior of Newstead and M. Richard de Cestria to provide William son of William de Guthmundham, a poor clerk, to a benefice in the gift of the prior and convent of Worksop. Cawood, 14 Nov. 1335.

793 Note of the like to the abbot of Kirkstall and prior of Bolton to provide William Vaysour of Leeds (*Ledis*), a poor clerk, to a benefice in the gift of the prior and convent of Lenton [see **857**]. Cawood, 23 Dec. 1335.

[86] A parchment measuring 28 by 6.5 cms. inserted opposite fo.386^{v}. The oath is written in a large hand, with a cross following *subscribo*. The memorandum is in a smaller hand. See **794**.

794 [*Presentation by Premonstratensian abbots of William de Aslaketon for blessing as abbot of Welbeck.*]
LITTERA PRO BENEDICTIONE . . ABBATIS DE WELLEBEK'. Reverendo [*etc.*]. suus humilis et devotus frater Alanus dei paciencia abbas ecclesie de Neuhous' ordinis Premonstratensis reverenciam tanto patri debitam cum honore. Venerabilem fratrem nostrum fratrem Willelmum de Aslaketon ecclesie de Wellebec' nostri ordinis et vestre diocesis canonicum in patrem et pastorem ejusdem ecclesie tunc vacantis per fratres dicte ecclesie rite et canonice secundum ordinis nostri instituta electum et a nobis ad quem ipsius confirmacio jure paternitatis legitime dinoscitur pertinere, prout nostri ordinis moris est, confirmatum vestre paternitati reverende presentamus per presentes a nobis plenitudinem sui officii plenarie recepturum, supplicantes dominacioni vestre humiliter et devote ut cum idem electus ad vos venerit cum presentibus munus benedictionis vestre sibi impartiri dignemini graciose. In quorum omnium testimonium et fidem presentes litteras sigillo nostro ac sigillis venerabilium fratrum de Croxton et Dala ecclesiarum nostri ordinis abbatum in dictis electione et confirmacione nobis assidencium signatis vestre reverende paternitati duximus presentandas. Conservet vos altissimus ad regimen eccclesie sue sancte per tempora diuturna. [Welbeck, 30 Dec. 1335.]

795 Commission to Henry [Burghersh], bishop of Lincoln, to institute John de Norhamton, clerk, to Warsop church, now vacant, on the presentation of Sir John, son of Sir William de Hamelak,[87] and arrange his induction, in the light of an enquiry by the archdeacon of Nottingham's official ordered by the archbishop, provided there is no canonical obstacle; reserving his obedience to the archbishop and reporting by letters patent. Bishopthorpe, 7 Apr. 1336.

796 Commission to the prior of Worksop and M. John de la Launde to provide Robert de Tyreswell (dioc. York) to a benefice in the gift of the prior and convent of Lenton. *Berewik,*[88] 1 May 1336.

797 Note of licence for absence for one year to John [de Leicester], rector of Tollerton, excusing him from personal appearance in synods. Drax, 26 July 1336.

798 [Folios 387v–389; N.F.467v–469] ORDINACIO CANTARIARUM IN CAPELLA DE SIBTHORP. Letters patent of the archbishop giving a detailed ordinance for chantries founded by Thomas de Sibthorpe, rector of Beckingham, in the chapel of Our Lady, St. John the Baptist and St. Thomas the Martyr in Sibthorpe church. Bishopthorpe, 10 June 1335.[89]

799 [Fo.389; N.F.469] Note of licence for absence for two years to John [de Clifton], rector of Clifton (*Cliffetun*), provided that he pays twenty shillings a year to his poor parishioners and resides in Lent and Advent. Cawood, 5 Sept. 1335.

[87] Preceded by *Ros*, cancelled. For John Ros [of Watton], see *Complete Peerage*, XI.122–3.
[88] Probably Barwick in Elmet. There was a convocation at York, 6 May 1336 (*HBC*, 595); see also below, **808–9**.
[89] Discussed by A.H. Thompson in *The English Clergy*, 247–51, and printed (with slight errors), 254–61; cf. **428**, an ordinance for this chantry in 1326.

800 Note of commission to the priors of Worksop and Blyth to provide Thomas son of William Barboch, senior, of Beckingham, to a benefice in the gift of the prior and convent of Nostell. Cawood, 21 Sept. 1335.

801 Institution [etc.] of Robert de Ilkeston, priest, as perpetual chaplain in the chapel of the Blessed Mary de Hethebeth by Nottingham, vacant by the resignation of William de Ambaldeston; presented by the prior and convent of Newstead. Bishopthorpe, 11 Oct. 1335.

802 Note of licence for absence for one year to M. Thomas Sampson, rector of Misterton; provided he is represented by proxy in synods. Bishopthorpe, 10 Oct. 1335.

803 Note of commission to the priors of Thurgarton and Newstead to provide John called Le Greyve of [Long] Riston, a poor clerk, to a benefice in the gift of the prior and convent of Worksop. Bishopthorpe, 23 Oct. 1335.

804 [*Exchequer writ suspending demands on the archbishop for arrears of scutages for Edward I's armies in Scotland in 1300, 1303 and 1306.*]
BREVE REGIUM AD SUPERSEDENDUM SCUTAGIA DOMINI REGIS. Rex collectoribus scutagiorum de excertibus Scocie de annis regni domini E[dwardi] quondam regis Anglie avi nostri xxviii, xxxi et xxxiiii in comitatu Not' salutem. Mandamus vobis quod demande quam facitis venerabili patri Willelmo archiepiscopo Ebor' Anglie primati de scutagiis predictis supersedeatis usque compotum nostrum proximum ad scaccarium nostrum de eisdem scutagiis, et districtionem si quam ei ea occasione feceritis interim relaxetis eidem. Teste H[enrico] le Scrop' apud Ebor' xxxi die Octobris anno regni nostri nono. Per rotulum de finibus factis per diversos pro servicio suo non facto in dicto exercitu Scocie anno xx[x]i in quo continetur quod Thomas[90] tunc Ebor' archiepiscopus fecit finem per centum libras pro servicio suo quinque feodorum militum, et rotulum de consimilibus finibus factis dicto anno xxxiii[i] in quo continetur quod Willelmus[91] tunc Ebor' archiepiscopus finem fecit per centum marcas pro servicio suo quinque feodorum militum non facto eodem anno, et per barones quoad scutagium de dicto anno xxviii quia dictus archiepiscopatus vacabat a xvi die Augusti anno xxvi dicti regis avi[92] usque xxx die Aprilis dicto anno xxviii et fuit in manu dicti regis E[dwardi] avy.[93] [York, 31 Oct. 1335.]

805 Note of commission to the prior of Thurgarton and John de Sandale, canon of Southwell, to provide John Graunt, a poor clerk, to a benefice in the gift of the prior and convent of Shelford. Cawood, 12 Nov. 1335.

806 The like to the priors of Thurgarton and Shelford to provide Richard Helye of Bradmore (*Bradmer*), a poor clerk, to a benefice in the gift of the prior and convent of Lenton. Cawood, 22 Jan. 1336.

[90] Corbridge (1300–4).
[91] Greenfield (1306–15).
[92] After death of Henry Newark (15 Aug. 1299).
[93] *Sic*, a dotted *y*.

807 Note of licence for absence for one year to [William de Lambley *alias* Flintham] rector of Cromwell to go on pilgrimage, excusing him from attending synods. Cawood, 26 Jan. 1336.

808 Note of mandate to the sequestrator in the archdeaconry to sequestrate all the income and offerings of the vacant church of Warsop from 17 April 1336 and to answer for them until instructed otherwise. Gargrave (*Gairgrave*), 25 Apr. 1336.

809 Note of licence for absence during the archbishop's pleasure to Robert Norays, rector of West Retford, while in the service of Maud, widow of Sir John Marmyon; granted at her request. Doncaster, 13 May 1336.

810 Note of commission to the dean of Nottingham to grant probate of the will of John Colier and commit administration of his goods to the executors it names. 18 May 1336.

811 Collation (by devolved right) and mandate for induction of John de Chadesden, the archbishop's familiar clerk, to the [east] mediety of Treswell church formerly held by M. John de Malton. Scrooby, 22 May 1336.

812 [*Commission extending the powers of Edmund le Broun, rector of Rossington, as penitentiary in Retford deanery.*]
[Fo.389v; N.F.469v] LITTERA AD ABSOLVENDUM PRO RECTORE DE ROSYNGTON. Willelmus permissione divina Ebor' etc. dilecto filio domino Edmundo le Broun rectori ecclesie de Rosyngton nostre diocesis salutem [*etc.*]. De vestris fidelitate et circumspecta industria plenius confidentes, ut quoscumque parochianos nostros ad te in foro penitencie accedentes eciam in casibus nobis reservatis juxta formam aliarum litterarum nostrarum vobis in hac parte pro decanatu de Retford tantummodo concessarum absolvere licite valeatis et pro modo culpe eis penitenciam injungere salutarem, vobis vices nostras committimus cum cohercionis canonice potestate. Valete. [Scrooby, 24 May 1336.]

813 Memorandum that on this date the same rector had a letter certifying his induction (*litteram testimonialem inductionis sue*), as was lawfully proved to the archbishop.[94]

814 Note of licence for absence for three years to John [de Clifton], rector of Clifton (*Clyfton juxta Not'*), farming its revenues to Sir Gervase de Wilford, attending synods by proxy, giving two marks a year to poor parishioners, maintaining services, etc. Scrooby, 24 May 1336.

815 Institution (in the person of Sir Adam de Ingoldby as proctor) and mandate for induction (to the archdeacon of York or his official) of M. Thomas Beek, canon of Lincoln, to Clayworth church, vacant by the resignation of M. Simon de Courtmajour; presented by Michael de Haynton, rector of

[94] See **280**. Edmund's possession had been challenged in 1326, when his deprivation was ordered on the suit of William de Pykworth, clerk, said to have been presented by Peter de Mauley (Reg. Melton, fo.571v; N.F. 711v).

Matlock and vicar general of M. Anthony Beek, dean of Lincoln, with power to present to all vacant benefices in the dean's gift. Clayworth, 29 May 1336.

816 Memorandum of the customary oath of obedience to the archbishop by the proctor of Peter de Campo Veteri, rector of [South] Scarle. Newark parish church, 5 June 1336.

817 Memorandum that the archbishop granted administration of the goods of William de Dalham, who died intestate, to John de Dalham, chaplain, and John Dand, according to the legatine constitution; they swore to indemnify the archbishop. Holme [Pierrepont] church, 17 June 1336.

818 Licence for absence for one year to John Gerad, rector of Ratcliffe on Soar, with provisions for his representation at synods, performance of services, the cure of souls and appointment of a responsible proctor. Thurgarton, 20 June 1336.

819 Note of licence to study in a *studium generale*[95] to William de Clyve, rector of Epperstone; fruits etc. of the church may be sold to suitable persons. Thurgarton, 21 June 1336.

820 Licence to study for three years from 7 April 1336 at a *studium generale* to John de Northampton, rector of Warsop; he need not be ordained save to the subdiaconate provided he supplies a vicar. Southwell, 24 June 1336.

Note that he had letters dimissory for all orders, and that the sequestration of Warsop church [see **795**, **808**] was released until the archbishop came *ad partes*. [Same date.]

821 Note of mandate for induction of William de Whitewell, chaplain, or his proctor, to Weston church to which he has been admitted by the bishop of Chichester (*Cicestr'*), by the archbishop's authority, in an exchange from Berwick (*Suthberewik'*) church; he has a letter as in the form above for the church of Barton-le-Street (*Barton in Ridale*) in the archdeaconry of York. Southwell, 25 June 1336.

822 Note of licence for absence for one year to [Robert de Burstwick] rector of Lambley; he may farm his church, appear by proxy in synods at Southwell, etc. Attenborough, 2 July 1336.

823 Note of licence during pleasure to the inhabitants of Chilwell village (*villula de Chilewell*) to have divine service celebrated in a chapel there, provided there is no prejudice to the parish church [Attenborough]. Same date.

824 MONICIO PRO RESIDENCIA RECTORUM ECCLESIARUM DE ADYNGBURGH GEDELYNG' ET CLIFTON.[96] Mandate to the dean of Nottingham to order Thomas

[95] No term is specified.

[96] Similar in form to no.90 of *Reg. Melton*, II.51–2; with addition (after *invigilet ut tenetur*) of 'quem terminum sic duximus moderandum cum notorie constet eundem Thomam

Vaus, rector of Attenborough, [Fo.390; N.F.470] to resume residence within two months or appear before the archbishop. Newstead priory, 7 July 1336.

Note of similar letters for the rectors of a mediety of Gedling [John de Glaston?] and Clifton [John de Clifton].

825 [*Licence to the prior and convent of Worksop, arising from the last visitation, to take measures for paying their debts* (see **760**, **832**).]
LITTERA FACTA PRIORI ET CONVENTUI DE WIRKESOP' PROPTER UTILITATEM DOMUS SUE. Willelmus etc. dilectis filiis priori et conventui monasterii de Wirkesop' nostre diocesis salutem etc. Necessitates domus vestre solicite advertentes ut ad relevamen domus predicte et ad solvendum debita ejusdem id quod in utilitatem et minus incomodum domus predicte cedere poterit, sicut per nos in ultima visitatione nostra quam exercuimus in eadem fuerat compertum fore necesse, licite possitis facere super quo consciencias vestras et cujuslibet vestrum in districti altissimi judicio oneramus vobis tenore presencium specialem concedimus facultatem. [Eastwood near Rotherham, 8 July 1336.]

826 Note of licence for absence for two years to John de Sculthorp, rector of Misson; with provisions to farm his church and be represented in synods. Birstall (*Bristall*), 20 July 1336.

827 Note of licence to the prior and convent of Shelford to farm a mediety of North Muskham church for five years, with proviso for its other charges ('dumtamen alio modo indempnitati monasterii quoad solucionem eris alieni et supportacionem aliorum incumbencium onerum mederi et prospici melius et levius nequeat, super quo eorum consciencia extiterat coram altissimo onerata'). Bramham, 27 July 1336.

828 [*Appointment of M. William de Langeley as sequestrator in the archdeaconry.*]
PREFECTIO SEQUESTRATORIS IN ARCHIDIACONATU NOT'. Willelmus etc. dilecto filio magistro Willelmo de Langeley clerico nostro familiari salutem [*etc.*]. De tuis circumspectione fidelitate et industria plenius confisi, te sequestratorem nostrum in archidiaconatu Notingham' et per totum ipsum archidiaconatum preficimus ac etiam tenore presencium deputamus, tibique ad exercendum sequestratoris officium in archidiaconatu predicto in omnibus et singulis articulis que de jure vel consuetudine illud concernunt officium quovis modo, necnon ad cognoscendum procedendum statuendum diffiniendum et exequendum in omnibus et singulis causis articulis vel querelis testamenta sive ultimas voluntates in dicto archidiaconatu omnium et singulorum decedencium contingentibus,[97] vices nostras committimus cum cohercionis canonice potestate; decanis et aliis ministris nostris ac subditis universis per predictum archidiaconatum constitutis firmiter injungentes quod tibi in hiis que ad hujusmodi officium pertinent de consuetudine seu de jure pareant humiliter et intendant.

moram trahere in loco a dicta ecclesia de Adyngburgh per sex dietas minime distante'; and (like **578**) omitting notice of dilapidations.

[97] The clause from *necnon* is in the margin, with marks for its insertion after *quovis modo.* Cf. **297**.

Alias commissiones quascumque quibuscumque personis in hac parte prius factas revocamus per presentes pro nostro beneplacito duraturas. Vale. [Drax, 26 July 1336.]

829 Note of commission to M. William de Langeley, rector of Carlton in Lindrick, and William, vicar of Harworth, to claim and receive clerks charged before the king's justices at Tickhill. 27 July 1336.

830 [*Commission to the archdeacon's official, the sequestrator and eight others, to sequestrate a third part of Langar church because Baldwin de Cokefeld, the rector, was violating a sequestration of tithes in the parts belonging to Lenton priory.*]
SEQUESTRUM TERCIE PARTIS ECCLESIE DE LANGAR.[98] Willelmus etc. dilectis filiis officiali archidiaconi nostri Notinghamie, sequestratori nostro in eodem archidiaconatu, decano nostro de Byngham, dominis Johanni de Byngham Hugoni de Radecliff super Trentam Thome de Estbrigeford Edmundo de Plumtre Roberto de Holme Andree de Brigeford ad pontem Ricardo de Wylegby ecclesiarum rectoribus ac domino Henrico rectori medietatis ecclesie de Cotegrave nostre diocesis salutem [*etc.*]. Cum dominus Baldewynus rector tercie partis ecclesie de Langare nostre diocesis pro eo quod sequestrum nostrum in duabus partibus decimarum agnorum lane feni garbarum et mortuariorum vivorum dicte ecclesie ad religiosos viros . . priorem et . . conventum de Lenton dicte nostre diocesis spectantibus ab antiquo legitime interpositum temere violavit et adhuc indies illud violat dampnabiliter et infringit, easdem decimas asportando contractando et de eis disponendo pro sue libito voluntatis, sit et fuerit majoris excommunicationis sentencia contra infringentes sequestra nostra ex constitucione synodali Ebor' proinde lata[99] involutus et pro excommunicato ea occasione publice et sollempniter nunciatus, et subsequenter sibi ne gregem dominicum tanquam ovis morbida inficeret labe sua fidelium comitivam in genere quam in specie inhibita et adiu est arcius interdicta donec rubore suffusus se ad reconciliacionis graciam inclinaret, quam quidem excommunicacionem et ipsius publicacionem predictus rector in suis obstinatus maliciis per plures menses sustinuit pertinaciter animo indurato et in ea adhuc contemptus ecclesie clavibus perseverat; nos attendentes quod nil obediencia prodesse videtur humilibus si contemptus et inobediencia contumacibus non obesset et quod illis proventus ecclesiastici sunt merito detrahendi quibus ecclesie communio denegatur, vobis et cuilibet vestrum in virtute obediencie firmiter injungendo mandamus quatinus fructus redditus et proventus dicte tercie partis ecclesie de Langare quos eidem Baldewino excommunicato ex causis premissis subtrahimus et tenore presencium sequestramus sub arto sequestro facia[ti]s fideliter custodiri, sequestro in dictis duabus partibus decimarum [Fo.390^{v}; N.F.470^{v}] ecclesie prius ut premittitur interposito in suo robore nihilominus duraturo, cujus custodiam sequestri sicut alterius vobis conjunctim et divisim cuilibet vestrum committimus per presentes cum cohercionis canonice potestate, inhibentes palam publice et expresse auctoritate nostra primo secundo et tercio ac peremptorio

[98] Followed by sixteenth-century marginal note: 'Langar tertia pars ad prioratum de Lenton pertinens.'
[99] MS. *latis*. See *Councils and Synods*, II (cited under **259**), I.495 (c.41).

ne quis vel qui[1] sequestraciones hujusmodi impedire seu fructus sequestratos quoquamodo occupare contractare vel auferre presumant absque nostra vel vestra seu ipsius vel eorum qui hujusmodi sequestrorum custodie per vos deputari contigerit licencia speciali sub pena excommunicacionis majoris, quam exnunc ut extunc in contrafacientes et rebelles canonica monicione premissa ferimus in hiis scriptis, aliasque contra eum et eos nihilominus gravius processuri prout justicia suadebit, quos cum vobis vel aliquo vestrum de eisdem constiterit faciatis et faciat ut excommunicatos publice nunciari seu fecerit unus vestrum, de quorum nominibus nobis constare faciatis seu unus vestrum[2] faciat quociens inde fueritis requisitus nos cum ex parte dictorum prioris et conventus de Lenton fueritis seu fuerit requisiti distincte et aperte certifices seu certificetis per vestras litteras aut suas patentes harum seriem continentes. Valete. [Worksop priory, 11 July 1336.]

831 Note of dispensation by authority of letters of Gaucelin, bishop of Albano, papal penitentiary, to Robert called Rest' of Kneeton, for being ordained priest before his twenty fifth year. Bishop Monkton, 7 Aug. 1336.

832 [*Decree for Worksop priory containing injunctions for the supervision of granges and audit of monastic accounts* (see **760**, **825**).]
DECRETUM DOMUS DE WYRSOP. Willelmus etc. dilectis filiis . . priori et conventui de Wirkesop nostre diocesis salutem [*etc.*]. Ex officii nostri debito monasterium vestrum nuper tam in capite quam in membris actualiter visitantes, inter cetera correctione digna comperimus quod injuncta vobis domino priori in ultimo decreto nostro licet gravis pene adjectione vallata servare contumaciter non sine nota inobediencie neglexistis, quodque edificia grangiarum vestrarum propter varias occupaciones quibus intenditis et in vestri defectum domine prior multipliciter corruerunt, terre jacent inculte et in eisdem instaurus animalium non habetur, ex quibus domus vestra malo supposita regimini ad irreparabilem dissolucionis opprobrium deducetur nisi occuratur celerius ex adverso. Propter quod premissis que vobis objecimus, provida deliberacione pensatis vestrisque responsionibus auditis et habitis super illis et demum vestro in hac parte interveniente consensu, decernimus statuentes quod decretum nostrum predictum servetis quatenus vos et quemlibet vestrum concernit et faciatis in omnibus suis articulis inviolabiliter observari et ut status ipsius monasterii a predictis dispendiis paulatim per provisum remedium valeat respirare. Fratrem Johannem de Ryby ex unanimi consensu conventus electum ad grangiarum vestrarum instauri bidencium boum equorum et quorumcumque animalium agriculture et aliarum rerum earumdem curam et custodiam deputamus, et una cum priore fratres Petrum de Danby suppriorem Robertum de Leverton et Willelmum de Hanay ad hoc tanquam saniores et sapienciores de conventu per eundem conventum vestro concurrente consensu unanimi preelectos dicto fratri Johanni grangiarum custodi ad ejus facta omnia et singula supervidenda tam in emptionibus et vendicionibus grossis quam in pecunia mutuo recipienda et ejus solucione facienda ac in omnibus[3] negociis magni ponderis et omnibus delib-

[1] Interlined.
[2] *unus vestrum* interlined.
[3] Underdotted (to cancel?).

eracionem solertem requirentibus assignamus, quem custodem et supervisores predictos absque causa probabili nobis ex parte tocius conventus vel majoris et sanioris partis ejusdem significanda, et tunc de mandato nostro nolumus nec permittimus ullatenus amoveri. Et per ipsos eciam deputatos et per priorem si interesse voluerit precepimus quod compotus quorumcumque ballivorum et ministrorum domus interiorum vel exteriorum supervideantur et audiantur quociens et quando fuerit oportunum, quibus ministris et ballivis arcius injungimus ut[4] dictis custodi et supervisoribus in predictis omnibus pareant et intendant. Injungimus eciam bursariis domus quod nullam omnino pecuniam sine dictorum deputatorum voluntate et assensu liberent cuiquam vel assignent. Inhibemus insuper vobis domino priori ne res domus certis usibus de vestro et conventus vestri assensu hactenus proinde assignate per vos nisi ad hoc dictorum deputatorum voluntas affuerit subtrahantur. Valete. [Westwood near Rotherham (*Westwod juxta Roderham*), 13 July 1336.]

833 Licence to the prior and convent of Felley to sell a corrody to Thomas Barry, provided it is to the advantage and profit of the house and the whole convent is in agreement. Cawood, 20 Aug. 1336.

834 QUARTA VISITACIO DECANATUUM DE BYNGHAM.[5] Mandate to the archdeacon or his official to cite the clergy and people of Bingham deanery to attend for visitation by the archbishop or his familiar clerks as follows: on Friday 7 June in Thoroton chapel; on Monday 10 June in Bingham church; on Tuesday 11 June in Barnstone (*Berneston*) chapel; on Wednesday 12 June in Colston Bassett church; on Thursday 13 June in [Upper] Broughton church; on Friday 14 June in Normanton [on Soar] church; on Saturday 15 June in Ratcliffe on Soar church; and on Monday 17 June in Holme [Pierrepont] church. Elkesley, 17 Apr. 1336.

DE NOTYNGHAM. Note of the like for Nottingham deanery, for attendance on Monday 1 July in Epperstone church; on Tuesday 2 July in St. Mary's, Nottingham; on Thursday 4 July in Strelley church; and on Tuesday 9 July in Warsop church.

DE NEWERK. The like for Newark deanery: on Monday 3 June in Clifton church; on Tuesday 4 June in [South] Scarle church; on Wednesday 5 June in Newark church; and on Thursday 6 June in Farndon church.

ET DE RETFORD. The like for Retford deanery: on Thursday 16 May in Bawtry chapel; on Wednesday 29 May in Retford church; and on Saturday 1 June in East Markham (*Magna Markham*) church.

835 [Fo.391; N.F.471[x] [6]] QUARTA VISITACIO PRIORATUUM DE WIRKESOP DE SHELFORD DE THURGARTON DE FELLEY ET DE NOVO LOCO IN SHIREWODE AC DE WELLANDWELL. Mandate [similar to **543**] to the prior and convent of Worksop for their visitation on Wednesday 10 July. Scrooby, 20 June[7] 1336.

[4] MS. *et*

[5] Similar in form to **606** but omitting religious claiming appropriated churches, etc.

[6] This folio is 9 cms. deep and its dorse is blank. The next folio is also numbered 471 in the new foliation.

[7] MS. *xii kal. Julii*, probably in error for 'June', *i.e.* 21 May: Melton was at Scrooby on 22 May (**811**). On 20 June he was visiting Thurgarton (**818**, **819**), as planned here.

Notes of similar mandates to Shelford, for Tuesday 18 June; Thurgarton, for Thursday 20 June; Felley, for Friday 5 July; Newstead, for Saturday 6 July; and the prioress and nuns of Wallingwells [omitting the date].

836 [Fo.392; N.F.471] Note of licence for absence until 2 Feb. 1337 to William de London, rector of South Collingham. Nottingham, 26 Sept. 1336.

837 Institution [etc.] of Reginald de Sibthorp, chaplain, to Kneeton church, vacant by the death of William de Gonaldeston; presented by the abbot and convent of Newbo. Gedling, 27 Sept. 1336.

838 Licence to the prior and convent of Lenton, rector of St. Mary's, Nottingham, to farm the fruits of the church for three years. Gedling, 27 Sept. 1336.

839 Note of licence to be absent for two years to William de Aslakby, rector of Sibthorpe; he may farm the church and be represented by proxy at synods. Gedling, 27 Sept. 1336.

840 Institution (in the person of his proctor, Adam de Ingoldesby, chaplain) and mandate for induction of Richard de Somerdby, chaplain, to Clifton vicarage, vacant by the resignation of Roger de Stowe sancte Marie; presented by M. Thomas Beek, prebendary of Clifton. Scrooby, 21 Sept. 1336.

841 Note of monition to [Adam de Preston] rector of Hickling to resume residence within a month, *sub pena juris*. Gedling, 27 Sept. 1336.

842 Note of licence to be absent for one year to [M.] Robert [de Neville], rector of Flintham; he may farm the church and be represented by proxy at synods. Same date.

843 Note of the like for two years to William de Ouley, rector of Eastwood. Same date.

844 Note of the like for one year to Thomas [de Casterton], rector of a mediety of Cotgrave; he may be represented by proxy at synods. Nottingham, 28 Sept. 1336.

845 [*Proceedings against John de Clifton, rector of Clifton* (see **824**, **852**).]
COMMISSIO CONTRA RECTOREM ECCLESIE DE CLIFTON. Memorandum quod Nonis Octobris anno domini MCCCXXXVI apud Thorp juxta Ebor' facta fuit commissio magistris Thome de Nevill et Johanni de la Launde ad corrigendum puniendum et reformandum excessus crimina et defectus contra rectorem ecclesie de Clifton comperta, ac ad relaxandum sequestrum in bonis ejusdem alias interpositum necnon ad impendendum eidem jam in extremis ut dicitur languenti absque beneficio a sentencia excommunicationis quam incurrerat propter suam contumaciam coram nobis contractam ac omnia alia et singula facienda et expedienda que premissorum qualitas exigit et natura conjunctim et divisim etc. cum cohercionis etc. [Bishopthorpe, 7 Oct. 1336.]

Ista rasura facta est precipiente magistro Ada.[8]

[8] Most of **846** was written over an erasure.

846 Institution (in the person of his proctor John Flemyng) and mandate for induction of Thomas Flemyng, clerk, to Bilborough church, now vacant; presented by Robert son of Robert de Strelley. Bishopthorpe, 11 Oct. 1336.

847 The like of Hugh de Morton, chaplain, to Barnby in the Willows church, vacant by the resignation of Jolanus de Nevill; presented by Jolanus de Nevill, kt. Bishopthorpe, 28 Oct. 1336.

848 The like of John de Cravenhou, chaplain, to Bulwell church, vacant by the resignation of M. Robert de Wyvill; presented by Edward III.[9] Bishopthorpe, 2 Nov. 1336.

849 [*Mandate excusing John de Sibthorpe, rector of North Collingham* (see **601**), *from attending meetings because of his age and infirmity*.]
LICENCIA PRO VICARIO DE COLINGHAM.[10] Willelmus etc. dilecto filio officiali archidiaconi nostri Ebor' salutem [*etc.*]. Quia dominus Johannes perpetuus vicarius ecclesie de Colingham senio est confractus ita quod propter impotenciam sui corporis non potest ut accepimus de cetero laborare, vobis mandamus quatinus dictum dominum Johannem pro suis non comparicionibus in capitulis et aliis convocacionibus habeatis totaliter excusatum, ita tamen quod unum clericum vel decentem personam vobis mittat qui vobis crimina et excessus loco sui denunciare poterit ut est justum. Valete. [Cawood, 12 Jan. 1337.]

850 PRO POLLUTIONE CIMITERII ECCLESIE DE ORSTON. Memoranda of licence to the rector and parishioners of Orston to have their churchyard reconciled by a catholic bishop, and of a letter to the dean of Bingham to enquire about this violence. Same date.

851 [Fo.392v; N.F.471v] Note of licence for absence until 1 August 1337 to Adam [de Preston], rector of Hickling, with licence for a proctor in synods. Cawood, 23 Jan. 1337.

852 Note of mandate to M. William de Langeley, sequestrator in the archdeaconry, to sequestrate the fruits of Clifton church from the time of its resignation by John [de Clifton], the last rector. Cawood, 6 Feb. 1337.

853 Institution [etc.] of M. John de Chilewell, subdeacon, to Clifton church, vacant by the resignation of John de Clifton; presented by Gervase de Clifton, kt. Bishopthorpe, 13 Feb. 1337.

854 Mandate to the archdeacon or his official to induct William son of Nicholas de Northaston, chaplain, to South Collingham church to which he has been instituted by Henry [Burghersh], bishop of Lincoln, by authority of the archbishop's commission for an exchange with William de London; presented by the abbot and convent of Peterborough. The bishop has certified London's admission to Noseley (*Nouesle*) church (dioc. Lincoln). Cawood, 25 Feb. 1337.

[9] *CPR 1334–6*, 315.
[10] Both North and South Collingham were rectories.

Memorandum that William [de Northaston] took the customary oath of obedience in the chapel at Cawood. Same date.

855 Institution [etc.] of John Hyne, chaplain (dioc. York), to Stanton on the Wolds church, vacant by the resignation of M. John de Chillewell; presented by Thomas de Wydmerpole. Cawood, 13 Mar. 1337.

856 [*Commission to M. William de Langeley* (see **828**) *to appoint tutors to all children and minors in the archdeaconry.*]
COMMISSIO MAGISTRO WILLELMO DE LANGELEY FACTA AD DEPUTANDUM TUTORES OMNIBUS LIBERIS IN ARCHIDIACONATU NOT'. Willelmus etc. dilecto filio magistro Willelmo de Langeley salutem [*etc.*]. De tua fidelitate et industria plenius confidentes, ad deputandum et assignandum tutores seu curatores omnibus et singulis liberis seu aliis in minori etate seu legitima infra archidiaconatum nostrum Not' constitutis tam ad tutelam et curam[11] corporum quam rerum et bonorum suorum custodiam, et ad committendum dandum et assignandum dictis tutoribus seu curatoribus administracionem liberam rerum et bonorum eorumdem in forma juris, necnon ad inhibendum quibuscumque subditis nostris et aliis qualemcumque inferiorem jurisdictionem excercentibus et cohercendum et compellendum eosdem ne exercicium jurisdictionis predicte exerceant quoquomodo, ad que cum cohercionis canonice potestate tenore presencium [tibi] committimus vices nostras. Vale. [Cawood, 17 Mar. 1337.]

857 COLLATIO ECCLESIE DE LINDEBY AUCTORITATE APOSTOLICA. Provision by the archbishop as executor of a papal grace to William Vaysour of Leeds, a poor clerk [see **793**], of Linby church, vacant by the death of Michael Normand;[12] in the presentation of the prior and convent of Lenton. Cawood, 18 Mar. 1337.

858 [*Inspeximus of the ordination of a vicarage in Edwinstowe church by Archbishop Godfrey Ludham dated 15 January 1261.*[13]]
ORDINACIO VICARIE ECCLESIE DE EDENESTOWE TEMPORE GODEFRIDI ARCHIEPISCOPI. Universis sancte matris ecclesie filiis ad quos presentes littere pervenerint Willelmus [*etc.*] salutem in eo quem peperit uterus virginalis. Noverit universitas vestra nos litteras bone memorie domini Godefridi dudum Ebor' archiepiscopi Anglie primatis predecessoris nostri ejusdem sigillo pendente signatas inspexisse eo qui sequitur sub tenore:

Universis Christi fidelibus presentes litteras inspecturis G[odefridus] miseracione divina Ebor' archiepiscopus Anglie primas salutem in domino sempiternam. Noveritis nos ad presentacionem virorum venerabilium decani et capituli Lincoln' dominum Ricardum de Melton presbiterum ad vicariam ecclesie de Edenestowe et capellarum ejusdem admisisse ipsumque instituisse perpetuum vicarium in eisdem ac in corporalem possessionem vicarie ipsius induci fecisse. Consistit autem vicaria ipsa in toto alteragio et omnibus minutis decimis ad ecclesiam et universas capellas spectantibus exceptis decimis curie

[11] *et curam* repeated.
[12] Instituted, as 'Michael Normannus', 1286 (*The Register of John le Romeyn*, ed. W. Brown, 2 vols., Surtees Society 123, 128, 1913, 1917, I.251, no.721).
[13] His register has not survived.

decani et capituli predictorum in Edenestowe. Item in una bovata terre cum competentibus mansis in Edenestowe et Peverelthorp. Et vicarius omnia ordinaria onera exceptis fortuitis casibus sustinebit et extraordinaria agnoscet pro rata porcione; solvetque quadraginta solidos per manus prepositorum decani et capituli pauperibus parochie erogandos. In cujus rei testimonium presentibus sigillum nostrum est appensum. Datum apud Scroby xviii Kalendas Februarii pontificatus nostri anno tercio.

In cujus inspectionis testimonium sigillum nostrum presentibus est appensum. [Cawood, 30 Mar. 1337.]

859 Licence to study for two years at a *studium generale* to Thomas Flemmyng, rector of Bilborough, dispensing him from promotion to orders higher than the subdiaconate, provided that he appoints a vicar. Cawood, 13 Apr. 1337.

860 [Fo.393; N.F.472] Note of mandate to the dean of Newark to warn Thomas de Stowe, vicar of Marnham, to resume residence within a month, and otherwise sequestrate his goods, on which [the dean] is to report. Escrick (*Estrik'*), 28 Apr. 1337.

861 Note of licence for absence [to study] *in forma constitutionis* for two years to John de Northwell, rector of a mediety of Rotherham, dispensing him from promotion to orders higher than the subdiaconate. Northallerton (*Alverton*) hospital, 23 May 1337.

862 Note of licence for absence for one year to Robert Norreis, rector of West Retford, while in the service of Lady Maud Marmion; also of a letter to the official of York and his commissary general or the receiver not to fine or prosecute him for previous absence in her service and to relax any censure, if inflicted. St. Martin's priory near Richmond, 19 June 1337.

863 Note of licence for absence until 29 September to [William de Whitewell] rector of Weston. Bishop Monkton, 27 June 1337.

864 [*Order for a weeekly payment to Gilbert [de Sancta Elena], rector of Finningley, despite writs to levy debts.*]

PRO NECESSARIIS RECTORIS ECCLESIE DE FINYNGLAY. Willelmus etc. dilecto filio rectori ecclesie de Babworth nostre diocesis salutem [*etc.*]. Volumus et tibi mandamus quatinus non obstante quocumque mandato nostro seu curie nostre Ebor' tibi auctoritate et pretextu brevium regis de levando debita facto de fructibus et bonis ecclesiasticis domini Gilberti rectoris ecclesie de Fyninglay nostre diocesis eidem . . rectori, ne in cleri opprobrium mendicet, facias de bonis suis pro vite sue necessariis xviii denarios singulis ebdomadiis ministrari et ecclesie sue predicte onera incumbencia debite supportari; proviso nihilominus quod dicta brevia regis fideliter absque fraude qualibet exequaris. Vale. [Cawood, 15 July 1337.]

865 Note of order to the receiver of York to pay £250 to Sir Thomas de Usflet for putting Sir John de Melton and his wife into possession of Fenton manor; John will pay £100 of this sum to the receiver. [Day and month omitted] 1337.

866 Note of licence for absence for one year to John de Wateby, rector of Maltby (*Malteby*), in the company (*comitiva*) of Lord Clifford and at his request. Cawood, 17 July 1337.

867 [*Certificate of the archdeacon's official that he has executed the archbishop's commission to summon objectors to the election of John de Rudstan as prior of Thurgarton to appear on 6 September.*[14]]

CERTIFICACIO ELECTIONIS DE THURGARTON. Venerabili in Christo patri ac domino domino Willelmo permissione divina Ebor' archiepiscopo Anglie primati domini . . archidiaconi Not' . . officialis obedienciam reverenciam et honorem. Litteras et commissionem nuper recepimus seriem infrascriptam continentes:

Willelmus [*etc.*] dilecto filio officiali archidiaconi nostri Not' salutem [*etc.*]. Presentata nobis electione nuper facta in capitulo monasterii de Thurgarton nostre diocesis ut dicitur de fratre Johanne de Rudstan canonico ejusdem monasterii ex parte . . supprioris et conventus monasterii de Thurgarton predicti, a nobis extitit humiliter et cum instancia postulatum ut electionem hujusmodi confirmare canonice dignaremur. Nos igitur volentes in ipsius electionis negotio statuta canonica sicut convenit observare, vobis committimus et mandamus quatinus infra triduum a tempore recepcionis presencium coelectum et compeditorem si sit et oppositorem si quis appareat nominatim, ac nihilominus in monasterio de Thurgarton predicto proposito publice monicionis et vocationis edicto si qui sint qui electioni predicte se opponere voluerint quovismodo, moneatis ac peremptorio citetis eosdem quod die Sabbati proxima ante festum Nativitatis beate Marie Virginis proximo futurum cum continuacione et prorogatione dierum subsequencium si necesse fuerit, quem diem eisdem et eorum cuilibet pro termino preciso et peremptorio assignamus et per vos volumus assignari, coram nobis compareat et compareant ubicumque tunc fuerimus in nostra civitate vel diocesi propondituri objecturi ac ostensuri quicquam canonicum habuerit seu habuerint quod proponere obicere et ostendere voluerit aut voluerint contra electi aut eligencium personas vel electionis formam quare non debeamus electionem hujusmodi prout ad nos pertinet confirmare decernere statuere et exequi ulterius quod est justum, facturi ulterius et recepturi quod justicia suadebit et secundum qualitatem et naturam ipsius negocii consonum fuerit rationi. Citacionem vero et terminum de quibus premittitur ad evitationem periculi animarum et ne dictum monasterium ex ipsius diutina vacacione paciatur in temporalibus incomoda et jacturas, et ut dilapidacionis excessus caucius evitetur que forsitan ex diffusiori termino imineret, ac ex causis aliis si necesse fuerit oportunis loco et tempore exprimendum sic duximus moderandum. Qualiter autem hoc mandatum nostrum fueritis executi nos citra dictum diem Sabbati per duos dies distincte et aperte certificetis per litteras vestras patentes harum seriem continentes. Valete. [Cawood, 28 Aug. 1337.]

Harum igitur auctoritate litterarum, quia de coelecto competitore aut oppositore aliquo nobis apparere non potuit quovismodo, in monasterio de Thurgarton predicto hujusmodi publice monicionis et vocacionis proposito edicto quod si qui essent qui electioni predicte se opponere vellent monuimus et

[14] See **135–6**, **208**, **222**, **353** for his previous term as prior. See also **880**.

citavimus peremptorio eosdem quod die Sabbati proxima ante festum Nativitatis beate Marie Virginis proximo futurum cum continuacione dierum subsequencium si necesse esset, quem diem eis et eorum cuilibet si qui essent auctoritate vestra assignamus, coram vobis ubicumque tunc essetis in vestra civitate vel diocesi compareat aut compareant propositeri objecturi et ostensuri quicquid canonicum habuerit vel habuerint contra dicti electi aut eligencium personas vel electionis formam quare vos electionem hujusmodi prout ad vos pertinet non deberetis confirmare decernere eciam statuere et exequi quod est vestrum, ac ulterius facturi et recepturi secundum naturam et qualitatem negocii quod justicia suadebit. Sicque mandatum vestrum reverenter sumus executi. Paternitatem vestram reverendam conservet altissimus per tempora feliciter successiva. Datum [Cottam, 31 Aug. 1337].

868 [*Confirmation of John de Rudstan's election as prior of Thurgarton, with his oath of obedience.*]

CONFIRMACIO EJUSDEM. In dei nomine amen. Presentata nobis Willelmo [*etc.*] electione nuper in capitulo monasterii de Thurgarton nostre diocesis per mortem fratris Roberti de Hathern ultimi prioris ejusdem vacantis facta de fratre Johanne de Rudstan canonico dicti monasterii in . . priorem ejusdem monasterii et pastorem, ipsaque electione et electi persona ac toto electionis negotio diligenter per nos examinatis, processu eciam debito et juris ordine juxta qualitatem ipsius negocii et naturam in omnibus observato, quia electionem ipsam de prefato Johanne de Rudstan viro utique provido et discreto presbitero et in dicto monasterio expresse professo litterarum sciencia morum et vite conversacione predito et commendato libero et de legitimo matrimonio procreato in [Fo.393^{v}; N.F.472^{v}] etate legitima constituto in spiritualibus et temporalibus circumspecto et aliis virtutum donis multipliciter insignito invenimus rite et canonice celebratam, ipsam electionem communicato jurisperitorum consilio auctoritate pontificali confirmamus, eidem electo per nos confirmato curam regimen et administrationem in spiritualibus et temporalibus dicti monasterii quantum ad nos attinet committentes. Quo facto obedienciam fecit in hunc modum:

OBEDIENCIA. Ego frater Johannes de Rudstan in priorem monasterii de Thurgarton Ebor' diocesis electus confirmatus ero fidelis et obediens vobis domino Willelmo [*etc.*] vestrisque successoribus ac officialibus vestris et ministris in canonicis mandatis. Sic me deus adjuvet et sancta dei evangelia. Et hoc propria manu subscribo.[15] Facte fuerunt confirmatio et obediencia supradicte apud Cawode in capella ejusdem viii Idus Septembris anno etc. XXXVII et pontificatus domini Ebor' archiepiscopi XX.

Note of two letters: (i) to the subprior and convent to obey John as prior; (ii) to the archdeacon's official to install him. [Cawood, 6 Sept. 1337.]

869 Note of licence for absence for one year to William [de Clyve], rector of Epperstone, excusing him from personal appearance at synods. Bishopthorpe, 11 Sept. 1337.

870 The like for three years to John [de Northampton], rector of Warsop; he may farm his church and not appear in synods in person. Bishopthorpe, 23 Oct. 1337.

[15] Followed by a cross.

871 (i) Appointment of Gregory [Fairfax], rector of Headon, as sequestrator in the archdeaconry of Nottingham.[16] Bishopthorpe, 27 Oct. 1337.[17]

(ii) Memorandum of a similar letter to M. John de Landa, rector of Arnold. [Cawood, 5 Nov. 1337.]

Memorandum quod ista littera emanavit generaliter et cancellata est superius de precepto domini.

872 Request to the prior and convent of Thurgarton to grant an annual pension to William de Wrelleton, the archbishop's familiar clerk, for his life, according to diocesan custom on the appointment of abbots and priors; he is a notary and his business acumen will be helpful.[18] Cawood, 12 Sept. 1337.

873 Note of mandate to the official of York or his commissary general to sequestrate the fruits and revenues of [Baldwin de Cockfield] rector of Langar until he has satisfied the sheriff of Nottingham for £5 for which he is to be distrained in Nottinghamshire. Cawood, 13 Jan. 1338.[19]

874 (i) Collation of Hugh de Oundele, chaplain, to Mattersey vicarage in an exchange [as below]. (ii) Note of mandate for his induction. (iii) Institution of Thomas de Foston, chaplain, to Bardney (*Bardeneye*) vicarage (dioc. Lincoln), quoting a commission of Simon de Islep, canon of Lincoln, vicar-general of Henry [Burghersh], bishop of Lincoln (dated Lincoln, 4 Jan. 1338) for an exchange of benefices between Thomas, vicar of Mattersey, and Hugh, vicar of Bardney, forwarding the report of an enquiry by the archdeacon of Lincoln's official; [Fo.394; N.F.473] presented by the abbot and convent of Bardney. (iv) Certificate to the bishop of Lincoln or his [above] vicar-general. Cawood, 23 Jan. 1338.

875 Note of mandate to the dean of Bingham to warn [Baldwin de Cockfield] rector of a mediety of Langar to resume residence within two months *sub pena juris*, 'in the same form as above for the rector of Attenborough' [**824**]. Cawood, 25 Jan. 1338.

[16] Practically identical to **828** (without its insertion) save that after *quovismodo* was a clause excluding testamentary estates exceeding £10 (as added in **297**). This clause was struck through, probably at the same time as the original date was cancelled and replaced, and the first memorandum written; this was done before **872** was written. The second memorandum, however, was squeezed into the half-line remaining after the first.

[17] Struck through, with the following date interlined over it.

[18] Similar in form to **537** and **651**, with this penultimate sentence: 'Ipse enim est publicus auctoritate apostolica notarius et aptus juvenis in agendisque negociis circumspectus et talibus insignitur virtutibus quod monasterio vestro vobisque et vestris indies tenere poterit magnum locum, quibus ac precibus quas ad presens intensis desideriis effundimus pro eodem attentis merito vestra in eo exuberare debet gracia et sibi larga et pinguis pensio assignari.'

[19] The remainder (15 cms.) of the last line had been filled with writing which was mostly erased, with only *abbas* still legible.

876 Institution [etc.] of M. Thomas de Nevill, chaplain, to Attenborough church, vacant by the resignation of Thomas de Vaus;[20] presented by Thomas Vaus, clerk. Cawood, 1 May 1338.

877 Note of licence for absence for seven years to M. Adam de Haselbech,[21] subdeacon, rector of Finningley; he need not be promoted to higher orders, for which he has a letter under the constitution *Cum ex eo*. He also has a letter to farm the church for five years. Cawood, 2 May 1338.

878 Note of licence for absence for two years to M. William de Langeley, rector of Carlton in Lindrick; he may farm the church. Cawood, 4 May 1338.

879 Institution (in the person of his proctor, Robert de Meaux, clerk) and mandate for induction of John de Hokesworth, clerk, to Thorpe church, vacant by the resignation of M. Roger de Heselarton; presented by the prior and convent of Haverholme. Cawood, 30 May 1338.

880 [*Resignation of John de Rudstan as prior of Thurgarton.*]
RESIGNACIO PRIORIS DE THURGARTON. In dei nomine amen. Ego Johannes de Rudstan prior monasterii de Thurgarton Ebor' diocesis statum et administracionem dignitatem et officium prioris monasterii antedicti in sacras manus vestras pure sponte simpliciter et absolute resigno in hiis scriptis. Anno domini MCCCXXXVIII et pontificatus nostri xxi mense Junii die quinto dictus prior coram venerabili patre etc. personaliter constitutus in camera dicti patris apud Cawode statum et officium prioris in sacras manus dicti patris resignavit, presentibus magistris Ada de Hasilbech Thoma de Nevill domino Ricardo de Otringham et multis aliis clericis familiaribus dicti domini. [Cawood, 5 June 1338.]

881 Certificate[22] of the archdeacon of Nottingham's official that he has executed the archbishop's mandate (quoted; dated Cawood, 20 June; received at vespers, 23 June) to publish the following 27 June as the date for making objections to Richard de Thurgarton, canon of Thurgarton, and his election as prior of Thurgarton. [Fo.394v; N.F.473v] Thurgarton, 25 June 1338.

882 Confirmation of Richard's election, and his oath of obedience, in the chapel at Cawood; with notes of letters to the subprior and convent to obey him, and to the archdeacon's official for his installation.[23] Cawood, 27 June 1338.

883 Note of licence for absence for one year to Peter de Bekering, rector of Tuxford. Cawood, 24 Oct. 1338.

884 The like for two years to John de Sculthorp, rector of Misson. Cawood, 25 Oct. 1338.

[20] This cause of vacancy is interlined over a cancelled one, that it was by exchange from Gisburn in Craven. Neville had been rector there since 1318 (*BRUO*, II.1351). Vaux was instituted to Attenborough in 1309 (*Reg. Greenfield,* IV.52, no.1772).
[21] See *BRUO*, II.883.
[22] Similar in form to **867**.
[23] All similar to **868**.

885 The like for one year to William de Northaston, rector of South Collingham, farming the church. Cawood, 29 Oct. 1338.

886 Institution [etc.] of Henry son of Geoffrey Breton of Awsworth, chaplain, to Egmanton vicarage, vacant by the death of William Lyouns; presented by the prior and convent of Newstead. Cawood, 7 Nov. 1338.

887 Note of licence to William [de Loscoe], rector of Selston, to be absent for one year in the service of the countess of Lincoln, farming the church. Cawood, 21 Nov. 1338.

888 Note of dispensation for bastardy to Hugh de Saundeby, clerk; he has a letter of dispensation. Cawood, 18 Dec. 1338.

889 Institution [etc.] of Richard de Radecliff, chaplain, to Nuthall church, vacant by the death of John [de Rempstone[24]]; presented by John de Cokefeld, kt. Cawood, 18 Jan. 1339.

890 Institution (in the person of his proctor Edward de Stapelford, rector of a mediety of Trowell) and mandate for induction of Roger de Wylughby, clerk, to Wollaton (*WOLASTON, Wollaston*) church, vacant by the death of Adam de Wellum;[25] presented by Richard de Wilughby, kt. Cawood, 25 Jan. 1339.

891 Dispensation to Peter son of William de Estdratton, chaplain, to minister in orders received while under legitimate age, a penance having been enjoined. Bishopthorpe, 21 June 1339.

892 [Fo.395; N.F.474] Note of grant to William de Loscow of custody of the sequestration of Greasley church, to which he has been presented, until it is learnt about the vacancy and the death of John de Mont', the late rector. He has a letter to the sequestrator in the archdeaconry. Cawood, 29 Jan. 1339.

893 Commission granting Thomas son and heir of Thomas son of William de Radecliff' administration of the goods of his father, who is said to have died intestate; he is to make an inventory and render account, indemnifying the archbishop against any [claimants], provided that the defunct did die intestate. Cawood, 17 Feb. 1339.

894 Institution [etc.] of Richard son of Richard de Whatton, clerk (dioc. York), to Widmerpool church, vacant by the death of Hugh de Cruland; presented by Roger Beler'. Bishopthorpe, 11 Apr. 1339.

895 Note of licence to study for one year at a *studium generale* to Thomas Flemyng', rector of Bilborough. Bishopthorpe, 13 Apr. 1339.

[24] Instituted 1317 (*Reg. Greenfield*, IV.276, no.2882).
[25] Instituted 1291 (*Reg. Romeyn* (cited under **857**), I.294, no.828*n*.).

896 INSTITUTIO CANTARIE FRATERNITATIS DE NEWERK'. Institution (in the person of his proctor, Henry de Evesham, clerk) and mandate for induction of Thomas de Alreton, chaplain, as perpetual chaplain of the chantry of the fraternity of the Holy Trinity, Newark, newly ordained and confirmed by the archbishop; presented by Henry Mous of Newark, provost of the fraternity, in accordance with the ordinance. Bishopthorpe, 17 Apr. 1339.

897 Note of licence to the prior and convent of Lenton to farm the fruits, rents and income of St. Mary's, Nottingham, for three years. Cawood, 15 May 1339.

898 Note of licence for absence for three years to M. William de Langeley, rector of Carlton in Lindrick, farming the church and excused from personal appearance at synods. Cawood, 1 June 1339.

899 [*Mandate for induction of William de Bekford to Beeston vicarage.*[26]]
INDUCTIO VICARIE DE BESTON. Willelmus etc. dilecto filio archidiacono nostro Notinghamie vel ejus officiali salutem [*etc.*]. Quia dominus Willelmus de Bekford capellanus ad presentationem domini nostri domini Edwardi dei gracia regis Anglie domini Hibernie et ducis Aquitanie per magistrum Simonem de Bekyngham rectorem ecclesie de Melsamby nostre diocesis virtute commissionis nostre in hac parte sibi facte ad vicariam ecclesie de Beston dicte nostre diocesis per mortem domini Willelmi de Wilvesthorp ultimi vicarii ejusdem vacantem admissus [sit] et salvo jure cujuscumque perpetuus vicarius cum onere personalis residencie juxta formam constitutionis legati edite in hoc casu institutus canonice in eadem, vobis mandamus quatinus dictum dominum Willelmum vel procuratorem suum ejus nomine in corporalem possessionem dicte vicarie cum suis juribus et pertinenciis universis ut premittitur inducatis seu faciatis induci. Valete. [Bishopthorpe, 20 June 1339.]

900 [Common Pleas] writ *admittatis* ordering the archbishop to admit the king's presentee to Beeston vicarage because he has recovered his presentation against the prior of Lenton by judgment of the court. Tested by John de Stonore, Westminster, 2 June 1339.

901 [*Certificate (under the seal of the official of Richmond) of M. Simon de Bekyngham that he has executed the archbishop's commission to institute William de Bekford as vicar of Beeston if there were no lawful impediment.*]
CERTIFICACIO SUPER INSTITUCIONE VICARII DE BESTON. Venerabili [*etc.*] suus humilis et devotus filius Simon de Bekyngham rector ecclesie de Melsamby vestre diocesis obedienciam cum omni reverencia et honore debitis tanto patri. Litteras vestras nuper recepi eo qui sequitur sub tenore:

Willelmus etc. dilecto filio magistro Simoni de Bekyngham rectori ecclesie de Melsamby nostre diocesis salutem [*etc.*]. De vestris fidelitate et circumspecta industria plenius confidentes, ad admittendum dominum Willelmum de

[26] The presentation to Beeston was now in the gift of the crown because the temporalities of the alien priory of Lenton were in the king's hands on account of the war with France. See *CPR 1338–40*, 244; A. Cossons, 'William de Bekford, King's Clerk', *Transactions of the Thoroton Society*, XXXIX (1935), 43–52.

Bekford capellanum vel procuratorem suum ejus nomine ad vicariam ecclesie de Beston nostre diocesis ad eandem nobis per dominum nostrum dominum Edwardum dei gracia regem Anglie dominum Hibernie et ducem Aquitanie presentatum si[27] sibi et nulli alii de jure debeatur, prout per breve regis et inquisitionem . . officialis archidiaconi nostri Not' ad mandatum nostrum in hac parte captam liquere vobis videbitur que vobis mittimus inspicienda nobis per eundem illico remittenda, ac instituendum canonice in eadem cum onere personalis residencie juxta formam constitutionis legati edite in hoc casu, inductione ipsius in corporalem possessionem ejusdem ac canonica obediencia nobis omnimodo reservatis, vobis committimus vices nostras. Et nos de omni eo quod feceritis in premissis expedito negotio unacum dictis brevi regio et inquisicione distincte et aperte certificetis per litteras vestras patentes harum seriem continentes. Valete. [Bishopthorpe, 19 June 1339.]

Cujus auctoritate mandati vestri reverendi, predictis brevi regio et inquisicione ac aliis evidenciis in hac parte coram me exhibitis ad plenum visis et instancius recencitis, prefatum dominum Willelmum de Bekford ad vicariam de Beston predictam per dominum Edwardum regem Anglie dominum Hibernie et ducem Aquitanie ratione temporalium prioratus de Lenton in manu sua occasione guerre inter ipsum et illos de Francia mote existencium hac vice patronum vestre reverende paternitati presentatum auctoritate michi in hac parte commissa admisi ac ipsum vicarium salvo jure cujuscumque canonice institui in eadem, prestito ab eodem juramento corporali quod more humano in forma constitutionis legati in dicta vicaria residenciam faciat personaliter. Predictum vero breve regium et inquisicionem vestre dominacioni duxeram transmittenda. Ad ecclesie sue sancte regimen altissimus vos conservet per tempora feliciter duratura. Datum Ebor' sub sigillo officialis Richem' xii Kalendas Julii anno domini supradicto [20 June 1339].

902 [Fo.395v; N.F.474v] CERTIFICACIO COLLACIONIS PREBENDE DE ROSCOMP' IN ECCLESIA SARUM'. Certificate to Robert [Wyvil], bishop of Salisbury, that the archbishop has executed his commission (quoted; dated Woodford (*Wodesford*), 12 May 1339) for an exchange of benefices between M. Thomas Beek, canon of Salisbury and prebendary of Ruscombe, and William de Feriby, rector of Brompton (dioc. York). The archbishop invested William 'by our biretta', reserving his installation and obedience to the bishop. He also instituted M. Thomas to Brompton (*Brumpton in Pikeringlyth*) in the person of his proctor, M. John de Notingham, rector of Elkesley (*Elkeslee*).[28] Bishopthorpe, 23 June 1339.

903 [*Institution of William de Feriby as rector of Clayworth, in the exchange with M. Thomas Bek.*]

INSTITUCIO ECCLESIE DE CLAWORTH. Willelmus [*etc.*] dilecto filio domino Willelmo de Feriby presbitero salutem [*etc.*]. Ad presentacionem reverendi viri magistri Bernardi Sistre canonici ecclesie beati Illarii Pictaven' archidiaconi Cantuar' apostolice sedis in Anglia nuncii ac custodis decanatus Lincoln' apud

[27] Interlined.

[28] For the letter of institution, see *Reg. Melton*, II.189 (no.512), which shows that Thomas exchanged two more benefices for Brompton (as in **903–4**). See also **908**; *BRUO*, I.154.

sedem apostolicam vacantis[29] et in manibus domini nostri pape existentis et ad conferendum beneficia quecumque ad collationem decani Lincoln' qui pro tempore fuerit seu presentandum ad eadem in hac parte commissarii, te de cujus meritis et virtutibus sinceram fiduciam in domino obtinemus ad ecclesiam de Claworth nostre diocesis per resignacionem magistri Thome Beek ultimi rectoris ejusdem ex causa permutacionis canonice facte cum ecclesia de Brumpton quam tu prius obtinebas vacantem admittimus et rectorem instituimus canonice in eadem. Vale. [Bishopthorpe, 23 June 1339.]

[margin] Note of mandate for induction to the archdeacon, etc. Same date.

904 (i) To M. John de Hale, canon of the collegiate church of All Saints, Derby, and vicar of Wirksworth, quoting letters of Bernard Sistre, canon of St. Hilary, Poitiers (*Pictave'*), papal nuncio and keeper of the deanery of Lincoln with authority to collate to benefices in its gift [Fo.396; N.F.475] (dated London, 8 June 1339). On behalf of Bernard and by papal authority, the archbishop has collated William de Feriby to the canonry and prebend in All Saints resigned by M. Thomas de Beek in an exchange for Brompton church. Mandate for William's induction. (ii) Collation of the same to William [repeating much of the mandate, adding that M. John de Notingham had resigned as Beek's proctor]. Bishopthorpe, 23 June 1339.

905 Institution [etc.] of William de Lascou, chaplain, to Greasley church, vacant by the death of John de Monte [see **892**]; presented by Walter de Faucomberge, kt., who is empowered to present to all churches in the patronage of Nicholas de Cantilupo, kt. Cawood, 15 Sept. 1339.

[William] took the oath due on the gospels, and he swore to go to the cardinals to be absolved for incurring excommunication by his delay in paying their procurations.[30] Meanwhile he was absolved and has a letter in form, etc. Same date.

906 Institution [etc.] of William de Ros, acolyte,[31] to Selston (*Seleston*) church, vacant by the resignation of William de Loscou; presented by William de Faucomberge, kt., [etc., as in **905**]. Cawood, 23 Sept. 1339.

907 Note of licence for absence for one year to William de Northaston, rector of South Collingham, farming the church. Cawood, 10 Oct. 1339.

908 Institution [etc.] of Thomas de Riplyngham, chaplain, to Clayworth church, vacant by the resignation of William de Feriby in an exchange for Stokesley church; presented by M. Bernard Sistre, canon [etc. as in **903**].[32] Cawood, 4 Nov. 1339.

909 Note of licence for the said Thomas to be absent for one year and excused from personal appearance in synods. Cawood, 8 Nov. 1339.

[29] By the provision of Anthony Bek as bishop of Norwich.

[30] See *Reg. Melton*, I.110–11, nos.371–5; III.173–9, no.292.

[31] Corrected from *magistro Willelmo de Ros clerico*; but *magistrum* remains in the mandate for induction.

[32] See *Reg. Melton*, II.190, no.520.

910 [*Undated inspeximus and confirmation of the indenture (dated 25 Sept. 1339) by which the prior and convent of Felley undertake to provide an annual income to the secular chaplain serving at the altar of Our Lady founded by Robert Stuffyn in Mansfield Woodhouse chapel, in return for his grant to them of the advowson of Attenborough.*]
[Fo.396^{v}; N.F.475^{v}] ORDINATIO CANTARIE IN CAPELLA DE MAUNNESFELD WODEHOUSE.[33] Universis sancte matris ecclesie filiis ad quos presentes littere pervenerint Willelmus etc. salutem in eo quem ad multorum salutem peperit uturus virginalis. Illorum devocionem sinceram convenit pia mentis intencione jugiter confovere qui ad divini cultus augmentum multiplicandum numerum ministrancium in ecclesia sancta dei et instituendum missarum celebraciones in quibus sacrorum ministerio sacerdotum quod peccatis populi immolatur deo patri filius sanctis orationibus complacatur altissimus et commissorum remissio impetrantur perpetuam sufficientem portionem de suis possessionibus et facultatibus libertate cupiunt gratuita elargiri. Cum itaque scriptum dilectorum filiorum prioris et conventus de Felleye nostre diocesis ecclesiam de Annesley[34] in usus proprios optinencium concessionem et promissionem eorumdem factam nuper super quadam cantaria in ecclesia sive capella de Mannesfeld Wodehousse dicte nostre diocesis ad divini laudem nominis sui cultus augmentum et pro salute animarum perpetuis temporibus facienda sigillo communi eorumdem signatam inspeximus in hec verba:

Universis Christi fidelibus quibus presentes exhiberi contigerit vel intimari frater Johannes prior de Felley et ejusdem loci conventus Ebor' diocesis ecclesiam de Annesley in proprios usus optinentes salutem in domino sempiternam. Divini cultus augmentacionem pro desiderio dilecti nobis in Christo Roberti Stuffyn de Neuwerk' affectatam attendentes ac donorum largiciones tam videlicet adquisitionis juris patronatus et advocacionis ecclesie de Adinburgh dicte Ebor' diocesis quam aliorum multiplicium bonorum munificenciam nobis et domui nostre per eundem liberaliter collatas memorie commendantes, unanimi consensu et voluntate capituli nostri pro nobis et successoribus nostris concedimus et promittimus per presentes quod nos prior et conventus supradicti et successores nostri sustentabimus et inveniemus unum capellanum secularem pro ipso Roberto et Alicia uxore sua dum vixerint et animabus Ricardi Stuffyn patrum et matrum eorumdem antecessorum eciam suorum et pro anima Johannis filii Hugonis de Portesmouth de London et animabus omnium pro quibus tenentur ac omnium fidelium defunctorum, et post mortem dictorum Roberti et Alicie pro animabus eorumdem ac omnium aliorum superius nominatorum, ad altare beate Marie in ecclesia sive capella de Mamesfeld Wodehousse missam singulis diebus quibus congrue et absque impedimento legitimo poterit modo qui sequitur celebraturum sustentandum presentandum

[33] The text has been collated with another copy in the Felley Cartulary (British Library, Additional MSS, 36872), ff.122–5. The latter is the better copy: significant variations have been noted and the cartulary reading has been preferred where the register is defective.
[34] The context suggests that Attenborough might be intended here: Annesley had been appropriated to Felley *c.*1191–1212, while Attenborough was to be appropriated 11 March 1344 and a vicarage ordained 13 June 1344 (*VCH Nottingham*, II.109–12; Thoroton, *Notts.* (cited under **410**), II.177–9, 266–7; Borthwick Institute, York, Register 10 (of Archbishop Zouche), fo. 108). The acquisition of the advowson was a vital stage in the process of appropriation; see also *CPR 1338–40,* 203. On the other hand provision is here made for the chaplain to be compensated from the fruits of Annesley if his stipend is unpaid.

et admittendum[35] perpetuis temporibus infuturum; concedentes eidem capellano et successoribus suis pro omnibus oneribus sibi et cantarie predicte incumbentibus sex marcas argenti a nobis et successoribus nostris per manus celerarii nostri qui pro tempore fuerit vel alterius procuratoris domus nostre annuatim apud Mamesfeld Wodehousse persolvendas in festis sancti Martini in yeme et Nativitatis beati Johannis Baptiste per equales porciones, ita quod solucio cujuslibet termini se referat ad tempus sequens sic videlicet, quod si contingat capellano qui pro tempore fuerit in dicta cantaria pro aliquo terminorum predictorum de predicto redditu satisfieri in parte vel in toto ac ipsum decedere ante terminum[36] solucionis proximo sequentem faciende, successori suo capellano[37] qui pro tempore fuerit in eadem cantaria de bonis ejusdem defuncti satisfiat competenter.

Idem vero Robertus dum vixerit quociens dicta cantaria vacaverit, unum capellanum ydoneum archiepiscopo Ebor' sede plena seu decano et capitulo Ebor' sede vacante presentabit; qui quidem archiepiscopus vel capitulum ut premittitur ipsum presentatum prout ad ipsos pertinet ad dictam cantariam admittat et canonice instituat in eadem. Post decessum vero ipsius Roberti cum dictam cantariam vacare contigerit, Ricardus Robertus Willelmus et Jacobus filii ejusdem Roberti qui supervixerint dum vixerint unum capellanum idoneum archiepiscopo Ebor' vel decano et capitulo ejusdem ut premittitur infra proximos xv dies ab ejusdem vacacione successive presentabunt, videlicet unus post mortem alterius; ita tamen quod semper senior eorum in hujusmodi presentacione preferatur et infra predictum terminum xv dierum dum vixerit singulariter presentet. Et si senior eorum qui pro tempore fuerit in hujusmodi vacacione minime presentaverit in forma predicta, nos dicti prior et conventus et successores nostri infra alios xv dies proximo numerandos ad dictam cantariam presentabimus sub modo et forma antedictis, vel alias extunc potestas providendi eidem cantarie et ipsam illa vice conferendi ad archiepiscopum Ebor' sede plena seu decano et capitulo Ebor' sede vacante absque prejudicio futuri temporis devolvatur. Et post mortem quidem predicti Roberti ac filiorum suorum prenominatorum, nos prior et conventus de Felley supradicti et successores nostri ad memoratam cantariam quociens et ex quacumque causa vacare contigerit infra predictum terminum xv dierum post ipsius vacacionem prefato archiepiscopo Ebor' vel decano et capitulo ejusdem ut premittitur presentabimus imperpetuum. Et si infra xv dies non presentaverimus, tunc vicarius perpetuus qui pro tempore fuerit in ecclesia de Mamesfeld infra alios proximos xv dies illa vice presentabit, alioquin archiepiscopus Ebor' qui pro tempore fuerit vel decanus et capitulum ejusdem ut premittitur de uno capellano idoneo pro predicta cantaria illa vice providebit vel providebunt.

Predicti vero capellani sic successive presentandi admittendi et instituendi pro predictis Roberto et Alicia ac animabus antedictis singulis diebus plenum servicium mortuorum videlicet Commendacionem Placebo et Dirige dicere tenantur et dicant, et in festis principalibus ac dominicis diebus missam celebrabunt de die vel de sancta Trinitate et semel in septimana de sancta

[35] MS. *admittandum*

[36] Interlined over *mortem*, cancelled; cf. *terminum* in Cartulary.

[37] Interlined.

Maria, ita quod in qualibet missa memoriam et orationem pro defunctis antedictis faciant speciales. [A missis vero matutinis et vesperis ac aliis horis canonicis in dicta ecclesia sive capella de Manefeld Wodhous cotidie interesse teneantur et precipue diebus dominicis et festivis nisi causa rationabili excusentur.][38] Et ad premissa omnia facienda et pro viribus adimplenda capellanus qui pro tempore fuerit in admissione sua per archiepiscopum vel decanum et capitulum ut premittitur oneretur et residenciam juret inibi facere personalem.[39] Et si forte capellanus qui pro tempore fuerit in ipsa cantaria in premissis faciendis et exequendis necgligens remissus aut incorrigibilis repertus fuerit et super hiis aut aliis excessibus notabilibus legitime convictus, confestim pro suis demeritis ammoveatur et alius capellanus ydoneus ad dictam cantariam in forma predicta presentetur et eciam preficiatur.

Ad quem quidem annuum redditum sex marcarum predicto capellano qui pro tempore fuerit in dicta cantaria terminis antedictis fideliter persolvendum et faciendum obligamus nos et successores nostros ac omnia bona nostra temporalia cum pertinenciis infra archidiaconatum Not' apud Whetebergh et Kirkeby Wodehous inventa sive penes nos retineantur sive ad firmam dimittantur districtioni cujuslibet capellani qui pro tempore fuerit in dicta cantaria, ita videlicet quod quantumcumque contigerit quod absit predictum annuum redditum per culpam nostram vel defectum a retro fore non solutum per unum mensem proximum post terminos statutos antedictos, libere et absque contradictione quacumque liceat predicto capellano in prefata cantaria pro tempore existenti in omnibus terris et tenementis nostris predictis pro voluntate sua distringere, districtiones captas abducere et retinere quousque eidem de omnibus arrreragiis predicti annui redditus una cum dampnis et expensis si quas ea occasione fecerit aut sustinuerit plenarie fuerit satisfactum. Volumus insuper et concedimus pro nobis et[40] successoribus nostris[41] quod quocienscumque et quandocumque dicta pecunia sex marcarum per mensem ultra predictos terminos statutos ob culpam nostram seu defectum fuerit non soluta, quod quiscumque [Fo.397; N.F.476] loci ordinarius, quem dictus capellanus qui pro tempore fuerit elegerit, possit fructus ecclesie nostre de Annesley predicte quoscumque sequestrare[42] et de bonis sic sequestratis sine reclamatione nostra et absque omni strepitu et figura[43] judicii dictam pecuniam non solutam levare et dicto capellano liberare, et ita fructus nostros predictos sub sequestro retinere donec eidem capellano de pecunia tunc retro debita fuerit persolutum; quodque idem ordinarius nos et successores nostros in premissis vel eorum aliquo in contrarium venientes aut contra ea aliqualiter attemptantes arbitrio suo punire valeat censura ecclesiastica quacumque juris remedio non obsistente. Si vero per viam sequestri aut alia via quacumque dicto capellano infra duos menses post lapsum alicujus termini statuti de predicta pecunia nullatinus satisfiat, volumus et concedimus pro nobis et successoribus nostris . . nos teneri . . domino archiepiscopo Ebor' sede plena vel decano et capitulo ejusdem sede vacante in xl

[38] As in Cartulary; in MS. this clause follows *facere personalem.*
[39] See previous note.
[40] Interlined.
[41] Interlined.
[42] Preceded by *usque*, cancelled.
[43] MS. *fugura*

solidis argenti[44] necnon et archidiacono Not' vel ejus officiali qui pro tempore fuerit in xx solidis argenti nomine pene persolvendis et applicandis, renunciantes in premissis omni appellationi excepcioni defensione regie prohibicioni et omni alii juris remedio quod nobis contra premissa competere poterit quovismodo. Ad hec eciam volumus et de expresso nostro consensu concedimus pro nobis et successoribus nostris quod per archiepiscopum Ebor' sentencia excommunicacionis majoris exnunc in[45] priorem celerarium et ceteros officiarios ac suspensionis in conventum et interdicti in capitulum domus nostre de Fellay antedicte si in solucione dicte pecunie per tres menses post lapsum cujuscumque termini statuti [per] culpam nostram defecerimus in toto vel in parte, necnon sentencia excommunicationis majoris in omnes et singulas alias personas que contra premissa aut aliqua premissorum venire vel ea aliqualiter infringere presumpserint, promulgetur eciam et fulminetur.

In quorum omnium testimonium hoc presens scriptum fecimus tripplicari, quorum unus penes nos retinemus[46] pro habenda memoria perpetua premissorum, et aliud penes capellanum[47] predictum qui pro tempore fuerit in dicta cantaria et tercium penes predictos Robertum et Aliciam heredes et executores suos volumus perpetuis temporibus remanere. Datum apud Felley in capitulo nostro septimo Kalendas Octobris anno domini MCCCXXXIX.

Nos Willelmus permissione divina Ebor' archiepiscopus Anglie primas supradictus litteras concessiones et promissiones dictorum prioris et conventus de Felley de quibus predicitur et omnia et singula contenta in eis ac cantariam predictam et ordinacionem super ea factam causis consideratis predictis quatenus ad nos attinet acceptamus ratificamus et confirmamus et ipsa sic fieri debere et esse.

911 Institution [etc.] of Thomas le Eyr, clerk, to Bilsthorpe church, vacant by the death of John Bulaux; presented by Lady Alice de Loudham. Cawood, 12 Mar. 1340.[48]

912 [*Commission to investigate the report of an enquiry into the vacancy of Gamston church and, if lawful, institute Roger de Wilughby.*[49] *William Tony, who claims the church, is to be invited to attend their proceedings.*]

[Fo.397v; N.F.476v] COMMISSIO SUPER ADMISSIONE AD ECCLESIAM DE GAMELSTON. Willelmus etc. dilectis filiis magistris Johanni de Landa juris civilis professori Radulpho de Yarewell officiali archidiaconi nostri Notinghamie et domino Gregorio de Hedon ecclesiarum de Arnale de Cotum et de Hedon nostre diocesis rectoribus salutem [*etc.*]. De fideli industria vestra et consciencjarum puritate plenius confidentes, ad intuendum inspiciendum et diligenter examinandum litteram inquisicionis ecclesie de Gamelston dicte nostre diocesis nuper auctoritate nostra per vos . . officialem predictum super ejusdem vacacione jure presentantis et presentati ac aliis articulis debitis et consuetis

[44] Interlined.
[45] *exnunc in* interlined over *extunc*, cancelled.
[46] From Cartulary; cf. MS. *remittimus*
[47] From Cartulary; cf. MS. *capitulum*
[48] The remaining half of the recto of this folio is blank.
[49] See note under **922**.

nuper capte, quam vobis mittimus hiis inclusam; et si presentatus ad ipsam ecclesiam inventus fuerit ydoneus sciencia moribus et etate ipsaque ecclesia de Gamelston nulli auctoritate apostolica de jure debeatur presertim Willelmo Tony qui se asserit ad dictam ecclesiam jus habere, quem coram vobis vocari volumus ut toti processui vestro in hac parte habendo intersit si sua viderit interesse et sibi in omnibus fieri justicie complementum nec aliquid in ejus juris injuriam attemptari, et in eo eventu si nullum canonicum obsistat ad admittendum dominum Rogerum de Wilughby clericum ad ecclesiam predictam et ipsum rectorem instituendum canonice in eadem et ad ipsum vel procuratorem suum ejus nomine induci faciendum in corporalem possessionem ejus ecclesie cum suis juribus et pertinenciis universis per ipsum cui id de jure seu consuetudine dinoscitur pertinere, et omnia alia et singula facienda et expedienda que in premissis et circa ea necessaria fuerint seu eciam oportuna, vobis vices nostras committimus cum cohercionis canonice potestate. Quod si non omnes vos hiis exequendis contigerit interesse, duo vestrum qui presentes fuerint ea nichilominus exequantur. Et nos de omni eo quod feceritis aut duo vestrum fecerint in premissis expedito negocio distincte et aperte certificetis aut certificent duo vestrum qui presens negocium fuerint executi per litteras vestras aut suas patentes harum et tocius processus vestri in hac parte habendi seriem continentes. Valete. [Cawood, 23 Oct. 1339.]

913 Institution [etc.] of Bro. John de Leverton, chaplain, to Newark vicarage, vacant by the death of Bro. Rocelinus; presented by the prior and convent of St. Katherine outside Lincoln. York, 19 Nov. 1339.

914 INTIMACIO ET NOTIFICATIO GRACIE WILLELMI DE GOTHMUNDHAM IN FORMA PAUPERUM. Memorandum that William son of [William] de Guthmundham informed the archbishop that he had bulls of grace and a process thereon concerning a provision to a benefice in the gift of the prior and convent of Worksop [cf. **792**]. Bishopthorpe, 13 Dec. 1339.

915 Institution (in the person of his proctor, John de Ekynton) and mandate for induction of Richard de Hakynthorp, chaplain, to Hickling church, vacant by the resignation of Adam de Preston; presented by William de Gray, kt., lord of Seagrave (*Segrave*). Cawood, 23 Dec. 1339.

916 [*Grant of administration to the widow of William de Claworth, who died intestate.*]
ADMINISTRACIO BONORUM WILLELMI DE CLAWORTH. Memorandum quod sub data apud Cawode viii Kalendas Marcii anno domini MCCCXXXIX scriptum fuit sequestratori nostro in archidiaconatu Not' ad liberandum Isabelle fuitz Wauter relicte Willelmi de Claworth nuper ab intestato decedentis administracionem in bonis que fuerunt dicti Willelmi sub sequestro nostro existentibus ut creditoribus satisfaciat et pro anima ejusdem defuncti distribuat prout secundum deum et conjecturatam voluntatem defuncti viderit expedire, recepta primitus ab eadem securitate sufficienti de conservando nos indempnes contra quoscumque creditores[50] dicti Willelmi et quoscumque alios racione bonorum ejusdem. [Cawood, 22 Feb. 1340.]

[50] From *contra* repeated.

917 Institution [etc.] of Bro. William de Upton, canon of Worksop, to Normanton on Trent (*Normanton juxta Trente*) vicarage, vacant by the death of Bro. Thomas de Branton; presented by the prior and convent of Worksop. Cawood, 27 Feb. 1340.

918 [*Commission to enclose a recluse at Kneesall.*]
AD INCLUDENDUM ISOLDAM DE KNESALE APUD KNESALE. Willelmus etc. dilectis filiis . . abbati de Rughford nostre diocesis et decano nostro de Newerk' salutem [*etc.*]. De vestris fidelitate et circumspecta industria plenius confidentes, ad includendum Isoldam de Knesale cujus mores et vita merita conversacioque honesta apud nos fidedigno testimonio comprobantur in loco ad id honesto et aperto, scilicet in quadam domo muro ecclesie parochialis de Knesale dicte nostre diocesis contigua de voluntate et consensu patroni et rectoris dicte ecclesie et aliorum omnium quorum interest noviter ea occasione constructa et ubi ipsa Isolda vitam ducendo solitariam affectat jugiter domino famulari, vobis conjunctim et divisim vices nostras committimus per presentes sigilli nostri appensione munitas. Valete. [Cawood, 18 Mar. 1340.]

919 Note of licence for absence for one year to Robert de Brustwyk, rector of Lambley, farming the church. Cawood, 20 Mar. 1340.

920 [Fo.398; N.F.477] Institution [etc.] of William de Estdrayton, chaplain, as perpetual chaplain of the chantry recently founded in St. Peter's, Nottingham, vacant by the death of Richard de Staunton; presented by Richard de Wylughby, kt., according to its ordinance. Cawood, 23 Mar. 1340.

921 Note of licence to John de Norhampton, rector of Warsop, to be non-resident and farm his church for three years from 28 March 1340.

922 Institution [etc.] of Robert de Remston, chaplain, to Wollaton church, vacant by the resignation of Roger de Wilughby;[51] presented by Richard de Wilughby, kt. Cawood, 1 Apr. 1340.[52]

[51] Following his institution to Gamston (**912**) after nine months at Wollaton (**890**). He returned there by an exchange with Robert, effected 31 Oct. 1341. A second exchange dated 7 Feb. 1342 restored Roger to Gamston and Robert to Wollaton. Roger ultimately exchanged from Gamston to St. Denis Walmgate, York, in 1367 (Borthwick Institute, Register 5A (vacancy, 1340–2), fo.113, 113v). See also *Lists of the Clergy of Central Nottinghamshire*, ed. K.S.S. Train (Thoroton Society, Record Series, XV, 1953–5), III.49; *Lists of the Clergy of North Nottinghamshire*, ed. K.S.S. Train (Thoroton Soc., Rec. Ser., XX, 1961), 75, and sources quoted there.
[52] The remainder of the folio is blank.

INDEX OF PERSONS AND PLACES

As in previous volumes of this edition, names of persons as well as places have been ordered in their modern form, when they could be identified without ambiguity. The abbreviations YER, YNR and YWR denote the Yorkshire ridings.

References are to the numbers of entries; some are supplemented with references to pages or numbered parts of longer entries.

INDEX OF SUBJECTS

[1] From *c.*1331 similar licences were often noted with licences for absence and for study (cf. Synod below).